Maya Potters' Indigenous Knowledge

Maya Potters' Indigenous Knowledge

COGNITION, ENGAGEMENT, AND PRACTICE

Dean E. Arnold

UNIVERSITY PRESS OF COLORADO
Boulder

© 2018 by University Press of Colorado

Published by University Press of Colorado
245 Century Circle, Suite 202
Louisville, Colorado 80027

All rights reserved
First paperback edition 2020

 The University Press of Colorado is a proud member of the Association of University Presses.

The University Press of Colorado is a cooperative publishing enterprise supported, in part, by Adams State University, Colorado State University, Fort Lewis College, Metropolitan State University of Denver, Regis University, University of Colorado, University of Northern Colorado, Utah State University, and Western State Colorado University.

ISBN: 978-1-60732-655-7 (cloth)
ISBN: 978-1-64642-042-1 (paperback)
ISBN: 978-1-60732-656-4 (ebook)
DOI: https://doi.org/10.5876/9781607326564

Library of Congress Cataloging-in-Publication Data

Names: Arnold, Dean E., 1942– author.
Title: Maya potters' indigenous knowledge : cognition, engagement, and practice / Dean E. Arnold.
Description: Boulder : University Press of Colorado, [2017] | Includes bibliographical references and index. | Contents note from ECIP table of contents.
Identifiers: LCCN 2017021804| ISBN 9781607326557 (cloth) | ISBN 9781646420421 (pbk) | ISBN 9781607326564 (ebook)
Subjects: LCSH: Maya pottery—Mexico—Ticul. | Mayas—Material culture—Mexico—Ticul. | Cognition and culture. | Potters—Mexico—Ticul.
Classification: LCC F1435.3.P8 A755 2017 | DDC 972/.65—dc23
LC record available at https://lccn.loc.gov/2017021804

Cover photograph by Dean E. Arnold

Contents

List of Figures ix

List of Tables xiii

Preface xvii

1. INTRODUCTION 3
   POTTERY PRODUCTION AND PARADIGMS 7
   ENGAGEMENT THEORY 8
      Why Engagement Theory? 9
   COMPONENTS OF THE THEORY 14
      The Behavioral Chain (The *Chaîne Opératoire*) 14
      The Semantic Structure of Knowledge 15
      Customary Muscular Patterns 17
      Feedback 18
      Technological Choice 23
   THE STRUCTURE OF THIS BOOK 26

2. HOW WAS THE DATA COLLECTED? 30
   THE METHODOLOGY AND ITS HISTORY 31

3. THE POTTERS' ENGAGEMENT WITH THE PERCEIVED LANDSCAPE — 50

ETHNOECOLOGY — 50
GEOLOGICAL CONTEXT — 51
SOURCES OF RAW MATERIALS — 53
   The Forest (*k'aash*) — 54
      Ethnoecological Zones in Northern Yucatán — 57
   Ethnogeology — 64
      Ch'e'en (a Well or Sinkhole) — 71
      Chultun (a Cistern) — 72
      Aktun (a Natural Cave) — 73
      Sah Kab (a Marl Mine) — 73
      Tantan Lu'um (a Hole in the Earth) — 76
   Ethnopetrology — 77

4. THE POTTERS' ENGAGEMENT WITH RAW MATERIALS — 79

ETHNOMINERALOGY — 79
K'AT (CLAY) — 80
   An Alternative Clay Source — 85
SAK LU'UM (WHITE EARTH) — 88
SAH KAB (WHITE POWDER) — 89
   Sah Kab for Construction Purposes (Natural Marl) — 91
      Sources — 92
      Preparation — 93
      Ancient Uses of *Sah Kab* for Construction Purposes — 93
   Sah Kab for Pottery Temper (Culturally Constituted Marl) — 94
      Temper Components and Their Subclasses — 96
      Preparing Temper — 100
      Sah Kab Temper Variability — 100
      Quality Tests for *Sah Kab* Temper — 103
   An Ancient Distinction — 108
HI' (CRYSTAL) — 108
   The Technological Advantages of *Hi'* Temper — 109
   Ancient Use and Exploitation of *Hi'* — 111

SPECIALIZED KNOWLEDGE	113
A COMMUNITY OF PRACTICE	115

5. THE POTTERS' ENGAGEMENT WITH PASTE PREPARATION — 121
PREPARING RAW MATERIALS	122
PASTE PREPARATION BEHAVIOR AS MATERIAL ENGAGEMENT	123

6. THE POTTERS' ENGAGEMENT WITH VESSEL FORMING — 129
THE FORMING TECHNOLOGY	137
FOUR TRADITIONAL VESSELS	141
The Water-Carrying Jar	142
Rim Variation and Its Meaning	144
Individual Variation in Rim Form	149
Other Traditional Shapes	149

7. THE POTTERS' ENGAGEMENT WITH DRYING AND FIRING — 154
GENDER AND FIRING	155
FIRING COOKING POTTERY	157
BUILDING A KILN	158
Kiln Sizes	164
Parts of the Kiln	166
PREPARING FOR FIRING	168
Drying Pottery	168
Slipping	169
Final Drying	170
Fuel Preparation	171
Selecting Wood for Firing	177
Loading the Kiln	177
FIRING	183
The Warming Stage (*chokokinta'al*)	183
The Final Stage (*ts'ooksa'al*)	186
VARIATIONS IN THE FIRING PROCESS	190
FIRING ACCIDENTS	191

8. TICUL POTTERY AS A "DISTILLED LANDSCAPE" / "TASKSCAPE"   198

The Religious Dimensions of Raw Materials and Their
Sources   199
  Clay (*Yo' K'at*)   199
    History   201
  Temper for Cooking Pottery (*Aktun Hi'*)   203
  Temper for Noncooking Pottery (*Yo' Sah Kab*)   204
  Red Slip (*Tantan Lu'um*)   204
  Water (*Che'en*)   205
  Fuel for Firing (*K'ash*)   205
Ritual Pottery as Symbols of a Distilled Landscape: The
Day of the Dead Rituals   206
Ancient Pottery from Ticul: A Distilled Community of
Practice   207

9. CONCLUSION   215

What Is Indigenous Knowledge?   215
Summary   216
Indigenous Knowledge and Learning   220
Ethnoarchaeology as Cultural Heritage   221
Implications for Methodology   223
What Drives Changes in Indigenous Knowledge?   226
Final Reflections   227

References   231
Index   257

Figures

3.1. Map of Yucatán showing major cities, towns, archaeological sites, and pottery-making communities between the late 1960s and 1994 — 51
3.2. View looking west-northwest along the north side of the *puuk* ridge between Ticul and Hacienda Yo' K'at in 1984 — 52
3.3. View showing the abrupt rise of the *puuk* ridge from the *kabal che'* zone and the *chak'an* zone on the north side of the ridge from Hacienda Yo' K'at in 2014 — 53
3.4. From the top of the *puuk* ridge looking south along the road from Ticul to Santa Elena in 1997 showing the *chak'an, kakab, ya'ash k'ash,* and *wits* ethnoecological zones — 54
3.5. A *milpero* at the top of the *puuk* ridge transporting firewood to Ticul from his cornfield from south of the ridge in 2008 — 55
3.6. Looking north from the top of the *puuk* ridge in 1970 toward the town of Muna showing the *chak'an* and *kabal che'* ethnoecological zones — 62
3.7. The semantic structure of the openings in the landscape with reference to the sources of raw materials used by the potters of Ticul up until about 1990 — 72
3.8. The marl quarry of San Juaquín northwest of Ticul in 1965 — 75
3.9. A *tantan lu'um*, a hole used to mine *k'an kab* used as a red slip for pottery and to make the mortar and plaster for building kilns in 2008 — 76

4.1. Surface subsidence north of the entrance of the clay mine at Hacienda Yo' K'at in May 1965 — 81

4.2. A potter's clay source dug into the clay deposit at the base of an abandoned marl (*sah kab*) quarry near Calkiní in 1994 — 83

4.3. The wall inside the clay mine at Hacienda Yo' K'at in 1968 showing the profile of a collapsed mining tunnel and sherd of a bolster rim basin on top of a large piece of clay — 86

4.4. Restored potsherd of Puuc (Medium) Slate Ware found in the collapsed mine tunnel in the Yo' K'at clay mine in 1968 — 87

4.5. Chunks of *sak lu'um* (palygorskite) mined at Yo' Sah Kab in 2008 — 89

4.6. Workers preparing the structure for heating rocks (limestone) to make lime in 1965 — 94

4.7. Close-up of the detail of the first layer of the structure used to make lime from limestone — 95

4.8. A miner digging tailings (*ta'achach*) at Yo' Sah Kab in 1966 that are used to mix with *nooy* from the mines to prepare pottery temper — 101

4.9. Inside one of the temper mines at Yo' Sah Kab in 2008 showing the tunneling into the marl deposit that contains a mixture of calcite, dolomite, and palygorskite — 102

4.10. Screening the mixture of *nooy* and the weathered tailings (*ta'achach*) at the temper mines (Yo' Sah Kab) in 1966 — 103

4.11. A potter testing a small amount of temper to determine its quality before it is mixed with the clay (1966) — 105

4.12. A large grinding stone for crushing *hi'* temper (1966) — 110

4.13. Highway workers about to use the tailings from preparing pottery temper for surfacing on the road between Ticul and Chapab (1967) — 114

5.1. The first stage of mixing temper with clay (1966) — 123

5.2. A potter evaluating the characteristics of the paste in an early stage of its preparation (1966) — 124

5.3. Adding more water to the mixture of temper and clay in order to achieve the appropriate texture and moisture content for wedging the clay (1966) — 125

5.4. Mixing the newly moistened clay/temper mixture (1966) — 126

5.5. Wedging the newly mixed paste that has been formed into cylinders (1966) — 127

FIGURES   xi

5.6.	The final stage of the wedging process in which the clay is rolled into cylinders in preparation for forming the vessels (1965)	128
6.1a.	Potters' working position while making a water-carrying jar (1984)	132
6.1b.	When a low stool is not available, potters still maintain the same working position for making pottery by sitting on an object of appropriate height—in this case a sack or clay or temper in 1988	133
6.1c.	A young boy resting in a squatting position in 1970	134
6.1d.	A man in a squatting position trims a *huano* palm frond for repairing the thatched roof of a house in 1984	135
6.2.	A potter using a traditional *k'abal* in 1984 using his foot to move the turntable while he shapes the vessel with both hands	139
6.3.	Potters seated on stools while slipping pottery in 1965	140
6.4.	Four women seated on low stools to slip pottery on a sunny day prior to firing in 1984	141
6.5.	Named parts of a traditional water-carrying vessel (*p'uul*, or *cántaro* in Spanish)	142
6.6a.	Cutaway images of the two rim forms on the water-carrying jar (the *cántaro* or *p'uul*) in Ticul	145
6.6b.	A potter demonstrates how he makes his own unique rim signature on a water carrying vessel (1984)	147
6.6c.	The rim style of water-carrying vessels of Máxima Tzum de Uc in 1984 that are different from those of her nephew (compare with Figure 6.6b)	148
6.7.	The traditional water storage jar (*kat*, or *apaste* in Spanish) showing the different named parts	150
6.8.	Another traditional water storage jar (*tinaja* in Spanish, no Maya name) showing the different named parts	152
7.1.	Diagram of a plan view of the Ticul kiln showing the named parts	167
7.2.	Slipping a water storage vessel (*tinaja*) before firing in 1966	170
7.3.	Loading a kiln with water storage jars, water-carrying jars, water storage / maize-soaking vessels, and figurines in 1965	181
7.4.	View inside a kiln in 1984 showing flower pots resting on a base of wasters and rocks, and waster fragments used to stabilize the pottery to keep it from collapsing	182
7.5.	Potter throwing wood into the kiln at the very beginning of the firing process in 1965	184

7.6a.	The blackening of the pottery during in the early part of the warming stage of firing in 1988	185
7.6b.	The blackening pottery at the end of the warming stage of firing in 1984	185
7.7.	Leveling the embers inside the kiln after it is hot and the wood in the *pach k'aak'* has spontaneously burst into flames (1966)	187
7.8.	Throwing split wood into the kiln during the early part of the last half of final substage of firing called "fire in the door of the kiln" (1966)	188
7.9.	Throwing split wood into the area behind the pots (the *pach k'aak'*) on either side of the door during the "fire in the door of the kiln" phase of firing	189
7.10.	Moving burning embers close to the door of the kiln in preparation for pushing them into the *pach k'aak'* behind the pots at the sides of the door of the kiln	190
7.11.	Pushing burning embers behind the pots (the *pach k'aak'*) at the sides of the door of the kiln during the "fire in the door of the kiln" phase	191
7.12.	Leveling the burning coals in the kiln during the "fire in the door of the kiln" phase of firing	192
7.13.	An illustration of the *bosh ela'an* type of firing accident in which the vessel has a large black spot with tiny cracks in it (1965)	193
7.14.	An illustration of the *bu'ul* accident in which a vessel has broken apart during firing (1965)	194
7.15.	An illustration of the *waakal* type of firing accident in which a circular-shaped flake has popped off the surface (1984)	194
7.16.	An illustration of a *k'e* type of firing accident when a large portion has popped off a vessel (1965)	195
8.1.	A household altar for the Day of the Dead ceremonies showing food bowls, incense burners, and candle holders of pottery that link the present with the spirits of the dead ancestors that come back to the land of the living from the earth during these ceremonies (1984)	207
8.2.	Map showing the area of the taskscape of Ticul potters before 1970	209
8.3.	Map showing the area of the taskscape of ancient potters who lived in San Francisco de Ticul during the Terminal Classic Period	210

Tables

3.1. The ethnoecological zones in northern Yucatán and the trees that grow in each zone — 58

3.2. The trees that grow in each ethnoecological zone organized by zone — 60

3.3. Botanical names for the trees used for firewood in Ticul — 65

3.4. The ethnopetrology of rocks according to Ticul potters showing their name, their use, and where each type was found — 77

4.1. The folk taxonomy of *sah kab* (white powder) and its division into pottery temper and marl for construction purposes — 90

4.2. Percent of clay in samples of *sah kab* for construction purposes collected during 1965 and 1966 — 91

4.3. Percent of clay in samples of *sah kab* for pottery temper collected in 1965 and 1966 — 91

4.4. Folk taxonomy of *sah kab* temper used among Ticul potters — 97

4.5. Percent of clay in samples of *ta'achach*, one of the principal components of pottery temper — 97

4.6. Percent of clay in *nooy*, one of the principal components of pottery temper — 98

4.7.	The plastic and liquid limits of kaolinite, smectite, and palygorskite arranged in the order of increasing plastic limits (from White 1949)	104
4.8.	The plastic and liquid limits of smectite, kaolinite, and palygorskite arranged in order of increasing plastic limits (from Liberto de Pablo 1964)	104
4.9.	Summary of the categories of raw materials used for making pottery in the 1960s and their physical foundations	116
6.1.	Nomenclature of the size categories for making traditional vessel shapes	130
6.2.	The units of measurement that potters use to make traditional vessels	131
6.3.	Postural patterns potters used for making pottery in Ticul from 1951 to 2008 documented from photographs	136
6.4.	Sequence of the stages of fabrication for vessels with a concave profile	138
6.5.	The stages of fabrication required to form the *apaste (kat)*, *tinaja*, and *cántaro (p'uul)*	138
6.6.	Potters' choices of different sizes and the appropriate measurements used for forming the stages of the water-carrying jar	143
6.7.	Potters' choices of different sizes, their use, and the appropriate measurements used for forming one variety of the *kat* shape (*apaste*)	151
6.8.	Potters' choices and their measurements for making a second variety of the *kat* (*apaste*) shape	151
6.9.	Potters' choices of size categories and the appropriate measurements used for each stage of the water storage jar (*tinaja*)	151
7.1.	Kilns and their characteristics for each production unit from 1965 to 1966 and 1984	160
7.2.	Direction of the prevailing winds in Mérida, Yucatán	161
7.3.	Kilns and their characteristics for each production unit in 1997	163
7.4.	Variability of kiln construction observed in 1965	165
7.5.	The burning characteristics of the varieties of firewood used for firing pottery	172
7.6.	Equivalent choices of firewood that have similar characteristics according to potters	175
7.7.	The burning values for the firewood from different types of trees that were common to potters in Ticul and *milperos* in Quintana Roo and their perceived quality	175

7.8. The ideal type of firewood used for each part of the firing process 178
7.9. Kinds of firing accidents identified by Ticul potters 193
8.1. The taskscape of the ancient and modern potters of Ticul, and their religious association that are materialized into pottery as a distilled landscape used for the rituals for the Day of the Dead 200

Preface

We live in a rapidly changing world that is replacing ways of life that have much to teach us. Like agricultural expansion and monocropping that are destroying biological diversity and hampering the ability of domestic plants to adapt to changing conditions, globalization is destroying indigenous knowledge that can provide solutions more closely attuned to the culture and environment of traditional peoples than uncontextualized scientific knowledge (e.g., see Faust 1998; Killion 1999).

This book is an exploration of the indigenous knowledge of traditional pottery making in Ticul, Yucatán, Mexico, as it is expressed in the Maya language and behavior, and described in terms of material engagement theory (Malafouris 2004, 2013; Renfrew 2004). It is a book about potters' knowledge, skill, and their engagement with their environment, their raw materials, and their process of making pottery. Some call this kind of knowledge "ethnoecology" (Nazarea 1999a, 1999b), "local knowledge," or "traditional environmental knowledge" (or TEK; Hunn 1999; Menzies 2006; Ratner and Holen 2007). In Ticul this knowledge is not changeless or shared outside of the population of local potters, but it is both cognitive knowledge, of which the potter is aware, and the actual practice and performance of that knowledge, of which the potter may have limited conscious awareness.

Defining this knowledge more specifically, Ratner and Holen (2007, 45) called it "locally specific and cumulative knowledge that Native peoples possess about their homelands." In this work I operationalize this definition of indigenous knowledge as traditional knowledge that is passed down from generation to generation in

Maya households and rooted in the pre-Columbian Maya past, but not necessarily unchanged from it.

The indigenous knowledge of Ticul potters is embedded in the native language of Yucatán, Yucatec Maya, and is usually, but not always, labeled in that language, often with subtleties unknown and unused in Spanish. Some knowledge of that language is essential to grasp the meanings that someone from outside the culture might miss. Translation, of course, does help, but it can obscure distinctions that the natives themselves make. An example of this difference involves the meanings of the Maya term *sah kab*, which potters freely translate as "white powder," or is geologically identified as marl. Transliterated as *sascab* in Spanish, this phrase refers to a material widespread in Yucatán, but the hispanicized word as well as its geological reference obscures a variety of meanings essential for understanding potters' indigenous knowledge (see chapter 4).

Learning and using Maya indigenous knowledge gave me a great sense of personal satisfaction, and learning conversational Yucatec Maya brought surprising consequences. I had spent six months in Yucatán in early 1965 learning about pottery firing, and in the course of that experience learned both conversational Spanish and some Yucatec Maya—particularly that related to making pottery. Returning to Ticul in January 1966, I was walking toward a house of one of the potters when a man stopped me and asked me a standard conversation-starting question in Yucatec Maya. I immediately responded in Maya, but after doing so, I realized that I had given the wrong answer. I corrected myself in Maya, and apologized in Spanish, but he responded by saying: "It's OK. You're Dean (or *din* as they called me). You know Maya."

His compliment stunned me. I had never see this man before, and I had no idea who he was. Yet, he knew me and knew my name. Indeed, I was so surprised that I never forgot the incident.

At the time, however, I contemplated what had happened. In 1966 Yucatán was still very isolated from the Mexican heartland, and non-Yucateco Mexicans were not highly regarded. They were called *huachis* because the word mimicked the squeaking sound of sandals of the highland mercenaries that invaded Yucatán in the years following the Mexican revolution of 1910 (see Joseph 1980, 150).

On the other hand, Yucatecans regarded North Americans with a genuine fondness. This affection seemed to have its roots as much in the distaste for those from highland Mexico as from their desire in the mid-nineteenth century to be independent from the central government of Mexico, secede from the Mexican nation, and become part of the United States (Alisky 1980, 249; Orosa Díaz 1994, 178). Desiring to preserve their unique regional and ethnic identity, Yucatecans viewed any attempt by a North American to learn Maya as an affirmation of that identity, and thus was greatly appreciated. The man I encountered must have heard that there was a *gringo* who, in the process of working with potters, was learning Maya.

When I returned to Yucatán in 1984, however, the culture had changed. Most obvious was the presence of the Mexican central government, along with the national culture from the heartland. Yucatec Maya was starting to disappear, and in Ticul, at least, children were discouraged from using it. Perhaps emblematic of this central Mexican dominance was that I never heard the term *huachi* again.

Is there a true "indigenous knowledge," or is it an illusion? Some criticize the notion of traditional knowledge, as if it went back into time immemorial and was immutable. Such critiques, of course, are straw men because traditional knowledge is changing even though its roots may be centuries old. Recognizing that indigenous knowledge and its practice in making pottery have changed over the last fifty years does not mean that this knowledge is so flexible, changeable, and relative that it is unknowable and cannot be discovered.

In many respects there is an objective way of establishing that some of this knowledge is, in fact, traditional, ancient, and goes back centuries. In Ticul, for example, the social memory of the sources of raw materials is verified by archaeological evidence that indicates that they extend back 1,000 years to the Terminal Classic Period (AD 800–1100; Arnold 2005a; Arnold and Bohor 1977). Similarly, before massive social change eliminated the demand for some vessel shapes, some of them were also produced in the pre-Hispanic period (e.g., in Smith 1971; see also chapter 6 in this volume).

By way of contrast, the firing of pottery represents a more complicated picture of traditional indigenous knowledge. The kiln used by the Ticul potter, for example, is of probable Moorish origin and is consistent with the origin of most of the postconquest Spanish immigrants who came from Andalusía, in southern Spain, a region that Islamic culture dominated for more than 800 years. Nevertheless, this apparently Moorish kiln in Ticul has a Maya name (*kot*), and the technology, nomenclature, and classes of fuel are tied to Maya classifications of earth, rocks, and trees.

Indeed, many changes have occurred in the firing process since my original data were collected in 1965, such as new types of kilns, firewood, and kiln furniture, and the addition of cement facing. Many of these changes (but not all) were described in a previous book on Ticul (Arnold 2008, 281–307). This book, however, focuses on the traditional, indigenous knowledge as it was embodied and expressed in the last half of the 1960s. Whereas traditional potters were engaging this knowledge in the 1960s to select raw materials, mix their paste, and form and fire their pots, most of it has now disappeared.

Nevertheless, the potters' craft continues, and will probably persist for many decades to come, but in a way different from it was in the late 1960s. Sadly, more than five decades later, only a pale reflection of this traditional knowledge remains. Consequently, this work is as much an attempt to describe and preserve this knowledge as Cultural Heritage as it is a desire to provide a different theoretical perspective about indigenous knowledge of pottery production that is useful to some of the current theoretical issues in archaeology and material culture studies.

This book is thus a synthesis and distillation of the indigenous knowledge of Maya potters of Ticul as I encountered, engaged, and recorded it in the last half of the 1960s. Some of this material has been published before, but all of it has been revised, enriched, rethought, and expanded into a coherent monograph with a unifying theoretical focus. Previously published work has been rewritten, smoothed, corrected where appropriate, and updated with additional information gleaned from field notes and Yucatec Maya language texts recorded in the 1960s.

Because this presentation involves a cognitive dimension, comprehending the craft involves understanding how the potters understood it, and it is essential to express some of this information in the way in which the potters themselves express it—using the words of Yucatec Maya, their native language. Using such words expresses the rich knowledge embedded in the potters' language. Yucatec Maya uses several sounds different from those in English, and an additional set of orthographic symbols needs to be employed. Rather than representing these sounds using a Spanish orthography, I use a phonetic transcription that expresses the integrity of the Yucatec Maya language apart from the colonial influence of Spanish. Such symbols that are different from Spanish orthography include the apostrophe ('), which indicates a glottal stop when placed between vowels. Following a consonant, it indicates that the consonant is glottalized. Vowel length is marked by single or double vowels.

Since so much knowledge of pottery making is embedded and expressed in Yucatec Maya, as the language disappears, much of the knowledge of the craft will also disappear. Since 1965 this loss has been dramatic. Much of the information that I obtained between 1965 and 1970 was in Yucatec, but by 1984 the craft had changed greatly. Older potters still possessed the full range of knowledge and skills about the craft, but young potters had a much narrower range than their older counterparts and were limited in their ability to speak Yucatec Maya. My principal informant, for example, said that though his children understood the language, they could not speak it because those who used it in school were the subject of discrimination. By 1994 all of his children had grown, and although they understood Maya, they did not speak it or use it. None became potters. Much of the potters' knowledge described here thus will disappear when my principal informants in 1965 (and their generation) pass from the scene.

One metaphor of the loss of Maya indigenous knowledge in Ticul was the disappearance of references to Xtabay, a vixen who lures men (often drunk ones) to their death or to suffer serious injury (see Peniche Barrera 1992, 103–5; Redfield 1941, 90, 116; 1950, 125; Redfield and Villa Rojas 1962, 41, 207). In 1965 I was single, and my Yucatecan friends often teased me about this seductive creature by saying that if I went out at night, she would certainly lure me to fall into one of the large drainage holes located at street corners. Needless to say, I never encountered Xtabay, but I carefully eyed those holes and their position whenever I passed them, not knowing if I would ever need to draw upon that knowledge on some dark, moonless night.

After 1965 I never heard anything about Xtabay again. This absence revealed more of the loss of indigenous knowledge than I realized because it coincided with the abandonment (after 1970) of the *novena* for Saint Peter, the patron saint of the hacienda where, up until very late 1991, clay for Ticul potters had been mined for almost a thousand years (Arnold 2008, 154–164; Arnold and Bohor 1977).

This volume is another of my contributions to the intersection of ethnology and archaeology called ceramic ethnoarchaeology. The research for this work began two years before the term "ethnoarchaeology" entered the literature (Oswalt and VanStone 1967), and long before most of the research and publications labeled "ethnoarchaeology" occurred. A literature in contemporary ceramic production and its relationship to archaeology already existed, most prominently with the publications of Thompson (1958) and Foster (1948, 1955, 1960a, 1960b, 1965). Others, however, had been describing contemporary pottery making and applying it to archaeology for years. A section in George W. Brainerd's, *The Archaeological Ceramics of Yucatán*, described pottery making in contemporary Yucatán and suggested that it provided insights for the ancient pottery there (Brainerd 1958, 66–68). Similarly, Anna O. Shepard's, *Ceramics for the Archaeologist* (Shepard 1965), reprinted in the same year as my initial research in Yucatán (1965), included examples of contemporary pottery production from the Southwest and applied them to archaeology. Having written brief reports about ceramic technology (e.g., Shepard 1952, 1958) in Yucatán for the annual yearbooks of the Carnegie Institution of Washington, she was convinced of the importance of studying modern Yucatán pottery making in order to preserve part of the Maya Cultural Heritage and recognized its relevance to archaeology. Shepard's correspondence with me in 1966 and 1967 and a letter to Bruce F. Bohor in 1967 underscored that desire (Shepard 1967).[1]

Some of the early literature on ethnography of pottery production had its origin in a Wenner-Gren Conference in 1961 that aimed to put the human element back into understanding pottery. The papers from this conference were eventually published as an edited volume (Matson 1965a) including several chapters—such as those by Frederick Matson (1965b), Robert Ehrich (1965), George Foster (1965) and Hélène Balfet (1965)—that became part of the nascent development of what has come to be known as "ceramic (or pottery) ethnoarchaeology."

In the 1970s more archaeologists turned to studying modern societies to understand the relationship between their material residues and the nonmaterial patterns responsible for those residues, and explore the relationship between style and learning networks (e.g., Stanislawski 1977; Stanislawski and Stanislawski 1978). Originally, two terms described this approach: "living archaeology" (Gould 1980) and "ethnoarchaeology" (Donnan and Clewlow 1974; Gould 1978). Only the term "ethnoarchaeology," however, has survived as the approach that studies contemporary societies from an archaeological perspective. Pioneers in these approaches—William Longacre (1991), Nicholas David (1972), David and Hennig (1972), Richard Gould (1978), and the late Carol Kramer (David and Kramer 2001; Kramer 1979, 1985, 1997)—are well known, and these scholars and their students have produced excellent research that virtually defined the field.

More recently, however, ethnoarchaeology has greatly expanded in content, areal extent, and methodology (e.g., P. Arnold 1988, 1991a, 1991b; Arthur 2006; Bowser 2000, 2005; Deal 1998; Gosselain 1992, 1998, 2000; Gosselain and Smith 2005; Sillar 2000; Stark 1991a, 1991b; Thieme 2007, 2009; Underhill 2003; Williams 1992, 1994a, 1994b, 2006; among many, many others) with many excellent summaries (P. Arnold 2000; Costin 2000; David and Kramer 2001; Hegmon 2000; Roux 2007; Stark 2003) and many edited volumes (Donnan and Clewlow 1974; Gould 1978; Kramer 1979; Longacre 1991; Longacre and Skibo 1994; Van der Leeuw and Pritchard 1984).[2] Ethnoarchaeology has moved beyond the study of residues to encompass larger issues of social and economic adaptations, technological choice (and the *chaîne opératoire*), and identifying political and social groups using material and stylistic features.

Even with the massive amount of literature in ceramic ethnoarchaeology, this work is different and "outside the box." If one measures the pulse and history of this subfield by its content and methodology, this work, like much of my research, is outside of the tradition of ethnoarchaeology as practiced in America during the last forty years.

Several reasons contribute to this perception. First, as explained above, the research for this volume began in 1965 before most studies of ethnoarchaeology began and before the term "ethnoarchaeology" existed. Much of the research reported and analyzed here antedates virtually all of the research in ceramic ethnoarchaeology done in the last forty-five years, and certainly before almost all of it was published.

Second, I did not come to the study of the ceramic production of living peoples from archaeology, but rather from linguistics and cultural anthropology, and those approaches are evident in the current volume. I am largely an ethnographer who is intent upon understanding potters and their production before I relate those data to archaeological questions. Even my research that focused on tight research questions related to archaeology (e.g., Arnold 1999, 2000; Arnold, Neff, and Bishop 1991; Arnold et al. 2012; Arnold and Bohor 1975, 1976; Arnold and Nieves 1992) was predicated upon a deep understanding of the production process first obtained through participant-observation. Some of the applications of my research to archaeology were serendipitous consequences, but they came out of deep ethnographic research.

A third reason that this work differs from traditional ethnoarchaeology is that though the scholars of ceramic ethnoarchaeology have done excellent work that is extremely important to archaeologists, I have done no work on the topics that have dominated so much of recent research (e.g., Beck 2006). Rather, my focus has been on the ecological context of production (Arnold 1975a, 1993, 1978b); the community and social organization of potters (Arnold 1989, 1991, 2008, 2012, 2015a; Arnold, Wynne, and Ostoich 2013); their indigenous knowledge (Arnold 1971); their raw materials (Arnold 1971, 1972a, 2000; Arnold, Neff, and Bishop 1991); the nature, structure, and choices of ceramic design (1983, 1984); and the relationship of some of these phenomena to archaeology (Arnold 2005a, 2005b; Arnold et al. 2007). My fieldwork has covered more than four decades of research on contemporary potters in Peru, Mexico, and Guatemala. My first publication (Arnold 1967b) linked the practices of contemporary potters in Ticul to the ancient pigment Maya Blue, showing that a semantic category used by the potters there corresponded to the clay mineral palygorskite (then called attapulgite), one of the critical components of Maya Blue. At least some of the ancient palygorskite used in Maya Blue appears to have come from a source known and used by the modern Maya (Arnold and Bohor 1975, 1976; Arnold et al. 2012) and perhaps from a source used by modern Ticul potters as well (Arnold 2005a; Arnold et al. 2012).

Nevertheless, the most important focus of ethnoarchaeology is to try and understand the past by using the present, not necessarily in a strict analogical perspective, but rather to see the present from the point of view of an archaeologist. Some ethnoarchaeologists claim that only archaeologists can do that, and perhaps they have a point. But, where is the potter's perspective in all of this? Doesn't that perspective also provide understanding of ceramic production uncontaminated by cultural and theoretical bias of the present? Because archaeologists are experts at dealing with residues of ancient societies, it is understandable that they have special expertise in dealing with those residues in the present. But, what are the cultural and social patterns responsible for those residues? Do archaeologists have special insights borne from the study of the past that privileges their understanding of the cultural patterns affecting material culture in the present? Without reflection on the methodology and approaches to contemporary societies, archaeologists might be prone to inexplicit cultural and theoretical bias.

The approach taken in this work reflects the idea that in order to understand the indigenous knowledge of the potter, one must use methodological approaches and descriptive tools of cultural anthropology that privilege the native's own cognitive structures. Long ago, however, Lewis Binford (1965) claimed that a concern with cognition in archaeology was paleopsychology and unworthy of a scientific approach, presumably because it was nonmaterial—a classic emulation of the mind/matter dichotomy and the primacy of a material approach. Cognition, however, has material consequences in potters' use of the landscape, their selection of raw materials, and their choices in making a pot—a point I made decades ago (Arnold 1971, 38–39).

This monograph thus tries to reclaim a point of view that puts the potter, his or her cognitive classifications, and his or her behavior into a broader perspective of indigenous knowledge in which he/she engages the landscape, the raw materials, and the processes that shape and fire pottery vessels. Even though much of the research for this work was done before the popularity of perspectives of technological choice, agency, and engagement, I never lost a recognition of the importance of the potter's viewpoint of the process in my subsequent research in Yucatán, using their classifications, and understanding their technological choices.

One may ask, "Why publish material that was largely collected fifty years ago?" The answers to this question are not simple. Probably the most significant reason is that except for my own work about Maya potters' ethnomineralogy (Arnold 1971)—which is expanded, rewritten, corrected, and updated here—no one since then (to my knowledge) has written a monograph about potter's indigenous knowledge of the entire pottery-making sequence (i.e., the *chaîne opératoire*) like that found in this volume. In spite of a resurgence of studies of indigenous knowledge, and a massive literature of ceramic ethnoarchaeology, the study of potters' indigenous knowledge that has archaeological relevance has received little attention.

A second, and perhaps a more instrumental reason in the delay in publication of this material, was a distraction stimulated by my discovery that the Maya knew and used one of the unique materials for making Maya Blue, an ancient pigment with unique properties. It was one of the great inventions of the ancient Maya (Arnold 1967a, 1967b, 2005a; Arnold and Bohor 1976; Arnold et al. 2007; Arnold et al. 2012) and is "one of the great technological and artistic achievements of Mesoamerica" (Miller and Martin 2004, 252). This discovery was a serendipitous consequence of participant-observation and the use of Yucatec Maya in collecting my data. Although this discovery was made more than fifty years ago, Maya Blue is so unique that chemists and material scientists are still trying to fully understand the nature of this pigment, with many hundreds of pages of analyses devoted to trying to figure out the kind of chemical bonding that exists between the indigo molecule and the clay mineral palygorskite that accounts for its unusual properties (Arnold 2015b).

Because no one had any idea that the Maya still used one of the materials for Maya Blue, it became the focus of my master's thesis (Arnold 1967a), and for a while I went off on a tangent to work on it. Research in Peru, Guatemala, a PhD thesis, my early years of teaching, a Fulbright lectureship in Peru, changing universities, and testing the assumptions of compositional analysis using ethnographic data focused my research elsewhere. Further, there were no paradigms to describe what I had done in Ticul. Ethnoarchaeology had not become popular yet, and though pioneers such as Raymond Thompson (1958) and George Foster (1948, 1955, 1960a, 1960b, 1965) had collected ethnographic data on pottery making with an eye toward using that data for archaeological interpretation, the study of what is now called ethnoarchaeology was very new. (It was not called "ethnoarchaeology" back then.) As important as those works were, they did not relate well to my data. Further, archaeology itself had moved toward a materialist dimension, and again, though that change was important and useful, it did not provide me with a paradigm for writing up my data because the cognitive approach was "out-of-style" in archaeology. Still, no one had used my approach to pottery technology, and no paradigms existed to describe it except for the limited perspective of cognitive anthropology that I had used to collect the data. The emergence of engagement theory in the first decade of the twenty-first century provided the first really effective way to describe and explain what I had done more than thirty-five years before.

It wasn't until I read Tim Ingold's book *Making* (Ingold 2013), that my data and experience dramatically fell into place. Some of my work already had anticipated Ingold's and Malafouris's (2013) work and laid the groundwork for my thinking. In *Ceramic Theory and Cultural Process* (Arnold 1985), I tried to show that the widespread but culturally relative assumption that pottery was purely a product of the mental template of each culture was overstated, if not untrue. This assumption comes from the belief that because pottery was the product of plastic clay, it was the result of a mental template of the maker and an infinitely plastic product of the potters' culture. As I said then, this view has deep roots in American anthropology as a metaphor for the plasticity of the human personality, a foundational belief of the Cultural and Personality School of anthropological thought of the early twentieth century. Ruth Bunzel, who reflected this view in her work *The Pueblo Potter* (Bunzel 1929), was a contemporary and colleague of Ruth Benedict and others at the time who were noted for their work in culture and personality, and for their belief that cultural patterns were totally relative, and that there were no cultural universals (Harris 1968, 393–448).[3] This perspective was a direct consequence of their focus on values and beliefs from inside their informants' heads. Once focus in anthropology shifted to a more etic and materialist perspective, cross-cultural regularities and patterns began to emerge (see Harris 1968, 605–87).

In ceramic studies, the view that clay used by potters is so plastic that it only reflects the culture and the choices of the makers is implicitly contradicted and nuanced by the work of Anna O. Shepard, whose pioneering work in ceramic technology, *Ceramics for the Archaeologist* (Shepard 1965), showed that though there certainly was a culturally relative dimension to making pottery (particularly in decoration such as design structure and symmetry), pottery was also affected by the mineralogical composition of pottery raw materials, the ratios of clay and temper within the paste, and what is now called the *chaîne opératoire* of the production sequence of mixing, forming, drying, and firing—a fixed sequence that exists across pottery-producing societies around the world.[4] This was reiterated in O. S. Rye's (1981) book, *Pottery Technology: Principles and Reconstruction*, which further affirms the fixed sequence of ceramic production and that there are cross-cultural regularities and patterns in the *chaîne opératoire* of ceramic production with, of course, choices and variability at various points within that sequence. This same perspective was further developed, expanded, and elaborated by Prudence Rice's encyclopedic work *Pottery Technology* (Rice 1987, 2015) that upon close examination shows the deep technical foundation of pottery production in the mineralogical characteristics of clays and how those characteristics can potentially affect their variability, and place constraints on the pottery-making process. Rice, however, also reviewed the cultural (and more relative) dimensions of pottery within that technological process.

Tim Ingold's (2013) book, however, matched my own experience as a participant-observer in working with the potters in Ticul, and I began to realize that much of the data that I had collected there showed that potters' practice is not just the reflection of relativistic, culturally and socially appropriate choices, but rather consists of the way that the potter transforms his raw material into pottery based upon his previous knowledge as well as the sensory feedback that comes from the nature and limitations of the raw materials and from that of the entire production process. In retrospect, I had already described the potters' engagement with their raw materials (Arnold 1971), but I erroneously interpreted these data using the mental template model that argued potters' simply materialized their cognitive categories. Lambros Malafouris's work (2004, 2013) on material engagement theory further encouraged me to put my experience into this new theoretical context because it helped me make sense out of my engagement with Ticul potters during the last fifty years, but especially during my research in 1965. It also provided me with a vocabulary ("material agency") for how to talk about what I had experienced both in the field and what I had tried to develop in *Ceramic Theory and Cultural Process* (Arnold 1985).

Finally, these data are part of the Cultural Heritage of the contemporary Yucatec Maya. As I have already stated, most of this knowledge and practice no longer exist, but the Maya language embodies, and is the key, to that knowledge. As I have already briefly anticipated here, this work also shows that this knowledge has created the platform for archaeological discovery that enhances knowledge of the ancient Maya, one of the most obvious forms of Cultural Heritage for the modern Maya. Sadly, the indigenous knowledge of the Maya potter has largely disappeared even though the craft continues in Ticul, though in a greatly attenuated form from its more traditional practice of fifty years ago. The extent of these changes was the subject of two previous monographs (Arnold 2008, 2015a).

So, this book has been a pilgrimage. It began when I worked with potters, learned their language of potting, and then learned how to use that knowledge to transform clay into a marketable vessel. Working on this book also illustrates the very process that Ingold (2013) describes: the transformation of data from texts, question-and-response frames, photographs, and participant-observation into a cohesive treatise of Maya indigenous knowledge. Such is the nature of "making" according to Ingold.

I am grateful to many people and organizations that encouraged and supported this work and helped with transforming these data into this monograph. The late Duane Metzger sent me to Yucatán in 1965, gave me total freedom to do my research and to follow it wherever it took me. My academic advisor at the University of Illinois, the late Donald W. Lathrap, encouraged me immeasurably to continue that research and reinforced this freedom. Correspondence with the late Anna O. Shepard also provided encouragement to continue my study of pottery making in Yucatán and to delve into deeper technical issues concerning the analysis of ceramic raw materials. She uniquely recognized the role of the study of Yucatec Maya pottery making as a part of the Maya Cultural Heritage that was disappearing. Our letters and a brief visit to her lab in Boulder in 1966 reaffirmed that perspective, though she did not believe that Ticul potters recognized the properties of palygorskite as a unique cultural category. My discovery of that link, however, turned out to be one of the important and unique forms of Maya Cultural Heritage that links the present Maya people to their ancient past.

Other individuals and organizations provided support for this research. The late Fred Strodtbeck, formerly of the Social Psychology Laboratory of the University of Chicago, provided some of the original funds for this research via the Midwestern Universities Consortium from a grant from the Ford Foundation. This funding was part of a larger package that established a research institute in Yucatán that greatly facilitated my fieldwork (and that of many students and scholars) between 1965 and 1970. The late Asael "Hans" Hansen and the late Herman Konrad, who were the directors during those years, provided logistical support and helped make my short research trips to Yucatán at that time extremely productive.

The research upon which this volume is based was also funded by a variety of other organizations, and I am very grateful for their support. In addition to the Social Psychology Laboratory at the University of Chicago mentioned above, the Department of Anthropology at the University of Illinois funded research in 1965. In 1966, field research received support from the Department of Anthropology at the University of Illinois. In 1967 a brief visit upon my return from Peru was funded by a NDFL Title VI Fellowship. In 1968 the University of Illinois Research Board funded a trip to Yucatán with B. F. Bohor of the Illinois State Geological Survey. In 1970, stopovers to and from Guatemala were underwritten by a grant from the Pennsylvania State University College of Liberal Arts. An American Republics Research Grant awarded under the Fulbright Program supported my work in Yucatán in 1984. Field research in Yucatán in 1988 was underwritten by the Human Needs and Global Resources Program and the G. W. Aldeen Memorial Fund at Wheaton College, and in 1994, fieldwork was made possible by a grant from the Wheaton College Alumni Association. Field Research in 1997 was supported by the Wenner-Gren Foundation for Anthropological Research (Grant No. 6163), The National Endowment for the Humanities (Grant Number RK 20191–95), and the Wheaton College Alumni Association. I am particularly grateful to the administrators of Wheaton College: Ward Kriegbaum, Stanton Jones, Patricia Ward, and Dorothy Chappell for their support of this research and the preparation of this manuscript by means of the G. W. Aldeen Memorial Fund and Wheaton College Faculty Development funds. The National Endowment for the Humanities (Grant Number RK 20191–95) provided a two-year grant that supported the analysis and write-up of much of these data and that used for my previous two books (Arnold 2008, 2015a), releasing me from two-thirds of my teaching responsibilities between 1995 and 1997 and making the preparation of the early stages of this book possible. A return trip to Yucatán in 2008 obtained a wide sample of palygorskite for comparison with samples of Maya Blue and was funded by the National Geographic Society (No. 7433-08). It provided an opportunity to use some of the indigenous knowledge that I had acquired more than forty years beforehand and that had been reinforced many times since my original research in 1965. This experience demonstrated to me that I had indeed internalized some of the Ticul indigenous knowledge in selecting raw materials.

Bruce F. Bohor, formerly of the Illinois State Geological Survey and the United States Geological Survey, did the original X-ray diffraction analyses of potters' raw materials from Ticul. Our work together in the field helped me understand the geological context of the ceramic raw materials used by Maya potters. Richard E.

Bisbing, a volunteer in the Conservation Department of the Field Museum, used several techniques to analyze one of the samples originally described by informants as chert or flint, and confirmed an earlier analysis that it was dolomite. Lic. José Luis Sierra Villarreal, director of the Centro Regional del Sureste del Instituto Nacional de Antropología e Historia; Professor Salvador Rodríguez, director of the Escuela de Ciencias Antropológicas, Universidad de Yucatán; and the entire staff of the Centro Regional del INAH and the Escuela de Ciencias Antropológicas provided collaboration and cooperation in facilitating and supporting this research. In 1987, and again in 1989, a small grant was received from the Alumni Association of Wheaton College to hire a student (Delores Ralph Yaccino) to put all of the field notes, informal surveys, and linguistic texts from this project into electronic form. Other teaching and research assistants over many years have helped me immeasurably in the analysis of these data and in preparing the illustrations for publication: Heidi Biddle, Helen Woodey, Charlie Shrack, Lindsay Wiersma, Christy Reed, Christa Thorpe, Sara Sywulka, Matt Wistrand, Susan Crickmore, Becky Seifried, Masako Kawate, Hilary Mulhern, and Hayley Schumacher. They and others whose names I may have forgotten have assisted in many ways, providing library assistance and preparing photos, charts, and graphs. I am also grateful to Kostelena Michelaki, who gave me copies of Tim Ingold's (2000, 2013) books, and whose work in Calabria, Italy, inspired me to think differently about my data. Charlie Kolb, along with three anonymous reviewers, read this manuscript and made many helpful suggestions for revision. My daughter, Michelle Arnold Paine (http://www.michellepaine.com/), made several of the drawings in this work and took some of the photographs in it when she worked with me in Yucatán. This book would not have been possible without the kindness, help, and cooperation of all my potter-friends in Ticul. I trust that this publication will provide increased visibility of their craft that will ultimately benefit their economic well-being. Finally, I wish to thank all of the staff of the University Press of Colorado who have made publishing this book enjoyable. Darrin Pratt and Jessica d'Arbonne provided much encouragement throughout the process, and the artistic talents of Dan Miller have converted less-than-excellent images from 2 × 2 slides, 35 mm B&W negatives, and 120 roll film into stunning images for publication. Laura Furney was very patient and encouraging with my questions and changes during the editorial process. Beth Svinarich graciously answered my pesky concerns about copyright and marketing.

To my late parents and to my wife, June, and my daughters Michelle and Andrea, I am deeply grateful, for without them and their help, patience, grace, and encouragement, this work could not have come to fruition.

Finally, this work is my third book-length monograph about pottery making in Ticul, Yucatán. In many respects it is a prequel to my previous two books by articulating the baseline of potters' indigenous knowledge that had subsequently changed substantially. My first book about Ticul potters (Arnold 2008) described the relationship between social change and the changes in the demand, distribution, and production of pottery from 1965 to 1997. Much of that volume was a quantitative description of the changes in the population of potters. This quantitative material was supplemented by a narrative description of the potters, their families, and their production units from 1965 to 2008 in a second volume (Arnold 2015a). Because all technology is socially embedded and somatically embodied, those works provided the social context for the indigenous technology described here. The knowledge described here, however, was found exclusively among the traditional household potters in the late 1960s that most likely were rooted in the Terminal Classic Period. Ticul was, and is, a community of practice that differs from the knowledge and practice of other such communities of potters in Yucatán.

NOTES

1. In a letter to clay mineralogist, Bruce Bohor, then of the Illinois Geological Survey, Shepard (Arnold 1991, 339–30; Shepard 1967) emphasized the importance of describing pottery making in the Maya area before it disappeared. About the same time she wrote to Norman McQuown of the University of Chicago in an attempt to lure me away from the University of Illinois to focus on Yucatán pottery making rather than write a dissertation on Peru from my fieldwork in 1967 under Lathrap. By that time, I already had an NDFL Fellowship that was renewable for three years and was already working on data from Peru. Copies of the complete letter can be found in the Dean E. Arnold correspondence in the Wheaton College Archives and Special Collections (Series 2, Box 1, Folder 4), and in the papers of the Anna O. Shepard Collection in the University of Colorado Museum of Natural History, Boulder (Drawer 13, File F13, as referenced in the "Anna Osler Shepard Papers: Content and Organization" flier from the museum).

2. The Van der Leeuw and Pritchard volume focused on both ancient and modern pottery.

3. The notion that cultural patterns are totally relative to each culture is itself a universal. In other words, this assumption implies that there are no universals except the relativity of cultural patterns—a philosophical contradiction.

4. The *chaîne opératoire* of making pottery really has two different, but related meanings. One consists of the basic pottery-making sequence of collecting raw materials, preparing them, forming them into a pot, and then firing the pot (a perspective utilized in Arnold 1985). This dimension has material agency for potters' production. The second meaning consists of many sequences within that basic *chaîne opératoire* that are culturally, socially, and individually relative and potentially can be used to identify social groups. This latter meaning seems to be the meaning used by most who focus on the *chaîne opératoire* in their research.

Maya Potters' Indigenous Knowledge

1

Introduction

Academic interest in indigenous (or "local") knowledge has grown in recent years, particularly for those interested in grassroots development and natural resource and wilderness management (Menzies 2006; Menzies and Butler 2006; Mistry and Berardi 2016; Ratner and Holen 2007). Based upon work by Harold Conklin (1961), Charles Frake (1962), William Sturtevant (1964), and Brent Berlin (Berlin 1973, 1992; Berlin et al. 1966, 1968; Berlin and Kay 1969), anthropologists have looked to indigenous knowledge, not just as a way of affirming the deep experience that indigenous peoples develop in their own environmental context, but also as a way to explore ways to identify and encourage sustainability in an environment with pressures of population, acculturation, and dwindling resources (e.g., Brondizio and Le Tourneau 2016; Lauer and Aswani 2009; Ratner and Holen 2007; Sillitoe 1998). Most of these studies have focused on subsistence and agriculture (e.g., Benz et al. 2007; Berlin, Breedlove, and Raven 1974; Faust 1998; Ford 2008; Ford and Nigh 2009; Johnson 1974; Lauer and Aswani 2009), crops such as potatoes (Brush 1980; La Barre 1947), maize (Benz et al. 2007; Butler and Arnold 1977), manioc (Kensinger et al. 1975, 43–51), plants (Berlin et al. 1974), ethnomedicine (Ortiz de Montellano 1975), medicinal plants (Caamal-Fuentes et al. 2011; Hirschhorn 1981, 1982), nutritious wild plants (Felger and Moser 1973), fish (Begossi et al. 2008; Chimello de Oliveira et al. 2012), and insects (Oltrogge 1977). Indigenous knowledge also provides a close-up of intimate knowledge of subsistence practices in hostile climates such as the Arctic and perceptions of climate change (Couzin 2007).

To my knowledge, however, little attention, if any, has been devoted to the study of the indigenous knowledge of crafts and the way in which potters, in particular, perceive and engage their material world in the process of making pottery. Even though my own foray into this world (ethnomineralogy) was published more than four decades ago (Arnold 1971), no book-length study of the indigenous knowledge of crafts, and that of potters, in particular, exists.

Anthropologists and development specialists, however, are concerned with craft production in cultural, environmental, and economic contexts in which agriculture is not possible or is insufficient for survival (e.g., Goff 1990). Indeed, government intervention for developing pottery production in Ticul, Yucatán, in the past tended to ignore local knowledge (both overt and covert) that resulted in repeated failures after investing thousands, if not millions, of pesos (Arnold 2008, 238–39, 245–46; 2015a, 201–12). Such failures are not uncommon in the Third World, and the tendency is to believe that scientific knowledge is superior to local knowledge (described in López Varela 2014) and that natives are ignorant, incapable of learning, or resistant to change. Such prejudicial attributions are, of course, not true because indigenous populations are not ignorant, nor do they resist learning new practices. Native peoples have sustained themselves for hundreds and hundreds of years using their traditional knowledge, and they have adapted to changing circumstances throughout the past (see Killion 1999). This traditional knowledge, however, may be incompatible with top-down development projects that fail to take it into account, fail to respect the local people, and do not understand or appreciate the indigenous perspective (e.g., López Varela 2014; Sillitoe 1998).

Indigenous knowledge is also critical to the study of the historic and prehistoric past. A recent review of an exhibition at the British Library in London documenting the search for the Northwest Passage in the nineteenth century noted that Inuit indigenous knowledge led to the discovery of one of the ships of Sir John Franklin, who set out to find an Arctic route around North America in 1845. Both Franklin's ships and all of his men were lost, and though Inuit accounts of the tragedy at the time were widely disbelieved and denounced, they ultimately proved to be correct and led to the discovery of one of Franklin's ships in September 2014 (Fahrenkamp-Uppenbrink 2015). Similarly, Jean Polfus used traditional ecological knowledge of the Dene First Nation to study the morphological, genetic, and ecological variability of three species of Caribou in the Canadian Northwest Territories (Merkle 2016).

Indigenous knowledge also has relevance to archaeology. The Society for American Archaeology's *The SAA Archaeological Record* devoted an entire issue to indigenous knowledge and its role in archaeological practice (Whitley 2007). Ethnoecological studies of plant use and forest use in Belize have shown that the

Maya subsistence practices reveal their long-term management of the tropical forest (Ford 2008). Indigenous knowledge has also been used to identify archaeological sites in dense tropical forest and to enhance local history for local indigenous populations (Duin et al. 2015). Kelli Carmean et al. (2011) have suggested that local indigenous knowledge, based upon the different types of stone gleaned from the Maya Cordemex Dictionary, indicate that different Maya classifications of stone were differentially distributed within and around Sayil and that high-quality construction stone may have been a natural resource that was controlled and distributed in a manner similar to water and land. Besides providing a description of ancient Maya perceptions of soil, land and earth, Christian Wells and Lorena Mihok (Wells and Mihok 2009) summarized contemporary and ethnohistoric classifications of these phenomena, providing a substantial contribution to those interested in Maya agricultural development.

The use of Maya dictionaries is an important and innovative way to understand the perceptions of the environment of the ancient Maya, but it is only a first step and can miss semantic variability. Dictionaries are no better than the specialized knowledge (or lack thereof) of the informants used to produce them. When meanings are specific to specialists such as potters, masons, and swidden agriculturalists in local communities of practice, however, understanding Maya traditional ecological knowledge must be understood with reference to specific local communities, their unique landscapes, and the variability of the raw materials found within them. Any description of Maya perceptions of their environment and raw materials is, of course, important for understanding ancient Maya culture and modern agricultural development, but classifications vary from place to place, from ethnic group to ethnic group, and from the present to the past. As this work shows, classifications of the landscape and the raw materials from it are specific to distinct communities of practice. There are, of course, commonalities between such communities in the present and those in the past as the works cited above have shown, but classifications appear to be specific to communities of practice that are bounded by local landscapes and internal interaction. Moreover, such classifications are unique to specialists in a community that use those resources. A close examination of Raymond Thompson's classic work (Thompson 1958) on Yucatec Maya pottery making, for example, reveals that though he tries to lump local classifications into larger behavioral units such as clay, temper, and paint, his detailed descriptions of the local variations indicate that each pottery-making community in Yucatán recognizes different Maya classifications of raw materials, defines them differently, and uses them in unique ways. This observation indicates that though variability exists within communities of practice, there is less variability within a community in the labeling and the selection of raw materials than there is between communities.

The study of craft production of a specific community of practice is, of course, critical for archaeologists because inferences of ancient pottery production are loaded with assumptions about the distribution of craft resources, or lack of them, how pottery is made, how production is organized, how technology (and its products) are transmitted from culture to culture, and how pottery relates to the populations that made and used it. Further, the study of craft production and the indigenous knowledge about it can reveal great insights into the past, not just about ceramic production, but for all crafts as well. Unfortunately, many archaeological descriptions of ancient craft production seem to exist in a parallel universe that is largely unrecognizable from the perspective of the actual knowledge and practice of crafts such as pottery making.

Critical to the study of crafts is how potters engage their landscape in order to produce pottery. What kind of knowledge do they embody about the natural world around them, about the materials that they use, and about the process by which they turn these materials into finished vessels? How do they engage their world using this knowledge?

These questions may seem to be simple and obvious to an archaeologist with equally simple and obvious answers. Although the ethnographic and ethnoarchaeological literature is filled with descriptions of what potters do and what they make, there is little emphasis about how they think, how they perceive and classify the world around them, and what they know. Many of the descriptions include the native words for raw materials and vessels, as well they should, but such references represent only the tip of the iceberg of what the potter knows, both consciously and unconsciously.

Knowledge, however, is not behavior, and anthropologists for generations have recognized that what humans say they do, and what they actually do, are not necessarily the same. Rather, actual behavior may vary from stated practice (Lauer and Aswani 2009), and actual outcomes may vary from the rules of behavior (Johnson 1974). This is no less true for pottery production than it is for ethnoecology and the study of kinship (Gillespie 2000a, 2000b, 2000c). My own description of patterns of kinship, inheritance, and residence among Ticul potters, for example, does not reflect elicited rules or verbal responses, but rather resulted from my deep experience of more than four decades of personal knowledge of individuals, their relatives, the composition of their households, and the changes, or lack thereof, of the locations of these households (Arnold 1989; 1991; 2008, 31–91; 2012; 2015a). These patterns were verified by records of birth, marriage, and death from municipal and church records as well as by the actual composition of the households over the years. In brief, they represented the behavior of actual household composition and house lot inheritance, not just the ideal rules of such composition and inheritance.

The focus on practice and behavior rather than knowledge has recently become popular and characterized as practice theory (Bourdieu 1978, 1980), but the concern about studying actual behavior is not new (except perhaps in Europe), and has been the concern of anthropologists in America for decades. In reality, both the knowledge *and* the practice of crafts need to be the focus of study in order to understand them holistically and to apply them to the remote past.

POTTERY PRODUCTION AND PARADIGMS

Like anthropology itself, the study of ceramics has been fraught with changing theories and paradigms that lurch from one perspective to another. Paradigms are constantly replaced by other, newer, more fashionable ones. Cognitive anthropology (D'Andrade 1995), cultural materialism (Harris 1968, 1979), cultural ecology (Steward 1955), ceramic ecology (Arnold 1985; Kolb 1976, 1988, 1989; Matson 1965a, 1965b), technological choice (Lemonnier 1986, 1992, 1993; Sillar and Tite 2000; Van der Leeuw 1993), *habitus* (Bourdieu 1978; Mauss 1976), behavioral chain analysis (Schiffer 1975, 2005; the *chaîne opératoire*), practice theory (Bourdieu 1978, 1980), and engagement theory (Malafouris 2004, 2013; Renfrew 2004) have all been advanced as presumably novel and exciting ways to describe what people know, what they do, and why.

No theory and paradigm, however, have an exclusive corner on explanatory validity. Most are limited, focus on one aspect or another of human behavior, and usually cannot incorporate opposing views. Nevertheless, they are not, as some would have us believe, in competition with one another and are best understood as additive. Rather, like the proverbial apples and oranges, they are incommensurable and complement and explain different aspects of the phenomenon being studied like the metaphor of the blind man and the elephant. Any craft such as pottery making, like the remainder of human culture, needs to be embraced and studied holistically. Technological choice, for example, is not incompatible with an ecological approach in which potters receive information from the environment, their raw materials, and the pottery-making process in order to make their pottery (Arnold 1985) as some have claimed (Gosselain 1998, 79–82; Loney 2000; Van der Leeuw 1993). All can contribute significantly to a holistic understanding and explanation of ceramic production and distribution and its variability. Different paradigms and theories of ceramic production all have truth value and need to be integrated together into a unified whole.

All of these approaches to the past have value, but the study of material culture should not be simply subject to the theoretical fads and then discarded when paradigmatic fashion changes. Emphasizing each new paradigm in order to appear "trendy" or "in style" (see Arnold 1991), and ignoring the value of previous ones, suggests that there is no objective, verifiable truth, that truth about the past is merely relative to the observer's position and has no transcendent value beyond the theoretical fad at the moment. For those archeologists who believe that the past has an objective reality that exists beyond our ability to adequately know and describe it, focusing exclusively on such a relativistic stance challenges the notion that there is such a thing as a real knowable past—albeit one that can never be described fully nor completely.

Some archaeologists spend time affirming the obvious that objects have meaning, that they affect behavior, that humans have agency, that ideas are reflected in material culture, and that the technology is embedded within a social and political structure. These notions are elementary and obvious to anyone with anthropological training and ethnographic experience, and probably to any thoughtful person. It is obvious that humans materialize ideas and semantic structures in material objects and that cognition is reflected in material culture because of human agency and that technology is socially embedded. What is significant about these truisms is not that they exist or are new, but rather that anthropologists need to figure out how they are manifested and applied in a particular time, place, and circumstance.

Some modern paradigms merely dress up traditional ideas in new terminological clothing. Some of this new terminology provides a vocabulary to talk about these ideas, but one should not be mesmerized with their seeming novelty and newness. That being said, engagement theory is an encompassing explanation that can incorporate a number of paradigms that tie human agents formally to material culture in new and thoughtful ways by recognizing both the action that humans have on the material world, the resulting artifacts, and the reflexiveness of that world, the artifacts, and their context, on human knowledge and action.

ENGAGEMENT THEORY

This book presents indigenous knowledge of Maya potters of Ticul, Yucatán, from the perspective of engagement theory. Still in its nascent stages, engagement theory has the potential to be a truly unifying theory for the study of material culture and ceramic production by incorporating many different perspectives. As described by Colin Renfrew (2004) and Lambros Malafouris (2004, 2013), engagement theory concerns itself with the relationships between humans and the material world that stress the knowledge-based nature of human action, and the reflexiveness that the material world exerts on the mind.[1]

Engagement theory, like cultural ecology (which also deals with relationships) is also holistic and unifying, but rather than focusing on how cultures choose to adjust to environmental, social, and political conditions, engagement theory provides a different emphasis. Rather, both Colin Renfrew (2004) and Malafouris (2004, 2013) are concerned about the effect that artifacts ("things") have on humans and upon their minds, recognizing that the human mind extends beyond the brain.

Why Engagement Theory?

Learning to make pottery depends upon engagement with the material world, and a theory about that engagement has the potential to draw together different strands of cognitive anthropology, cultural ecology, notions of *habitus* (including motor habits), technological choice, behavioral chain (or *chaîne opératoire*) analysis, data from the landscape, and the inherent characteristics and constraints of the raw materials. This work thus is an attempt to combine such approaches into a coherent whole to describe the traditional knowledge of the Maya potters of Ticul, Yucatán.

In some respects, material engagement theory is more useful in ethnoarchaeology than it is in archaeology and needs to be more rooted in the actual engagement with artifacts in the empirical world of ethnography before it is applied to the past. This approach is not always possible, but it is possible with technological processes such as making pottery because the basic behavioral chain (*chaîne opératoire*) of making pottery is isomorphic between the present and the past. Production follows the same universal sequential process of procuring raw materials, preparing them, mixing them to make the paste, forming them into a vessel, and then drying and firing them. This sequence transcends space and time, even though there is great variability in each of these steps with behavioral sequences within them that have social significance. Further, based upon ethnographic cases among societies throughout the world, there are highly probable limits to distances to ceramic resources, constraints on production intensity by weather and climate, the amount of drying space available, and the effect of the degree of sedentariness on pottery production that can aid the archaeologist in interpreting the past (Arnold 1985, 2015a, 243–76). In this sense the process of making pottery has at least some material agency in its production (see Malafouris 2013, 207–26). As both Malafouris (2013, 20726) said and Tim Ingold (2013) illustrated throughout his work with examples from architecture and basket making (among other activities), the engagement of the material world involves both human and material agency.[2]

Engagement theory can provide a useful approach to describing potters' indigenous knowledge that relates to many of the themes of contemporary archaeology. To do so, one must understand the way that potters categorize their raw materials, the culturally relevant characteristics of those materials, and their sources in the landscape (e.g., Arnold 1971). It also takes into account the role of the environment and landscape in providing choices for production (cultural ecology and technical choices) and the actual physical properties of raw materials learned by the potter. Further, engagement theory can take into account the habitual nature of human cultural behavior. Although part of this notion is *habitus*, there is a firm physiological basis for habitual working postures and muscle syntax (e.g., motor habits). Finally, engagement theory has the potential to incorporate feedback (Arnold 1985, 1–19) from aural, visual, and tactile *percepta* derived from the potter's interaction with the raw materials, the behavioral chain of the pottery-making process, and the language of other humans. The notion of feedback developed in *Ceramic Theory and Cultural Process* (Arnold 1985), for example, was one way of describing the engagement of potters with the social and natural environment that recognizes that they are agents, that they are not oblivious to the social and natural world around them, and that potters recursively receive information (feedback) from it in a way that affects the pottery-making process. The point of that book was to restore a neglected perspective to ceramic studies that potters live and work in a natural world—not just a social, or socially constructed, one—and that the natural world of making pottery (e.g., weather, raw materials, and the process of making pottery itself) has some material agency in its production. Pottery nevertheless still embeds and materializes relativistic social and cultural patterns, but those aspects of production can be inferred more credibly if the material agency of the raw materials and of the process is understood first.

I am attracted to engagement theory because of my experience participating in the practice of making pottery when I came to understand the way in which potters engaged the behavioral chain of pottery making. First, by participating in the process of mining and selecting raw materials, I learned how to select raw materials and then selected them myself, thus understanding the way in which the potter engages both the landscape and the raw materials in it. Further, my experience with the material agency of weather and climate in Peru (Arnold 1975a; 1985, 61–98; 1993, xxiii–xxvi; 2011), Yucatán (Arnold 2015a, 243–76) and in Guatemala (Arnold 1978a, 336, 338–39, 341–42, 346–47, 351–53, 357, 365, 369, 371, 380, 384) showed me that failure to take weather into account may lead to erroneous conclusions about inferences of the intensity of craft production in ancient societies. Intensive pottery production cannot be done full time during a period with heavy rains and damaging winds without great changes in the potters' built environment (Arnold 2015a, 243–90). This perspective only occurred to me in retrospect after deep reflection on my field experiences and on the lack of pottery production during the rainy and hurricane season.

From this engagement, I learned lessons about the procurement process that I would not have understood as deeply had I not participated in it. When geologist

B. F. Bohor and I visited the clay mine at Hacienda Yo' K'at in 1968, we crawled through an entrance tunnel that was barely fifty centimeters wide and twenty centimeters high (Arnold 2008, 175; Arnold and Bohor 1977). It was so small that I had to move through it on my stomach with arms stretched out in front, propelling myself forward by the action of elbows and toes. As my toes dug into the bottom of the tunnel, my heels simultaneously scraped its ceiling. Although the tunnel opened up inside the mine into a large excavated room, getting there was not for the claustrophobic. The air was bad, and the audio recording that I made there revealed my rapid breathing. Reflecting on this experience afterward proved to be psychologically traumatic. When I showed slides of the interior of the mine to my classes and played the audiotape made there, it had devastating effects on my mental state. Nightmares about claustrophobia in the mine and the potential danger of its collapse plagued me for years afterward. ("Things" really do change the mind!) Nevertheless, experiencing the embodiment of the technology and engaging in the mining process enabled me to learn firsthand about the experience of a clay miner. As traumatic as my experience was, engaging in the actual practice of the technology created a genuine understanding of the great challenges and dangers of underground clay mining (Arnold 2008, 15–16, 158). After hearing about several deaths and near fatal accidents in the clay and temper mines during the course of my research from 1965 to 2008, I realized how dangerous such mining can be. My engagements illustrate how one cannot truly understand technological practices unless one actually participates in them (Arnold 2008, 15–16), a point also made explicitly and implicitly by Ingold (2013).

Visiting the Ticul clay source again in 1984 also provided a stimulus to reflect on the importance of bodily engaging in the technology of clay procurement. By this time the 1968 mine was abandoned, and clay was extracted through a series of vertical shafts sunk approximately three to five meters into the ground to reach the clay layer. I lowered myself into one of these shafts, as miners had instructed me, by wrapping the rope around one hand, grabbing the rope with the other, and using the footholds on the shaft wall to provide support for my body as I changed hand positions on the rope.

Climbing out of the shaft was much more difficult. Using the rope to raise myself from foothold to foothold was a daunting task, and I had to rest frequently by placing my back against the side of the shaft by pushing my feet against the opposite wall.

Miners had insisted that I remove all my clothes except my underwear to descend into the shaft, but I refused and only removed my shirt. When I ascended the shaft, however, I had to force my back against its wall as I pulled myself up the rope. In doing so, I loosened a considerable amount of marl behind me that was forced into my jeans and shorts because of the horizontal or near-horizontal position of my legs used to move me up the shaft. By the time I reached the top of the shaft, I was carrying considerable extra weight. In order to remove the marl from my jeans and underwear, I had to take off all my clothes anyway and then had to put them on again—soiled from my descent into the mine. The miners, however, only needed to remove their underwear to empty them of any marl that had accumulated in them, but they donned clean clothes—untainted because they did not wear them during mining (Arnold 2008, 15–16, 172–80). The miners' advice took on a new meaning after I descended into the mine myself. Rather than having just a dirty body that could easily be brushed off like the miners did, I had a dirty body and dirty clothes and had expended unnecessary energy in carrying marl up the shaft in my clothes!

In examining the images of my earlier visit to the clay mine in 1968, I noticed that the miner that accompanied us wore only underwear. This seemingly strange behavior finally made sense to me. As a result, I was able to gain insight into the daunting task of going up and down the shaft into the mine and raising the raw clay to the surface (Arnold 2008, 170–80).

This experience also taught me that clay mining in the shafts could not be done by a single miner, but required two men—one to mine the overburden and clay in the shaft and another to raise it to the surface. I had noticed that miners worked their shafts in two-man teams, but going down into the mine myself revealed that a single miner working in the shafts would be difficult if not possible, and such shaft mining was best accomplished by a two-man team.

When my visit to the clay mines in 1984 ended, the miners offered my informant and me a ride on the truck that transported the clay back to Ticul. In the morning we had ridden bicycles the approximately six kilometers to the mines within Hacienda Yo' K'at, and I remembered how relieved I was that did not have to ride my bicycle back to Ticul in the heat of the day. So, we placed ourselves and our bicycles on top of the load of clay, and the truck took us to my informant's house in Ticul. This seemingly simple act was a great relief, but it also made me appreciate the role of the distance traveled to clay sources and how difficult it must have been to carry virtually any amount of clay back to ancient Ticul (San Francisco de Ticul, see chapter 8) on one's back during the Terminal Classic Period (see Arnold and Bohor 1977).

I had a similar experience during my first trip to the temper mines in 1965 except that two informants and I rode bicycles to the mines during the heat of the day in the hottest season of the year. Even as a young man of twenty-two, I found the bicycle trip exhausting and was pleasantly surprised that we didn't have to bring the sacks of temper (probably weighing more than 30 kg) back with us on our bicycles (Arnold 2008, 217). Rather, informants left the sacks of prepared temper for a hauler to bring them to the potters' houses with his horse cart. If they had carried the temper on their backs when they returned to Ticul, the amount that they could carry would probably be less than thirty kilograms, and the trek back to Ticul would have been exhausting.

I also learned how to fire pots by first eliciting descriptions of the process in Yucatec Maya and then doing it by myself under the watchful eye of my informant. The result of this practical engagement aided me in understanding the nature of technological "knowledge," how it is learned, how it is practiced, and how it is passed on to others. After firing five times by myself, I learned just how complicated a seemingly simple technological process can be by understanding the multifaceted nature of human engagement with that process. This engagement helped me bridge the gap between cognitive knowledge of firing and its actual practice, and how the actual practice of firing affected the mind, specifically the cognitive structure of firing.

Similarly, on one April morning in 1965, I got up at 4:00 a.m. to accompany a potter who was taking his water-carrying jars to Oxkutzcab to sell. He had purchased space on a truck that was taking ice from the factory in Ticul, and the truck owner rented space to the potter to transport his pots. After we arrived I watched him bargain with buyers and then sell his remainders at a discount at midday so that he would not have to pay the additional cost of transporting his vessels back to Ticul.

My experience with the embodiment of knowledge and participation with potters and their craft thus have enriched this description greatly and illustrates why participant-observation is so important in anthropological research. Because technology is artifact, activity, and knowledge, actual participation in the culture permits a degree of understanding beyond questioning, verbal interaction, and observation. It provides a foundation for understanding the engagement of the potter with the craft and the sale of his products.

The lack of actual engagement as a participant-observer in the pottery-making process is one reason some archaeologists have a difficult time understanding ethnographic perspectives such as those embodied perspectives of sensory feedback presented in works such as "Ceramic Ecology of the Ayacucho Basin, Peru: Implications for Prehistory" (Arnold 1975a, 1975b), and *Ceramic Theory and Cultural Process* (Arnold 1985). Some do not understand why the effort required to carry more than thirty kilograms of clay from the source to their houses for more than five kilometers is so difficult, because they have not done it themselves. These are some of the reasons that I find archaeological descriptions of pottery production and their relationship to ancient society so incongruent with my own experience in studying pottery making in Yucatán, Guatemala, and Peru. Some archaeologists have not had the experience of actually studying or working with the potters in the field themselves and have never bodily engaged the craft enough to see the material agency of the process and its environmental context. As both Ingold (2013) and Malafouris (2013, 207–26) have shown both experimentally and theoretically, actual engagement of the archaeologist in artifact production does reveal a different and unique perspective that is helpful in understanding the production and use of material culture.

COMPONENTS OF THE THEORY

Although greatly influenced by the insights, perspectives, and theories of Ingold (2000, 2013), Renfrew (2004) and Malafouris (2004, 2013), what follows does not engage those perspectives in detail. Rather, like my other work on pottery production, it follows a synthesis based upon my own experiences in the pottery-making process with limited theoretical jargon yet without losing the importance of linking theory and data. This presentation thus is more of a grounded theory, based first on my own description and engagement in the pottery-making process of Ticul and elsewhere, and then using some of the theoretical concepts in order to try and understand that engagement from a theoretical and generalizing perspective.

THE BEHAVIORAL CHAIN (THE *CHAÎNE OPÉRATOIRE*)

If engagement theory is holistic, what are its components? First, engagement theory must include an understanding of the universal dimensions of the behavioral chain of pottery making. This sequence of activities is unique to making pottery because it follows from the unusual characteristics of clay minerals that require a fixed sequence consisting of obtaining raw materials, mixing them, adding water, and then shaping, drying, and firing them. Although the general sequence is fixed by the nature of the raw materials and the desired outcome of the final fixed form, there are numerous choices within each link of the chain. Some of these have material agency in the practice of the craft; others do not, but reflect cognitive agency influenced and modified by cultural, social, and individual factors. There are also subsequences within this master sequence that reflect individual, social, and cultural patterns that are not influenced by the material constraints of the raw materials or the pottery-making process.

The material agency of raw materials and of the pottery-making process often appears to be excluded or ignored—particularly in discussions of technical choice and the *chaîne opératoire*, as if there was no material agency at all. Making a usable paste to form pottery requires enough plasticity to form a vessel, but not so much that the shape will sag after forming. So, functioning nonplastics must be added to reduce plasticity. Then, the paste is fabricated into vessels, and then they must be dried carefully. This loss of water in the paste is a critical step in the process, and thus the humidity, temperature, and the amount of sunshine affect successful completion of the pottery-making process (Arnold 1985, 61–98). These conditions may exist in the natural environment, or they may be the result of changing the built environment to increase covered space and using special drying areas such as shelves in order to protect the pottery from the damage resulting from risks of inclement weather and those from household activities such as playing children, domestic animals, and clumsy adults (Arnold 2015a, 243–76).

The Semantic Structure of Knowledge

The second component of the theory involves the semantic structure of indigenous knowledge that is reflected in language. Language is the users' guide to understand potters' engagement with their landscape, their raw materials, and the pottery-making process. I originally approached the potter's craft through the language of the potters (Yucatec Maya) in which my informant structured the description of ceramic technology through questions that he formulated. This began even before I knew Spanish and was possible through a technique known as ethnoscience (described in the next chapter). Using this technique, I eventually learned the Maya names and indigenous semantic structure of Yucatec Maya ceramic technology that were part of the potters' indigenous knowledge.

Understanding the semantic structure was critical for understanding the native categories used in making pottery. Categorization is an integral part of human epistemology, foundational to any culture, as well as necessary for any serious scientific study. So, engagement theory should take into account the way in which the potters categorize their environment, their raw materials and their sources, and their characteristics. This categorization does not just proceed one way from the mind to the object but, as Malafouris has pointed out, involves the influence that the external world (the environment, landscape, raw materials, and pottery-making process) has on those categories. Native categories of phenomena are critical because if one also wants to approach pottery through the perspective of technical choice and discover the potter's choices, one cannot do that unless one knows the options.

In Ticul, some of the potters' semantic categories are general cultural categories known to others in the culture, but potters also utilize specialized classifications that come from their unique engagement with the process of making pots. Such knowledge is learned through experience by engaging the environment, the raw materials, and the production process itself. In many cases these categories are labeled in the native language and consist of their classifications of ecological zones, rocks, clays, tempers, firewood, vessels, parts of vessels, parts of the kiln, and parts of the firing process. The community of potters in Ticul is thus a community of practice circumscribed by potters' own interaction and by the unique landscape that they engage. It is different from other communities of practice in Yucatán that make pottery (such as Mama and Tepakán), are different interacting populations, have virtually no contact with Ticul potters, and engage a very different landscape to obtain their raw materials.

Ticul potters, for example, describe clays by the five color terms that are used in all Maya languages (Berlin and Kay 1969), but they use other more specialized categories that cut across these colors (see chapter 4). They separate high-quality clay for making pottery from ordinary clay that is not used for making pottery using properties such as taste and the manner in which the clay dries. Similarly, potters use a major class of raw materials (temper) that has the same Maya term as a widely available calcareous marl, but which they differentiate by the source from which it comes and by the presence or absence of a critical ingredient they call "white earth." Similarly, though potters share the knowledge of the categories of firewood with Maya swidden agriculturalists, they have specialized knowledge about the wood, such as speed at which each burns, the height of its flame, and whether it burns with a lot of smoke.

The culturally relative nature of these cultural and linguistic categories raises a significant issue in using them across time and space. As interesting as they might be, their usefulness for understanding the technology and for doing archaeology is limited. How can such categories be applied to the past? This study thus engages the knowledge of the potter from both the emic and the etic perspectives (Harris 1964; 1968, 568–604; 1990; Headland et al. 1990; Lett 1990; Pike 1990) that reflect complementary epistemological and methodological approaches to human culture. If one relies on verbal data, one's ability to generalize cross-culturally will be limited. Verbal data is, of course, better than no data at all, but the emic categories obtained by verbal data should be related to etic units of observation if they are to have any validity across time and space. Furthermore, etic and emic perspectives provide complementary viewpoints that enhance understanding technologies in the present, and provide a translation of the potters' technology useful in studying the past, and an epistemology for comparing it with that of other cultures in the present and in the past.

Another way of looking at the complementary perspectives of emic and etic epistemologies is to see the emic perspective as what potters say and the etic perspective as what they actually do. Further, the etic perspective thus does not just involve the translation of the emic categories, but rather is also the material results of actual practice. The results thus can be represented as scientific categories by using units of observable behavior such as minerals and chemical elements. Emic and etic approaches, however, are only ways of knowing and are not the same as actually engaging the pottery-making process. Furthermore, understanding etic categories (scientific knowledge) is not an attempt to validate useful indigenous knowledge (Brouwer 1998), but simply a way of translating indigenous (emic) categories into meanings that can be more easily understood in a different cultural context and used in the study of the past.

Customary Muscular Patterns

Engagement theory should also take into account the habitual nature of human culture called *habitus*. *Habitus* consists of at least two different aspects. First, it includes customary and habitual muscular patterns that come from repeated behaviors such as working and carrying positions (Arnold 1985, 147–50; 2008, 236–37, 240–42, 244–45). Marcel Mauss (1976) first noted that different muscular patterns existed among cultures of the world, and he called these patterns *habitus*. Gordon Hewes (1955, 1957), motivated by Mauss's work, classified worldwide postural patterns and found that over 1,000 were possible and that certain ones were common to particular regions. Hewes did not use the term *habitus*, but rather recognized them for what they were: postural patterns. Although not clearly influenced by Mauss, Robert Spier (1967) expanded the notion of working postures to include muscular patterns of motion called motor habit patterns. Arnold (1985, 147–49) applied the notion of motor habits and postural patterns to ceramic production and pointed out how these traditional patterns can inhibit the introduction of new technology such as the wheel (Arnold 2008; Arnold, Wilson, and Nieves 2008). Pierre Bourdieu (1978) reintroduced the term *habitus*, one that involves the nature of muscular patterns of position and action that were habitual. Bourdieu's use of the term, however, is broader than muscular patterns of position and action, but American anthropologists sometimes use as a simpler term. It simply appears to be the power of habitual ways of thinking called "tradition."

Muscular patterns are social in that they are learned from others, are reinforced by furniture and the lack thereof, and are consistent across different activities in a culture (Arnold 1985, 147–51; Spier 1967). With respect to pottery production in Ticul, potters work either squatting to mix the paste, or seated on the floor, or on a low stool (a *k'an che'*) to form the pottery on a turntable. As is true with work patterns in general (Arnold 1985, 147–48; Spier 1967; see also table 6.3, this volume), the postural and motor habit patterns of making pottery in Ticul are the same as those used for other activities as well. With the location of the hearth on the ground, cooking and tending the fire are done in a squatting position. Further, relaxing, cutting pond fronds, or other activities are all accomplished by using the same squatting position or by sitting on a low stool (see table 6.3 in this volume).

Second, *habitus* also involves sequences of muscle use that have created a habitual syntax of behaviors that are largely unconscious. These sequences consist of the behavioral rules and strategies that combine categories for preparing raw materials, mixing them to make the paste, using the paste to construct a vessel, and firing the vessel to forever fix its shape. These sequences could also be regarded as one aspect of the *chaîne opératoire*. Sometimes these positional and motor patterns are referred to as "muscle memory," but in reality, muscles don't remember; rather, habitually patterned positions and motor habits are the results of the syntax of synapses firing in the brain.[3] This motor learning involves the increased production of myelin, a substance that surrounds and insulates axons in the central and peripheral nervous systems. The increased production of myelin increases the speed of electrical communication among neurons in the brain and hence its computational power (Long and Corfas 2014; McKenzie et al. 2014). One view of why motor learning is habitual is that newly generated myelin is laid down preferentially in circuits that are engaged during that learning (Long and Corfas 2014; McKenzie et al. 2014). It thus alters the internal neural structure of the brain and results in habitual behaviors. The habitual use of technology and "things" thus really do change the brain just as Malafouris (2013, 119–49, 227–49) argued.

Feedback

Finally, engagement theory ties all of the phenomena of ceramic production together by incorporating feedback. Feedback consists of the information flowing to the human agent from other humans as well as that coming visually, aurally, and in tactile form from the raw materials, the environment, the landscape, and the potter's engagement with the behavioral chain (the *chaîne opératoire*) of the pottery-making process. It is simply the information perceived by human agents from their engagement with the social and physical world in a way that affects their behavior. Feedback also comes from the use of, and demand for, pottery in the form of information when it is used by a population. According to cybernetic theory, this information is not *really* feedback unless it actually affects the agent's behavior or performance or has the potential to do so.

Although first proposed more than sixty years ago by Norbert Weiner (1948, 1954), the notion of feedback or feedback loops has become a widely used scientific concept across many scientific disciplines. A search of the scientific content of journals of the American Association of the Advancement of Science for articles that deal with feedback, for example, returned references to 12,009 articles across all of the biological, physical, and social sciences, and an additional 1,238 articles in their other journals established since 1999.[4]

Feedback has become a common way to express mutually causal relationships across the natural and social sciences with discoveries that use the concept appearing almost weekly in *Science*, the flagship journal of the American Association for the Advancement of Science. A review of how *feedback* is used is beyond the scope of this work, but a brief survey of some articles in *Science* reveals that feedback loops are particularly important in natural systems such as the deviation amplifying relationship of clouds, air-sea dynamics, and ozone-temperature-wind to global warming and climate change (e.g., Clement et al. 2009; Kerr 2009b); the deviation amplifying effect of solar variations on climate variations (Kerr 2009a; Meehl et al. 2009); the mutual feedback between climate change and vegetation (Peñuelas, Rutishauser, and Filella 2009); climate change and soils (Amundson et al. 2015); feedback between the light-dark cycle, behavior, and metabolism (Ramsey et al. 2009; Wijnen 2009); and between behavior, environmental complexity, and movement strategies in mussels (de Jager et al. 2011). Feedbacks are also invoked to describe the complex relationship between fire, rainfall, and vegetation in the transitions between forest, savannas, and grasslands (Hirota et al. 2011; Mayer and Khalyani 2011). A positive feedback loop is also used to describe the social attachment between humans and dogs that is stimulated and modulated by mutually gazing at one another and mediated by the production of increased concentrations of the "trust hormone," oxytocin, in each species. Such feedback is believed to have been involved in the domestication of dogs (MacLean and Hare 2015; Nagasawa et al. 2015).

Negative or regulatory feedback loops have been advanced to describe and explain cellular responses and internal "tuning" (Justman et al. 2009) and the regulation of intracellular stress-induced proteins in *Drosophila* that prevents age-associated pathologies by a variety of factors (Lee et al. 2010). Further, regulatory feedback is invoked to describe the effect of human prefrontal cortex and hippocampus on monitoring errors ("mistakes") in learning when a human genetic variant inhibits dopamine uptake in the brain (Holden 2007; Klein et al. 2007).

Similarly, among humans a feedback model has been invoked to describe "system-dependent selection" in which "ecological feedback in a dynamical system can lead to environmental regulation, stable phenotypic diversity and an increase in mean fitness" (Lansing et al. 1998). Gregory Bateson (1958, 287–90) used the notion of feedback for what he called "circular causal systems." Malafouris (2013, 225) uses sensory feedback to describe the engagement of the potter with the clay, and Arnold (1985) has used it to describe what is now known as the material agency between pottery raw materials, the process of making pottery, weather, and a host of cultural patterns that result from the engagement of the potter in pottery production. The feedback mechanisms described in *Ceramic Theory and Cultural Process* can be viewed not only as mutually causative mechanisms for the relationship of pottery, environment, and society, but also as factors that have material agency in the pottery-making process, its seasonality, and its implication for production (see also Arnold 2011), just as Malafouris (2013) argued that the material world external to the brain can profoundly affect and change the "mind" and can be viewed as an extension of it.

Feedback for humans is, of course, different from that of natural systems in which relationships are activated by internal triggers. Unlike in nonhuman systems, humans obviously make choices, and they can choose whether or not to use the information coming from the raw materials, the pottery-making process, the weather, and the demand for vessels. If they choose to ignore this information, however, they may jeopardize the use of their craft to supply their subsistence needs. If, on the other hand, they choose to accept such information and act on it, potters must have either prior long-term memory, experiential knowledge, and working memory to deal with it, and have a problem-solving ability in order to incorporate the feedback coming from the pottery-making process to complete a pot successfully.[5]

When potters engage their craft, the information for producing pottery does not just flow from their mind through their muscles and the syntax of body movement for shaping the paste. Rather, consonant with engagement theory (Arnold 2008, 13–17; Malafouris 2004, 2013; Renfrew 2004), information about the raw materials and the process itself also flows from potters' senses back into their brains, where they make decisions about paste preparation, fabrication, shape, decoration, and firing. This feedback thus is not just a way of describing the multiple and mutually causal links between cognition, behavior, and objects, but it also has a certain ontological validity: it occurs in the minds of potters with information coming from the senses, and they must make choices based upon it. Malafouris (2013, 119–49) calls this "material agency."

On a macroscale, this kind of information flow has been documented and elaborated elsewhere (Arnold 1985) and can be described as a series feedback loops that provide information that the potter can use in making choices in the production process. When such feedback from the performance characteristics of the production process (usually from information through sight, taste, and touch) reveals that some problem has occurred, the potter must modify her behavior in order to achieve a desired result. This recursive information flow thus enables the potter to make and distribute her pots successfully (Arnold 1985).

I have seen this kind of engagement of the potter again and again in Ticul since 1965. Potters, for example, may unknowingly add inferior temper to their paste and, seeing the problems that it has caused, modify the performance characteristics of the paste by adding more *sak lu'um* (palygorskite) to it (Arnold 1971; 2008, 204–12). During the firing process, potters may face problems with excess blackening of the pottery or the failure of the wood behind the pots (i.e., the *pach k'aak'*) to burst into flame at the right moment. Throughout the entire production process, potters are receiving information from their senses, and they must make behavioral choices to ensure a successful outcome (see Arnold, Wilson, and Nieves 2008). Such information flow does not in itself cause changes in potters' behavior (as some believe), but rather provides information for them to make decisions to maintain or change their behavior in order to successfully complete the pottery-making process. This same pattern of feedback from technological processes in the process of firing occurs in the Tuxtlas in Mexico (Pool 2000), in Peru (Arnold 1972a; 1993, 106–7), and in Guatemala (Arnold 1978a), though not always described as such.

Some technological choice proponents, however, appear to argue that feedback related to raw materials and the weather is deterministic (e.g., Loney 2000; Van der Leeuw 1993). Environmental determinism, however, has not been a part of anthropology for more than a century (see also Arnold 2008, 11–13). The notion of choice, on the other hand, is really an old concept in anthropology. In his classic work *Theory of Culture Change*, Julian Steward (1955) recognized that societies and their members made choices to adjust to the environment, and that the task for the anthropologist was to discover what those choices were. Do potters, for example, have a narrow range of choices or a broad range of choices? As I stated over forty years ago: "Environment does not determine the occurrence of ceramic production, but provides choices which either favor or limit the development of pottery making and its evolution from a part-time to a full-time activity" (Arnold 1975b, 201). Rather, as potters engage their environment, their experience has provided them with the knowledge that certain choices have adverse consequences, and they use that information to make decisions about future production. Further, the environment, far from a passive backdrop for ceramic production as some technological choice theorists appear to believe, exerts selective pressures over time on those choices that are viable and those that are not viable. To use Malafouris's perspective, one aspect of the engagement of the potter with his raw materials consists of "material agency" of the raw materials, the environment, and the production process.

If potters make their vessels during rainfall, fire during rain, or lose all of their unfired pottery because of a hurricane, they soon learn that choosing to make, dry, and fire their pottery during wet weather is futile, or they build structures to shelter the process until rainy weather passes (Arnold 2015a, 243–76). Potters would regard anyone who chooses to ignore the adverse consequences of drying and firing pottery during rainy weather as foolish, naive, or stupid, even though sometimes they must fire in such circumstances because of their need for subsistence returns.

In such a case, they try to dry their pottery as much as possible in a sheltered environment and wait, if they can, to fire it on a relatively dry day.

Pottery requires drying before firing, but how much and under which conditions is highly contextual (see Arnold 1985, 61–98; Rice 1987, 152–53; 2015, 152–53). Potters can choose to make and dry their pots outside in the rain, for example, but if they do so, they are foolish and are wasting their time. The generalizations about drying thus involves understanding of the daily and seasonal patterns of weather because it inhibits the physical and molecular processes of making, drying, and firing clay objects. More important for archaeologists, however, is the availability of sufficient space to dry their pottery to avoid damage to it (Arnold 2015a, 243–76). The more objects that potters make in adverse conditions, the greater the amount of covered space that they require. This generalization has direct correlates for the archaeology of production space.

Another source of feedback comes from the embodiment of habitual tasks such as energy use. If potters use their own bodies for transporting clay and temper, their energy expended is not limitless, and the feedback from carrying a forty-kilogram sack of clay more than one kilometer affects their choice of source and type of raw material (Arnold 1985; 2008, 153–89; 2011). The amount of energy carrying clay and temper doesn't determine location of production as some archaeologists believe (Kelly, Watkins, and Abbott 2011).[6] Rather, as I have said before, the distance to ceramic resources are probabilistic and require some understanding of statistical probabilities (Arnold 2005b, 2006; see also Arnold 1991) that are consonant with a statistical "power law" (Arnold 2011). Over time, the energy costs of transporting clay and temper exert a selective force against traveling more than seven kilometers to obtain raw materials except under conditions of animal, motorized, or water transport that extends that distance using a similar amount of energy (Arnold 2011). In some cases obtaining pottery raw materials can be combined with travel for subsistence activities or moving into and through a niche with ceramic resources (Arnold 1985, 199–20), and this activity can have the effect of extending the distance to ceramic resources (i.e., an "energy extender"; see Arnold 2011). Further, distances to resources appear to have some regional variability (Druc 2013; Heidke et al. 2007), but within the general ranges of the high frequencies of distances in the model already presented, for reasons that are unclear.

Finally, feedback comes from a variety of social channels that involve anticipated demand and methods of distribution. Potters must have some information from buyers, middlemen, or other potters concerning which pots will be desired and will sell if they are to use their craft to make a living.

Feedback thus is simply the recursive flow of information from the raw materials, the paste, the pottery-making process, the environment context, and demand through the potters' senses. This information influences, but does not determine, their choices

(Arnold 1975a, 1975b, 1985). Potters monitor and evaluate such information to ensure their success in making a pot (D. Arnold 2000), and they may modify their behavior in order to achieve successful fabrication of a vessel (Arnold 1985). Using the notion of feedback simply recognizes that the relationship between social, environment, and material context and humans is not unidirectional, but is recursive with tactile, aural, and visual information flowing back to the potter from the materials, the production process, demand, and method of distribution. The notion of feedback is thus part of the information that influences technological choices. Human agents utilize the feedback from their memory, the behavioral chain, social factors, motor habit patterns, and the social and physical environment in order to make their choices for making pottery. It is the mirror image of materialization and involves at least some material agency that can affect the production of pottery (Malafouris 2013). Both materialization and feedback are necessary to understand the production process.[7]

In my earlier work I argued that the information that flows between the environment, the production process, and the potters (Arnold 1985) provided the basis for making generalizations about the relationship between pottery, the environment, and social and cultural patterns. Although the pottery production is a universal process requiring raw materials, water, temper, forming, drying, and firing, generalizations about that process and their relationships to the environment are still highly contextual and need to be related to the mineralogy of the local clays, the clay/temper mixture, and the local weather and climate.

The one qualification about feedback that was missing from my earlier work (Arnold 1985) was that the information coming from the environment, the raw materials, or the pottery-making process comes through the senses of the potter to his/her mind. In other words, the potter has agency in the choices to act or not act upon the information from feedback. I did not express this as such because it was so obvious to me. I never dreamed that some archaeologists would be so deterministic that they would see my work as being so. Determinism is in the eye of the beholder, but now Malafouris (2013) and Ingold (2013) also recognize the material agency in artifact creation. Further, one cannot be a participant-observer with potters and not recognize their agency. Only those who have not had this experience can call the effect of weather on making pottery, and the sagging and broken pots that result from it, as being deterministic.

Technological Choice

Recently, scholars have tried to emphasize the importance of the social dimensions of choice as opposed to the technological basis of choice by separating technological from nontechnological, or social choices. Social choices (or technological choices, depending upon how they are defined) in such instances are those choices made based upon other criteria than the physical constraints of the raw materials and the forming technology (Lemonnier 1986, 1992, 1993; Loney 2000; Van der Leeuw 1993). In reality, however, the physical constraints of the raw materials, and potters' engagement with them and with the production process provide the foundation for many of their choices (Arnold 1993, 106–7; Pool 2000). The result of this engagement means that every forming technology cannot successfully produce every shape as I have already shown for Ticul (Arnold 2008, 229–79; cf. Van der Leeuw 1993). Rather, the forming technology, the plasticity of the clay, the paste, the kind of temper used, and the kind of vessel produced are all interdependent.

All so-called technological choices thus really have multiple causes. Potters learn their options by social means, and they choose to make particular vessels from a combination of their indigenous knowledge about shapes, from feedback coming from social interaction about the anticipated demand for the vessels, from the constraints of the raw materials, and from the process of pottery making itself. Forming a pot is not predetermined or technically based because of raw material or climate restraints, nor are choices exclusively based upon nontechnical (social) criteria, but rather are based upon the interaction with, and the engagement of, motor and postural habits, indigenous knowledge, the raw materials, and the process of making the pot. These are then affected by the feedback of visual and tactile experience with raw materials and the pottery-making process that may require experimentation and modification (Arnold 1978b, 347; 1993, 80). Because the raw materials have different potentialities and constraints for making particular vessel shapes such as the working ranges, and the plastic and liquid limits of clay materials (Rice 1987, 61; 2015, 67–70; see also White 1949 and tables 4.7 and 4.8), different forming techniques work best with specific clay minerals, or combinations thereof.

It is thus impossible to isolate a single cause of any particular choice to make it social, technological or ideological; technical choices involve all of these dimensions in one way or another. Choices of traditional raw materials from Ticul (Yo' K'at and Yo' Sah Kab), for example, could be argued to have a social basis since they come from traditional sources of clay (Yo' K'at) and temper (Yo' Sah Kab), both of which were significant places for potters in the 1960s. Is the reason for choosing these sources then a strictly nontechnological one? The importance of the sense of place of those locations was, of course, a significant explanation, but further analysis revealed that both of these places have unique materials that are superior for making pottery compared to those from other locations (Arnold 1971; see also chapter 3 in this volume). Choices that potters make have multiple levels of explanation. Social choices may have technological reasons as their basis, even though the potters may not know or understand those reasons.

This combined social and technological dimension of choice can be illustrated in Quinua, Peru, where design structures reflect both community-based standards of design and the ecological and social structure of the community (Arnold 1970b; 1983; 1984; 1993, 147–96), but with great variability of the choice of design within that structure. Although the potters' choice of design structure, design motifs, and bands would seem to be exclusively socially derived with considerable choice involved, the social organization, irrigation organization, and the socially perceived environment also influence the design structure (Arnold 1983, 1984). To put it differently, the behavioral chain of pottery design has many levels of social, environmental, and technological criteria that are embedded within it. Separation of the social dimensions of choice from its technological dimensions is thus artificial and is the product of analysis, not cultural reality.

Some scholars argue for the determinative role of culture in ceramic production because clay is so plastic and thus reflects the imprint of the culture with no intervening factors. This notion is a flawed assumption and was reviewed and critiqued more than thirty years ago in the introduction to *Ceramic Theory and Cultural Process* (Arnold 1985, 1–19). It has a long history in American anthropology and goes back at least to the early twentieth century. Ruth Bunzel (1929) brought it into the study of pottery, and it was believed that it metaphorically paralleled the notion of the total plasticity of the human personality that emerged from the influence of Freud on the American Culture and Personality School of thought in early twentieth-century anthropology (Arnold 1985, 1–19). Indeed, *Ceramic Theory and Cultural Process* was written to show that pottery was not totally plastic, and the pottery-making process itself also had agency in the cultural patterns necessary in its production. In retrospect, that work was an early statement and example of what is now called "material agency" (Malafouris 2013, 148).

Based upon experimental archaeology and a review of the literature of the previous fifteen years, Tim Ingold (2013) made an identical point in his book, *Making: Anthropology, Archaeology, Art and Architecture*. Material culture, he argued, does not passively reflect makers' ideas or designs, but rather materials are transformed by the maker into a usable product within the constraints of the materials and the technical challenges of the actual "making" process. Malafouris (2013) made a similar point in his detailed elaboration of engagement theory and went further to say that the mind extends beyond the brain and that the external world changes the brain and, by extension, cognition.

Pottery thus is the result of interaction of many factors that enable potters to engage their technology to produce a pot. Culture (or human agency) is certainly one important factor, but it is not the only factor influencing production, instead including many generalizable (nonrelativistic) factors from the natural and social environment. The chemical and mineralogical characteristics of clay minerals, and the process of forming clay into pottery, for example, have generalizable relationships with the pottery-making process (Arnold 1985). Consequently, the potter's choices (and culture) are not simply imprinted on the raw clay but are rather the product of the bodily engagement of the potter and the raw materials involving the potter's training and tradition and his interaction via feedback from the raw materials, the environment, and the process of the emerging pottery product.

THE STRUCTURE OF THIS BOOK

The remainder of this book unfolds the indigenous knowledge of the Maya potter of Ticul with reference to engagement theory just laid out. The next chapter details how the data for this book were gathered. Although much of the data were collected more than fifty years ago, my experience with cognitive anthropology, and its separation from archaeology until relatively recently, meant that the paradigms for presenting this research at the time were too divergent from prevailing paradigms for publication. Part of my problem was my own disillusionment with cognitive anthropology. Eventually, supplementing cognitive categories with a more active engagement in the process of pottery making in the field, I was able to use the Maya categories that I learned, but there was no way to put it all together into a more unified and holistic approach until now. The development of engagement theory (Malafouris 2004, 2013; Renfrew 2004) and Ingold's (2013) description of his students' experiential engagement with making artifacts excited and encouraged me to present my cognitive data along with the experience I gained by actually engaging in the pottery-making process.

Chapter 3 presents the potters' perception of the landscape around Ticul. The details of the landscape—with its culturally defined land forms, forest, and the openings in the landscape—are critical components of the way in which the potter engages the environment to obtain the raw materials to make pottery.

Chapter 4 is an exploration of the Maya potters' ethnomineralogy, the way in which they engage, conceptualize, and classify their raw materials. To make this analysis more relevant to archaeologists and non-Maya, I have also described these data in ways that relate to actual minerals and their physical properties.

Chapter 5 describes the potters' engagement with the changing properties of their raw materials once they are prepared and mixed with water in preparation for forming. In this case, the mental template often regarded as a "paste recipe" is, in reality, at best a rough guide, and the potter must change the amounts of raw materials in the paste as he engages the performance characteristics of the paste. Again, the imprint of a mental template on paste preparation fails as an explanation for how potters make their objects.

Chapter 6 describes the way in which the potters conceived of making a pot and the way in which they produced it. Although Ticul potters produced different vessels in the 1960s from what they do now, the chapter focuses only on the major traditional vessels that potters made in 1965 but were largely abandoned after 1970.

The theme of Maya perceptions and indigenous knowledge of firing is presented in chapter 7 and describes the way in which potters built their traditional kiln and how they named its parts. After an elaborate preparation for firing, potters load the kiln and fire their vessels through a series of named stages and substages using certain types of firewood to achieve the desired effects necessary for the successful completion of the process.

Chapter 8 utilizes the perspective of "pottery as distilled landscape" to synthesize some of the data in this work. This notion originally was developed by Ingold (2000) and then modified as "congealed landscape" by Kostalena Michelaki et al. (2012, 2014). Because of great social and technological changes that have occurred in Ticul in the last fifty years, some of the points in the synthesis are speculative. Nevertheless, it does show that the notion of pottery as distilled landscape has some validity in the rich ethnographic data from Ticul. Because of the uniqueness of its landscape, cognition, and practice of making pottery in Yucatán, the chapter argues that Ticul pottery, before the late twentieth century, distilled portions of the local landscape as a "taskscape" and thus was the product of a unique community of practice circumscribed by distances not exceeding seven kilometers. This application reinforces its value for archaeological contexts as well.

Finally, the conclusion ties the work together and argues for the importance of understanding the engagement of the potter in the making process if one is to understand the past. Showing the value of engagement theory, this chapter applies and summarizes the work as a contribution to refining ideas about technology. It reiterates that the potters' perception of the environment around Ticul and the cognitive categories used by potters in their engagement with the landscape, their raw materials, and the pottery-making process are the product of a unique community of practice that is different from other such communities in Yucatán.

This chapter also reveals how ethnoarchaeological research among Ticul potters during the last fifty years has enriched Maya Cultural Heritage. Unfortunately, much of this heritage has now disappeared because of great social changes, the changes in demand for many ceramic vessels, and the potters' loss of the Yucatec Maya language.

Finally, the chapter recapitulates Malafouris's notion that cognition extends beyond the brain. Indeed, it is the interaction of cognition with the feedback of landscape, raw materials, and the pottery-making process that gives rise to the semantic categories that constitute part of indigenous knowledge that the potter used to make pottery. That this knowledge has changed verifies Malafouris's idea that "things"—whether landscape, raw materials, or vessel shapes—change the mind. In Ticul, however, this change also results from task segmentation in which potters no longer have direct interaction with the landscape and the market.

NOTES

1. Malafouris's theory is much more complex than that which is described and applied here. In light of the lexical elaboration that he uses in his book, this presentation engages that theory generally. What I have done here is to apply his theory to my own fieldwork experience but without the elaborate lexical semantics. In doing so I have failed to elaborate the detailed richness of his theory, but I hope to have made it clearer and more accessible.

2. Ingold made this point very eloquently when he said: "Human endeavours, it seems, are forever poised between catching dreams and coaxing materials. In this tension, between the pull of hopes and dreams and the drag of material constraint, and not in any opposition between cognitive intellection [sic] and mechanical execution, lies the relation between design and making. It is precisely where the reach of the imagination meets the friction of materials, or where the forces of ambition rub up against the rough edges of the world, that human life is lived" (Ingold 2013, 73).

3. Maléne Lindholm et al. 2016 also cast doubt on the notion of muscle memory as a result of muscle-training experiments: "We found no coherent evidence of a skeletal muscle transcriptome memory, even though there were some data indicating a training-induced memory mechanism" (Lindholm et al. 2016, 40). The source of such memory may be in the brain as I have suggested here.

4. These journals included *Science* (11,017 articles), *Science Signaling* (begun in 1999, 992 articles), *Science Translational Medicine* (begun in 2009, 241 articles), *Science Advances* (begun in 2015, 91 articles), and *Science Immunology* (begun in July 2016, 1 article). All but 26 of these articles occurred after 1952, with most of them published since 1977 (http://science.sciencemag.org/search/feedback?, accessed October 1, 2016).

5. Working memory consists of the brain system that is necessary for the concurrent storage and processing of information necessary for complex cognitive tasks such as language comprehension, learning, and reasoning (Baddeley 1992, 556). Standing "at the crossroads between memory, attention, and perception" (Baddeley 1992, 559), working memory consists of the central executive that coordinates the visuospatial sketch pad, the phonological loop, and as more recently proposed, the episodic buffer (Wynn and Coolidge 2010a). To explore these components in relation to the engagement of the Maya potters with their indigenous knowledge is beyond the scope of this work. Suffice it to say, however, that some of the literature on working memory and its proposed relationship to the evolution

of cognition reveals the dramatic role that human engagement (rather than a preexisting mental template) with vocalization, visual images, and action has in the development of the modern human mind (Wynn and Coolidge 2010b). If indeed engagement appears to be so significant in the development of the modern human mind, then is it reasonable, if not obvious, that the relationship between Maya cognition and Maya pottery as proposed in this work is not just the materialization of a mental template, but rather the engagement of Maya cognition with the environment, raw materials, and process of making pottery.

6. Sophia Kelly et al. (2011) believe that the threshold model of ceramic resources is deterministic but provide no evidence that this is indeed the case, and they do not understand the probabilistic nature of the model as evident in the graphical distribution of distances to resources (Arnold 1985) and as a statement of statistical probabilities cited in works published well before their article was published (Arnold 2005a, 2006). Nevertheless, the distances to resources in their case study do precisely fit the curve of my probabilistic model of such distances (Arnold 2005b, 2006, 2011).

7. Flint knapping was the model that was used for the development of the notion of the *chaîne opératoire*. For anyone who has done any rudimentary stone knapping themselves, or watched someone with these skills, visual feedback also occurs in the production of stone tools. Choices, for example, depend upon (among other factors) the results of previous blows to the raw material that are visible to the maker.

2

How Was the Data Collected?

The methodology for collecting the data used in this work reflects more of a pilgrimage of trying to understand my data about potters' indigenous knowledge and my experience with engaging the potters' technology than it is the result of a methodology derived from a tightly conceived and executed research question. This chapter documents that pilgrimage. Now spanning more than fifty years, this pilgrimage has shown me that deep involvement with a culture and their technology is not easy, simple, or succinctly explained. Rather, the paradigms, theories, and techniques that I used early in my fieldwork were simply inadequate to explain my own experience in which I had learned how to think and behave as a potter. Since the turn of the twenty-first century, however, new paradigms and theories have emerged in both anthropology and archaeology that helped make sense of my engagement with the technology of the Maya potter.

This work thus is based upon a number of different methodologies that constitute a holistic approach to the indigenous knowledge of the Maya potter. Initially, my approach consisted of using the techniques of ethnoscience, now associated with what is called cognitive anthropology. I found these techniques, however, less than satisfying because they were entirely based upon language, and all behavior was forced into the conscious, verbal level. Much knowledge that drives behavior, however, is below the level of awareness and is often not understood without participation in the culture or a violation of cultural rules. Nevertheless, ethnoscience provided a foundation for participation, engagement, and observation of the pottery-making process, and it provided a framework that allowed me to see the process from the perspective of the Maya potter through the more than forty years of my experiences, interaction, engagement with, and observations of the process of making pottery in Ticul.

THE METHODOLOGY AND ITS HISTORY

The roots of this research began in fall 1964 during my first semester in graduate school. I had come to the University of Illinois to study linguistics, but I also enrolled in an anthropology course in ethnographic field methods. The professor (Duane Metzger) had recently returned from Mexico with two informants. One was a Tzeltal-speaking Indian from Tenejapa, Chiapas (Alonzo Méndez) and the other was a Yucatec Maya–speaking potter from Ticul, Yucatán (Alfredo Tzum Camaal). Metzger also brought local raw materials and pottery-making equipment from Ticul and set up Alfredo and his equipment in the basement of a university-owned house so that he could make pottery there. He also asked Alfredo to build a kiln behind the house using Illinois stone and clay. Its construction and the entire pottery-making process were observed by members of Don Lathrap's archaeology seminar, who also cut, measured, and drew sherds that Metzger brought from Alfredo's family kiln in Ticul. Another faculty member (Art Rohn) documented the production process for a proposed teaching museum in the department, and measured the firing temperatures using a pyrometer. The university's audiovisual service produced a film about the project called *Ollero Yucateco* (Metzger and Lathrap 1965; Nash 1966).

Metzger also used the informants for his field methods course so that the graduate students could gain proficiency in an elicitation technique called "The New Ethnography" or "Ethnoscience," pioneered by Metzger, Gerald Williams, Mary Black, and others (Black and Metzger 1965; Metzger and Williams 1963a, 1963b, 1966; see also Black 1963; Frake 1962; Sturtevant 1964, 99–101). Now considered to be a part of cognitive anthropology (D'Andrade 1995; Tyler 1969), this technique is based upon the assumption that culture is knowledge and is organized by language (Goodenough 1957, 1964). It thus emphasizes eliciting linguistically labeled semantic categories as a method of doing ethnography. Because the ethnoscience technique focuses on the categories that informants themselves know, this technique helps to eliminate the investigator's initial ethnocentric bias and enables her to elicit a wide variety of cultural information in the informant's native language (Metzger and Williams 1963b, 1076; Sturtevant 1964, 99–101).

The ethnoscience technique (as conceived by Metzger) begins by asking an informant to formulate a question in his native language using a language common to the informant and ethnographer (Spanish in this case). The ethnographer then asks that question of the informant, who responds in a culturally appropriate manner. By having the informant formulate significant questions and appropriate responses, the ethnographer builds the structure of his informant's worldview by using the categories that are free of the anthropologist's cultural and theoretical biases. Essentially, it eliminates a mass of irrelevant observations, and it identifies the cognitively significant information immediately *in the field*. Ultimately, this technique can uncover folk taxonomies and other semantic structures in any cultural domain.

Remarkably, the approach can be accomplished with a limited knowledge of the informant's native language. In Metzger's class, I worked with the Tzeltal informant. I knew no Tzeltal or Spanish, and my informant knew no English. Consequently, the task of eliciting the Tzeltal categories initially seemed impossible. But, I had come to the class with experience in basic descriptive linguistics that taught me the skills of phonetic transcription and morphological analysis. With a little help with question words (such as "who," "what," "when," "where," and "how"), and with some knowledge of Tzeltal grammar provided by Metzger, I was able to elicit an elaborate ethnotaxonomic scheme of pottery shapes in Tzeltal along with the informant's drawings of them. The process revealed a folk taxonomy of vessel function and distinctive features of the shape characteristic of each of the six Tzeltal pottery-making communities. All of these data revealed the structure of how a Tzeltal man who was not a potter understood and categorized Tzeltal pottery and recognized their distinctive features.

In spring 1965, Metzger sent me, another student, and the two informants to Mexico to return them to their communities and begin fieldwork in Yucatán. Metzger joined us in Puebla, and we then proceeded to Yucatán, where we were joined by two other students. Metzger's approach to fieldwork was "sink or swim," and after he set us up in a house in Ticul, he disappeared, only to resurface briefly to pay our informants and our rent. Still accustomed to the spoon-feeding approach that characterizes much of American undergraduate education, we found Metzger's approach to fieldwork caused us considerable anxiety. Initially, we were resentful and felt abandoned because we had little guidance and virtually no encouragement.

When Metzger first told me that learning a culture through its language was possible without first knowing the language, I was incredulous. My subsequent research in Ticul, however, demonstrated that Metzger was correct. I had mastered the ethnoscience technique in Urbana, and I was able to elicit frames and texts in Yucatec Maya with no initial knowledge of Yucatec or Spanish. Fortunately, I had also undertaken two independent studies in linguistics as an undergraduate. An intensive summer's training in descriptive linguistics and independent work with a Japanese informant at the University of North Dakota, and describing and analyzing glossolalia in a local Episcopalian Church during my senior year in college gave me the basic tools of linguistic analysis. At the University of Illinois, I had taken a field methods course in linguistics during the previous semester that consisted exclusively of independent work with a Malayalam-speaking informant.

In retrospect, these experiences prepared me well for working in Yucatec Maya. They increased my sensitivity to the subtleties of its phonemes and taught me how to transcribe them. Nevertheless, working with an entirely new language within a new cultural context provided a great challenge. A sympathetic linguist (Robert W. Blair; see Blair 1964), who was working in Ticul at the time, helped me with the subtleties of Yucatec tone, glottals, and grammar.

So, I began my research in Ticul using the ethnoscience technique, and during the course of six months, I learned both conversational Spanish and basic Yucatec Maya. I was so afraid of failure and worked so hard that I collected vast amounts of data. The amount and quality of these data still astounds me more than five decades later. Much of this information forms the basis of this book.

At the beginning of the field season, Metzger suggested that I might want to work on pottery firing using Alfredo Tzum Camaal, one of the informants we had brought back with us from Urbana. I followed his suggestion, and used the ethnoscience technique with great success. With very limited Spanish, I asked Alfredo to formulate an appropriate question about firing. I then asked the question, and he responded appropriately.

Metzger insisted that I transcribe both questions and responses because he argued that traditional ethnographies were the result of responses to unknown stimuli. As I learned the Yucatec question words and grammar, I formulated new questions that focused on building a folk taxonomy such as "What are the parts (P) of the firing process?" Responses (R) to this question (RP) were substituted into the question frame: "What are the parts of (RP)?" I also formulated questions that built a chronological sequence. This strategy began with a question such as "How do you fire pottery?" After the potter responded (R1), I formulated a question using his response, substituting it into the frame of the first question: "After you finish R1, what do you do next?" In this manner, I continued framing the same question with different substitutable items. This procedure continued until I reached the limit of Alfredo's knowledge.

Initially, I thought that I had formulated a rather small, tightly focused research strategy of learning how a Maya potter fired his pottery. Much to my surprise, however, firing pottery successfully was not just about firing but was tied to the entire production process from the selection of raw materials, their sources in the Maya landscape, and Alfredo's response to weather conditions. Early in my research, the questioning process led to information about raw materials because potters believed that certain types of clay, temper, and wood were critical for successful firing. Subsequent questions and responses dealt with how to select the appropriate raw materials and how to distinguish them from materials that were not used for making pottery. Other queries elicited the parts of a vessel, the kinds of raw materials, the sources from which they came, the steps of forming and firing, the parts of the kiln, the types of firewood needed to achieve a desired result, and the types of firing accidents and their causes. All of this information revealed detailed semantic structures of various cultural domains used by Ticul potters.

At various intervals I solicited multisentence texts in Yucatec Maya in order to provide a check on the questioning and to determine whether the categories in the texts were the same as those that emerged from the questioning. The question, "How do you make pottery?" for example, produced a text that yielded culturally recognized portions of the pottery-making process including the categories of required raw materials. Similarly, the question "How do you fire pottery?" resulted in a text that listed the main stages of the firing process that I followed up later with further questions.

All of this interaction largely took place in Yucatec Maya and was faithfully transcribed with few Spanish or English interlinear translations. When a puzzling word or phrase arose from the questioning or from the texts, I asked Alfredo about it with my growing knowledge of Spanish, and he provided concrete examples of categories, processes, and distinctions.

I soon learned that learning *about* the potter's indigenous knowledge of firing was different from learning the potter's actual engagement with the process. Learning the Maya categories of raw materials, parts of the kiln, and the stages of firing, as indispensable as they were, was insufficient to fully understanding the firing process and how the potter actually fired his vessels. Discovering what people actually do (real behavior) from what people say they do (ideal behavior) is probably the central epistemological issue both in ethnography and ethnoarchaeology. Nevertheless, it is possible to address this problem by using different techniques that address both emic and etic perspectives (Gould 1978; Harris 1964, 1968, 1990; Lett 1987, 61–67; 1990; Pike 1990) and those that focus on both validity and reliability (see Arnold, 1967a, 1967b, 1971; Pelto and Pelto 1978, 33–34). Validity concerns measuring what one purports to measure, whereas reliability refers to repeatability (Pelto and Pelto 1978, 33–34). Further, as I discovered later, the observations and actual practice of firing pottery turned out to be somewhat different from its semantic structure. This disjunction puzzled me, but it wasn't until I learned about motor habits and engagement theory—and especially read Ingold's (2013) book, *Making*, in early 2014—that I discovered that these new paradigms and theories helped explain the disconnect between the cognitive structure of making and firing pottery and its practice. Ingold's description of the actual engagement of selecting raw materials, and his description of the accounts of his students' attempts at making various objects, helped me make sense of my experience from almost fifty years earlier.

The emergence of the disconnect between cognitive anthropology and my engagement with the pottery-making process was serendipitous. During that first field experience, I was dutifully transcribing linguistic and semantic data in the confines of my house during the oppressive heat of the dry season. Many times I would fall asleep after lunch with pen in hand and retire to my hammock for a brief siesta while my informant, Alfredo, patiently waited for my mind to come back online. After about two months, I was tired of talking to a single informant inside my house and was exhausted and bored from eliciting a seemingly endless litany of Yucatec Maya semantic structures. I had also started to suffer the loneliness of culture shock—that crisis experience necessary for all who successfully adjust to the values of another culture. I thus decided to change my approach by visiting potters and learning firsthand how they actually fired their pottery in order to involve myself more intensively in the life of the potters and their craft. Several households were visited regularly, and field notes were transcribed documenting these visits. I also traveled to raw material sources, and observed the religious rituals (*novenas*) associated with potters' deceased relatives, and those for the patron saint of Hacienda Yo' K'at, where potters obtained their clay (see Arnold 1971; 2008, 158–59).

My switch to participant-observation also involved other methodologies. I conducted an informal survey of the potters in the community. Its overall purpose was to record the kind, size, and orientation of the kilns in Ticul, but other kinds of data were also collected. During this survey I photographed all of the kilns of each household I visited and in the process discovered that potters also possessed a sophisticated knowledge of weather patterns that informed the orientation of their kilns. I also visited the source location where temper was mined and prepared, photographing temper selection and steps of the process. I also witnessed firing as often as I could, and I photographed the stages of the firing process. These images visually illustrated the critical stages of the process and their associated behavior.

This change in strategy was, in retrospect, precisely that which was necessary for adapting to culture shock. I enjoyed my participant-observation experience so much that it completely changed my research design and methodology. Instead of focusing on transcribing queries and responses about firing in Yucatec Maya in my house, I observed every firing episode by my informant (Alfredo Tzum Camaal), his brother-in-law (Francisco Keh), his cousins next door (Elio and José Uc), and another potter I knew (Manuel Martín). Each time Alfredo told me that he, his relative, or his friend was going to fire, I would observe the process, sometimes sitting facing the kiln with my typewriter before me on a table. Each time the potter performed some activity related to firing, I described it in English, transcribed my informant's description of it in Yucatec Maya, and noted the time. This approach revealed some interesting patterns, but it turned out that the passage of time during the firing process was tertiary, if not irrelevant, from the viewpoint of the potter.

My eliciting process, however, revealed a very different pattern. Much of Alfredo's verbal account indicated that he performed certain sets of behavior at well-defined stages of the process, and he used these stages in his description of the process. From my observations, however, I had practically no idea of how he conceptualized firing but that he was subdividing the firing process according to what was happening inside the kiln. I noted several regularities in his behavior, but I was unable to gain any appreciation or understanding of the cognitive structure associated with them.

Fortunately, direct observations of kilns and firing practices eventually served as a means of checking my texts and question/response frames. When my observations did not fit the explanation that my informant had given me, I asked about the discrepancy and used it to probe more deeply into the potter's knowledge. By having the potter describe his behavior in Maya, transcribing it, and then questioning him about it in Spanish, I could compare it with my observations and with the data in Yucatec Maya that I had elicited previously. In most cases he had overgeneralized his description, and after my questioning, he explained more of the detail and structure of the process that were apparently too complex to explain previously. In order to verify the accuracy of my observations, I repeated this questioning at a later time to be sure that the information was complete and that my informant was truly describing his knowledge of the process, not just relying on his memory of what he had told me earlier.

Eventually, I began to see that the potter engaged the firing process as a sequence of steps with transitions to each step based upon visual feedback from what was happening in the kiln. As my comprehension of the Maya description of firing deepened, I began to see its relationship to my observations and was able to see how he used that feedback to make behavioral choices that influenced the successful completion of the process.

My observations of firing provided visual references of the Maya categories elicited earlier, and I began to be more confident about the verbal descriptions of firing that I had painstakingly described during the first two months of my research. Nevertheless, my observations led me to suspect that there was more to firing pots than my observations led me to believe, and more than I had recorded from Alfredo's semantic structures of the process based upon my linguistic data. So, I wanted to find out if my knowledge was sufficient to actually fire the pots. This concern reflected Ward Goodenough's (1957) assertion that "culture" consisted of what one had to know in order to get along in a culture and be accepted as one of its members. Adequate cultural description occurs when an anthropologist acquires enough knowledge to enable him to behave (or practice) in a way that the members of the culture consider appropriate (Goodenough 1957). I had learned the language of firing, the stages of the process, the kinds of behavior required, and the parts of the kiln. But, was my knowledge sufficient to fire successfully? Would my knowledge and behavior be acceptable to a Yucatec potter as Goodenough (1957) had proposed?

This question essentially concerned scientific validity (Pelto and Pelto 1978, 33–34). The semantic categories derived from my elicitation technique provided a rather abstract description of pottery production that, as important as these categories were, needed to be related to nonverbal behavior. I had already seen that informants *did* behave in the manner in which they said they did, but could I replicate that behavior myself based upon my knowledge and observations of the firing process? I had already made a number of observations of the nonverbal behavior of firing, but were my observations and knowledge of the linguistically labeled semantic categories sufficient to emulate that of a Maya potter in a manner that he considered appropriate and acceptable?

In order to answer these questions, I wanted to fire a kiln-load of pottery myself in order to evaluate my description of the potter's indigenous knowledge. Over a period of many weeks, I had observed many firing events. So, I asked Alfredo if I could fire his pots. Initially, he was skeptical, but ultimately he agreed to let me fire a partial kiln-load of mold-made figurines under his watchful eye. He explained that my attempt would be a test to see if I could do it without ruining them. So, he partially filled his kiln with mold-made objects that would be easy to fire. If I failed to fire the vessels properly, then he could fire them again, or repair them with plaster of Paris, and then sand and paint them. Fortunately, my attempt at firing was successful, and by the end of the first field season, Alfredo and his brother-in-law allowed me to fire five kiln-loads of their pottery by myself.

My actual practice of firing verified the linguistic and observational data that I had collected, but I also learned new insights and explanations of the potters' behavior. I learned many lessons about the relationship of cognitive knowledge to behavior and practice as well as becoming aware of the limitations of the cognitive approach. During my first attempt of firing, I was performing the tasks learned from verbal transcriptions. I had elicited the categories of firewood, the structure of the process, and the behaviors required for each part. But, I soon discovered that this knowledge was limited and insufficient to emulate the potter's behavior. Although I knew the names of the firewood categories, I could not identify them, and Alfredo gave me a crash course about the characteristics of the firewood so that I could use the appropriate types for firing his pots. Equally, if not more important, I did not realize that the potter possessed an underlying, and largely unconscious, set of cognitive rules or strategies of practice that were just below his threshold of awareness.

One such rule was expressed as a curious set of contradictions in my written transcriptions. They indicated that adding firewood to the kiln during the warming period was done by increasing the quantity of wood by a given number of pieces until a certain threshold was reached and the kiln was considered "hot." I elicited these data several times, and Alfredo responded with different amounts each time; his descriptions of the amounts of wood added appeared to be contradictory. All of these descriptions indicated that it was important to count the sticks of firewood added to the kiln during the initial stage of firing.

When I actually tried to follow one of the verbal recipes that I had elicited, and counted the pieces of firewood that I was about to throw into the kiln, Alfredo reprimanded me by saying that the number of the sticks of firewood added to the kiln was not important. Rather, he said, I should wait until the flame diminished to a point slightly above the wood and then add a little more wood than I added previously. Further, as the fire increased in intensity, I needed to add firewood evenly across the floor of the kiln with each new charge of fuel.

Alfredo reprimanded me because I replicated the recipe rather than engaging the process and applying the underlying strategies of practice. Because of my error, his threshold of awareness deepened, and he was able to describe the strategy to me. Originally, those strategies (one kind of *habitus*) had generated a detailed verbal description of firing, but the elicitation process had not produced the strategies themselves. In retrospect, the actual strategies of the practice of firing were just as important as the cognitive knowledge about it.

Besides its failure to reveal the behavioral strategies of throwing wood into the kiln, my elicitation did not discover the potter's motor habit patterns—another critical dimension of technological practice. Toward the end of firing, the heat of the fire from the door of the kiln was overpowering. Yet one must get close enough to its door to throw the firewood into the kiln to position it properly inside. During my first attempt at firing, I was fighting the oppressive heat of the flames and trying to get close enough to the kiln door to add more firewood. As I threw the wood into the kiln, it hit the pots on the far side. Again, Alfredo reprimanded me because hitting the vessels with the wood would damage them. Pushing me aside and taking wood in hand, he snapped it into the kiln with a short wrist motion, rather than using the full arm swing that I had used, and the wood fell precisely in the desired location without hitting any pots. He briefly demonstrated the motion to me, and soon, I too was throwing wood to a precise location inside the kiln using the same technique. In all of the weeks of eliciting the terminology and chronology of the firing process, he had never revealed this motor habit pattern to me. Once my behavior threatened to damage his pots, however, the detail and importance of this skill quickly emerged into his level of awareness, and he was able to describe it to me. Again, my experience revealed that understanding pottery firing was much more than just observing the process or eliciting Alfredo's knowledge about it.

Another example of the value of practice beyond mere description and observation concerned the strategies that the potter uses to terminate firing. After the pots become totally black and the wood behind the pottery has completely burned, the potter considers the kiln hot, and the final stage begins. During this stage, wood is thrown into the kiln evenly in a series of intermittent additions after the fire burns down after each addition of fuel. After feeding the kiln this way three or four times, the potter lets the wood burn completely until no more than glowing embers remain. Then, he bends down to look into the kiln. If he sees that the pots are black in several places, he has several choices to make. If they are black in the back of the kiln near the floor, then that part of the kiln got too hot, and he must avoid throwing more wood into that area. If he sees blackness in other areas, however, it means that the pottery is not completely baked, and he must continue adding wood targeted to that area. If, on the other hand, the pots are all glowing red, firing is complete and he can end the process.

Unfortunately, my verbal data of this stage of the process indicated that the potter's behavior was fixed and did not vary with the conditions inside the kiln. It is unlikely that I would have discovered these strategies for firing if I had not actually fired myself. Potters' choices during firing are deeply influenced by visual feedback from the kiln.

Probably the most interesting aspect of this research was the discovery of the complexity of the potter's technological knowledge. He knew the burning characteristics of forty-seven different types of firewood, and he knew how to use each type effectively during the firing process to achieve the desired effect during each stage. In addition, his understanding of firing accidents and what caused them demonstrated that he also had a practical knowledge and understanding of firing and its consequences. Further, he had some control over the process and achieved the desired affects despite variations in firewood and seasonal weather, and what he saw happening inside the kiln. Most important for me, however, was that firing pottery was not just placing wood in a kiln full of pots and lighting the fire. Rather, it consisted of a large body of knowledge about materials and processes and of the engagement and interaction with them that produced the desired effect in the face of a variety of modifying influences and stimuli. It was not the imposition of a mental template on the firing process, but rather the engagement of the potters' knowledge and practice with the feedback from the process. This knowledge and practice, both explicit and implicit, also encompassed the entire pottery-making process from the selection of the raw materials to the removal of the fired pot from the kiln.

In retrospect, my practice of firing was precisely the kind of engagement that Ingold (2013) described from a series of experiences that his students encountered in making artifacts using a variety of materials. The making of a fired pot involved a transformation of the dried clay pot into an inflexible solid one, and this involved my engagement with the qualities of the raw materials and problem-solving the interaction of weather, firing, and raw materials. Finally, after more than forty-five years, my experience with firing in Ticul made sense to me in a conceptual and explanatory way.

By far one of the clearest demonstrations that Alfredo's knowledge about firing did not take the precise form of my elicited knowledge became evident as he reflected on his experience firing back at the University of Illinois in the fall of 1964. Because it appeared that the potters' firing behavior reflected a complex interaction of knowledge, his engagement with materials, and the process itself, I asked Alfredo about his firing at the University of Illinois. He had built a kiln there and fired it using local materials. He said that he was unfamiliar with the wood used, but he was able to fire successfully by using his basic principles of firing. These principles were essentially those strategies that I had learned during my own experience with firing in Yucatán but were applied to the Illinois context without any of the knowledge of the local materials or the environment in which he was working.

My personal experience with the practice of firing also clarified the meaning of some puzzling behavior. Although Alfredo never described it during the elicitation of Maya verbal data, I noticed that after each firing episode, he disappeared inside his house and shut the door. Knowing that Latin American peasants used ontological categories of "hot" and "cold" that organized their world of food, disease, body states, and external conditions (Foster 1979, 184–88; McCullough 1973; Neuenswander and Souder 1977), I thought that such behavior might be related to these beliefs. States of "hot" and "cold" must be properly balanced for good health and to forestall disease, and the best way to achieve this balance was to modify the external conditions gradually toward cold.

This explanation seemed to be an obvious one for a potter who had just completed firing. The potter was very hot, and it seemed that the best way to regain balance in his body state was to cool slowly by retiring into the relative cool of a thatched house and resting. After I had fired myself, however, Alfredo's behavior became clear. After spending six hours in front of a kiln with its temperature exceeding 1,000 degrees Celsius, the front of my body was extremely hot and I was exhausted. It was all I could do to stumble into Alfredo's house, collapse into a hammock, and fall asleep. There were no hot and cold categories at work here—just simple exhaustion.

These experiences sensitized me to the firing process, and during the course of more than four decades of ethnographic research on pottery making, I have seen more than 100 different firing events in widely separated parts of Latin America.

These varied from open firing in Guatemala (Arnold 1978a), to the use of an updraft kiln firing in Peru (Arnold 1972a; 1993, 100–8), and firing in a beehive kiln in Ticul (Arnold 2008, 281–307). Besides the firing events that I have witnessed, I talked to many potters about firing and probably have seen hundreds of kilns and firing areas. As a result, I have amassed an immense amount of data about the process.

The practical experience of firing thus revealed an important fact about the study of human behavior, whether it was ethnography or ethnoarchaeology: although language was an important tool for understanding and discovering cultural behavior, using only semantic categories embedded in the native language to describe that behavior was insufficient. Further, using one's own language and cultural categories (such as time) can bias description toward criteria that do not exist in the technology of the indigenous culture. Firing also demonstrated the socially embedded and somatically embodied nature of technological knowledge (e.g., the motor habit patterns of cultural practice) and how those patterns cannot be elicited through the use of semantic categories alone. The cognitive approach to technology thus proved to be helpful and to be a critical first step in approaching indigenous knowledge, but not totally sufficient for understanding pottery firing or pottery making in general. It was not until I actually fired the pottery that I learned the practical strategies about the process that the semantic categories did not reveal. Further, the elicitation process did not uncover nonverbal behavior—especially the motor habits that were often below the potter's threshold of awareness. Rather, my experience of firing on my own convinced me that ethnoarchaeological methodologies that rely exclusively on verbal data from questioning informants using interviews, surveys, and questionnaires can never arrive at a sufficient understanding of the study of technology. Rather, learning the potters' language and semantic categories, participating in the potter's activities, learning the craft in informal contexts, and observing it are probably the best ways to truly understand the cognitive as well as the behavioral dimensions of the potters' technology.

From the passing of fifty years since this research was done, this conclusion also illustrates the value of practice theory (Bourdieu 1978, 1980) as more a formal and more elaborate explanation of Goodenough's (1957) challenge that "culture" consisted of what one had to know in order to get along in a culture and be accepted as one of its members; adequate cultural description thus occurs when an anthropologist acquires enough knowledge to enable her to behave in a way that the members of the culture consider appropriate. These issues of cultural practice are very old in anthropology, but they are equally important in the study of technology as well as for understanding other aspects of culture. They antedate Bourdieu's (1978) notion of practice theory that emphasizes the importance of describing culture (or pottery making in this case) in the way in which it is practiced, not just by describing knowledge. Archaeologists have been attracted to practice theory because the pottery that they study actually reflects the *practice* of making pots, not just the knowledge of doing so. Moreover, the knowledge of the craft is very difficult, if not impossible, to tease out of ancient pottery apart from the practice of the way the pottery was made (e.g., the *chaîne opératoire*).

Practice theory also involves understanding how the motor habit patterns and their syntax drive human behavior. More recently, Ingold (2013) reinforced this position by showing experimentally that engagement of craftsman in the actual practice of producing objects reveals that production was more about problem solving, the engagement of raw materials, and the process of "making" than materializing a mental template in the mind of the maker.

Fieldwork after 1965 marked the beginning of the shift from cognitive anthropology, observation, and practice to a focus on topics of more interest to archaeologists. My goal for the 1965 research was not clearly or directly related to archaeology. As a result, the archaeological implications of much of those data were not initially obvious. While the semantic structure of firing was interesting and gave me respect for the knowledge of the Maya potter, the ethnotaxonomic data initially appeared to provide little help in understanding the relationship of ceramic technology to either Maya archaeology or to archaeological theory and practice. The data did reveal, however, that the selection of raw materials for the pottery fabric and for firing could significantly affect firing success. These data led to the more intensive study of the semantic structures of the raw materials and their associated procurement behavior. The results, as I would come to discover later, had profound archaeological significance.

When I returned to Urbana in fall 1965, I was assigned to Don Lathrap as my advisor because Metzger had left the university to go to the University of California at Irvine. I complained about Metzger's "sink or swim" method of teaching ethnography in the field, but Lathrap dismissed my complaints and tersely affirmed Metzger's approach to fieldwork as the best kind of training. It has taken me many years to see his wisdom and appreciate both Metzger's approach and Lathrap's affirmation of it, but in retrospect, I see that Lathrap was as accurate as he was wise. After all, I had been thrown into the metaphorical "deep end of the pool," I had learned to "swim" and learned to swim well. I was successful and had learned much using the approach of ethnoscience. I had collected vast amounts of data, and I am still mining that information fifty years later. Furthermore, after preparing scores of undergraduate interns to work abroad in Wheaton's Human Needs and Global Resources Program in development, health care, and AIDS treatment and prevention, I have come to appreciate the critical importance of developing tolerance of ambiguity, initiative, commitment, tenacity, drive, perseverance, and independence for working in a field situation. I first learned these qualities experientially in 1965 as a result of Metzger's sink or swim approach to training students in the field. Since then, I have also learned the importance of teaching students "how-to" skills to enable them to adapt to another culture rather than merely providing information "about" adapting. Many of my students, however, were content learners and were not comfortable with learning the how-to skills of practice such as curiosity and how to learn from experience. Unfortunately, one cannot teach curiosity.

Since I had signed up for credit for thesis research for my initial fieldwork in Yucatán, the main goal in late 1965 was to organize my ethnosemantic data into a master's thesis on firing. I saw Metzger at a party in the fall, and he suggested that I write my thesis about pottery firing in Yucatec Maya rather than English! The task was daunting, but not impossible. Another professor, Fred Strodtbeck, from the University of Chicago, whose grant financed our research, suggested that I write a thesis that provided advice to an unborn Maya potter. After showing Lathrap my data, we decided that it would be appropriate to write a manual of Maya pottery firing with an emphasis on descriptions in Yucatec Maya.

I had organized about 20 percent of my data into such a manual when I received the X-ray diffraction analyses of the raw materials that I had collected earlier that year. These analyses revealed that the substance that Ticul potters called "white earth" (*sak lu'um*) was the clay mineral palygorskite. It was called attapulgite back then (Bailey et al. 1971, 131), and a member of the Illinois Geological Survey had identified it in the raw materials that Metzger brought back from Yucatán in 1964. Lathrap knew that palygorskite had been identified as a constituent of the ancient Maya pigment called "Maya Blue" (Gettens 1962; Shepard and Gottlieb 1962). Blue was the color of sacrifice for the ancient Maya and was used on ritual objects such as pottery, figurines, incense burners, and murals (Shepard and Gottlieb 1962; Tozzer 1941, 117–19). The Maya Blue pigment was unusual because it was resistant to strong acids, and its color had remained rich and vivid for 800 years. Further, the clay mineral palygorskite was not very common, and in 1965 nothing had been published about its occurrence in the Maya area.

In late fall 1965, I learned that Strodtbeck was making a brief trip to Yucatán and he consented to ask my informant, Alfredo Tzum Camaal, to collect some more raw material samples for analysis. He and Asael "Hans" Hansen of the University of Alabama contacted my informant, Alfredo, who collected eight more samples for analysis in December 1965.

The possible relationship of the palygorskite used in Maya Blue and the Ticul potters' white earth category suggested an important link between the present and the past. This discovery changed the direction of my research and focused it on the connection between palygorskite and potters' ethnomineralogy in Ticul. Although the evidence was tantalizing, I had reason to doubt the certainty of the relationship between the Maya category "white earth" and palygorskite. First, only eleven samples formed the basis of the mineralogical analysis. Second, only one sample of white earth (*sak lu'um*) and *sah kab* pottery temper (that contained it) were analyzed, and the remainder of the samples did not represent the full range of the available culturally defined categories. Third, these samples were selected by one potter, and consequently they only represented the viewpoint of one person. These limitations reduced the significance of any general statements that I could make about the mineralogical basis of potters' knowledge and use of white earth for temper in Ticul.

I pondered many questions about the relationship of palygorskite and the white earth category of the Maya potters: Did potters consistently recognize its properties, and did these properties correspond to the unique characteristic of palygorskite? Alternatively, did the samples of white earth only coincidentally consist of the clay mineral palygorskite with no relationship to the potters' knowledge and behavior? Did the cooccurrence of palygorskite in samples of white earth exist simply because of methodological bias? Or, was the correspondence between palygorskite and white earth truly a cultural relationship understood by the potters? Was palygorskite consistently present in the raw materials used by the potters? Did the entire community of potters recognize the importance of white earth in pottery temper? Without answering these questions, it was impossible to establish the relationship of a population's cognitive category to material correlates with any scientific validity or reliability.

In order to demonstrate the validity of the relationship of white earth and palygorskite, I formulated several procedures to test my hypothesis of the relationship: If my hypothesis was valid, samples of white earth collected in the future should be pure palygorskite. In addition, if *sah kab* temper must contain white earth, this belief should be verified by talking with other potters and with every person who mined and prepared temper. If they said that *sah kab* temper must contain white earth, then it was a significant constituent of this temper. In order to verify this belief for the entire population of potters, I would also have to collect a sample of *sah kab* temper from each household of potters in Ticul that used it. If white earth (*sak lu'um*) was indeed palygorskite, then all of these temper examples should contain it. Also, I would need to collect samples of materials that did not contain *sak lu'um*, such as those marls (also called *sah kab*) used for construction purposes. If my hypothesis was correct that *sak lu'um* is palygorskite and my ethnographic data about *sah kab* for construction purposes were correct, then none of these marls (*sah kab*) for building purposes should contain it, and *sah kab* for pottery temper was different from *sah kab* for construction purposes. Finally, I would have to collect samples of material that those who mined temper selected as containing white earth (*sak lu'um*). If my hypothesis were correct, these samples should contain palygorskite. In the same way, I would need to collect samples of materials that the temper miners reject as *not* containing *sak lu'um*. These samples should not contain palygorskite. When these tests were accomplished, I could be certain about the validity of my hypothesis.

In January 1966, I returned to Ticul to collect the data necessary to answer these questions, employing several different methodologies to operationalize my hypotheses. I carried out a survey of structured observations of almost all (97 percent) of the households (28/29) that were making pottery at that time, and collected one or more samples ($N = 39$) of the temper from each. These samples represented the finished product of all of those who mined and prepared *sah kab* temper. Any household that I did not visit was noted, and information about it was provided by other informants. Members of each potters' household were asked what they knew about white earth (*sak lu'um*), from whom each had purchased raw materials, and other related information. Did potters consider white earth to be a significant constituent of their temper?

At each potters' house that I visited, I asked to buy a sample of temper and occasionally a sample of clay. In gratefulness for their cooperation, I asked the potters if they would like a picture of their family using a Polaroid camera that I had brought from the United States. The use of the photographs was a big hit, and word spread fast from house to house such that by the time I arrived at the next potter's house with my camera, the family, especially the women, were already dressed up in their best clothes ready to pose for my picture. Unfortunately, some households were not potters, and since I had limited Polaroid film I had to explain that I was only taking pictures of the potters. The use of the pictures, however, was a great way to build rapport, ask my questions, and buy a sample of temper in order to fulfill my research design.

I also visited the location where *sah kab* temper and white earth were mined and prepared (Yo' Sah Kab), and I interviewed most of those who mined and prepared it, observing their methods of preparation. Did the miners recognize the importance of white earth?

Linguistic texts and detailed notes were collected about all ceramic raw materials and about those materials that were semantically related to those used to make pottery. About 107 black-and-white photographs were taken, detailing the process by which raw materials are prepared, how white earth was incorporated into them, and how pottery was fired.

I talked with a variety of people in Ticul who were familiar with both *sah kab* as a temper and with *sah kab* as a building material. Most of these people were potters, but I talked with others, such as a well digger, who would be more familiar with *sah kab* for construction purposes.

I also collected a wide variety of materials that were selected by potters as being representative of specific cultural categories. These categories were those that were crucial in the preparation and composition of *sah kab* temper and related materials. Samples collected by my informants included the constituents of temper, *sak lu'um*, clays, stone, and *sah kab* for construction purposes. I also obtained samples of the materials rejected for use in the preparation of temper.

The samples of the materials collected were numbered and given to B. F. Bohor of the Illinois Geological Survey for mineralogical analysis by X-ray diffraction. As with Bohor's previous analyses, I compared them with their Maya name and with my ethnographic data about their origin and use.

The data from the 1966 season indicated that, with few exceptions, the cultural categories of raw materials were indeed those categories used by the entire population of potters. Conversations with, and observations of, several potters confirmed the definitions of categories and verified that the sources of raw materials were used by all potters. The survey reinforced these data, revealing that potters were consistently obtaining their temper from the source that had been identified earlier in the questioning.

Ticul potters did indeed identify *sak lu'um* (white earth) as a distinct Maya category and specified it as a significant component of pottery temper. They also recognized its unique properties (Arnold 1967a, 1967b, 1971, 2005a). The X-ray diffraction analyses of *sak lu'um* and pottery temper (by Bohor) revealed that the *sak lu'um* category corresponded to the clay mineral palygorskite. All of these data offered convincing evidence that *sak lu'um* was the crucial constituent of *sah kab* temper and that *sah kab* for construction purposes did not contain this substance. These results completely substantiated my hypothesis that *sak lu'um* was palygorskite and has been reaffirmed with every subsequent analysis of *sak lu'um* from Ticul and nearby Sacalum since 1965 (Arnold 2005a; Arnold and Bohor 1975, 1976; Arnold et al. 2007; Arnold et al. 2012).

These results revealed important implications for archaeology. They provided a link between scientific categories (minerals, in this case) identifiable by the archaeologist and the contemporary Maya potters' linguistic and raw material procurement behavior. As I said in my master's thesis (Arnold 1967a), these results revealed a link between modern Maya pottery production and between *sak lu'um* and palygorskite in both Ticul and the nearby community of Sacalum. This link provided important evidence that these two communities may have been ancient sources for palygorskite used in Maya Blue, and perhaps for Maya Blue itself (Arnold 1967a, 1967b, 1971, 2005a; Arnold and Bohor 1975, 1976). Subsequent analyses of Maya Blue revealed that Sacalum (and perhaps Ticul as well) were indeed sources of palygorskite used in Maya Blue (Arnold et al. 2012).

Although significant, the discovery of palygorskite in the Ticul area and its cognitive and behavioral significance to Maya potters created a tangent that precluded the write-up and publication of more than 98 percent of the data collected about firing and pottery production during the 1965 field season. These data are now presented in this work. Another reason for the delay in publication was the prevailing theoretical paradigm at the time. The late 1960s witnessed the development of a materialist paradigm that came to be known as processual archaeology. Paradigms that emphasized cognitive categories, whether they had material correlates or not, were considered to be too elusive for archaeologists. Further, cognitive concerns were repudiated as paleopsychology (after Binford 1965, 204), and this theoretical bias was repeatedly cited by others as a rationale for approaches that allegedly did not belong in archaeology.

It was clear to me, however, that such ethnosemantic categories were important for understanding Ticul ceramic production and in understanding some of the cultural context of the constituents of Maya Blue. Raymond Thompson's (1958) classic work provided an excellent survey of contemporary Yucatec pottery making, but deeper details of ceramic production in Ticul had emerged from my ethnoscience approach to Maya ceramic technology. Fortunately, the field of archaeology now recognizes the limitations of the materialist approach, and more recently a cognitive approach has become congruent with concerns of postprocessual approaches in archaeology and a newly developing focus called cognitive archaeology that was reified in the creation of a new journal, the *Cambridge Journal of Archaeology*, and in the publications of the McDonald Institute for Archaeological Research (e.g., DeMarrais, Gosden, and Renfrew 2004; Renfrew 1998; Renfrew and Scarre 1998).

I visited Ticul again in July 1967 on a return trip from studying contemporary potters in Peru (Arnold 1972a, 1972b, 1975a, 1983, 1984, 1993). Besides Ticul, other communities of potters (Mama, Maxcanú, Tepakán) were visited. Information about ceramic raw materials from these communities were elicited, and about thirty samples were collected. A brief reconnaissance of the temper mines near Ticul revealed that some of these mining areas were located less than fifty meters from an archaeological site dating to the Terminal Classic Period (about AD 800–1000; Arnold 2005a). Subsequently, miners expanded the mining area, tearing through the archaeological site and destroying it. Although this destruction was lamentable, temper mining underneath the archaeological site indicated that it lay directly over the palygorskite deposit that was probably used to mine temper and palygorskite during the Terminal Classic Period.

The occurrence of palygorskite in Yucatán stimulated the interest of clay mineralogist B. F. Bohor of the Illinois State Geological Survey. Bohor had done the X-ray diffraction analyses of samples collected in 1965, 1966, and 1967, and now he wanted to study the occurrence of palygorskite and Ticul potters' clay in the field.

In November 1968, Bohor and I made a two-week trip to Yucatán to collaborate on a study of ceramic raw materials. While Bohor visited raw material sources and collected geological samples, I interviewed potters with a tape recorder. Extensive information was obtained about different raw materials, and approximately 200 samples of raw materials were collected. Some of these were geological samples collected by Bohor that were not relevant to anthropological questions, but approximately fifty samples were linguistically labeled raw materials that were identified by, and collected from, local potters. In addition, we visited six other communities. Some of these had active potters (Maxcanú, Mama, Tepakán, Akil), whereas the craft had been abandoned in two others (Peto and Becal). Source locations of raw materials were visited in Ticul, Mama, and Tepakán, and samples of clays and tempers were collected. We observed and sampled clay deposits along the hill ridge from Maxcanú to Tekax and made a reconnaissance of the interior of Ticul clay mine at Hacienda Yo' K'at (Arnold 2008, 153–89; Arnold and Bohor 1977).

Different communities had different ethnomineralogical categories, gave them different names, and used them in different ways. These differences meant that ethnomineralogical categories, their linguistic labels, and their uses were unique to communities, even in a place such as Yucatán, where a common language and culture existed and where the geological environment was likewise similar from community to community (see Arnold 1971). Each of these pottery-making communities thus represented a unique community of practice.

Research out of step with prevailing paradigms can discourage publication and the dissemination of scientific knowledge, particularly for a young scholar, even if it is unique and creative. An early report of this work was my master's thesis (Arnold 1967a), which was published as a research report by the University of Illinois Department of Anthropology (Arnold 1967b). At the time, the reviews editor for *American Antiquity* was a faculty member in the department, and the publication was sent to the most qualified reviewer, but the review was never submitted, and no review was ever published. In retrospect, however, this unreviewed, obscure report was one of the early publications in the newly emerging subfield of ethnoarchaeology in the late 1960s and one of the first to use both rigorous hypothesis testing and a technique in the physical sciences to look at a comparatively large sample of ceramic raw materials that applied to the archeological issue of Maya Blue. Fortunately, a revised version of the work focusing on the potters' semantic categories of raw materials, but without the application to Maya Blue, was subsequently published in *American Antiquity* (Arnold 1971). Using these data, a paper inferring the cognitive structure of ancient ceramic raw materials during the Terminal Classic period was presented at the Society for American Archaeology meetings in Mexico City in 1970 (Arnold 1970a) but was never submitted for publication because its approach was out of step with the prevailing archaeological paradigms at the time. This paper and the data upon which it is based have been incorporated into this work.

The methodology used to collect the data in this work thus has a long history over many years. What is clear, however, is that all of my subsequent visits since the 1960s (i.e., 1970, 1984, 1988, 1994, 1997, and 2008) revealed that the original semantic data collected really did reveal the way that Ticul potters classified and used their raw materials, and made and fired their pottery. This viewpoint was dramatically brought home to me in 2008 when I visited Yucatán with clay mineralogist B. F. Bohor, formerly of the United States Geological Survey. The goal of our research was to expand the samples of palygorskite to establish a baseline for comparison with the analyses of Maya Blue. We hoped that our sample would provide data against which we could compare samples of Maya Blue and determine the source of the palygorskite used in the pigment (see Arnold et al. 2012). Many times during our raw material surveys, Bohor handed me a sample that he had collected and asked me: "Is this *sak lu'um*?" Much of the time I said yes, and this judgment was verified by my informant, Alfredo, who was with us. Furthermore, my identifications were almost always verified as palygorskite by X-ray diffraction of the samples done later by Bohor and Neff. I had learned how to identify *sak lu'um* from potters and had put that knowledge into practice as I collected samples for our analysis and study. My original concern of learning to behave as a potter using Goodenough's (1957, 1964) definition, and my experience with the practice of, and engagement in, the pottery-making process thus has continued to bear fruit.

In spite of my accurate identification of *sak lu'um* as palygorskite, my failures to identify the mineral revealed that my perceptions and those of the potters from whom I learned were tied to the local landscape around Ticul. My identifications of *sak lu'um* at Yo' Sah Kab and nearby Chapab were always identified as palygorskite. My identification of what I thought was *sak lu'um* at a roadcut near Oxkintok and in the railroad cut east of Maxcanú, however, were often wrong, and they turned out to be white smectite or some other mineral. These errors show how raw material classifications are tied to the potters' engagement with the local landscape around Ticul and cannot be easily transferred to other locations. This observation further confirms the notion that indigenous classifications of raw materials not only are tied to interactions with the local landscape, but also reflect a unique community of practice that is not easily transferable to other areas.

All of the samples collected for this work over the last fifty years are now archived and are part of the research collection of the Field Museum of Natural History in Chicago. Included with these samples are electronic copies of the sample lists and electronic copies of relevant publications. Copies of field notes, Maya linguistic texts, Maya question/response frames, all data sets, and photographs eventually will be deposited in the archives of Wheaton College.

3

The Potters' Engagement with the Perceived Landscape

ETHNOECOLOGY

One dimension of the indigenous knowledge of Ticul potters is based upon their perception of their landscape and how they classify it using their native language—Yucatec Maya. The categories that result from this classification inform and constrain potters' choices of raw materials and contribute to the successful practice of their craft. They form the foundation for potters' engagement with their material world to make pottery.

This chapter lays out the ethnoecology of Ticul potters by describing the landscape that potters use, their classifications of it, and how these categories relate to the raw materials that they use to make pots. One fundamental part of this ethnoecological knowledge is the way that they have classified the forest—the living portion of their landscape—and the manner in which the forest relates to pottery production. Potters also categorize the earth, or their nonliving landscape. So, besides the forest, potters obtain raw materials from openings in the earth. Their classification of these openings is one criterion for their choices of raw materials.

This and subsequent chapters seek to understand the engagement of Maya potters with the pottery-making process by using two complementary epistemologies. The first consists of the potters' indigenous, or traditional, ecological knowledge. This point of view consists of their perception of their environment and the basis for choosing the sources of raw materials by describing how they perceive, classify, and label their landscape categories (emic categories). The second kind of

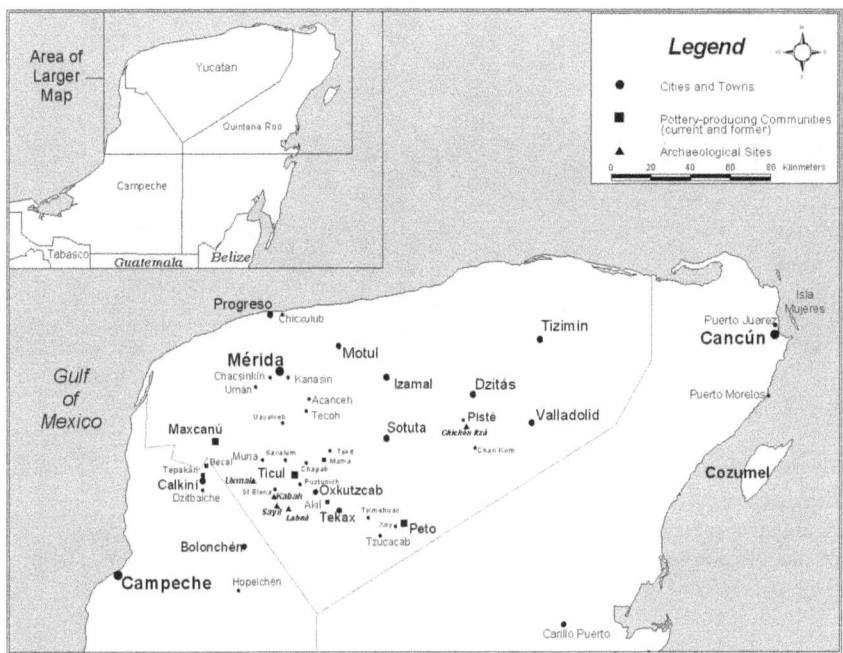

FIGURE 3.1. Map of Yucatán showing major cities, towns, archaeological sites, and pottery-making communities between the late 1960s and 1994 (map drawn by George A. Pierce). (From Arnold 2008, 34.)

epistemology consists of the scientific categories that enable outsiders and scientists to understand the potter's viewpoint more objectively. Whereas the major theme of this work is the indigenous (or emic) knowledge of the potter, it is not as useful to the archaeologist who does not have access to these categories in the past. So, this knowledge needs to be understood in terms of a cross-cultural, scientific epistemology (etic criteria) that is outside of the world of the Maya potter. The first of these etic criteria consists of the background geology, botany, and ecology of the Yucatán Peninsula necessary to understand their culturally relative knowledge.

GEOLOGICAL CONTEXT

The Yucatán Peninsula is a vast limestone platform that stretches 400 to 600 kilometers northward from the North American continent (figure 3.1). The extreme northern portion is relatively flat, but as one moves south from the coast, the elevation increases gradually with an average gradient of one meter per three kilometers (Isphording 1975, 240). Approximately eighty kilometers from the north coast and

FIGURE 3.2. View looking west-northwest along the north side of the *puuk* ridge between Ticul and Hacienda Yo' K'at in 1984. This image shows the *chak'an* ethnoecological zone consisting of the north slope of the ridge and the southern edge of the *kabal che'* zone at the bottom of the slope.

fifty kilometers inland from the western shore, the topography changes, and a ridge rises to an elevation of one hundred meters (Isphording 1975, 251; figures 3.2 and 3.3). Beginning just east of the town of Maxcanú, this ridge extends some 160 kilometers to the southeast (Isphording 1975, 25; West 1964, 71; Wilson 1980, 19) and is sometimes called the "hill ridge," the *sierrita de Ticul*, or simply, in Yucatec Maya, the *puuk* ("hill").[1]

Immediately south of this ridge, the terrain flattens out again with large areas of deep soils and little surface limestone (figure 3.4; Dunning 1994). Beyond these flat areas the undulating terrain begins again until approximately sixteen to twenty kilometers south of the hill ridge, a series of haystack-like hills (figure 3.4) dominate the landscape (Doehring and Butler 1974; Isphording 1975, 255; Wilson 1980) where the Maya centers of Uxmal, Kabah, Sayil, Labna, and Xkipché flourished between AD 800 and 1100 (Ball 1994; Kurjack 1994; Vallo 2002; figure 3.1).

Since the Yucatán Peninsula is underlain with limestone with numerous surface outcrops, the soils in much of Yucatán are residual from limestone, but they are also residual from volcanic ash (Quiñones and Allende 1974), probably from the volcanoes of highland Mexico and Guatemala.[2] Soil quality, however, varies from region to region and is not uniform (Isphording 1975, 240). In the region between the coast and the base of the *puuk* hill ridge (the Northwestern Coastal Plain), soils

FIGURE 3.3. View showing the abrupt rise of the *puuk* ridge from the *kabal che'* zone and the *chak'an* zone on the north side of the ridge from Hacienda Yo' K'at in 2014.

are largely restricted to areas between rock outcrops and small depressions on the pitted limestone (Isphording 1975, 240). In some areas soil coverage is less than 40 percent of the surface area. With a thickness rarely exceeding a few centimeters, its quality is unsuitable for most types of agriculture. Northeast of Ticul, however, this soil quality changes, and soils tend to be deeper and more productive (Isphording 1975, 244). The best soil for agriculture, however, lies immediately south of the *puuk* hill ridge (Dunning 1994, 11; figure 3.4).

SOURCES OF RAW MATERIALS

The first way that potters engage their landscape is through the sources of their raw materials. Their choices of these materials require a rather sophisticated knowledge of the living and nonliving landscape and an understanding of the larger environmental context.

Potters obtain their raw materials from two different parts of the landscape: the forest and the earth. Both types are elaborately classified and consist of a variety of culturally recognized subcategories. Knowledge of these subcategories provide the foundation for potters' traditional knowledge about their raw materials.

FIGURE 3.4. View from the top of the *puuk* ridge looking south along the road from Ticul to Santa Elena in 1997. This image looks down the through the *chak'an* zone, and the *kakab* zone, where the terrain levels out. The *ya'ash k'ash* lies beyond the *kakab* zone, and in the distance lie the hills of the Yucatan hill country (the *wits* zone) (photo by Michelle Arnold Paine). (From Arnold 2008, 97.)

THE FOREST (*K'A'ASH*)

The first source of raw materials consists of the potters' living landscape, the forest. The forest is ubiquitous in Yucatán, and up until the 1960s, many potters were also subsistence agriculturalists (*milperos*). They selected a portion of the forest, cut it down, let it dry, and then burned it near the end of the dry season (usually in late April). Once the rainy season started in June, they planted maize (and sometimes beans and squash) and then weeded the field several times thereafter. The field was harvested at the end of the rainy season beginning in November or December. It was planted again in the following year, but after an additional year or two, it was left fallow, and another field was selected, cut, and burned. After about twenty years, depending on location, the fallowed field could be used for agriculture again (see Steggerda 1941, 125–26). This technique provided the Maya with their most basic subsistence crop—maize—which was, and continues to be, the critical component of the traditional Maya diet.

In the past many potters made pottery intermittently, and pottery-making households multitasked between agriculture and making pottery, other crafts, and/or other

FIGURE 3.5. A *milpero* carrying firewood on his bicycle returning to Ticul from his cornfield in late May 2008 at the top of the *puuk* ridge on the Ticul-Santa Elena highway. Swidden fields in the *kakab*, and *ya'ash k'ash* zones on the south side of the *puuk* ridge are more productive than those in the *kabal che'* zone closer to Ticul, and swidden agriculturalists still prefer to travel the increased distance over the *puuk* to the south, even in 2008.

activities (Arnold 2015a). Shifting agriculture was ideal for such intermittent multitasking because it was compatible with making pottery in at least three ways.

First, growing maize was a significant buffer from the vicissitudes of the demand for the products of the potters' craft and provided a way to manage any downside risk from a lack of demand for their wares. Potters thus could always feed their families from their maize plot if returns from their craft were insufficient.

Second, shifting agriculture also provided one of the most critical resources for sustained ceramic production—fuel for firing. Since wood was left in the field after burning, each trip to the field for clearing, planting, and weeding was an opportunity to transport one or two bundles of firewood back to the household to use as fuel for firing (figure 3.5). After cutting, trees were removed to the edge of the field and allowed to dry for at least nine months so that cutting firewood would not interfere with the plants of next year's crop. Usually, firewood acquisition in any given field occurred the following January after the first crop of maize was harvested. It could be cut earlier, but *milperos* usually did not prepare firewood until after the rains had washed the charcoal dust from the burned trees so that they did not get dirty. Consequently, firewood had dried at least a year before it was brought to Ticul for firing pottery. Being an agriculturalist as well as a potter thus provided wood for firing—one of the most critical resources for sustained ceramic production as well as providing basic subsistence returns to supplement craft production.

Third, the scheduling of the activities required for shifting agriculture was also very compatible with making pottery. The amount of time required for shifting agriculture allows the potter to cultivate a maize plot and also make pottery intermittently. In a study of five different towns north and east of Ticul, Steggerda (1943a, 125–26) found that only 190 eight-hour days were required to cultivate the average field size of 39,692 square meters (99.23 *mecates*) necessary to feed a Maya family. The remaining 48 percent of the year could be devoted to other activities such as making pottery, though constraints from weather and climate can still limit the amount of time available to make pots (Arnold 2015a, 243–76).

Although the scheduling of the cycle of activities for shifting agriculture are constrained by the rainy season and the growth cycle of the plants, the exact timing of those activities within those constraints is flexible. Cutting and clearing the forest must be done early enough in the agricultural year so that the cleared field can be burned before the rainy season starts in late May or early June; planting needs to be done immediately before or immediately after the rains start. Weeding the field, however, can be done at any time during the growth of the plants but usually occurs about four times during the growing season. Finally, harvesting may take place anytime after the rainy season passes when the ears are dry so that they can be stored without spoiling.

On a daily level, the potter can schedule activities such as cutting the forest, burning, planting, cultivating, and harvesting so that they can complement, rather than compete with, pottery-making activities. In the early morning he can work in his field when fog and moisture may damage newly formed pottery and slow its drying (Arnold 1985, 66–99). Then, after returning to his house in the late morning, he can make pottery when sunshine and heat are required to dry clay, dry pottery, and fire.

The importance of shifting agriculture for potters has declined greatly since 1965. In 1965–66, many swidden agriculturalists still existed in Ticul, but even with the complementary nature of swidden agriculture and pottery making, few potters planted maize plots.

When women were potters, however, fewer problems existed with scheduling conflicts between pottery making and agriculture. Women could fit making pottery between household tasks and childcare, a pattern that is widespread in many parts of the world (Arnold 1978a; 1978b; 1985, 95–108). Nevertheless, weather and climate still provided constraints on producing more than a few pots (if that) during the rainy season. Further, the small footprint of traditional Maya houses restricted drying and storage space for pottery, and increased risk of breakage of fragile unfired pots (Arnold 2015a, 253–76).

The selection of appropriate land for a maize field requires a detailed knowledge about the forest and its variability. Such knowledge is not unusual among indigenous groups (Carneiro 1994; Kunstadter 1994). In the Maya community of X-uilub in eastern Yucatán, shifting agriculturalists (*milperos*) manage the forest knowing the changes in its composition from old forest to that of a recently abandoned field (Sánchez González 1993).

Similarly, Anabel Ford and Ronald Nigh (Ford and Nigh 2009) argue that the Maya forest garden results from a series of management practices that have sustained the forest for thousands of years. These practices result from the rich traditional knowledge used in the practice of milpa agriculture that the Maya have passed on for generations. They suggest that "the creation, intensification and maintenance of this resource-rich ecosystem . . . underwrote the development of the Maya civilization" (Ford and Nigh 2009, 214).

The Maya of Yucatán also appear to use traditional knowledge parallel to the Maya in Belize to utilize and maintain the forest for milpa agriculture (Ford and Nigh 2009). Such knowledge was critical for making pottery as well because potters knew the ethnoecological zones of the region, the kinds of trees within them, and the burning characteristics of the wood that came from them.

ETHNOECOLOGICAL ZONES IN NORTHERN YUCATÁN

Except for urban and agricultural areas, most of the northern part of the Yucatán Peninsula is covered with a secondary scrub forest. The first few kilometers inland from the north coast consist of marshes and/or very low vegetation less than two meters high, but further inland, a low forest begins. As one moves southward and eastward, its height increases from approximately four to five meters around Mérida, to approximately six to seven meters further south near the hill ridge. On the south side of the ridge, the forest height increases until one reaches the tropical forest in the state of Campeche. Similarly, as one moves eastward from the northwestern portion of the peninsula, the forest height also rises until one reaches the tropical forest near the border of the state of Quintana Roo.

Subsistence agriculturalists systematized and categorized this environmental variation into different ethnoecological zones that ranged from the northern coast of the peninsula to the tropical forest in the south. Some zones are more favorable for agriculture than others, but each has distinct characteristics with specific types of trees that occur in each zone (table 3.1).

TABLE 3.1. The ethnoecological zones in northern Yucatán and the trees that grow in each zone

Maya zone	Location	Description	Tree types
tsek'el	Extends from the sand on the north coast to south of Mérida	Many rocky areas with very little soil	No information
pok che'	Between tsek'el and kabal che'	Low forest	salche'
kabal che' (or kaba' che')	From the northern base of the hill ridge northward	Low forest	p'eres kuch, ts'ilts'il che' (infrequent), shahpuch, ha'abin, sak kaatsim, sutup, shkitin che', chukum, bakal che', shu'ul, k'anasin, sa'itsa, chon lok', k'ampurus che', ts'uts'uk, ki'i che', chakah, **ts'iu che'**, bo' chiich, chakte', tsalam, shpomol che', shtuha che', shbakal che', silil, sak bak, saya' che', shu' che', subin che', shya'ash ek', k'anchunup (infrequent), bohon che' (infrequent)
chak'an	The lower slope on the north and south side of the puuk hill ridge	The area of high grass (sacate) south of kabal che'	pimienta che', bosh kaatsim, chukum, ya'ash 'ek', chulul, ts'ilts'il che', pichi che', sabak che', nopal cactus, k'an chunup, tsiwil che', shtak'in che', chakah, shtuha' che', shya'ash k'is, sina'an che', subin che'
puuk	The high hill ridge immediately south of Ticul	The hill zone	shtak'in che' (more here than in other zones), chakah, **saknah che'**, **pimienta che'**, k'an che', shapuch, kiis, ch'imai, sak bak
kakab lu'um (or kakab)	Low places (bajadas) south of the puuk ridge about 2 km south of Ticul	Smooth (suave) fertile black soils that have few rocks	bosh kaatsim, ts'uts'uk, pishoy, bohon che', tsiswil che', chakte', shya'ash kiis, sabak che', saknah/k che', shya'ash ek, shku'upchel che'
ya'ash k'ash "green forest"	South of the puuk and the kakab zones and located about 14–16 km from Ticul	The region of high trees	k'an chunup, *tsaalam, *ha'abin, *chukum, *ts'iu che', *sakab che', chak te', saknak che', chulul che'
wits	The hill region 16–20 km south of the puuk ridge	The haystack-like hills south of the puuk ridge	saknak che', chulul che', k'anchunup
k'ana k'aash	The montaña: the tropical forest zone south of the wits zone		No information

Note: Most of the information for this chart was obtained in 1965 and 1970, and much of it was verified in 1984. Tree names with an asterisk indicate that they were attributed to this zone in 1984 but were not included in the lists from 1965 and 1970. One reason for this discrepancy may be that most of the firewood consumed by potters in 1984 came from the ya'ash k'ash and wits zones, about which my informants had little familiarity in 1965. Tree names identified in **bold** type were elicited in 1997 and probably were placed in the zones for the same reasons. Names are written with phonetic script, not with Spanish orthography. The h thus is not silent as it is in Spanish.

Some trees are unique to a particular zone, while others grow in several zones (table 3.2). As one would expect, potters are more familiar with the zones closer to Ticul than they are with those that are more distant.

Knowledge about the wood from the trees in the forest contributes to firing success. Each type of tree produces wood with certain burning characteristics. Some wood burns slowly or with a smoky flame, whereas other wood burns with a strong or high flame. Knowing these characteristics helps potters control the firing process so that they can conserve fuel and maximize its effects so that they will not overfire or underfire their pottery (see chapter 7). Knowledge of the ethnoecological zones and of the different characteristics of the wood from the trees in each zone thus contributes positively to firing success.

Those potters who are, or have been, *milperos* recognize nine distinctive ecological zones in northern Yucatán. The northernmost zone lies inland from the beach, scrub forest, and marshes along the north coast. Called *tsek'el* (table 3.1), it consists of many rocky areas with very little soil (*saman lu'um* or *saman milo'o*). This zone is also the *henequén*-producing zone that includes many haciendas (such as Yaxcopoil, Xtepén, and Ch'u'uyu') that formerly cultivated and processed *henequén* for its fiber (Baklanoff 1980; Joseph 1980). By 1984, however, most of the land previously devoted to growing *henequén* had been abandoned and returned to scrub forest or was converted to some other use.

South of the *tsek'el* zone, one encounters the *pok che'* zone, an area of low forest with fewer rock outcrops. The next zone further south lies near the hill ridge and is called the *kabal che'* (or *kaba' che'*) zone (table 3.1–3.2; figure 3.6). Consisting of low forest that extends northward from the base of the hill ridge, it includes much of the area around Ticul.

Immediately south of Ticul, the *chak'an* zone begins as the terrain rises slightly at the base of the hill ridge and includes the lower portion of its slope (figures 3.3 and 3.4). Near Ticul this zone is wide, with a substantial amount of grass. Because cutting the grass requires too much effort in order to prepare ground for a swidden field, the *chak'an* zone is not usually cultivated. The soil is also very damp because of the water runoff from the slope above.

The hill zone (*puuk*) begins where the terrain rises more steeply and continues up over the crest of the ridge. On top of the ridge, some areas are relatively flat and may be as much as 1.2 to 1.6 kilometers wide (as is that portion on the crest of the hills along the road between Ticul and Santa Elena). On the other side of the summit, the *chak'an* zone begins again where the terrain slopes downward (figure 3.4).

The fertile soils of the *kakab* (or *kakab lu'um*) zone begin at the base of the *chak'an* zone (figure 3.4). The soils here are deep, dark (often black according to potters),

TABLE 3.2. The trees that grow in each ethnoecological zone (table 3.1) organized by zone. Name variants of trees are grouped together in the same category. For explanation of the zones, see table 3.1.

Tree names	Zones						
	pok che'	kabal che'	chak'an	pu'uk	kakab lu'um	ya'ash k'ash	wits
salche'	x						
ts'ilts'il che'		x	x				
p'eres kuch		x		x			
shahpuch		x		x			
ha'abin		x				x	
sak kaatsim		x					
sutup		x					
shkitin che'		x					
chukum		x	x			x	
bakal che'		x					
shu'ul		x					
k'anasin		x					
sa'itsa		x					
chon lok'		x					
k'ampurus che'		x					
ts'uts'uk		x			x		
ki'i che'		x					
chakah		x	x				
ts'iu che'		x				x	
bo' chiich		x					
shpomol che'		x					
sak bak/ sak bak che'/ sah bak che'/ sabak che'		x	x	x	x		
chakte'		x			x	x	
tsalam		x				x	
shtuha che'		x	x				
shbakal che'		x					
silil		x					

continued on next page

TABLE 3.2—*continued*

Tree names	Zones						
	pok che'	kabal che'	chak'an	pu'uk	kakab lu'um	ya'ash k'ash	wits
shu' che'		x					
subin che'			x				
saya' che'		x					
bohon che'					x		
(sh)pimienta che'			x	x			
bosh kaatsim			x		x		
(sh)ya'ash 'ek'			x		x		
chulul/ chulul che'			x			x	x
shtak'in che'			x	x			
sina'an che'			x				
nopal cactus			x				
k'an che'				x			
ch'imai				x			
shku'upchel che'					x		
shya'ash k'iis			x		x		
pishoy					x		
saknah/k che'			x		x	x	x
sakab che'						x	
tsiswil che'	x	x			x		
k'anchunup	x	x				x	x
kiis				x			
pichi che'	x	x					

and have few rocks. Such soils are unusual in Yucatán, but the *kakab* zone supports a number of modern agricultural projects that have planted citrus groves, maize, and other crops (Dunning 1994). Citrus groves, however, cannot be sustained by rainfall alone during the dry season and must depend upon deep-well irrigation for moisture.

This zone also includes the former sugar plantation (Finca Tabí) that enslaved at least one of the ancestors of Ticul potters during "The Epoch of Slavery" in the late

FIGURE 3.6. View from the top of the *puuk* ridge in 1970 looking north toward the town of Muna showing the vegetation that covers the northern peninsula. The road in this picture is the road from Muna to Uxmal; the town of Muna lies at the base of the ridge in the center of the photograph, and a portion of the highway from Muna to Mérida can be seen at the extreme left of the photo. This image shows the *chak'an* zone on the north slope of the *puuk* ridge with a *henequén* field cultivated in it (*right center*), and the *kabal che'* zone at the base of the slope and extending northward.

nineteenth century (Arnold 2015a, 69; Meyers 2012; Rejón 1981a, 1981b; Strickon 1965, 48–52). Informants sometimes placed Finca Tabí in the *kakab* zone and other times within the *ya'ash k'ash* zone. So, its fields probably spanned both zones. All of the zones from the *puuk* zone southward, however, tended to be marginal for human settlement because of the scarce water sources accessible from the surface. Those natural sources that did exist, however, were in caves, in depressions on the surface (*aguadas*), and in openings in the surface rock that collected rainwater (*haltuns*). During the Terminal Classic, the Maya excavated cisterns (*chultuns*) to collect rainwater. After the Spanish Conquest, however, the use of metal tools and explosives to dig wells allowed access to the water level deep underground.

The next zone (*ya'ash k'ash*) begins approximately twelve to sixteen kilometers from Ticul near the archaeological site of Labná (figure 3.1). Literally translated as "green forest," this zone contains trees that are older and higher than the zones further north. Even though many rocks occur in this zone, the maize yield here is twice that from the *kabal che'* zone around Ticul. If a *milpero* cultivated 100 *mecates* (400 m^2) of land in *kabal che'*, for example, his yield was one sack of maize per *mecate*, whereas the yield in the *ya'ash k'ash* zone was two sacks per *mecate*.

Consequently, the *ya'ash k'ash* is regarded as the most desirable zone for swidden agriculture because of its fertility. Even with its distance from Ticul, travel to it was worth the extra effort because of the increased yields. In the late 1950s, one potter (Alfredo Tzum Camaal) and his father, Agustín, cultivated 100 *mecates* (40,000 m²) close to the ruins of Labná before they devoted their time more intensively to making pottery.

These fields were about six kilometers beyond Finca Tabí and were part of the commercial farms (*fincas*) of Skayum, San Francisco, and Oxloch. *Milperos* rented land from the *finca* of San Francisco, and the foreman charged them 10 percent of the crop, which was about one *carga* (one sack) of maize for each 10 *mecates* of land. Even in 2008, shifting agriculturalists still traveled to zones south of the hill ridge (figure 3.5) to tend their fields.

A subzone within this zone was *ya'ashom* ("green deep"), which was two kilometers south of the cave of Loltun, and is also favorable for agriculture because water was more accessible here than elsewhere in the *puuk* region (see Dunning 1988, 1994).

About twenty kilometers beyond the hill ridge, the Yucatecan hill country (called the *wits*) begins (figure 3.4). This zone consists of haystack-like hills and high trees and extends southward to the town of Bolonchén in the state of Campeche. The ancient Maya centers of Uxmal, Kabah, and Sayil flourished here between AD 800 and 1100 (Ball 1994; Kurjack 1994; Vallo 2002; figure 3.1). The soil is also better here than north of the hill ridge. Those potters who still had swidden fields in 1997 preferred to plant them in the *ya'ash k'ash* zone or in the *wits* zone beyond.

An ethnoecological niche consisting of a red soil (called *k'an kab*) and called *k'an kab che'* lies within many of these zones. Whereas pockets of this soil type exist within the low forest zone (*kabal che'*) around Ticul and beyond it to the north, they are also abundant on the south side of the hill ridge in the *kakab lu'um* zone about four kilometers south of Ticul. For the potter, this niche contains trees that are highly desirable as fuel for firing, including *chukum, sutup, shkitin che', sak* ("white") *katsim*, and *bosh* ("black") *katsim* because they burn with a high or quick flame and with no smoke (see chapter 9). Indeed, *sutup* and *shkitin che'* require a soil with abundant *k'an kab*.

In spite of the superiority of the wood from the trees that grow there, potters believe that the *k'an kab che'* soil type is not desirable for maize fields and has limited agricultural potential. Crops grown there need much rainfall because the sun dries out the soil. Too much rain, on the other hand, may cause the plants to die because the soil is not very porous and does not drain well. Consequently, maize and other crops planted in this niche will not survive, and *milperos* do not like to plant their fields in such low places (*ak'al che'*) where red soil (*k'an kab*) predominates. Rather, they prefer planting on higher ground where the soil drains better.

Potters recognize different types of trees from these zones (tables 3.1–3.2). In order to provide scientific names for these trees, I used their Maya names to search the botanical and anthropological literature of Yucatán for their scientific name (table 3.3). The results are probably not as reliable or accurate as collecting leaves, flowers, and seeds from these trees in the field and then having a botanist identify them, but most of the Maya tree names could be linked to specific species names. The integrity of these names was checked by Robin Foster of the Department of Science and Education (formerly the Department of Botany) at the Field Museum, and the spellings, botanical names, and hierarchical groupings were checked for accuracy in the taxonomic database of the Missouri Botanical Garden called "tropicos.org" (MBG 2014). After using many sources to obtain these names, the same botanical names kept coming up again and again for the Maya common names in the ethnobotanical literature. This redundancy suggested that either common bibliographic sources were used to obtain the botanical names, that there was agreement about the association of the common names with the scientific names, or perhaps both. The botanical names for some common names, however, were never found.

Common names of plants, however, do not necessarily have a one-to-one correspondence with a single botanical species. As Berlin and his colleagues (Berlin 1973, 267–69; Berlin et al. 1966, 1968) noted for folk taxonomies in general, indigenous names for plants may overdifferentiate or underdifferentiate a species. Further, the trees identified in the literature listed here were located in different parts of Yucatán, and may have different referents from those used by the Ticul potter, or may have different meanings in different locations because they come from different communities of practice. Finally, some names may underdifferentiate scientific species of trees so much so that the common names may extend to an introduced species (e.g., the orange tree, *Citrus Aurantium* L.). Indeed, two Maya names found in the literature were also listed as equivalent to a species in the *Ageratum* genus that is herbaceous and not a tree. Since the Maya names for these trees had other botanical names, the members of the *Ageratum* genus were dropped from the list.

Ethnogeology

Whereas the ethnoecological zones of the Yucatán forest are one source of potters' raw materials, the other source is their nonliving landscape: the earth. Potters obtain their clay, temper, and water through openings in the ground surface that are

TABLE 3.3. Botanical names for the trees used for firewood in Ticul. Names are written with phonetic script, not with Spanish orthography. The *h* thus is not silent as it is in Spanish. Synonyms for the Maya name (where they exist) are in parentheses in the first column.

Yucatec name	Scientific name (family)	Source
(sh) bakal che'	*Bourreria pulchra*, Millsp. (Boraginaceae, MBG 2014)	Rodríguez, Rodríguez, and Uhu 1992, 18; Barrera Marín et al. 1976, 49; Bradburn 1998, 321; Bricker et al. 1998, 24; Roys 1976, 215; Souza Novelo 1940, 7, 16; Standley 1930, 395–96
	Cordia sp. (Boraginaceae, MBG 2014)	Bradburn 1998, 332
(sh) bo' ch'ich'	*Hippocratea excelsa* HBK	Bradburn 1998, 323
	Hippocratea celastroides HBK (Hippocrateaceae; more recently placed in Celastraceae, MBG 2014)	Bricker et al. 1998, 33
bohon che'	*Coccoloba schiedeana*, Lindau (Polygonaceae, MBG 2014)	Souza Novelo 1940, 7, 17
	Cordia gerascanthus, L. Baria (Boraginaceae, MBG 2014)	Barrera Marín et al. 1976, 53; Roys 1976, 217; Standley 1930, 397
	Cordia alliodora (Ruiz et Pavo) Cham (Boraginaceae, MBG 2014)	Barrera Marín et al. 1976, 53
bosh kaatsim	*Prosopis chilensis*, Stuntz (Borangináceae, now placed in Fabaceae, MBG 2014)	Souza Novelo 1940, 7, 17
	Prosopis julifora, D. C. (Fabaceae, MBG 2014)	Barrera Marín et al. 1976, 54; Roys 1976, 224[a]
	Mimosa sp. (Leguminosae, now placed in Fabaceae, MBG 2014)	Barrera Marín et al. 1976, 54; Standley 1930, 279; Steggerda 1943b, 211
	Acacia gaumeri Blake (Leguminosae, now placed in Fabaceae, MBG 2014)	Rodríguez, Rodríguez, and Uhu 1992, 20; Barrera Marín et al. 1976, 54
chak te'	*Caesalpinia platyloba*, S. Wats; (Fabaceae, MBG 2014)	Barrera Marín et al. 1976, 62; Roys 1976, 231–32; Steggerda 1943b, 199
	Caesalpinia bijuga, L. Brasil (Fabaceae, MBG 2014)	Roys 1976, 231–32
	Caesalpinia velutina (Britton et Rose) Standley (Leguminosae, but assigned to Fabaceae, MBG 2014)	Barrera Marín et al. 1976, 62
	Sweetia panamensis Benth. (Leguminosae, assigned to Fabaceae, MBG 2014)	Barrera Marín et al. 1976, 62; Rodríguez, Rodríguez, and Uhu 1992, 22

continued on next page

TABLE 3.3—*continued*

Yucatec name	Scientific name (family)	Source
chakah (*palo mulato/ chacah*)	*Bursera simaruba* (L.) Sarg. (Burseraceae, MBG 2014)	Rodríguez, Rodríguez, and Uhu 1992, 21; Barrera Marín et al. 1976, 57; Bradburn 1998, 321; Bricker et al. 1998, 62; Rancho El Porvenir 2014, 90, 96; Roys 1976, 227–28; Standley 1930, 313; Steggerda 1943b, 199
	Bursera spp. (Burseraceae, MBG 2014)	Barrera Marín et al. 1976, 53
	Caesalpinia gaumeri (Fabaceae, MBG 2014)	Rancho El Porvenir 2014, 90
chon lok'		No information
chukum	*Pithecellobium albicans*, Benth. (Now called *Havardia albicans* (Fabaceae, MBG 2014), by Foster. Formerly, in Leguminosae)	Rodríguez, Rodríguez, and Uhu 1992, 23; Barrera Marín et al. 1976, 70; Roys 1976, 239; Souza Novelo 1940, 8
	Acacia riparioides (Britt and Rose) Standl. (Leguminosae, now in Fabaceae, MBG 2014) (Now called *Senegalia riparioides* by Foster)	Standley 1930, 277
	Havardia albicans (Kunth) Britton & Rose (Leguminosae, now placed in Fabaceae, MBG 2014)	Bradburn 1998, 323; Bricker et al. 1998, 74
chulul	*Apoplanesia paniculata*, Presl. (Leguminosae, now placed in Fabaceae, MBG 2014)	Barrera Marín et al. 1976, 71; Bradburn 1998, 320; Bricker et al. 1998, 75; Roys 1976, 239–40; Souza Novelo 1940, 8; Standley 1930, 290
	Apoplanesia reticulata Presl. (Leguminosae, but not listed in MBG 2014)	Barrera Marín et al. 1976, 71
ch'imai	*Acacia pennatula* (Schlecht. & Cham.) Benth. (Leguminosae, now placed in Fabaceae, MBG 2014)	Rodríguez, Rodríguez, and Uhu 1992, 24; Bradburn 1998, 320; Bricker et al. 1998, 54
ha'abin (*madera de hierro*)	*Piscidia communis* (Blake) Harms. (This taxon includes *Ichthyomethia communis*, Blake [Souza Novelo 1940, 9; Roys 1976, 242; Steggerda 1943b, 212–13] and *Piscidia erythrina*, L. [Roys 1976, 242], which were incorrectly classified according to Standley.) (Fabaceae, MBG 2014)	Barrera Marín et al. 1976, 78; Standley 1930, 301–2

continued on next page

TABLE 3.3—*continued*

Yucatec name	Scientific name (family)	Source
	Piscidia piscipula (L.) Sargent (Leguminosae, now in Fabaceae by MBG 2014)	Barrera Marín et al. 1976, 78; Bradburn 1998, 326; Bricker et al. 1998, 92; Rancho El Porvenir 2014, 93, 94, 95
	Leucaena leucocephala (Fabaceae, MBG 2014)	Rancho El Porvenir 2014, 91
	Piscida spp. (Leguminosae, now in Fabaceae by MBG 2014)	Barrera Marín et al. 1976, 78
k'ampurus che'		No information
k'anchunup	*Thouinia paucidentata*, Radlk. (Sapindaceae) (species not listed in MBG 2014, but species of the genus largely found in the Sapindaceae family)	Bradburn 1998, 327; Bricker et al. 1998, 145; Rancho El Porvenir 2014, 90, 93, 95, 96; Roys 1976, 251; Souza Novelo 1940, 10; Steggerda 1943b, 216; Standley 1930, 340
	Sebastiania adenophora, Pax. & Hoffman (Euphorbiaceae) (species not listed in MBG 2014)	Rodríguez, Rodríguez, and Uhu 1992, 33; Barrera Marín et al. 1976, 97; Roys 1976, 251; Standley 1930, 333
	Clusia Flava Jacq. (Clusiaceae, according to MBG 2014)	Rodríguez, Rodríguez, and Uhu 1992, 33; Barrera Marín et al. 1976, 97
k'anasin (k'ansin)	*Lonchocarpus rugosus*, Benth. (Leguminosae, now assigned to Fabaceae by MBG 2014)	Rodríguez, Rodríguez, and Uhu 1992, 33; Barrera Marín et al. 1976, 97; Rancho El Porvenir 2014, 91, 93, 95, 96; Roys 1976, 250; Souza Novelo 1940, 10, 20
	Randia longiloba (Rubiaceae, MBG 2014)	Rancho El Porvenir 2014, 93, 96
	Malmea depressa (Annonaceae, MBG 2014)	Rancho El Porvenir 2014, 91
	Metopium brownei (Anacardiaceae, MBG 2014)	Rancho El Porvenir 2014, 91
	Piscidia piscipula (Fabaceae, MBG 2014)	Rancho El Porvenir 2014, 91
k'an che'		No information
ki'i che'		No information
kits'		No information
pimienta che'		No information
p'eres kuch	*Croton glabellus* L. (Euphorbiaceae)	MBG 2014; Standley 1930, 320
pichi che'	*Psidium sartorianum* (Berg.) Niedenzu (Myrtaceae, MBG 2014)	Rodríguez, Rodríguez, and Uhu 1992, 40; Barrera Marín et al. 1976, 123; Roys 1976, 276; Standley 1930, 373; Steggerda 1943b, 214–15

continued on next page

TABLE 3.3—*continued*

Yucatec name	Scientific name (family)	Source
	Psidium yucatanense Lundell (Myrtaceae, MBG 2014)	Barrera Marín et al. 1976, 123
pishoy	*Guazuma ulmifolia*, Lam. (Sterculiaceae, now in Malvaceae by MBG 2014)	Barrera Marín et al. 1976, 123; Bradburn 1998, 323; Bricker et al. 1998, 218; Roys 1976, 276; Souza Novelo 1940, 12, 22; Standley 1930, 355
sa'itsa/sak'itsab' (sakitsa/ zacitza); tsaytza'	*Neomillspaughia emarginata*, Blake (Polygonaceae, MBG 2014)	Rodríguez, Rodríguez, and Uhu 1992, 45; Barrera Marín et al. 1976, 151; Bradburn 1998, 325; Bricker et al. 1998, 329; Souza Novelo 1940, 13, 23; Standley 1930, 254
	Hampea trilobata Standl. (Bombacaceae, now in Malvaceae according to MBG 2014)	Standley 1930, 353
sabak che'	*Exostema caribaeum*, Roem et Schult. (Rubiaceae; genus not in MBG, 2014)	Rodríguez, Rodríguez, and Uhu 1992, 41; Barrera Marín et al. 1976, 129; Souza Novelo 1940, 13, 22
	Sickingia aff. salvadorensis Standley (Rubiaceae, MBG 2014)	Rodríguez, Rodríguez, and Uhu 1992, 41; Barrera Marín et al. 1976, 129
sak bak		No information (same as above?)
sak kaatsim	*Mimosa hemiendyta*, Rose & Rob. (Leguminosae, now in Fabaceae by MBG 2014)	Roys 1976, 303; Souza Novelo 1940, 13, 23; Standley 1930, 279
	Mimosa bahamensis, Benth. (Leguminosae, now in Fabaceae according to MBG 2014)	Rodríguez, Rodríguez, and Uhu 1992, 42; Bradburn 1998, 324; Bricker et al. 1998, 239
sakab che'		No information
salche	*Cassia villosa* Mill. Irwin & Barneby (Leguminosae, now assigned to Fabaceae by MBG 2014)	Rodríguez, Rodríguez, and Uhu 1992, 42; Bricker et al. 1998, 242[b]
	Cassia sp. (Assigned to Fabaceae by MBG 2014)	Rodríguez, Rodríguez, and Uhu 1992, 42
sak(a)nah che'	*Colubrina reclinata* Brongn. (Rhamnaceae, MBG 2014)	Barrera Marín et al. 1976, 136
saya' che'		No information
shahpuch		No information
shk'atin che'		No information

continued on next page

TABLE 3.3—continued

Yucatec name	Scientific name (family)	Source
shkitin che' (kitinche')	*Caesalpinia gaumeri*, Greenman (Leguminosae, now assigned to Fabaceae by MBG 2014)	Rodríguez, Rodríguez, and Uhu 1992, 31; Barrera Marín et al. 1976, 171; Bradburn 1998, 321; Bricker et al. 1998, 129
shu' che'		No information
shu'ul	*Lonchocarpus xuul* Lundell (Leguminosae, now assigned to Fabaceae by MBG 2014)	Barrera Marín et al. 1976, 187; Bradburn 1998, 324; Bricker et al. 1998, 264; Rancho El Porvenir 2014, 93, 95, 96
	Jatropha gaumeri Greenman (Euphorbiaceae, MBG 2014)	Rancho El Porvenir 2014, 91
	Lonchocarpus yucatanensis Pittier (Leguminosae, now assigned to Fabaceae by MBG 2014)	Rodríguez, Rodríguez, and Uhu 1992, 50; Barrera Marín et al. 1976, 187
shku'upchel che'		No information
shpomol che' (pomolche')	*Jatropha gaumeri* Greenman (Euphorbiaceae, MBG 2014)	Rodríguez, Rodríguez, and Uhu 1992, 40; Bradburn 1998, 324; Bricker et al. 1998, 220
shtuha' che' (t uha')	*Cassia atomaria* L. (Leguminosae, now assigned to Fabaceae by MBG 2014)	Bradburn 1998, 321; Bricker et al. 1998, 281
	Senna uniflora Miller (I &B.) (Leguminosae, now assigned to Fabaceae by MBG 2014)	Rodríguez, Rodríguez, and Uhu 1992, 43
silil	*Diospyros cuneata* Standl. (Ebenaceae)	Bradburn 1998, 323; Bricker et al. 1998, 246
sina'an che'	*Alvaradoa amorphoides* Liebm. (Simaroubaceae, now assigned to Picramniaceae by MBG 2014)	Bradburn 1998, 320; Bricker et al. 1998, 246
subin che' subin	*Acacia collinsii* Safford (Leguminosae, now assigned to Fabaceae by MBG 2014)	Bradburn 1998, 320; Bricker et al. 1998, 250
	Acacia globulifera Saff. (Leguminosae, now assigned to Fabaceae by MBG 2014)	Barrera Marín et al. 1976, 143
	Acacia cornigera (L.) Willd. (Leguminosae, now assigned to Fabaceae by MBG 2014)	Rodríguez, Rodríguez, and Uhu 1992, 43
sutup	*Helicteres baruensis*, Jacq. (Malvaceae, by MBG 2014)	Roys 1976, 313

continued on next page

TABLE 3.3—*continued*

Yucatec name	Scientific name (family)	Source
	Citrus Aurantium L. (Rutaceae) (Species not found in MBG 2014)	Standley 1930, 307
	Calonyction aculeatum (L.) H. D. House (Convolvulaceae, MBG 2014)	Barrera Marín et al. 1976, 142
tsalam	*Lysiloma bahamense*, Benth. (Leguminosae, now assigned to Fabaceae by MBG 2014)	Barrera Marín et al. 1976, 150; Souza Novelo 1940, 14, 23; Standley 1930, 279
	Lysiloma Latisiliquum (L.) Bentham (Leguminosae, now assigned to Fabaceae by MBG 2014)	Rodríguez, Rodríguez, and Uhu 1992, 45; Bradburn 1998, 324; Bricker et al. 1998, 41
tsi(s)wil che'		No information
ts'ilts'il che'	*Gymnopodium antigonoides*, Blake (Polygonaceae, MBG 2014)	Barrera Marín et al. 1976, 155–56; Souza Novelo 1940, 14, 24
	Gymnopodium floribundum Rolfe var. *antigonoides* (Rob.) Standl. and Steyermark (Polygonaceae)	Rodríguez, Rodríguez, and Uhu 1992, 46; Bradburn 1998, 323; Bricker et al. 1998, 51; Rancho de Porvenir 2014, 91
	Pithecellobium dulce (Standley indicates that this might be *Pithecellobium unguis-cati*, see *tsiu che'* below) (assigned to Fabaceae by MBG 2014)	Standley 1930, 282
	Hampea trilobata (Malvaceae, MBG 2014)	Rancho El Porvenir 2014, 91
	Havardia albicans (Fabaceae, MBG 2014)	Rancho El Porvenir 2014, 91
ts'uts'uk (*tsutsuk*)	*Diphysa robinioides*, Benth. (Leguminosae, now assigned to Fabaceae by MBG 2014)	Roys 1976, 316; Souza Novelo 1940, 14, 24
	Diphysa carthagenensis, Jacq. (Leguminosae, now assigned to Fabaceae by MBG 2014)	Barrera Marín et al. 1976, 157; Bradburn 1998, 323; Bricker, Po'ot Yah, and Dzul de Po'ot 1998, 55; Roys 1976, 316
	Cissampelos pareira L. (Menispermaceae, MBG 2014)	Rodríguez, Rodríguez, and Uhu 1992, 46; Barrera Marín et al. 1976, 157
ts'iu che'	*Pithecellobium unguis-cati*, (L.) Mart. (Leguminosae, now assigned to Fabaceae by MBG 2014)	Barrera Marín et al. 1976, 156; Roys 1976, 315; Souza Novelo 1940, 14; Standley 1930, 281–82
	Pithecellobium dulce (Roxb.) Benth (Leguminosae, now assigned to Fabaceae by MBG 2014)	Barrera Marín et al. 1976, 156; Bradburn 1998, 326; Bricker et al. 1998, 53

continued on next page

TABLE 3.3—*continued*

Yucatec name	Scientific name (family)	Source
(sh)ya'ash k'is		No information
(sh)ya'ash 'ek	*Pithecellobium leucospermum*, Brandeg (This species taxon includes *Pithecellobium tortum*, Mart. [Souza Novelo 1940, 15, 24; Roys 1976, 299] and *Lysiloma sabicu*, Benth. [Roys 1976, 299] that were incorrectly classified according to Standley.) (Leguminosae, now assigned to Fabaceae by MBG 2014)	Barrera Marín et al. 1976, 190; Standley 1930, 281
	Pithecellobium mangense (Jacq.) McBride (Leguminosae, now assigned to Fabaceae by MBG 2014)	Bradburn 1998, 326; Bricker et al. 1998, 312

a This entry in Roys is listed as *katsim-ek* (*catsim-ek*). This means "*katsim* black" or "black *katsim*" and is another way of saying *bosh katsim*.

b Bricker identifies this species as an herbaceous plant rather than a tree as is implied by this list. This difference may indicate dialectical variability in the references for trees and plants, or species underdifferentiation (see Berlin 1973; Berlin et al. 1966).

classified by depth, location, and whether they are man-made or natural. Each kind of opening is the source of a different kind of raw material (figure 3.7).

CH'E'EN (A WELL OR SINKHOLE)

Because the northern Yucatán Peninsula is a karst landscape with no surface lakes or streams, drainage is subsurface with water disappearing into the ground within a few hours after a heavy rain (Doehring and Butler 1974, 562; Wilson 1980). The only permanent natural sources of water are natural depressions that retain seasonal rainfall throughout the year (*aguadas*) and sinkholes where the surface limestone has collapsed down to the level of groundwater.

The Maya refer to a natural sinkhole as a *cenote* (e.g., see West 1964, 72)—a hispanicized form of the Yucatec Maya word *dzonot* (*ts'onot*). Ticul informants, however, do not use this word because there are no natural sinkholes locally that contain water like those that occur further north where the water table lies near the surface and is exposed in relatively shallow sinkholes. As one moves south, however, the water table becomes deeper as the elevation of the ground surface rises, and usually is too far below the surface to be exposed in sinkholes.

With no sinkholes and *aguadas* around Ticul, the only reliable sources of water for household consumption are deep wells dug through many meters of soil, rocks, and clay using metal tools and explosives. So, the Maya of Ticul use the term *ch'e'en* to refer

72 THE POTTERS' ENGAGEMENT WITH THE PERCEIVED LANDSCAPE

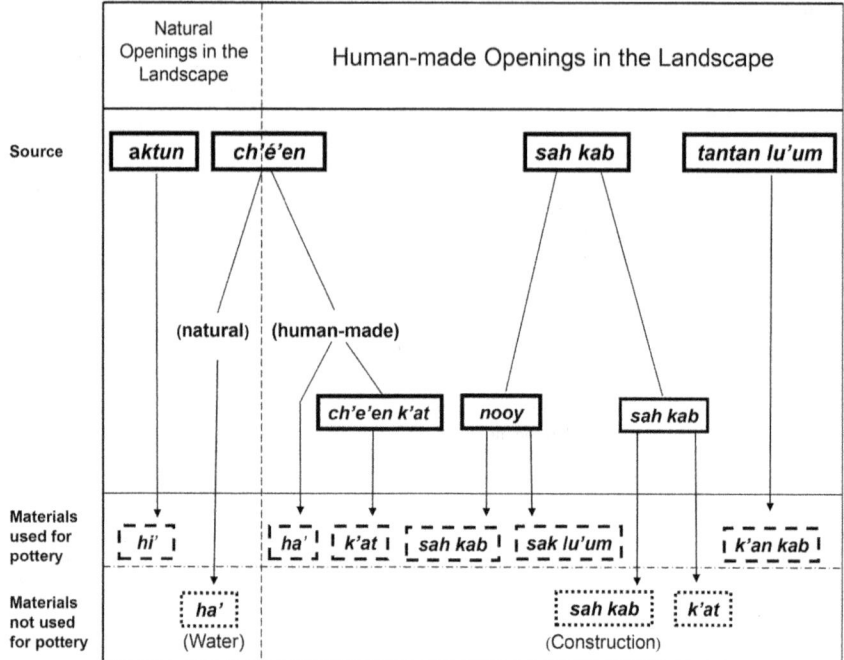

FIGURE 3.7. The semantic structure of the openings in the landscape with reference to the sources of raw materials used by Ticul potters up until about 1990 (see Arnold 2008, 153–220). (Modified from Arnold 1971, 28.)

to a well, as well as a natural sinkhole, but its meaning is broader and includes any hole of great depth such as the clay mine at Yo' K'at (*ch'e'en k'at*), even if water is not present.

CHULTUN (A CISTERN)

In the region immediately adjacent to the northern side of the *puuk* hill ridge and extending southward into the Yucatecan hill country, the geology and the seasonal scarcity of rainfall create a chronic problem of water availability (Dunning 1994; Isphording 1975, 244, 246, 251; McAnany 1990). Permanent sources of water are nonexistent to rare here because the water table is too far below ground level, and natural sinkholes are not deep enough to reach it (Dunning 1994; Isphording 1975, 244, 246, 251; McAnany 1990).

In Ticul, the water table lies twenty-five meters below the surface, and south of the hill ridge it is much deeper. Except for caves and a few sinkholes (such as one in the archaeological site Kiuik in the *wits* zone), rainfall provided the only water available prior to the conquest, and then only during the rainy season when it collected in seasonal pools of semiartificial origin (*aguadas*) and holes in impervious rock (*haltuns*, see E. H. Thompson 1895, 7). With little precipitation falling for most of the dry season, from January through early May (Arnold 2008, 99), the lack of a regular source of water throughout the year created a serious adaptive problem for human populations.

As a consequence of the lack of surface water and a deep water table, few major settlements existed in this region until the beginning of the Terminal Classic Period (about AD 800), when the Maya dug underground cisterns called *chultuns* to collect water in the rainy season and store it for use in the dry season when little rain falls (E. H. Thompson 1895; Zapata Peraza 1989). This technology provided water that supported larger populations, and as a consequence, these populations expanded into areas previously uninhabited because of the lack of reliable sources of domestic water (see McAnany 1990). *Chultuns* were used for storing other materials besides water, but when they were used for storing water, the Maya plastered them on the inside (E. H. Thompson 1895).

Chultuns also occur in archaeological sites around Ticul (Arnold 2005a; Brainerd 1958, 23, 30; Stephens 1996 [1843], 284–85; E. H. Thompson 1895) and were the only sources of water before the historic period. Today, they serve no modern purpose except that they may provide an opening through the limestone layer to dig a *sah kab* mine.

AKTUN (A NATURAL CAVE)

A third type of opening into the ground surface is the natural cave (*aktun*, or *gruta* in Spanish). Several natural caves are located around Ticul, and all of them are found in the hill ridge south and west of the city (see Hatt 1953; Mercer 1896; R. H. Thompson 1958, 70; West 1964, 84–121). Aktun Hi' is near the Ticul cemetery, whereas Aktun Lara lies further south near the road to Santa Elena. Aktun Ch'ak Tale'en and Aktun Shmak are located in the hill ridge near Hacienda Yo' K'at west of Ticul. Aktun Tzunu'um is one kilometer further west, and beyond it lie Aktun Osh and Aktun Boosh. Besides these larger caves, potters say that there are many more smaller ones.

SAH KAB (A MARL MINE)

The fourth Maya category of openings in the ground surface is a mine called a *sah kab* and is dug into the naturally occurring marl (Bates and Jackson 1987, 403) below the ground surface. The Yucatec phrase *sah kab* does not just refer to the mine, however, but also to the raw material that comes from it. So, a *sah kab* mine serves as a source for the marl that is also called *sah kab* (*sascab* in Spanish). As a raw material, *sah kab* is literally translated as "white powder," a friable material that is relatively soft and is quarried more easily than rock.

Sah kab mines are divided into two subcategories depending on their location. One subcategory is more inclusive and refers to any *sah kab* mine anywhere. The other type is also called *nooy* and exists only at Yo' Sah Kab ('over *sah kab*'), a place located along the road to Chapab that is a source of materials for preparing pottery temper (Arnold 2008, 191–220).

When potters refer to a *sah kab* as a source, they often refer to it as a *cueva* in Spanish. The Spanish word *cueva*, as it is used in Ticul, and its apparent similarity with its English cognate "cave," do not have the same meaning. One should not suppose that meanings that appear to be obvious in English should be imposed on a Spanish cognate that has been translated from Yucatec Maya. *Cuevas* are actually man-made (*hecha por personas*) mines and called *sah kabo'ob* in Yucatec Maya or *sascaberas* in Spanish. The English word "cave," however, refers to a natural cave (i.e., made by nature [*hecha por la naturaleza*]) and called *aktun* in Yucatec Maya or *gruta* in Spanish). In order to avoid confusion between the English and Spanish cognates of cave, a source of *sah kab* in this work is called a "*sah kab* mine," whereas an *aktun* (and the equivalent Spanish word, *gruta*) refers to a natural cave.

The *sah kab* mine and the natural cave are not only distinguished by the agency of their origin but also by the raw materials obtained from them. Each source and the raw materials from them are mutually exclusive. The raw materials from the *sah kab* mine do not occur in a natural cave. One cannot, for example, obtain *sah kab* from a natural cave. Whereas some rocks can be dug from a *sah kab* mine, they are different from those obtained from a natural cave.

In many places around Ticul, and elsewhere in Yucatan, *sah kab* mines exist on the edges of quarries, where miners removed the surface rock for construction of walls and buildings and exposed the marl below it. These quarries exist on the outside of settlements and leave large depressions in the landscape. They expand as mining continues into the walls around their edges to extract marl (*sah kab*) for construction purposes (figure 3.8).

In addition to using an extant marl quarry (*sascabera*), one who wants to obtain marl (*sah kab*) for construction purposes must first locate an appropriate location. *Sah kab* mines cannot be dug anywhere. Rather, a miner must first find the proper kind of rock outcrop (*tunich*). Potters, for example, recognize many different categories of rocks, but marl lies under a rock outcrop called *sah kab tunich* that protrudes slightly above the ground level. If the outcrop is soft (like *sah kab* itself) and one can dig into it easily, then the rock is *sah kab tunich*, and *sah kab* usually lies within a meter below it. If red earth (*k'an kab*) lies on the surface, however, marl deposits (*sah kab*) may be far below the surface because red earth deposits may be very deep. Similarly, if a very hard rock (*tok' tunich*) occurs on the surface, then no *sah kab* exists beneath it.

FIGURE 3.8. The marl quarry of San Juaquín northwest of Ticul in 1965 used to mine marl (*sah kab*) and rock for building purposes. The soil is scraped off the caprock before mining and is piled above it on the edge of the quarry. Once the caprock is removed, miners tunnel into the marl layer below it. When the caprock collapses into the mines, it is broken up and removed for building purposes, and mining continues into marl layer around the edges of the quarry. The floor of this quarry lies about 4 m below the normal ground surface and consists entirely of a clay, but its quality is too poor to use for making pottery.

Quarriers use other criteria to identify a suitable location to mine constructional marl (*sah kab*). Within towns and villages, marl (*sah kab*) lies within a few feet below the surface near an oak (*roble*) or avocado tree because the *sah kab* retains moisture and makes the avocado tree grow rapidly. It is likely that this explanation has a physical basis because the moisture-absorbing qualities of the clay mineral smectite (see next chapter) that occurs in the marl means that the subterranean *sah kab* actually does retain moisture that percolates into it and provides sustenance for the tree.

Several kinds of materials occur inside a *sah kab* mine: marl (*sah kab*), rocks (*tunich*), and sometimes pockets of clay (*k'at*). The rocks in the marl may be hard pieces of *sah kab* (*tunichil sah kab*) that potters consider different than the *sah kab tunich* that lies on the ground surface. Sometimes rocks in the mines may also consist of a harder rock called *tok' tunich*. An analysis of a rock called *tunichil sah kab* from inside of a *sah kab* mine revealed that it consisted of dolomite and the clay mineral montmorillonite (that is now called smectite, Arnold 1967b, 30). *Tok' tunich* consists largely of dolomite.

FIGURE 3.9. A *tantan lu'um*, a hole used to mine *k'an kab* used for a slip for pottery and for making the mortar and plaster for kilns. Dug in thick beds of *k'an kab*, mining sometimes uncovers some rocks below the surface. Located in a temper mining area near Yo' Sah Kab in 2008, the amount of *k'an kab* removed from this source suggests that it was used to build a kiln because only a much smaller amount is required for a slip for pottery. A deposit of ashes, charcoal, and a few kiln wasters on the edge of the hole (out of sight) further suggests that a potter used a truck to bring kiln waste to the location, dump it there, and then filled the truck with the mined *k'an kab* and returned to Ticul.

TANTAN LU'UM (A HOLE IN THE EARTH)

The fifth Maya category of an opening in the earth is the *tantan lu'um*. Unlike a *sah kab* mine, a *tantan lu'um* does not perforate the rock layer, is not a *sah kab* mine, and does not contain *sah kab*. Although it denotes a deep hole, potters also use the term to signify a small, shallow hole that is dug in an area where "red earth" (*k'an kab*) occurs on the surface (figure 3.9).

A *tantan lu'um* is a source of the rust-colored red earth (*k'an kab*) used as a red slip (Arnold 1971; R. H. Thompson 1958, 91; see chapter 8) and to make mortar for constructing and plastering kilns. *K'an kab* literally means "yellow powder," just as potters translate *sah kab* as "white powder." Some potters describe *k'an kab*, however, as *chak lu'um* (red earth) but prefer to use *k'an kab* rather than *chak kab* or *chak lu'um* for the category. *K'an kab* appears to be residual from the limestone and was identified as hematite by Bruce F. Bohor of the Illinois Geological Survey.

Although potters can procure this material almost anywhere, some obtain it in a deep deposit near the temper mines (Yo' Sah Kab) located along the road to Chapab northeast of Ticul. At a point 3.3 kilometers from Calle 24, an unimproved road leads south into the forest. After a short distance the road turns east, and along its south edge lies a large area of red earth (*k'an kab*). In 1965 and 1966, potters dug a small hole (45 cm wide by 25 cm deep) in a very low hillock and removed the red earth to use for their red slip. Another shallow source for *k'an kab* was found in the forest at Yo' Sah Kab in 2008, but it was also used as a dump for sherd wasters, charcoal, and ashes from firing (figure 3.9).

Ethnopetrology

Besides classifications of landscape and trees, potters also recognize many different kinds of rocks (table 3.4). These rocks have diverse uses and come from different locations, and some of them overlap with the potters' classification of minerals described in the next chapter. *Sak lu'um tunich*, for example, is given the "rock" designation because it looks and feels like a rock, and yet when it is wet it behaves differently (see chapter 4). Similarly, *hi' tunich* is a rock but potters may also simply refer to it as *hi'*.

TABLE 3.4. The ethnopetrology of rocks according to Ticul potters showing their name, their use, and where each type was found. The "use" column was a response to the frame *Ba'ash meyhul kubeeta'al yeetel _____?* (What part of the pottery-making process uses it? (Free translation), and the locations of each item in the "where found" column was a response to the frame *Tu'ush kucha'abal _____?* (Where is it found?) (This frame set was elicited in 1965 and was not elaborated or detailed in the years after that. There is some contradiction between the data here and the rocks used to make a kiln in chapter 7, for reasons that are unclear.)

Maya name	Use	Where found (general)
chak tunich (red rock)	Walls of houses made with rocks and plaster (*pak'il nah*)	Hill ridge (*puuk*)
boosh tunich (black rock)	Kiln (*koot*)	Hill ridge (*puuk*)
k'an tunich (yellow rock)	Walls (*pak'*)	Hill ridge (*puuk*)
hi' tunich (crystalline rock)	Temper for cooking pottery (*kum, shamach, caldero kum*)	Caves (*aktun*) along the hill ridge (*puuk*)
sakel baach tunich (white birds' egg rock)	Walls of houses made with rocks and plaster (*pak'il nah*)	Pulled out of the ground (*lak'bil ich lu'um*)
tok' tunich (hard rock)	Kiln (*kot*)	High hill ridge (*mul*)
boosh t'ok tunich (black hard rock)	Kiln (*kot*)	High hill ridge (*mul*)

continued on next page

TABLE 3.4—*continued*

Maya name	Use	Where found (general)
chak tok' tunich (red hard rock)	Kiln (*kot*)	High hill ridge (*mul*)
sak lu'um tunich (*sak lu'um* rock)	Temper for noncooking pottery (e.g., *p'uul* [water-carrying pot]), *hamak, kat* [water storage pot], *lak* [food bowl])	Marl mines (*sah kab*) at Yo' Sah Kab
tunich sak kab	*yu ch'u'ul puut'* (meaning unclear)	Marl mines (*sah kab*)
k'at tunich (*tunichil k'at*) (rocks in clay)	Not good for anything	Picked out of clay (*kupanal k'at*)
k'an kab tunich (red earth rock)	Kiln (*kot*)	No response
sah kab tunich (marl ('*sah kab*') rock)	Walls of houses (*pak'il nah*)	*lakbil u beeta'al lu'um* (Pulled out of the ground)
chak sah kab tunich (red '*sah kab*' rock)	Walls of houses (*pak'il nah*)	In the earth (*lu'um*)
nen us tunich (crystal rock)	Cooking pottery (*kum*)	Over very hard rock (*yo' tsek'el tunich*)
tsek'el tunich (hard rock)		Hill ridge (*puuk*)
hal tun tunich (rock with hole that catches water)	Not used for making pottery (*ma' ti'a'al meyahil*)	Where there is hard rock sticking out of the ground (*tu'ush yan yo' tsek'el tunich*)
kab tunich	Grinding nishtamal (*hu'uchul ku'um*)	Small hills on the hill ridge (*chan puuk*)
tunich ka'anab	To polish pottery (*yult'al meyah*)	Seashore (*tuhal kana'ab*)
tunichil aktun (rocks in natural caves)	Washbasins (*polbil tunich*)	In natural caves in the hill ridge (*aktun*)

NOTES

1. The hill ridge known as the *puuk* in Yucatec Maya is usually and more commonly written as *puuc* rather than its more phonetic pronunciation as *puuk*. I have used a phonetic orthography here to be consistent with my transcription of Yucatec Maya used in this work.

2. Although the role of volcanic ash in Yucatán soil development appears to be unexplored except for H. Quiñones and R. Allende (Quiñones and Allende 1974), analyses of palygorskite collected from approximately two meters below ground level at Yo' Sah Kab indicate the presence of volcanic minerals, in turn suggesting that palygorskite was altered volcanic ash (Arnold et al. 2012).

4

The Potters' Engagement with Raw Materials

ETHNOMINERALOGY

The Ticul potter's indigenous knowledge of their raw materials involves a subset of the larger corpus of their traditional environmental knowledge. Although they draw some of their knowledge about those materials from the larger repertoire of Maya categories of earth (*lu'um*), clay (*k'at*) and rock (*tunich*), they select and use them in a way quite different from nonpotters. Their knowledge thus is specialized, unique to potters, and generally not possessed by other members of the community. Rather, it is based upon their own practical experience and engagement with the physical properties of their raw materials and the sources from which they come.

The potter's knowledge of raw materials does not just consist of the choices that they make when they select them but also involves a foundational problem-solving skill as they engage and use them. This engagement is not just based on knowledge of sources and the phenomenological distinctions that are important to potters but also involves evaluating tactile and visual feedback from the raw materials, enabling them to select and use materials to make pots successfully, and involves what to do if those materials are inferior. This feedback thus is evaluated by their knowledge that they have received from tradition and from previous engagements with making pottery. Their choices of raw materials are not only the materialization of a previously existing mental template, or the result of immutable cognitive categories, but also result from their engagement with those materials to evaluate their suitability for making pottery. It is a part of their working memory.

K'AT (CLAY)

Clay, of course, is basic to pottery production, and potters recognize five different colors of it that correspond to the five color categories in Yucatec Maya: white (*sak*), black (*boosh*), blue/green (*ya'ash*), red (*chak*), and yellow (*k'an*).[1] Although color is a convenient factor in describing clay, it is not important in assessing the quality of the clay for making pottery.

In the 1960s, potters recognized two major classes of clay distinguished by their suitability for making pottery. One class was superior for making pottery, whereas the other type was useful only for making small items if it could be used at all. Distinguishing the quality of clay was especially critical for fabricating large vessels.

Historically, high-quality clay for making pottery consisted of two colors—white (*sak*) and yellow (*k'an*)—and came only from Hacienda Yo' Kat (literally, "over clay" in Yucatec Maya) located five kilometers northwest of Ticul. Up until about 1970, it came from a single deep mine (Arnold 2008, 153–59; Arnold and Bohor 1977). By 1984, however, miners had procured it through several vertical shafts that were used up until late 1991, when clay mining at Yo' K'at was abandoned and clay was imported from the state of Campeche (Arnold 2008, 153–59).[2]

Clay was widespread and abundant at Yo' K'at. Although its areal extent was unknown, potters removed a massive amount of it from the mines there, judging by the large mined-out cavities in the underground mine in 1968 (Arnold 2008, 174) and by the surface subsidence adjacent to the mine entrance in 1965. This subsidence suggested that the surface had collapsed into a sizable underground cavity created by the extraction of clay (figure 4.1).

When Bohor and I explored the Yo' K'at mine in 1968, we found that potters had tunneled into a large bedded deposit (approximately 2 m thick) of kaolinite and a random mixed layering of the clay minerals kaolinite and smectite.[3] Based upon other surveys of accessible clay deposits by geologist Bruce F. Bohor and myself in the 1960s, the Yo' K'at deposit appeared to be the only large such deposit accessible to potters in the immediate area of Ticul (Arnold 1967a, 1967b, 1971; Bohor 1975).

Although this mixed layer clay is found elsewhere in Yucatán, it is not widely distributed. In our survey and analysis of clays in northern Yucatán, Bohor and I found that it occurred only in very specific and limited localities such as Tepakán and Yo' K'at. Schultz and his colleagues (Schultz et al. 1971, 56) identified it in Raymond Thompson's samples from Becal and Yo' K'at, and Isphording and Wilson (1974, 486) also reported its occurrence at Yo' K'at, Tepakán, and Becal and in soil samples obtained near Mérida.

Unlike the few sources from which high-quality clay can be mined, deposits of the clay mineral smectite are much more widespread, but this clay is inferior for making pottery, and in some cases useless.[4] Such deposits are found in small pockets

FIGURE 4.1. The surface subsidence north of the entrance of the clay mine at Hacienda Yo' K'at in May 1965 that suggests the surface collapsed into a large underground cavity from clay mining. (From Arnold and Bohor 1977, 577 [fig. 3].)

in the mines and quarries dug to obtain marl (called *sah kab*) used to make mortars, plasters, and surfacing materials (see also Arnold 1967a; 1967b; 1971, 25), but it also occurs as a thick bed at the base of the marl (*sah kab*) quarries (figure 4.2). Up until the 1990s, potters generally did not use such clay because they considered it to be inferior for making pottery (Arnold 2008, 153–89). After clay mining at Yo' K'at was abandoned in late 1991, procurement moved to locations north and east of Calkiní in the state of Campeche (Arnold 2008, 156–70), and those areas became the source of clay for Ticul potters, even though its quality varied greatly.

Potters engage the quality of the clay by using two practical criteria to distinguish good pottery clay from ordinary clay: its salty taste and its drying properties. Good clay has a salty taste. Inferior clay, on the other hand, does not have a salty taste; it opens up and falls apart when it is dried in the sun.

These two practical criteria reflect the chemistry, mineralogy, and geology of the local clays. First, saltiness comes from the presence of sodium chloride in the clay.[5] Using silver nitrate to assess the presence of the halogen group of ions (such as chlorine), the soluble residues were tested after the clays had been mixed with distilled water, boiled with charcoal, and then filtered.[6] All (3/3) of the samples of potter's clay from Yo' K'at contained the chloride ion, whereas most (4/5) samples of ordinary clays from elsewhere did not (Arnold 1971, 30).[7] The Fischer Exact test (for a contingency table with cells less than five) revealed that the difference between the potters' perception of the presence and absence of the chloride ion in the two types of clay was marginally significant ($p = .07$), but that it was probably a reasonably accurate test to differentiate the clays (see Goodman 2016). Additional tests revealed that even though the chloride ion was present to a certain degree in some of the ordinary clays, the Yo' K'at clay had the highest concentration of the ion in the samples judged by the amount of silver chloride precipitate produced by the tests.[8]

The relative presence or absence of sodium chloride in clay is probably due to the accessibility of the clay deposit to the leaching action of groundwater. Originally, the sodium chloride probably came from the marine origin of the geological deposits of northern Yucatán. Therefore, one might expect that all of the clay deposits would test positive for the chloride ion. Clay deposits exposed to percolating rain water from the surface would leach out any soluble salts (such as sodium chloride) from these deposits. This leaching would also occur in beds that were residual from the limestone, where clay was redeposited in the marl from the movement of groundwater through the marl deposits.

The clay deposit at Yo' K'at, however, is 1.5–2 meters thick, and because such clay deposits are relatively impervious to groundwater, its soluble salts probably were not leached out. Consequently, the differential accessibility of a clay deposit to leaching is probably responsible for the salty taste for the Yo' K'at clay and its absence in ordinary clay. The potters' taste test thus appears to have a valid chemical basis grounded in the geological realities of clay sources around Ticul; it was a very useful criterion for identifying the quality of the clay for making pottery.

Although the taste test was largely a rule-of-thumb test for potters, it also provided technological benefits. Ticul pottery has a substantial amount of calcium carbonate in its temper, and when fired to 900 degrees Celsius, the heat drives off the carbon dioxide from the carbonate to form calcium oxide that easily takes up moisture from the air. This change creates molecules of calcium hydroxide that occupy more space than the original carbonate minerals in the paste, and as they expand, they put stresses on the vessel walls, causing them to spall and crack (Rice 1987, 98; 2015, 81, 109, 377; Shepard 1965, 22, 30). The presence of sodium chloride in the paste, however, can ameliorate the potential adverse effects of this change. In experiments with New Guinea pottery, Owen Rye found that small amounts of salt in the paste appeared to lower the sintering temperature of clays, effectively sealing off the calcium oxide from water and thus inhibiting the formation of calcium hydroxide from the calcium oxide after firing (Rye 1976).

FIGURE 4.2. A hole in the clay deposit at the base of an abandoned marl (*sah kab*) quarry near Calkiní that was used as a clay source by Fidencio Huicab in 1994. Ticul potters did not use such deposits as sources of their clay before 1991 because this kind of clay was considered "ordinary clay" and not suitable for making pottery. When the clay from Yo' K'at became exhausted, however, potters and specialist miners began obtaining clay from abandoned marl quarries between Calkiní and Dzitbalché, and used their indigenous knowledge to engage the properties of the new materials and adapt them to making pottery, often by changing their paste preparation techniques and recipes (see Arnold 2008,155–70; Arnold et al. 1999).

The second test that potters use to identify high-quality clay is its drying properties. This test uses the visual feedback that the potter receives from the drying clay. If it opens up and falls apart when it is dried in the sun, then it is inferior for making pots because it causes drying vessels to crack because of excessive shrinkage.

This test relates to the differences in the crystal structure between the clay minerals smectite and kaolinite and their effect on adsorption of water on their molecular surfaces. The potters' clay from Yo' K'at consists of kaolinite and a random mixed layering of kaolinite and smectite, whereas the ordinary clay just consists of smectite. Smectite has a distinctive atomic structure in which a weak negative charge resides on the surface of each of the individual clay layers because of the unequal substitution of certain metallic ions within the crystal lattice (Grim 1962, 16–18; Rice 1987, 47–49; 2015, 55; Van Olphen 1963, 66). In order to compensate for this unbalanced charge, cations and polar molecules (such as water) are readily taken up between the layers. In fact, layers of water from one to several molecular units thick may develop between the individual layers of smectite. This property, called interlayer swelling, expands its molecular structure in the presence of water and greatly increases its volume (Grim 1968, 265–69; Rice 1987, 48–49; 2015, 50, 55; Shepard 1965, 8–10). When smectite dries, much of this water is lost, and the volume of the clay greatly decreases (Rice 1987, 49; 2015, 55, 103; Shepard 1965, 377). This characteristic explains why ordinary clay contracts and opens up when it is dried in the sun and why vessels made from it crack during drying because the dried vessels simply shrink too much.

Kaolinite, on the other hand, has a different crystal structure. Because there is no substitution of metallic ions of unequal charge within its crystal lattice, no negative charges exist on the surfaces of its individual molecular layers (Grim 1962, 16; Rice 1987, 45), providing little opportunity for ion substitution in their structure (Rice 2015, 51). As a result, cations and water molecules are not attracted into positions between the layers of the clay. Rather, the chemical structure of kaolinite consists of one or two molecules of interlayer water that are tightly bound to the clay layers and cannot be lost at temperatures less than sixty degrees Celsius. Kaolinite thus has two basic differences from smectite: (1) the quantity of the interlayer water in the kaolinite is only a fraction of the water present in smectite, and (2) the interlayer water of the kaolinite, in contrast to that in the smectite, is not lost in air drying and is only lost during firing. Consequently, changes in volume during drying are greatly reduced using the mixed-layered clay compared to pure smectite. Since the Yo' K'at clay does not break open and crack as much when it is dried in the sun, vessels made with the Yo' K'at clay are stronger and do not crack as easily as those made from ordinary clay.

There have been occasions in the past, however, when the clay at Yo' K'at was inaccessible due to difficulties with the manager of the hacienda, or because the mine yielded poor-quality clay and rocks (*shish k'at*) (Arnold 1971; 2008, 153–89). In these cases potters attempted to use the taste test and drying test for finding suitable clays for making pottery from elsewhere. Even then, potters could not be sure that their vessels would not crack.

Although clay from Yo' K'at was preferred for all pottery, and was critical for making large vessels, ordinary clays were not entirely unusable. Even though many sources of ordinary clay were identified (such as in nearby marl [*sah kab*] mines), most potters did not use it, but rather obtained their clay from Hacienda Yo' K'at until mining was abandoned there at the end of 1991. Some ordinary clays, though not desirable, are satisfactory for making small vessels such as bowls and figures. Small vessels made with inferior clay do not crack as much as large ones. Furthermore, because many smaller vessels (such as coin banks) are painted with an enamel paint after firing, cracks can be repaired with plaster of Paris, sanded, and then covered with paint to hide the crack. Even though potters occasionally may use ordinary clay for small vessels, they typically avoided it totally.

Potters had discovered the superior quality of the clay from Yo' K'at at least by AD 800–1000 during the Terminal Classic Period. When Bohor and I crawled into the clay mine there in 1968, we were surprised to find sherds on the floor of the mine about fifty meters from the entrance and about three meters below ground level (see Arnold 2008, 154–80; Arnold and Bohor 1977). We noticed that more were embedded within the wall (figure 4.3). Bohor examined the area around the sherds in the wall and concluded that they appeared to be in situ in the clay deposit. Miners apparently had encountered the sherds during mining and discarded them on the floor of the cavity. When we reconstructed the sherds later, they formed a large triangular sherd of a bolster rim basin from the Terminal Classic Period (figure 4.4). When we examined the photograph that we took in the mine, however, we saw what appeared to be a collapsed mine tunnel with a large chunk of clay in it covered by the large sherd (Arnold and Bohor 1977; figure 4.3). Because of the cramped quarters of the mine and the meager light from our flashlights, we could not see the entire context of the sherds embedded in the wall. The sherd was indeed in situ, but the photograph revealed that the sherd was not in the larger clay deposit, but rather was sealed in what appeared to be a profile of a mine tunnel that had filled with marl from the layer of marl above the clay deposit during the thousand years between our visit in 1968 and when the clay miner left the sherd in the mine tunnel during the Terminal Classic Period.

An Alternative Clay Source

The relationship of potters' ethnomineralogical knowledge to their engagement with their raw materials is also illustrated in their use of alternative clay sources. The tactile and visual feedback that comes from engaging these new materials also affirms the lack of a preexisting mental template. Rather, it demonstrates the importance of the problem-solving dimension of choosing a clay that involves the feedback from their actual engagement with it.

Probably the most important alternative clay source to Yo' K'at was one that was located only a few blocks away in the Barrio of Mejorada. In 1965 it was about ten meters northwest of the principal house on the north side of Calle 15, midway between Calle 28 and Calle 30 (Arnold 2008, 166). In the distant past, the clay mine was reportedly owned by Gómez Canul. In 1952, however, a potter named Julián Huicab bought the property after he married the daughter (Josefina Mex) of a potter (Cesario Mex) who lived directly across the street (Arnold 2015a, 183, 195).

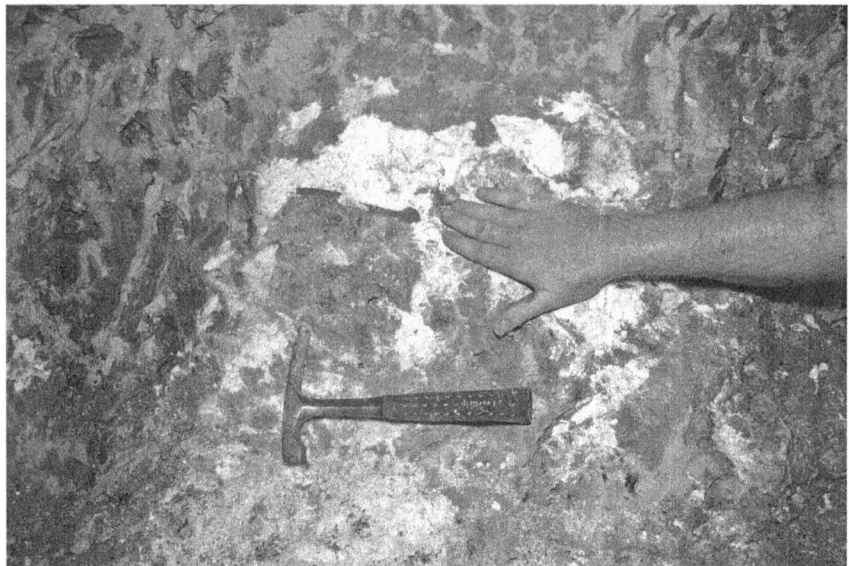

FIGURE 4.3. Image of the wall inside the clay mine at Hacienda Yo' K'at in 1968 showing the profile of a collapsed mining tunnel and a sherd of the bolster rim basin covering a piece of clay in it. During the 800 years since the mining tunnel was used, several kinds of debris washed into it, filling in around the sherd-tool that covered the lump of clay: (1) solid calcareous material (*sah kab*) from above the clay deposit, (2) pieces of clay, (3) a mixture of clay and calcareous marl (*sah kab*). The occurrence of a large piece of clay on the concave underside of the sherd suggests that the restored sherd-tool was used to gather clay in the mine after it was removed from the mine face (see also Arnold 1985,63; 2008,174–76; and Arnold and Bohor 1977). Although the tunnel profile indicates a small size, it is no smaller than some of the mine tunnels used by miners in the 1968 mine (see Arnold 2008,174–75).

I visited this source in 1965 and again in 1966 (Arnold 2008, 165–67), and the clay deposit there appeared to be part of a deposit encountered in Plaza of Mejorada in the late 1960s, when vertical shafts were dug at street corners to provide drainage after heavy rains. Julián still owned the clay source in 1997, but by this time, all evidence of clay mining had disappeared (see Arnold 2008, 165–67). He died about 1998 (Arnold 2015a, 195), and by 2008 construction activity on the lot had totally covered the area of the former mine.

In 1965, potters' engagement with the Mejorada clay revealed different characteristics from the Yo' K'at clay. First, the Mejorada clay had a different taste; it was sweet and did not have the saltiness of the Yo' K'at clay. Second, it was white whereas the Yo' K'at clay was yellow. Third, potters said that it did not have the strength (*fuerza* or *muuk'* in Yucatec Maya) of the Yo' K'at clay and was therefore inferior to it. So, to

FIGURE 4.4. The restored sherd-tool of Puuc (Medium) Slate Ware found in the collapsed tunnel (figure 4.3) in the mine at Yo' K'at in 1968. The original basin from which this sherd came was twenty-six centimeters in diameter. Slight use wear along the broken edges of the original sherd suggest that the sherd was a scraper to gather clay in the mine after it was removed from the mine face. (The remaining fragment necessary to complete the triangular shape was the result of a fresh break and, like the broken character of the remainder of the sherd, was probably the work of modern clay miners.)

compensate for these characteristics, the owner mixed the Mejorada clay with the Yo' K'at clay in a ratio of 1:1 to make pots, but he said that fired vessels made from it eventually fell apart when water was placed in them. The clay was, however, acceptable for making small figures that did not hold water.

These beliefs about the quality of the Mejorada clay are consistent with the mineralogical analysis of the clay by clay mineralogist B. F. Bohor. It revealed that the clay consisted of 85 percent smectite and 15 percent dehydrated halloysite. Since L. G. Schultz et al. (1971) found that the clay that Bohor had called "halloysite" was a random mixed layering of kaolinite and smectite, the halloysite in the Mejorada sample was likely a combination of 85 percent smectite and 15 percent random mixed layering of kaolinite and smectite (Arnold 1967b, 30).[9] This composition indicates that its quality was not as poor as the common ordinary clay (smectite) in the area, but neither was it as good as the clay from Hacienda Yo' K'at.

When a sample of the Mejorada clay was mixed with water and temper, the paste had a brighter yellow color than the Yo' K'at paste. Comparing the texture of the two pastes by rubbing them between the fingers revealed that the Yo' K'at paste had more grit (called *ta'achach* or *shish*) than that made with the Mejorada clay.

Making a vessel was the ultimate test by which potters evaluated the quality of a new clay. If the vessel was dried and fired successfully, then it was tested by placing water in it. If the vessels did not leak within twenty-four hours, then the clay was deemed acceptable for making water pots.

The Mejorada clay passed these tests. It was successfully formed into three small water storage vessels (*apastes*) and two small water-carrying vessels (*cántaros*) that were then fired. When water was placed in them, they did not leak. So, informants concluded that the clay was very good for forming pottery, and they were thinking about asking the owner if he would sell some of the clay to them. To my knowledge, however, my informants never bought clay from the owner and never used it, but continued using the clay from Yo' K'at. Again, these experiments with the Mejorada clay reveal that potters do not follow a preexisting mental template, but rather make their technological choices after they receive feedback from engaging the properties of the raw clay and from the performance characteristics of the dried and fired vessels.

SAK LU'UM (WHITE EARTH)

Sak lu'um (white earth) is a second category of Ticul potters' indigenous knowledge of raw materials for making pottery and is identified by their engagement with its properties. It looks like a rock (figure 4.5) that is often white but may also be yellow or cream. It is very hard and has a chalky texture. It weighs less than a rock of the same size but becomes soft and pliable like clay when it is wet. These properties differentiate *sak lu'um* from rocks (*tunich*) or clay (*k'at*). Rocks (*tunich*) do not become soft and pliable when they are wet, and clay (*k'at*) is not as hard and occurs naturally in a more moist state. Unlike clay, white earth is dry when it is mined and is difficult to mine because it is very hard and cannot be crushed easily (Arnold 1967a, 1967b, 1971).[10]

Analyses of approximately 180 samples of *sak lu'um* by X-ray diffraction collected since 1965 have confirmed that *sak lu'um* is entirely different from the rocks and other clay materials of the area. *Sak lu'um* is palygorskite (Arnold 1967a, 1967b, 1971; Arnold and Bohor 2008; Arnold et al. 2007; Arnold et al. 2012). Rocks (*tunich*), on the other hand, consist of calcite and/or dolomite, and the clays (*k'at*) are composed of a small amount of kaolinite and a random mixed layering of kaolinite and smectite, or just smectite.

Whereas palygorskite is classed as clay mineral and is plastic like that of other clay minerals, it has a very different structure. Most clay minerals have a plate-like

THE POTTERS' ENGAGEMENT WITH RAW MATERIALS   89

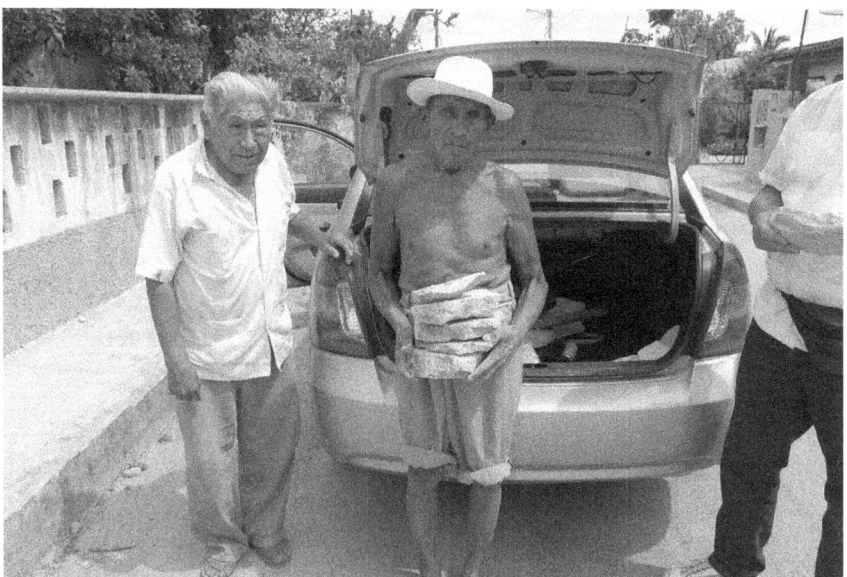

FIGURE 4.5. A Ticul potter holding chunks of *sak lu'um* (palygorskite) mined at Yo' Sah Kab in 2008. This image shows the visual characteristic of *sak lu'um* (white earth): it looks like a white rock. Without one's engaging its properties in a tactile manner, however, *sak lu'um* does indeed seem like a rock. Even though it's hard and difficult to break up like a rock, it is light in weight but becomes plastic when enough water is added to it. This potter soaked it in water, dried it, and broke it up to sell to potters as a supplement to paste preparation when the temper purchased from specialist miners was inferior quality. This particular form of palygorskite came from the base of a one meter deposit of the mineral.

morphology, whereas palygorskite and its close relative, sepiolite, have a fibrous and needle-like morphology (Grim 1968, 44–45; Rice 1987, 50; 2015, 57).[11] This structure gives both minerals unusual properties.

Potters' indigenous knowledge about *sak lu'um* thus has a physical and mineralogical basis. The potter's practical knowledge of, and engagement with, the properties of *sak lu'um* correspond to the known scientific properties of palygorskite (Arnold 1967a, 1967b, 1971).

SAH KAB (WHITE POWDER)

The Yucatec Maya expression *sah kab* refers to both a source and to the raw material that comes from that source (figure 3.7). This distinction is more clearly expressed in Spanish as *sascab* (*sah kab*, the material), and *sascabera* (*sah kab*, the source).

TABLE 4.1. The folk taxonomy of *sah kab* (white powder) and its division into pottery temper and marl for construction purposes. For a folk taxonomy of pottery temper, see table 4.4.

sah kab (white powder)			
sah kabil meyah (pottery temper)	*chen sah kab* (construction purposes)		
	sak sah kab (white)	*chak sah kab* (red)	*kut sah kab* (inferior)

Potters recognize two subcategories of *sah kab* sources. One category is a mine of a naturally occurring marl (*chen sah kab*) used for constructing roads and buildings.[12] The other subcategory (*nooy*) serves as a mine for materials used to prepare pottery temper (*sah kabil meyah*).

Besides two different categories of the sources, potters also classify the material from them (*sah kab*) differently, even though they translate both types as "white powder" (table 4.1). Whereas the *sah kab* for construction purposes is a naturally occurring marl, *sah kab* for pottery temper is a deliberately created cultural and behavioral mixture that contains *sak lu'um*. Potters say that "white earth" (*sak lu'um*) gives the pottery strength (*muuk'*) and is essential to prevent sagging and cracking. Potters either use materials that naturally contain *sak lu'um* to prepare their temper or they add it to the temper deliberately.

The other subcategory of *sah kab* is simply a natural marl and does not contain *sak lu'um*. Instead, it is used only for construction purposes (e.g., mortars, plasters, and surfacing materials for patios, floors, and roads). In contrast to mines of *sah kab* temper that are located only at Yo' Sah Kab located northeast of Ticul along the road to Chapab (Arnold 1971; 2005a; 2008, 194–98), mines for constructional *sah kab* are found throughout the area.

Besides having different meanings, the mineralogy of the two categories of *sah kab* are also different. Although two minerals are common to both groups (calcite and dolomite), the kind of clay mineral in each of these materials is different. *Sah kab* for construction purposes contains the clay mineral smectite (Arnold 1967b, 28; 1971), whereas *sah kab* temper contains palygorskite and only occasionally smectite (Arnold 1967a; 1967b; 1971, 34). Palygorskite only occurs in *sah kab* temper, and does not occur in the *sah kab* for construction purposes (Arnold 1967a; 1967b; 1971, 32–33). Analyses of the thirty-five samples of *sah kab* for pottery temper collected from Ticul potters revealed that they all contained calcite, dolomite, and the clay mineral palygorskite, and all eleven samples of *sah kab* for construction purposes contained the clay mineral smectite and calcite and/or dolomite and no palygorskite (Arnold 1967a, 1967b, 1971). Twenty-four samples of *sah kab* temper contained minor amounts (from a trace to 30 percent of clay content) of smectite in addition

TABLE 4.2. Percent of clay in samples of *sah kab* for construction purposes collected during 1965 and 1966. Acetic acid was used to dissolve the carbonate fraction. Percentages are the weight of the dried insoluble residue minus the beaker weight divided by the total of the weight of the dried untreated sample × 100 (mean = 14.12 percent).

Sample number	% Clay	Subcategory	Source of sample
7	6.57%	*chak* (red)	Marl quarries of San Juaquín
41	21.67%	*chak* (red)	Mine in house lot of Mejorada clay mine

TABLE 4.3. Percent of clay in *sah kab* for pottery temper collected in 1965 and 1966 (see Arnold 1971, 33–34). Acetic acid was used to dissolve the carbonate fraction. Percentages are the weight of the dried insoluble residue minus the beaker weight divided by the total of the weight of the dried untreated sample times 100. The mean percentage of clay in these samples is 37.14 percent clay.

Sample number	% Clay	Source of sample
20	35.27%	House of temper miner Eusevio Yeh (sifted)
18	38.98%	House of a potter, but mined by Crecencio Sima, who was the potter's WiSiHu
8	37.17%	House of a potter, but mined by Crecencio Sima who was the potter's sister's husband

to the carbonate minerals (i.e., calcite and dolomite) that were common to the group. Besides the different clay minerals in each type of *sah kab*, the amount of clay present was also different. After using hot acetic acid to dissolve the carbonate minerals, *sah kab* for construction purposes had a mean of 14.1 percent clay (N = 2, table 4.2),[13] whereas *sah kab* for pottery temper had a mean of 37.1 percent clay (N = 3, table 4.3).

Sah Kab for Construction Purposes (Natural Marl)

The first type of *sah kab* (white powder) is a natural marl used for construction purposes (*chen sah kab*). It is well suited for mortars, plasters, and surfacing because the smectite found in it has excellent film-forming and case-hardening properties, making it a useful material for creating a hard-packed surface (Bruce Bohor, personal communication; Rice 1987, 49; 2015, 55).

Sah kab for construction purposes consists of three basic subclasses (table 4.1). Two of these differ on the basis of color: one is red (*chak*) and the other is white (*sak*). Both are used as a filler for mortars and plasters similarly to the way that sand, crushed rock, or gravel are used as a filler elsewhere (Arnold 1971). Some informants say that both colors possess the same quality for construction, but others believe that the red variety has more "strength" for this purpose.

A third subclass is *kut sah kab*. This type has a finer texture than other subclasses, does not contain many rocks, and may be encountered just as often as the higher-quality red or white varieties. It is easy to dig, and a small blow can loosen a large chunk of it. During mining, it falls slowly from the ceiling of a mine even when one is not digging there. By way of contrast, other types are more difficult to mine and only a small amount can be loosened at a time. If a clay pocket occurs in a *sah kab* mine, the *sah kab* around it is *kut sah kab*.

Kut sah kab is inferior for making mortars and plasters because it has no "strength" (*fuerza*) and is used for surfacing and leveling patios, floors, and roads. Preparing such surfaces first involves placing a layer of large rocks on the ground as a foundation. Then, smaller rocks are packed into the empty spaces between the larger ones, and *kut sah kab* is spread over them. Informants say that this technique was also used to construct the ancient Maya roads called *sak beh* (*camino embutido*) found in and around many archaeological sites. Before the streets of Ticul were paved with asphalt, they were surfaced in this same manner.

Sometimes masons mix *kut sah kab* with water and use it as a filler for a portion of the house foundation, floor, or wall beneath the ground that is not exposed to the elements. It should not be used, however, for mortar, plaster, or a filler for any portion of a structure above ground level. When a mason laid the tile floor of an informant's house in the late 1960s, he mixed the white variety of *sah kab* with lime, but his workers also used a little *kut sah kab* as well. For portions of a building exposed to rainfall, however, "red" or "white" *sah kab* must be used because these types are said to resist the moisture better than *kut sah kab*. If one uses *kut sah kab* for mortars and plasters, however, the building will eventually collapse.

Kut sah kab may be white (*sak*) or yellow (*k'an*). Yellow *sah kab* is always considered to be *kut sah kab*. When it is white, pieces of it resemble chalk. The *kut sah kab* from the clay mine at Hacienda Yo' K'at, for example, is very white and resembles chalk, while the *kut sah kab* in Ticul has a slightly yellowish color. Distinguishing white *kut sah kab* from white (*sak*) *sah kab* must be done carefully because mistakenly using *kut sah kab* for mortars and plasters can produce disastrous results.

SOURCES

Sah kab for construction purposes (marl) usually comes from quarries located within house lots and on the outskirts of cities, towns, and villages (see also Folan 1982). In the 1960s and before, masons often dug a mine in a house lot in order to procure marl for building a new house or for an addition to an existing one (see also Erasmus 1965). Obtaining *sah kab* in this way, however, was risky because mines that produced good-quality *sah kab* for mortars (i.e., *sak sah kab* or *chak sah kab*) were not as common as those that produced *kut sah kab* that is only suitable for surfacing. So, the quality of the marl (*sah kab*) from a mine in a house lot must be evaluated carefully, and that from mines on one's own property should not be used hastily.

Purchasing at least some marl (*sah kab*) when undertaking a building project is often a better choice than mining it in one's own house lot. The mason who built an addition to my informant's house in the late 1960s, for example, said that *sah kab* from the mine in the lot was *kut sah kab* and was unsuitable for mortars and plasters. If he had used it, he could not have guaranteed his work. To illustrate this point, my informant showed me the crumbling wall of the house next door made with the marl from the same mine. The quality of marl for construction purposes thus can only be assured if builders purchase it from professional quarriers.

PREPARATION

The preparation of *sah kab* for making mortars and plasters is a relatively simple process. After mining, it is sifted to remove the rocks (*tunichil sah kab*) and then mixed in a ratio of four parts *sah kab* to one part lime.

Lime is critical for mortars and plasters used in the construction of buildings and is produced by heating certain categories of local rocks using wood from certain trees. This same practice for lime making also occurred in Quintana Roo in eastern Yucatán (Sánchez González 1993, 58–59).

Producing lime involves constructing an elaborate circular structure of layers of wood about 1.5 meters high that are oriented around a central pole. Broken rocks are placed on the wood infrastructure, and gasoline is poured down the central pole (figures 4.6 and 4.7; see also Redfield and Villa Rojas 1962, 55, 64). Then, the wood is ignited and allowed to burn until it is totally consumed. If the wood infrastructure is prepared properly, then only a pile of lime remains at the end of the process.

ANCIENT USES OF *SAH KAB* FOR CONSTRUCTION PURPOSES

Since the marl (*sah kab*) below the surface rock is so easily quarried and useful for construction purposes, it is likely that it was also used by the ancient Maya. In the sixteenth century, Diego de Landa (Gates 1978, 8, 85; Tozzer 1941, 18, 171) noted that the colonial Maya used a white earth (probably *sah kab*) for building purposes, and Shepard (1952, 263) and William Folan (1982) noted the existence of *sah kab* mines around the ancient site of Mayapán. Earl Morris (Morris et al. 1931, 223) reported extensive *sah kab* quarries around Chichén Itzá. Several *sah kab* mines are also located around the site of Ek Balam north of Valladolid and in and around the site of Cobá (Folan 1978, 1982). Because *sah kab* for mortars and plasters comes from mines below the surface, and because mortars and plasters were so critical for

FIGURE 4.6. Workers preparing the structure for converting rocks (limestone) into lime in 1965 and a pile of prepared lime from the process (*lower right*). The structure consists of alternating layers of wood and limestone that are arranged around a central pole. When the structure is completed, a fire is ignited in the center and may burn for several days until the rocks are converted into lime.

constructing the monumental architecture of the ancient Maya, marl mines and quarries probably exist around every archaeological site in Yucatán as well as in and near every modern city, town, and village.

Although studies of ancient mortars and plasters exist (Littmann 1958, 1960), it is difficult (if not impossible) to find definite evidence of the ancient exploitation of such marl around Ticul that is unaltered by modern mining. Modern construction practices use marl so extensively that mining leaves large open, quarry-like depressions in the landscape but destroys all evidence of earlier mining.

SAH KAB FOR POTTERY TEMPER (CULTURALLY CONSTITUTED MARL)

Unlike that used for construction purposes, the second major category of *sah kab* consists of a culturally defined mixture of materials that is used only for pottery temper. Up until about 1990, this temper was mined and prepared exclusively at Yo' Sah Kab (literally "over *sah kab*"), located along the road to Chapab beginning 3.3 kilometers from Calle 24 (Arnold 2008, 191–220; Thompson 1958, 68) and was the only location within the immediate area of Ticul where *sak lu'um* was found. In the late 1980s, however, *sak lu'um* was discovered on private land nearer the village of Chapab, and much of the temper mining moved there beginning in the 1990s (Arnold 2008, 191–220).

FIGURE 4.7. Close-up of the detail of the first layer of the structure used to convert limestone into lime (see figure 4.6).

The extensive mining and preparation areas at Yo' Sah Kab suggest a long period of temper exploitation in this location, and this was confirmed by the presence of an archaeological site there (Arnold 2005a). After being told about the site in 1967, I asked my informant to take me there, and I noted several *chultuns* and a Terminal Classic (AD 800–1000) occupation on top of, and around, a large hole in the surface. After inquiring about the site in 1984, and being told that it had disappeared because temper mining had churned through it, it was clear that it was located over the *sak lu'um* deposit, indicating that the ancient inhabitants probably mined *sak lu'um* and *sah kab* temper there. This inference is further supported by a discovery of a house structure and Terminal Classic sherds (Puuc Unslipped Ware) within the temper preparation areas near the site, but on the other side of the road to Chapab. Potters had mixed the Terminal Classic sherds (Puuc Unslipped Ware) with the tailings of previous preparations, apparently crushing and sifting them for temper. Yo' Sah Kab thus probably served as a source of *sak lu'um* and *sah kab* temper for potters since the Terminal Classic Period (Arnold 2005a).

In order to distinguish these mines from those used to obtain *sah kab* for construction purposes, potters also refer to a mine at Yo' Sah Kab as a *nooy* (or plural *nooyo'ob*). These mines are technically *sah kab* mines, but at Yo' Sah Kab, the material obtained from them is also called *nooy* to distinguish it from naturally occurring marl (ordinary *sah kab*) used for construction purposes.

TEMPER COMPONENTS AND THEIR SUBCLASSES

Sah kab temper (*sah kabil meyah*) ideally consists of two component parts (table 4.4). The first part, called *ta'achach* (meaning "cast-offs," or "garbage" in Yucatec Maya), consists of the coarse and weathered screenings discarded from earlier temper preparation and can be freely translated as "tailings" from the preparation process. *Ta'achach* has no subclasses except that which contains *sak lu'um* and that which does not. X-ray diffraction analyses of *ta'achach* ($N = 2$) revealed that it contained palygorskite and a combination of calcite and dolomite (Arnold 1967b, 7). Acid dissolution of the carbonate minerals revealed that the *ta'achach* samples ($N = 3$) contained a mean of 31.07 percent clay (table 4.5).

The second component of temper consists of the fine powdery substance called *nooy* excavated from underground mines tunneled into the marl layer about 1–1.5 meters from the surface. As with the general meaning associated with the word *ta'achach*, *nooy* also has a meaning that refers to something that is desirable and useful, and it also can refer to other materials such as the white succulent portion of a coconut, in contrast to its discarded shell.

Unlike *ta'achach*, *nooy* is classified much more elaborately and has numerous subclasses (table 4.4). The two most inclusive subclasses are good-quality *nooy* (*nooy ma'alob*) and inferior *nooy* (*kut nooy*). Good-quality *nooy* contains *sak lu'um*, whereas *kut nooy* does not.

GOOD-QUALITY *NOOY*

Good-quality *nooy* is subdivided into several subcategories that are distinguished by color (white ([*sak*] and red [*chak*]), hardness, and a crystalline, "sugarlike" appearance (table 4.4). X-ray diffraction analyses of good-quality *nooy* ($N = 6$)

TABLE 4.4. Folk taxonomy of *sah kab* (white powder) temper used among Ticul potters and its subdivision into different types. The *kut nooy* category includes all of the subcategories of *sah kab* for construction purposes that occur at the temper mines (see table 4.1).

sah kabil meyah (*sah kab* for pottery temper)						
nooy (freshly mined material from the mines)						*ta'achach* (tailings)
nooy (good)				*kut nooy* (unsuitable *nooy*)		
sak nooy (white)	*chak nooy* (red)	*hi' nooy* (sugarlike)	*tok' nooy* (hard, flintlike)	*ta'anooy* (fine-grained)	other	

TABLE 4.5. Percent of clay in samples of *ta'achach*, one of the principal components of pottery temper. The samples analyzed were collected in 1965 and 1966 (see Arnold 1967a, 7; 1967b, 7), and acetic acid was used to dissolve the carbonate fraction. Percentages are the weight of the dried insoluble residue minus the beaker weight divided by the total of the weight of the dried untreated sample times 100. The mean percentage of clay in these samples is 31.07 percent.

Sample number	% Clay	Source of sample
10	32.70%	Yo' Sah Kab (portion in communal [*ejido*] land)
6	21.55%	Yo' Sah Kab (*ejido* portion)
33	38.95%	Venancio Huicab (*sah kab* temper)

contained palygorskite and calcite or a combination of calcite and dolomite (Arnold 1967b, 7–8). Acid dissolution of the carbonates from five samples of good-quality *nooy* revealed that these samples had a mean of 27.58 percent clay in them (table 4.6).

Besides color, potters use hardness to identify another subcategory of *nooy* called *tok' nooy*, which contains pieces of a very hard rock called *tok' tunich*. Potters translate *tok' tunich* as "flint" (*pedernal*; Arnold 1967a, 1967b, 30) because striking it with a pick produces sparks. An analysis of it by X-ray diffraction, however, revealed that it was not quartz but a very hard dolomite. Pulverizing it and dissolving a portion of it with acetic acid revealed that 66.9% of it dissolved, and 33.1% of it did not ($N = 3$). Reanalyzing the same sample of *tok' tunich* in 2015 revealed that it had a hardness (Mohs' scale) of 6.0, which is not as hard as quartz or flint (7.0). Using a polarized light microscope and attenuated total reflection Fourier transform for infrared spectroscopy (ATR-FTIR) also revealed that the sample contained no quartz at all, but only carbonates.[14]

Potters believe that temper prepared with *tok' nooy* is more fire resistant and that pottery made with it will not become overfired (*sakalel*; see chapter 7) as quickly as

TABLE 4.6. Percent of clay in *nooy*, one of the principal components of pottery temper. The samples analyzed were collected in 1965 and 1966 (see Arnold 1971, 33–34), and acetic acid was used to dissolve the carbonate fraction. Percentages are the weight of the dried insoluble residue minus the beaker weight divided by the total of the weight of the dried untreated sample × 100. The mean percentage of the clay fraction in these samples is 27.58 percent.

Sample number	Insoluble in acetic acid(%)	Subcategory	Source of sample
4	10.15	*kut*	Yo' Sah Kab (*ejido* portion): sifted
2	28.85	*tok'*	Yo' Sah Kab (*ejido* portion): sifted
1	37.38	*tok'*	Yo' Sah Kab (*ejido* portion): unsifted
5b	16.94	*chak*	Yo' Sah Kab (*ejido* portion): can be used to mix with *ta'achach* to add to clay to make small pottery
3	36.31	*chak*	Yo' Sah Kab (*ejido* portion)
2b	35.85	*sak*	Yo' Sah Kab (*ejido* portion): can be used to mix with *ta'achach* to add to clay to make large pottery

pottery made with ordinary *nooy* and *ta'achach*. Consequently, vessels made with *tok' nooy* are placed in the hottest portion of the kiln (the *tan k'aak'*, see figure 7.1). Pottery made with ordinary *nooy*, on the other hand, is placed in the top or sides of the kiln, where there is less heat. If, however, a potter only makes one trip to the mines to obtain *tok' nooy* for each pile of tailings (*ta'achach*) prepared, then he doesn't need to place the pottery made with it in the hottest part of the kiln. If, on the other hand, the potter makes two or three trips to the mines to obtain *tok' nooy* for each pile of *ta'achach* prepared, then the pottery made with it will require more heat during firing.

A fourth subcategory of *nooy* is *hi' nooy*. This category has a distinctive crystalline appearance (table 4.4) that is somewhat similar to *hi'* (chapter 3), the temper used for making cooking pottery. Both materials have an obvious crystalline appearance but are distinguished by two important criteria. *Hi' nooy* comes from a man-made *sah kab* mine at Yo' Sah Kab and contains *sak lu'um*. *Hi'*, on the other hand, comes from a natural cave (*aktun*, see below) in the hill ridge (*puuk*) and does not contain *sak lu'um*.

Although *hi' nooy* and *tok' nooy* are potential ingredients of temper, potters do not choose to use them very often, because they are difficult to mine. Both *hi' nooy* and *tok' nooy* make the temper heavier than other types of *nooy*, and the pottery made with them does not sag.

The physical property of heaviness was demonstrated to me in 2008, when Bruce Bohor and I were collecting samples of palygorskite at the temper mines (Arnold and Bohor 2008; Arnold et al. 2012). I was in a mine digging samples of *sak lu'um* from the mine face when my hammer struck a rock and produced sparks. My informant called this rock *tok' tunich*. Scooping up some of the mined talus from the mine floor beneath the area in which I was digging, he put it in my hand, saying, "This is *tok' nooy* and it's heavy. Can you feel it?" I could. A handful of *tok' nooy* was indeed heavier than the handful of regular *nooy* that he placed in my other hand.

Although all of these categories of *nooy* are distinct from one another, their attributes are not mutually exclusive (table 4.4). Hardness and crystalline appearance, or lack thereof, are more important in distinguishing different types of *nooy* than is color. *Hi' nooy*, for example, can be white (*sak*) and can be described as *sak hi' nooy*, but generally, *hi' nooy* is not identified by color. White (*sak*) or red (*chak*) *nooy* is a noncrystalline (non-*hi'*), nonhard (non-*tok'*) material. Hard *nooy* is *tok' nooy*, and crystalline *nooy* is *hi' nooy*, regardless of color.

POOR-QUALITY *NOOY*

Poor-quality *nooy* that does not contain *sak lu'um* is collectively called *kut nooy*. It is thus an inferior and undesirable material, and generally potters reject it for preparing temper. This designation also includes all classes of *sah kab* for building purposes that may also occur at the temper mines.

Besides not containing *sak lu'um*, *kut nooy* has other defining characteristics. It may be several colors but is not usually identified by color. It is not heavy and can be mined easily, but potters avoid mining and using it because they believe it causes pottery to sag, crack, and break. X-ray diffraction analysis of *kut nooy* ($N = 4$) revealed that it contained calcite and dolomite,[15] the clay mineral smectite, and sometimes palygorskite (Arnold 1967a; 1967b, 8, 25). The amount of clay minerals in the one sample analyzed was only 10.15% (table 4.6).

Potters say that *kut nooy* does not have the strength to support a tall vessel body during forming. Temper prepared with *kut nooy* thus is not used for large vessels such as large water-carrying jars (*p'uul*, or *cántaros*), water storage jars (*tinajas*), or large plant pots (*rectos* and *cubanos*) because even if they do not sag, crack, or break, they may still leak without the presence of "white earth." Even though *kut nooy* has rather drastic effects on these larger vessels, it can be used as a temper for small items of pottery such as figurines and small food bowls (*cajetes*) that do not have high vessel walls, but potters must add other *nooy*, or *ta'achach* that contains *sak lu'um*, so that the amount of "white earth" in temper exceeds the amount of *kut nooy*.

One variety of *kut nooy* is very fine grained, is powdery, and has a texture similar to ashes (*ta'an*). This material (called *ta'anooy*) is easy to mine and can also be described by color such as "red" (*chak ta'anooy*). It does not make the temper heavy, and it is not used for preparing temper, because potters say that it does not contain *sak lu'um*. This assessment is verified by the X-ray diffraction analysis of a sample of *ta'anooy* that contained calcite, dolomite, and the clay mineral smectite, but no palygorskite (Arnold 1967b, 25).

In mineralogical terms, all *nooy* contains calcite and/or dolomite (Arnold 1967a, 1967b). Good-quality *nooy* with *sak lu'um* also contains palygorskite and no smectite, whereas *kut nooy* contains smectite, though it may or may not contain palygorskite. Potters' distinctions between good-quality *nooy* and *kut nooy* highlight the different physical characteristics between smectite and palygorskite, and these practical distinctions thus have a mineralogical basis. Combining the ethnographic and mineralogical perspectives, potters appear to reject materials that contain smectite for preparing temper, whereas they prefer using materials that contain palygorskite though some smectite, in fact, may also be present (see Arnold 1967a; 1967b, 25–26).

PREPARING TEMPER

Potters prepare temper by mixing *nooy* from the temper mines with the discarded screenings (*ta'achach*) from previous preparations (figure 4.8; see Arnold 2008, 193–98, 204–15). Accomplishing this process involves selecting a preparation area with screenings that have mines nearby. The selection process involves first engaging the physical properties of the tailings by trying to crush the screenings in their hands. If they can, then they are good for making temper. If potters cannot crush them, they move to another area to test the *ta'achach* again.

This engagement with the screenings of previous temper preparations by means of the potter's tactile feedback appears to have a foundation in their mineralogy. Those that contain the clay mineral palygorskite (*sak lu'um*) break up and fall apart with rainfall. Consequently, they become more friable as time passes and can be easily crushed by hand. Those screenings with just calcite and dolomite, on the other hand, cannot be crushed as easily with the hands.

After the potter has selected the appropriate preparation area, he digs up some of the tailings and gathers them in a pile. Then, he goes to one of the mines nearby to dig for *nooy* (figure 4.9) and brings it to the preparation area and dumps it on the pile of tailings.

Using a log (called *shpuchu che'* ["pole for beating"]) made from a tree called *chak te'* (*Caesalpinia platyloba* Wats, according to Steggerda 1943b, 199, 218), the potter beats the pile of tailings and *nooy* (see Arnold 2008, 204–12). When he is finished, he screens the mixture and fills a sack with the sifted temper (figure 4.10). After a sack is filled, it is closed and placed by the side of the road for transport to Ticul.

SAH KAB TEMPER VARIABILITY

Temper preparation varies among potters and miners (Arnold 2008, 206–12). Some use more tailings (*ta'achach*) and others use more *nooy*. Although they say that the

FIGURE 4.8. A miner digging and accumulating tailings (*ta'achach*) at Yo' Sah Kab in 1966. As is evident here, after weathering, these tailings are mined for mixing with *nooy* from the mines and then crushed. The hole in the tailings pile at the right was also mined for this preparation event. The pole used for crushing the mixture of tailings and *nooy* lies at the center left of the image (see also Arnold 2008, 205, 207).

mix between tailings and *nooy* is equal, they do not appear to measure the proportions precisely. Rather, it appears to be quite variable depending upon the potters' engagement with the temper constituents, the evaluation of them based on visual and tactile feedback, and the anticipated consequences of their choices.

By using tailings exclusively, the miner avoids any possibility of inadvertently using the *kut nooy* that causes his pottery to crack and break (see also Arnold 1971, 33–34). Because the plastic limit of smectite (tables 4.7 and 4.8) is lower than that of the palygorskite, it degrades and washes away at a rate faster than the palygorskite, and the palygorskite endures longer. On the other hand, using more *nooy* than tailings, one potter said, can cause the pottery to break, dry more slowly, and requires more "fire" (*fuego*) and "strength" (*fuerza*) of the flame during firing.

Sometimes miners choose to add dirt (*tierra*) to the temper, but this choice creates another problem of quality. Potters say that such temper does not moisten well. It requires a lot of water, and large vessels made with it crack and break when they are placed in the sun. Unlike using *kut nooy*, however, using temper prepared with dirt does not create as many drying and cracking problems with small vessels as it does with larger ones.

FIGURE 4.9. Inside of one of the temper mines at Yo' Sah Kab in 2008 showing the tunneling into deposit that contains a mixture of calcite, dolomite, palygorskite, and occasionally small amounts of smectite. These mines are the source of one of the components of temper called *nooy*. Mined-out rooms and tunnels of the mine can be quite large, extending as many as ten meters into the deposit. A solid palygorskite layer underlays the floor of this mine. I encountered *tok' nooy* at the rear face of this mine. (See also Arnold 2008, 206.)

Another variation consists of mixing *sah kab* for construction purposes with tailings (*ta'achach*) or *nooy* from the temper mines. In 1966 three potters reportedly used the naturally occurring marl (*sah kab* for building purposes) to prepare temper. One temper miner was said to have brought tailings from Yo' Sah Kab, mixed them with *sah kab* for construction purposes, and sold it to potters. In another case a potter reportedly mixed *sah kab* for construction purposes with the screenings from the temper (*ta'achach*) that had been used to dust molds before clay was pressed into them.

These reports of using *sah kab* for construction purposes were the only ones that I have heard during the span of my forty-four years of research in Ticul. When one of these potters was confronted with the rumor that he had used *sah kab* for construction purposes in his temper, he denied it. In practice, however, I have never actually observed *sah kab* for construction purposes *ever* being used in any way for pottery temper.

FIGURE 4.10. Screening the mixture of *nooy* from the temper mines and the weathered tailings (*ta'achach*) from previous preparations (1966). The pick behind the miner is used to loosen the tailings (*ta'achach*) in the preparation area, dig the *nooy* from the mines, and mix the two components together. He uses the long pole to pound the mixture and break it up to prepare for sifting it (Arnold 2008, 205).

QUALITY TESTS FOR *SAH KAB* TEMPER

In order to ensure that temper contains *sak lu'um*, the potter has devised a series of tests to identify materials which contain *sak lu'um* in order to avoid damage to his vessels. Initially, the potter selects the appropriate materials at the temper mines by the most obvious physical properties of *sak lu'um*. Subsequently, he uses other tests to evaluate its quality. These tests are based upon the visual and tactile feedback the potter receives from his engagement with wetting the temper. They became very important when potters no longer mined their own temper but purchased it from specialists and needed to assess its integrity for making pottery.

The first test consists of moistening a small portion of temper with water (figure 4.11). If it becomes very sticky (*kotsk'alak*) when a limited amount of water is added to it, then a sufficient amount of *sak lu'um* is present.[16] If, on the other hand, the temper does not become sticky but instead becomes very fluid and watery and does not feel similar to clay, then little or no *sak lu'um* is present, and the temper is not good for making large vessels. It can, however, still be used for figurines and food bowls (*cajetes*).

TABLE 4.7. The plastic and liquid limits of kaolinite, smectite, and palygorskite arranged in the order of increasing plastic limits (rearranged and condensed from White 1949, 510). The terminology in the original source is used with the new classification in parentheses.

Clay mineral	Source	Particle size (microns)	Plastic limit (%)	Liquid limit (%)	Plastic index
Kaolinite	Twiggs Co., GA	whole	29.9	35.0	5.1
Kaolinite	Union Co. IL	whole	36.3	58.4	22.1
Kaolinite	Union Co., IL	< 1.0	37.1	64.2	27.1
Kaolinite	Union Co. IL	0.5	39.3	71.6	32.3
Montmorillonite (Smectite)	Pontotoc, MS	whole	81.4	117.5	36.1
Montmorillonite[a] (Smectite)	Belle Fourche, SD	whole	97.0	625–700	528–603
Montmorillonite (Smectite)	Pontotoc, MS	< 1.0	109.5	177.6	66.1
Attapulgite (Palygorskite)	Quincy, FL	whole	116.6	177.8	61.2

a Although sodium montmorillonite has a higher plastic and liquid limit than other montmorillonites (also called smectite), it is so gelatinous that it could not be used for making pottery.

TABLE 4.8. The plastic and liquid limits of smectite, kaolinite, and palygorskite arranged in order of increasing plastic limits (abstracted and translated from Liberto de Pablo 1964). The terminology in the original source is used with the new classification in parentheses.

Clay mineral	Plastic limit (%)	Liquid limit (%)
Kaolinite	26–38	34–73
Montmorillonite (Smectite)	51–97	125–700[a]
Attapulgite (Palygorskite)	100–124	161–232

a This higher liquid limit is for sodium montmorillonite, and is different than that for other smectites (table 4.7). This very high range means that adding water up to this range would result in a material that is so gelatinous that it could not be used for making pottery. It is not the kind of smectite found around Ticul.

A second test of temper quality involves the amount of water that the temper absorbs when it is mixed with the clay. In this process, clay is first soaked in water and then mixed with the dry temper. Temper that contains abundant *sak lu'um* requires much water during paste preparation; potters say that it "sucks" a lot of water and absorbs 50 percent more water than inferior temper. If the temper remains dry during this process, then the temper is good quality and more water must be added. If, on the other hand, the temper becomes moist and sticky quickly during this process, then the temper is inferior. It likely contains *kut nooy* and requires only

FIGURE 4.11. Testing a small amount of temper to determine its quality before it is mixed with the clay (1966). By using a small amount of temper and adding water, the potter engages the different plastic limits of the clay minerals of smectite and palygorskite by using the tactile feedback of the plasticity of resulting mixture. Although palygorskite is a clay mineral, it acts as a nonplastic in the paste. Inferior temper, however, contains enough smectite to adversely affect the paste by increasing its plasticity.

a little water because the paste can easily become liquid. In that case water must be added a little at a time or the paste will become useless; the potter must also add *sak lu'um* to the mixture.

The tactile and visual feedback that the potter receives from his engagement with the quality control tests reveals that his indigenous knowledge reflects a practical understanding of the different liquid and plastic limits of smectite, kaolinite, and palygorskite (tables 4.7 and 4.8). The plastic limit is the lowest percentage of water that the dry clay will absorb before it becomes plastic and allows it to be rolled into a small coil without breaking into pieces (White 1949, 508–9). The liquid limit, on the other hand, is the lowest percentage of water that the dry clay will absorb before it begins to flow when it is jarred slightly (White 1949, 508). The more water that is necessary for a particular clay to become plastic, or to become liquid, the greater the plastic or liquid limit of that clay.

The different plastic and liquid limits for clays thus have two important practical implications. First, the clay mineral palygorskite, which Ticul potters identify as *sak lu'um*, has a higher plastic and liquid limit than either smectite or the random mixed-layering of smectite and kaolinite (tables 4.7 and 4.8). It thus does not become plastic in the preparation of the paste, but takes up water from it. This characteristic is responsible for the potters' perception that *sak lu'um* in the temper "sucks" a lot of water in paste preparation but does not become plastic. The palygorskite thus acts as a nonplastic in the prepared paste and reduces its plasticity.

The second practical implication, on the other hand, is that temper containing smectite (i.e., inferior temper) becomes plastic (and hence sticky) when it is mixed with the body clay during the paste preparation. By the time good-quality temper (i.e., temper containing palygorskite, but without smectite) becomes plastic with added water, the body clay (the random mixed layered kaolinite-smectite) would have exceeded its liquid limit and become fluid and unworkable (tables 4.7 and 4.8). The use of smectite-containing temper thus increases the plasticity of the paste rather than reduces it, and when the potter tests his temper by adding water to it, temper that contains smectite becomes fluid and watery with less added water than temper that contains palygorskite and no smectite. The potter thus has developed two practical tests for assessing temper quality based on physical properties that clay mineralogists know as the plastic and liquids of palygorskite. These properties distinguish palygorskite from the other clay minerals in Ticul.

The potter obviously does not see these tests as the difference in the properties of two clay minerals and their plastic and liquid limits, but rather as indicators of the presence or absence of *sak lu'um*. In reality, the physical characteristic that potters see as the absence of *sak lu'um* actually is the presence of smectite, even though some palygorskite (*sak lu'um*) may be present as well (see Arnold 1967a; 1967b, 26; 1971). Even a small amount of smectite in the temper causes it to behave differently than that which contains only palygorskite. As a result, the potter believes that his temper is inferior and says that it does not contain *sak lu'um* (or enough of it), even though, in fact, the temper usually does contain it. The potter's test, then, only engages the obvious and useful physical properties of his materials and is not based on knowledge of their mineralogy.

The presence of the smectite in the inferior temper also accounts for the potter's belief that inferior temper causes his vessels to sag and crack. Sagging is caused by a highly plastic paste, and plasticity is usually reduced by adding more temper. When inferior temper is added to the clay, it actually increases the amount of smectite in the paste. Since smectite absorbs larger amounts of water between the clay layers, the clay expands, becomes more plastic, and causes the clay body to sag after forming (Rice 1987, 49; Shepard 1965, 377).

Even if the pottery made with inferior temper does not sag, it may still crack and break during drying and firing. When the interlayer water in the smectite is lost during these processes, the clay body contracts greatly and creates stresses in the vessels, causing them to crack. Adding more nonplastics to the clay will, of course, alleviate this problem because it reduces plasticity, but if one uses a temper that contains smectite, adding more of it perpetuates and confounds the problem because it makes the paste more plastic.

If a potter finds that he is using inferior temper, then she can restore the quality of the temper (i.e., its strength—*muuk'*), by either adding good-quality temper that contains *sak lu'um*, tailings (*ta'achach* that also contains *sak lu'um*), or tiny pieces of pure *sak lu'um*. With all three of these choices, the potter increases the amount of the palygorskite in the paste. Because of its higher plastic limit than either the mixed-layered smectite/kaolinite in the clay or the smectite itself, the palygorskite absorbs some of the extra water in the paste without becoming plastic because of its higher plastic limit and functions as a nonplastic along with the calcite and dolomite. Increased nonplastics in the paste reduces the proportion of plastic material, reduces plasticity, and prevents the sagging of the newly made vessels caused by the smectite.

Furthermore, by absorbing more of the free water in the paste without becoming plastic, less is available to the highly plastic smectite clay, and it would expand and contract less. Stresses in the newly formed vessels would be fewer, and they would not crack as much.

These observations reveal the way in which potters engage the raw materials to prepare temper for making pottery. Learning how to recognize and respond to the feedback coming from that engagement is a fundamental part of their indigenous knowledge about temper. Again, they do not act on a mental template that is simply materialized in the choices of a raw material. Rather, potters engage the raw materials using tactile and visual feedback to make decisions of quality. They use their indigenous knowledge to engage and evaluate the raw materials before they are mixed and made into pottery.

An Ancient Distinction

The distinction between *sah kab* for construction purposes and *sah kab* temper appeared to be recognized as early as the Terminal Classic Period (AD 800–1100). In 1967, one small sample of eroding mortar was collected from a structure in the archaeological site at the temper mines (Arnold 2005a). Analyses of this sample by X-ray diffraction revealed that it contained calcite, dolomite, and a small amount of smectite that was qualitatively identical to the modern *sah kab* for construction purposes. The existence of a plaster with no palygorskite even in a location directly over the palygorskite deposit suggests that during the Terminal Classic Period, the site's inhabitants distinguished two similar materials that today are known as *sah kab*. Given the availability of both materials under and near the site, they could be easily confused by nonpotters. Apparently the Maya living at this site during the Terminal Classic had already found that smectite-containing *sah kab* had certain advantages for mortars and plasters such as its bonding ability and its case-hardening structure (B. F. Bohor, personal communication) and its contrast with the palygorskite-containing *sah kab* from underneath the site that was used for pottery temper.

HI'

A fourth major category of raw materials is called *hi'* and is used as a temper for cooking pottery. *Hi'* is a kind of rock (*hi' tunich*) that potters define as a crystalline, sugary-like material that comes from a natural cave (*aktun*) in the nearby hills (usually Aktun Hi' or Aktun Lara). Ticul potters distinguish between *hi'* and *sah kab* temper on the basis of their different sources, their different uses, the obvious crystallinity of the *hi'*, and the belief that *sah kab* temper must contain white earth (*sak lu'um*). *Hi'* does not contain it and is more difficult to mine than the materials needed to produce *sah kab* temper. X-ray diffraction analyses of two samples of *hi'* revealed that it consisted of crystal fragments of calcite (Arnold 1971, 33–34).

Although potters distinguish three types of *hi'* on the basis of color—yellow (*k'an*), white (*sak*), and red (*chak*), one potter said that white (*sak*) *hi'* was superior to the other two colors for pottery temper. Pottery made with white *hi'* is said to be harder and more heat resistant. Pots made with it supposedly do not crack or break easily and are more durable.

The choice of one color of *hi'* over another for tempering cooking pottery does not appear to have a technological foundation and reflects the notion of technological style. As with many such choices, it is unclear what other factors besides color may influence this option. Human choices are seldom, if ever, made in isolation using a single criterion.

Mining the *hi'* involves removing chunks of it from walls of the caves. Potters then crush them in their house lot using a circular boulder on a rock outcrop (figure 4.12). This feature may also be used for grinding *sak lu'um*, mined temper, and temper screenings (*ta'achach*) from sifting temper to produce a finer paste.

The Technological Advantages of *Hi'* Temper

Does the choice between *hi'* temper for cooking pottery and *sah kab* for noncooking pottery have a practical technological basis? Or, is the choice simply a matter of technological style or choice? Both types of pottery contain calcite (calcium carbonate), which, if fired above 900 C°, drives off the carbon dioxide and forms calcium oxide in a process called calcination. After firing, the calcium oxide rehydrates in the presence of water to form calcium hydroxide. This molecule occupies more space in the paste than the original calcite and puts stresses on the vessel wall, eventually creating spalls and cracks (Rice 1987, 98; 2015, 81, 109, 377; Shepard 1965, 22, 30). Consequently, both types of temper would presumably create the same problem, and thus macrocrystalline calcite would not appear to have a more advantageous use for tempering cooking pottery. Consequently, the crystalline calcite temper for cooking pottery and the calcareous temper for noncooking pottery would seem to be a choice without technological foundation. Anna Shepard (1952, 265) said that thermal tests of different kinds of temper did not support the potters' belief that *hi'*-tempered pottery was superior for cooking pottery. If this interpretation were really true, then this choice between the two types of temper would indeed be a case of technological choice based upon style rather than functional considerations.

Nevertheless, Ticul potters have persisted in their use of *hi'* temper for cooking pottery as they have done since the Terminal Classic Period until metal pots replaced clay cooking pots, and the production of cooking pottery was abandoned. Why did this calcite tempering persist for so many centuries, particularly when calcination would be a persistent problem for the durability of cooking pottery during heating? Potters' knowledge and use of raw materials are often (but not always) practical and reflect a basic understanding of, and engagement with, the properties of the materials involved. Since Shepard wrote her report suggesting that the potters' choice of the temper for cooking pottery had no technological basis, more information has accumulated about the importance of calcite as a pottery temper. In contrast to the temper used for noncooking pottery (calcite, dolomite and palygorskite), using pure calcite as a temper for cooking pottery has a significant advantage for cooking. Compared to other minerals, calcite expands at a rate closest to that of a low-fired clay matrix (see Rye 1976, 117). When the clay and temper expand at different rates with firing, the vessel may crack and break. When the clay

FIGURE 4.12. A grinding stone for crushing *hi'* temper in 1966. The potter (Ramón Aguilar) used a large spherical rock on a rock outcrop to crush *hi'* and the screenings produced from sifting *sah kab* temper to create a more fine-grained paste.

fabric and tempering materials expand at the same rate during firing, however, the fabric resists thermal fracturing (see Rye 1976, 117).

The similarity of the expansion rates of calcite and the clay body, however, does not address the problem of calcination in the temper. O. S. Rye (1976, 121–31) found that adding salt (sodium chloride) water to calcite-tempered paste generally mitigates the decomposition of calcite by raising the temperature at which calcite decomposes (see also Arnold 1985, 26–28). Salt can either occur naturally in the paste, as it does in the Yo' K'at clay, or it can be added by the potter as it is in New Guinea (Rye 1976), in North Africa (Hudson 1997, 136), among Arab potters (Rye 1976, 125), and in some areas of Pakistan (Rye and Evans 1976, 39).

Rye (1976, 122, 131) also argued that the presence of sodium chloride in the Yo' K'at clay produces the same effect and explains that the sodium from the salt acts as a flux and lowers the vitrification temperature of the clay within the range of traditional firing methods. Vitrification produces two important effects: (1) it produces a stronger fabric that is able to resist the hydration of calcium oxide after firing, and (2) it seals some of the pores, restricting the access of water to the calcium oxide. Since the salts in the paste move to the surface and are deposited there when the water evaporates, these effects would be greatest on the vessel surface—that part with the highest temperature during firing and cooking.

The amount of salt necessary to achieve this affect is minimal. Only 1 to 5 percent of the volume/weight of the total paste was sufficient to raise the temperature of calcination and avoid spalling (Rye 1976, 133). Since the Yo' K'at clay already contained a small amount of sodium chloride (Arnold 1971, 29–30), it may likewise inhibit calcination enough to make calcite temper useful for cooking and mitigate its adverse effects (see Arnold 1971, 30; 1985, 24–28).

Other evidence indicates the superiority of calcite tempered pottery for cooking. M. S. Tite and Y. Maniatis (Tite and Maniatis 1975) showed that clays from England with calcite, either naturally present or added to them, reduced the temperature which vitrification first occurred from 960° C to 840° C. This range is well within the range of firing in many pre-Industrial potters such as those in Ticul. Since vitrification stabilizes the structure of the clay product, it is likely that this process would protect the structure of the calcite-tempered pottery from calcination. This hypothesis, however, has yet to be tested experimentally with calcite-tempered clay. Unfortunately, the original Yo' K'at clay is no longer available, but this research does suggest that a combination of sodium chloride and calcite in the Ticul clay provides beneficial effects for cooking that are not just a difference in technological style.

Although temperature data are not available for firing either the cooking or the noncooking pottery, it appears that firing temperature of cooking pottery is low enough to reduce the risk of calcination in the paste. Two factors contribute to this inference. First, because the door of the kiln for firing cooking pottery is much larger than that for the kiln for noncooking pottery, more heat is lost from the kiln from firing cooking pottery than from firing noncooking pottery. Second, firing cooking pottery takes less time than firing noncooking pottery. Noncooking pottery requires as much as six hours of firing, during which the kiln is slowly heated and then fueled at a feverish pace until the pots glow red (see chapter 7). For cooking pottery, however, the kiln is preheated, and then the pots are placed on, and then removed from, the coals in the kiln. Cooking pottery thus appears to be fired at a lower temperature for a shorter duration than noncooking pottery and therefore has lesser risk of calcination than does noncooking pottery.

Ancient Use and Exploitation of *Hi'*

Tempering pottery with *hi'* is an ancient practice that dates at least to the Terminal Classic Period. Three lines of evidence support this inference. First, one of the paste variants of the Puuc Unslipped Ware from the Terminal Classic Period contains inclusions of crystalline calcite (Smith 1971, 2:171). The amount and type of these inclusions do not occur naturally in clays of the area but were probably added by the ancient potter just as they are by the modern potter. Indeed, modern potters describe this ancient pottery as *hi'* tempered because it contains such an obviously crystalline material.

Just as two different pastes were produced in Ticul in the present, so it appears that two analogous types of pastes were made during the Terminal Classic Period. Even at Yo' Sah Kab, where *sah kab* temper was presumably mined during the Terminal Classic Period, *hi'*-tempered pottery lay on the surface of the site. This ware (Puuc Unslipped Ware) was probably used for cooking, and it contrasts with the Medium Puuc Slate Ware, also found at the site, that did not have these inclusions (Arnold 2005a). Macroscopically, the slateware paste had a finer texture and did not contain macrocrystalline inclusions. Instead, it appeared to be similar to the contemporary *sah kab*-tempered pottery that contains calcite, dolomite, and palygorskite (Arnold 2005a).

The second kind of evidence for *hi'* tempering in antiquity comes from the evidence of *hi'* mining in the caves along the hill ridge south and west of Ticul (see chapter 3). First, this mining occurred in the recent past. In the late nineteenth century, Henry Mercer (1896, 66) reported *hi'* mining in Aktun Hi' and Aktun Lara.[17] Aside from these two caves, Mercer found no direct evidence of *hi'* mining in any of the other caves that he visited in Yucatán. In 1929 Hatt also noted evidence of mining activity at Aktun Hi' and said that miners had almost completely denuded the cave by carrying out "most of the cave earth and chipped rock of the sides and ceiling" that he erroneously thought was gypsum (Hatt 1953, 16). Later in the twentieth century, others reported that *hi'* came from Aktun Hi' (Barrera Vásquez 1937, 164; Thompson 1958, 70). I visited Aktun Hi' briefly in 1965 and found evidence of *hi'* mining on the wall near the entrance. Since then, those few potters who occasionally made cooking pottery have said that they obtained their *hi'* from Aktun Hi'.

Further, the mining of *hi'* in these caves dates to the Terminal Classic Period (AD 800–1100). Both Mercer (1896) and Robert Hatt and his colleagues (Hatt 1953) excavated portions of these caves and suggested that *hi'* mining dates at least to a prehistoric level now called the Terminal Classic Period. At Aktun Lara, Hatt and his colleagues opened two trenches. In the first trench potsherds of the Terminal Classic Period occurred throughout the debris down to 50 cm, and in the second trench sherds occurred from 15 to 130 cm, but they were not described nor identified (Hatt 1953, 26–27). In excavations at Aktun Ch'ak Tale'en (Aktun Chekt-a-leh), Mercer (1896, 68) found many crystals together with sherds that appeared to be Puuc Unslipped Ware, in the first sub-surface level.[18] The bones of a historic horse and dog, however, were found in that level and in the level below it. Since these animals were introduced after the Spanish Conquest, the preconquest integrity of these two levels is dubious, in spite of the presence of apparently Puuc Unslipped Ware in them. At Aktun Shmak, however, Mercer (1896, 73, 80) put in two small trenches. In the first trench he found crystal fragments in levels 2 and 3 at depths of twenty-five to forty centimeters below the surface. In all three levels he found potsherds that he described as "decorated with scratches" (Layers 1 and 2) or "decorated with incised lines" (Layer 3). These sherds were probably Puuc Unslipped Ware from the Terminal Classic Period just like the similar collections from Aktun Ch'ak Tale'en, but there was no reason to question the integrity of the prehistoric levels here because there was no evidence of postconquest disturbance.

Aktun Hi' and Aktun Lara are relatively close to Ticul and were accessible to ancient potters who lived there. Distance to these caves fit the model of distance to ceramic resources that resources for most pottery-making communities occur within a distance of four to five kilometers from the potters' household (Arnold 1985, 32–60; 2005b; 2011; Heidke et al. 2007, 145–49, 151). Indeed, the disturbance of the levels and the extent of *hi'* mining both on the surface and below in these caves suggest that the Maya have probably mined *hi'* in some of these caves continuously from the Terminal Classic until well into the ethnographic present.

SPECIALIZED KNOWLEDGE

The Maya ethnotechnology of pottery production in Ticul is local to Ticul and specialized within the population of the potters there. Nonpotters generally do not possess this knowledge. They do not recognize, for example, the distinction between *sah kab* for pottery temper and *sah kab* for construction purposes. Discussions of these distinctions with nonpotters in the 1960s revealed that they did not know that the *sah kab* for temper and that for construction were different entities. A conversation with a well digger at that time revealed that he did not refer to *sah kab* for construction purposes in the same way that a potter did. When he used the term *chen sah kab* ("only" *sah kab*), for example, he was referring to marl (*sah kab*) for construction purposes and to pottery temper (*sah kab*) to the exclusion of other kinds of material. The potter, however, uses that same term to refer exclusively to *sah kab* for construction purposes.

This specialized knowledge was graphically demonstrated to me when I visited the temper mines (Yo' Sah Kab) in July 1967. At the time, the road to Chapab that passed the mines was unimproved with rock outcrops and potholes, and workers were making repairs on it. They had backed up a dump truck to one of the preparation areas and were shoveling the discarded screenings (*ta'achach*) into a truck in order to use them to surface the nearby road (figure 4.13).

114 THE POTTERS' ENGAGEMENT WITH RAW MATERIALS

FIGURE 4.13. Highway workers shoveling the tailings (*ta'achach*) from preparing pottery temper into a truck to use for surfacing the road between Ticul and Chapab in 1967. They mistakenly thought that the tailings were *sah kab* for construction purposes, and their actions incited protests and anger from the potters. Although not immediately evident, careful examination of this image reveals that the material is being loaded from the ground surface, not from a marl quarry, as it would be if the marl (*sah kab*) had been mined for construction purposes.

When I returned on the following day, a large pile of brush obstructed the entrance road to the mines and preparation areas. One member of the road crew was arranging rocks on the road in preparation for receiving a final layer of *sah kab* (see discussion of *kut sah kab* in this chapter), but none of the other workers were present.

What had happened? The road crew's use of the screenings from the temper mines had incensed the potters. On the previous evening, several potters had alerted others that the highway crew was exploiting their temper resources, and they organized a mass protest. Since the temper mines were on communal (*ejido*) land, a group of potters that included a representative of each family approached the president of the ejido and asked him to stop the road crew from removing the screenings (*ta'achach*) from the location. Those screenings would be used again in temper preparation.

The next day the potters appealed to the president of the nearby village of Chapab and then went to the temper mines themselves to stop the road crew from removing material from the mining area, erecting the roadblock of brush at its entrance. By the time that I arrived later in the day, the roadwork had stopped.

Had the road workers known about the basics of the potters' temper categories and their method of preparation, they could have avoided the conflict with the potters. The road crew knew that *sah kab* was used for a surfacing material, and they apparently thought that there was no difference between the *sah kab* used by potters at the temper mines and the marl for construction purposes mined elsewhere.

Potters understood that the variety of *sah kab* from the temper mines, however, occurred nowhere else because *sak lu'um* (palygorskite), the critical component of the temper, was only found there. The road crew's removal of the discarded screenings (the *ta'achach*) of the preparation process effectively destroyed one of the potters' crucial resources for future temper preparation by using them to surface the road. Unlike the marl used for construction purposes, the screenings from the temper preparation would be used again and were too unique to be used in road surfacing, whereas *sah kab* for construction purposes was more common and more widespread. The conflict between the potters and the road crew thus dramatically demonstrated the existence of potters' specialized knowledge that separates naturally occurring marl for building purposes (called *sah kab*) from the cultural mixture of materials that potters use for pottery temper (also called *sah kab*). In this light, it is easy to understand the potters' protest.

A COMMUNITY OF PRACTICE

Even though a detailed comparison of the Ticul raw material categories in this chapter with pottery-making communities elsewhere in Yucatán is beyond the scope of this chapter, the source names and the use and meaning of these raw materials are unique compared to those of other communities of potters in Yucatán (D. Arnold 1971, 2000; Thompson 1958, 65–71). This difference suggests that raw material procurement and paste composition were localized in antiquity when communities were even more isolated from one another than they were in the 1960s. Nevertheless, at least some archaeologists assume that pottery represents the product of a population that extends beyond the local community with multiple communities of potters having the same knowledge and producing the same pottery. This assumption is reified somewhat in the use of ceramic typology as it is traditionally practiced in the Maya area (Aimers 2012; Sabloff and Smith 1969; Smith 1971). Further, in Shepard's critique of my identification of palygorskite as part of the indigenous knowledge of the Ticul potter, she thought that I believed that all Maya potters in Yucatán possessed knowledge of palygorskite (Arnold 1991, 328–30). They do not. The mineral palygorskite is indeed widespread, but the Maya knowledge of *sak*

TABLE 4.9. Summary of the categories of raw materials used for making pottery in the 1960s and their physical foundations. The "potter's distinctions of category" are those that the potter makes exclusive of differences of use and source (modified and updated from Dean E. Arnold, 1971, "Ethnomineralogy of Ticul, Yucatan Potters: Etics and Emics." *American Antiquity* Vol. 36, p. 38).

Category Pottery	Category Nonpottery	Use	Potter's distinctions of category	Minerals common to each category
hi'		Temper for cooking pottery	Crystallinity	Macrocrystalline calcite
sah kab		Temper for noncooking pottery	Contains *sak lu'um*	Calcite, dolomite, palygorskite
	sah kab	Mortars, plasters, surfacing materials	Does not contain *sak lu'um*	Calcite and/or dolomite and smectite
k'at		Pottery clay, light-colored slip	Salty taste, does not open up readily when sun dried	Kaolinite and random mixed layering of kaolinite and smectite
	k'at	If used for making pottery, used only for small items; otherwise not used	No salty taste, opens up when sun dried	Smectite
sak lu'um		Most important constituent of *sah kab* temper	White, hard, light in weight, does not become plastic or fluid readily	Palygorskite
k'an kab		Red slip for noncooking pottery	Red powder	Hematite

lu'um (palygorskite) does not exist beyond Ticul and neighboring Sacalum.[19] Even a community of potters that uses materials containing palygorskite (such as those in Mama) do not recognize its properties, and they do not know the category *sak lu'um*.

This realization makes generalizations about Maya ceramic technology in antiquity difficult. Rather, all indigenous knowledge is local, and the pottery that results from it is the result of the potters' engagement within a social, geological, and mineralogical context that is local. This consequence is consonant with practice theory (Bourdieu 1978, 1980), which argues that understanding of human behavior must take into account the way it is practiced. Indigenous knowledge involved in selecting raw materials (table 4.9) in Ticul, however, is not just the way that knowledge is practiced but also the way that those raw materials are perceived, categorized, classified, and engaged using characteristics important to the potters. A theory of practice must involve a cognitive dimension. The communities of potters in Yucatán (like Ticul) are thus distinct communities of practice. This conclusion is not only true of Yucatán but also was evident from my research in communities in the Valley of Guatemala and in the Valley of Ayacucho Peru (Arnold 1972a, 1978a, 1978b, 1993).

NOTES

1. All of the Maya languages share these same color categories (Berlin and Kay 1969, 31), but more recently, the blue/green category in Yucatec Maya has separated into green (*ya'ash*) and blue (*ch'ooh*; see Bricker et al. 1998, 86), the word for the indigo plant (*Indigofera suffruticosa*; Barrera Vásquez et al. 1980, 139). This change fulfills Berlin's (1970, 12–13) prediction about the evolution of color terminology for all languages that the first addition of a basic color term in languages with only five basic color terms (white, black, red, yellow, and blue/green) consists of the bifurcation of colors in the blue/green category.

2. I visited Hacienda Yo' K'at again in 2014, when I was invited to attend the inauguration celebration of its conversion to a boutique hotel (Hacienda YoKat 2014) and to help cut the ribbon of a small Museum of Clay there (Museo Casa de Barro 2015). The owners dedicated two panels to my research on the clay mine on the hacienda and my discovery (with Bohor) that the ancient Maya used the clay from a mine three meters below ground to make pottery during the Terminal Classic Period (AD 800–1000). Sadly, the previous owner (the Consul of the Principality of Monaco in Cuba) had backfilled all of the mines formerly used for clay extraction.

3. When B. F. Bohor of the Illinois Geological Survey originally analyzed the clay using X-ray diffraction (Arnold 1967a; 1967b; 1971, 29), he concluded that it was partially dehydrated halloysite. Subsequently, Anna O. Shepard and her colleagues at the US Geological Survey also analyzed the Yo' K'at clay and found that it consisted of random mixed-layering of kaolinite-montmorillonite (93.8 percent), kaolinite (2.9 percent), quartz (2.6 percent), anatase (a titanium oxide, 0.7 percent), and trace amounts of calcite and K-feldspar (Schultz et al. 1971, 140). Bohor's subsequent reinterpretations (Bohor 1975) of the X-ray diffraction data of this clay are consistent with those of Shepard and her colleagues (Schultz et al. 1971) and Wayne Isphording and E. M. Wilson (Isphording and Wilson 1974, 48) that the clay is a mixture of kaolinite and a random mixed layering of kaolinite and montmorillonite (now called smectite). Clay mineralogists R. E. Grim, W. Bradley, and W. A. White also examined the X-ray diffraction patterns of the Yo' K'at clay in the late 1960s and affirmed this interpretation.

From this point on in this work, I will use the term "smectite" to refer to "montmorillonite" for consistency and to reflect the changes in terminology.

4. These conclusions are similar to those of Isphording and Wilson (1974) in their clay survey except that they say that smectite "was found in thin beds in the limestones of

the northern Yucatán plain and in the soil samples from the Classic site [*sic*] of Mayapán (Isphording and Wilson 1974, 486). Bohor and I, however, found that the smectite beds could be quite large and are often found at the base of the marl layer. When this marl layer and the rock above are removed, a clay layer is exposed on the floor of these quarries. In 1994 and again in 1997, visits to clay quarries near Dzitbalché' (see Arnold et al. 2000, 303–4) indicated that a thick clay layer lies at the base of marl (*sah kab*) in these locations (Arnold 2008, 167–70). In these cases clay was easily accessible because rocks and *sah kab* had been stripped off for construction purposes, leaving the layer of clay underneath.

Further, the data presented here contradict the statements of George Brainerd (1958, 66), who said, "No striking differences among types of body clay are recognized by the potters in modern Yucatán, nor would such be expected from the geological uniformity of the area." As is shown here, Ticul potters do indeed recognize differences in body clay, and my research with Bohor indicates even greater variability of clays outside of Ticul. Further, the geology is more complex than one might think, even though the most common minerals are calcite, dolomite, and the clay mineral smectite.

5. There are several complications with the empirical verification for the potters' taste test. Clays may contain other salts besides sodium chloride, and these salts could conceivably affect the taste of the clay, even though one would expect that sodium chloride would be at least partly responsible. Second, the potters' taste threshold may complicate this test. Sodium chloride could be present in all clays, but potters' taste test may have a higher threshold than the chemical test for the chloride ion, and they can detect it only when the amount present exceeded this threshold.

6. These tests were carried out by Stanley Anderson, who was then a graduate student in chemistry at the University of Illinois. He is now research associate/lecturer in the Department of Chemistry at the University of California, Santa Barbara.

7. Because informant's taste tests of dried clays did not yield predictable results in all cases, he said that the test is only valid with fresh clays. (In actual fact, whether or not the clays are newly mined should not affect the presence of the sodium chloride in the clay that is the basis for its salty taste.)

8. This outcome was evaluated by the amount of white precipitate when silver nitrate was added to the soluble portion of the clay. Given the issues of taste versus chemical thresholds of the chloride ion, the results of the chemical test reported here suggest that the taste test was probably a reasonably accurate way to differentiate the two different types of clay even though there was a 7 percent chance that there was no difference between them. See Steven Goodman (2016) for a discussion of *p* values and scientific reasoning.

9. Bohor's analysis of this clay revealed that it consisted of 85 percent smectite and 15 percent dehydrated halloysite. Since the analysis of this clay occurred in 1966 before the different interpretation of the composition of the Yo' K'at clay by Schultz et al. (1971) had been published, and was also found to be kaolinite and a random mixed layering of kaolinite and

smectite (see n. 3 above), it is assumed that the "halloysite" in the sample from this source could be better interpreted as a random mixed layering of kaolinite and smectite.

10. One potter identified *sak lu'um* as *sak lu'um tunich* (white earth rock) when I elicited a list of rocks in 1965 (table 3.4). This attribution and its unique physical properties affirm it as a unique material that has rocklike properties, but it is not really a type of "earth" (*lu'um*) either. That the material is not really rock (*tunich*) or clay (*k'at*) indicates its unique qualities for potters and its unique Maya name, even though it is a clay mineral.

11. Palygorskite (also called attapulgite) and sepiolite formerly were grouped under the family of clay minerals called palygorskite. The Clay Mineral Society Nomenclature Committee, however, recommended that clay mineralogists relegate the name "attapulgite" to synonymy, since the name "palygorskite" has priority for the mineral member itself (Bailey et al. 1971, 131) because it was first found near the Ural Mountains in Russia. The illustration of palygorskite in Prudence Rice (2015, 57) dramatically shows the needle-like structure of palygorskite in contrast to the morphology of other clay minerals.

12. Generally, potters use the expression *chen sah kab* ("only" *sah kab*) to refer to *sah kab* for construction purposes and *sak kabil meyah* (to refer to *sah kab* for making pottery), though the use of these two expressions and their meanings can overlap in certain contexts. The expression *chen sah kab* (only *sah kab*), for example, means *sah kab* apart from anything else such as lime or clay, and in certain specific situations, and can be used to refer to either type of *sah kab*. In the rather specific context of distinguishing clay and temper, for example, *chen sah kab* can refer to "*sah kab* pottery temper" rather than "for *sah kab* for construction purposes":

Q: "Should I bring the clay and the temper (*sah kab*)?"
A: "No, *chen sah kab*." (Only the *sah kab*)

During my survey of potters' households in 1966, for example, I asked for a sample of temper from each household I visited. Sometimes, the response was "*chen sah kab*?" (only *sah kab*?) In other words, "You only wanted a sample of *sah kab* and not clay?" At the temper mines (Yo' Sah Kab), however, *chen sah kab* specifically refers to *sah kab* without any *sak lu'um* in it and consists of one of the varieties of *sah kab* for construction purposes such as *sak*, *chak*, or *kut sah kab*.

13. Sample numbers 1, 2, 3, 4, 6, 7, 8, and 10 were each weighed into ten gram samples. Each was placed in a beaker after the beaker was weighed, and then acetic acid was added, mixed, and heated off and on over a sand bath for several days, and then allowed to settle. After settling, the water and acid remaining were poured off and more acid was added and then heated and occasionally stirred again after several more days. After the water and acid mixture were poured off, the samples were dried and weighed. The weight of each beaker was subtracted from the final weight and then divided by ten grams (the weight of the original sample) to get the decimal fraction of clay (and the few other noncarbonate minerals present). That fraction was multiplied by 100 to obtain the percentage.

14. Flint, of course, is quartz, and I was puzzled why this rock (*tok' tunich*) was so hard but did not appear to contain quartz, particularly since archaeologists in the Maya area refer to hard rocks and the stone tools made from them as "chert" or "flint" (Masson and Peraza Lope 2014, 369–77). To settle this issue, this same sample of *tok' tunich* was analyzed again by Richard E. Bisbing, a volunteer in the Conservation Department of the Field Museum using techniques other than X-ray diffraction. He found that it scratched steel but did not scratch a glass plate, indicating that it had a hardness of 6.0 in the Mohs Scale, a hardness consistent with producing sparks when it was hit with a rock hammer. Chips of the rock also dissolved slowly in acetic acid with effervescence, indicating the presence of carbonates. The residue was collected with a ball of adhesive (a mounting medium) and transferred to a microscope slide, dispersed, and then prepared for examination by a polarized light microscope. This analysis revealed that no quartz was present. In addition, the sample was placed on the diamond sample interface of the Smiths Detection Identifier, pressed until it crushed against the diamond, and then analyzed by ATR-FTIR (attenuated total reflection Fourier transform for infrared spectroscopy). The harder chips contained mainly carbonates (calcite or dolomite), and there was no indication of quartz or other silicates in the infrared absorption spectrum of the harder chips.

Two other samples of material that informants said were "like" (*parecido*) *tok' nooy* were also analyzed by Bisbing and also had no quartz, or the hard dolomite seen in the rock sample of *tok' nooy*. They appeared to be similar to other samples of *nooy*.

15. This number included the sample of *ta'anooy* described below since it is a kind of *kut nooy*.

16. One potter also says that during this test one will see small pieces of white material present and that this material is *sak lu'um*. The darker pieces in the temper are *ta'achach*.

17. In the orthography that Mercer (1896) and Hatt (1953) used, Aktun Hi' is written as Actun Ji, in conformity with a Spanish orthography. Others use a slightly different orthography in Spanish for *hi'* and write it as *jib* (Morales Valderrama 2005, 122, 127). The last phoneme is a glottal stop that is sometimes written and sometimes not, but it freely varies with a voiceless bilabial stop "p," which may be heard as a "b" and thus written that way.

18. H. C. Mercer (1896, 68) said that these potsherds were "decorated with scratches." A small sample of these sherds ($N = 2$) were later identified by Brainerd (Brainerd 1958, 110, 111) as belonging to the Florescent period, which is now called the Terminal Classic Period in Yucatán. They are probably Puuc Unslipped Ware (Smith 1971, 145–48). Although the sample size selected by Brainerd is unfortunately small, the date is consistent with that of most of the other pottery that Mercer excavated from the Yucatán caves.

19. The alteration of the landscape of Yucatán using explosives, metal tools, and heavy machinery (such as bulldozers) has exposed palygorskite in several other locations, but it is unlikely that palygorskite was available to the ancient Maya in these locations. Rather, informants reported that white earth (*sak lu'um*)/palygorskite from Sacalum was widely valued as a cure from various illnesses, and peddlers carried it all over the peninsula to sell to local inhabitants for this purpose.

5

The Potters' Engagement with Paste Preparation

In the previous chapter I described how potters engage their raw materials using their indigenous knowledge and the feedback that they receive through their senses from working with them. This engagement reveals that some choices of raw materials are equally viable for producing pottery; others are not. Some have technical constraints on them; others do not. Any particular raw material selected, however, does not necessarily determine a successful outcome but can have unintended consequences and create challenges that potters must engage to ensure successful paste preparation, as well as forming, drying, and firing their vessels.

Such consequences often appear when the potter mixes the clay and temper to form the paste (*ya'achta'al le k'at*). During this stage, the potter engages the physical properties of his raw materials in new ways. Rather than just selecting one raw material over another, the potter now must deal with new properties resulting from combining temper, clay, and water. Being aware of these new properties and assessing their implications for the rest of the pottery-making process, are based both upon the potter's previous knowledge and experience and upon the sensory feedback received from the changes in the performance characteristics that occur during the paste preparation process. Paste preparation is no less an engagement of the raw materials than the actual fabrication of a pot, but it does not simply reify or materialize potters' preexisting notion of a paste recipe. Rather, it requires the evaluation of tactile and visual feedback of the properties of the paste to solve problems that may hinder the successful completion of a usable vessel.

DOI: 10.5876/9781607326564.c005

Traditionally, potters had two paste choices: one for making cooking pottery (using *hi'* temper) and the other (using *sah kab* temper) for making noncooking pottery. Each of these technologies traditionally resided within particular families (Arnold 2008, 110–12; 2015a, 177–96). Since that time, however, the families that made cooking pottery have either abandoned the craft entirely or switched to making noncooking pottery (Arnold 2015a, 177–96).

PREPARING RAW MATERIALS

Assessing the quality of the clay and temper continues with preparing them to mix the paste. Clay must be dried in the sun so that when it is combined with water and temper, the mixture will be uniform. If the clay opens up and dries too quickly (see previous chapter), the potter has additional challenges.

Evaluating the drying clay affects the potter's decision to proceed to the next step of pottery production. Vessels made from poor-quality clay may crack severely when they are dried. If they survive drying, the consequences may not appear until after the firing process is over. As a result, assessing the quality of the clay during drying is essential to avoid cracking and breaking the vessels during drying and firing.

When asked how long they dry their clay, potters used the criteria of time: good-quality clay requires more time to dry than poor-quality clay. In reality, however, the length of the process is defined by the visual feedback that the potter receives from the properties of the drying clay, such as the size of the chunks that break apart during the drying process.

Assessing drying time also involves feedback from the weather. Rainfall and humidity prevent the clay from drying sufficiently and prolong the process. During the rainy and hurricane season (June through November)—with its high humidity, heavy rainfall, and cloudiness—several days are required to dry the clay whereas during the dry season, only one day is necessary (e.g., see Arnold 2015a, 250–52).

Drying the clay may also serve another purpose that involves potters' engagement with it. Clay quality may be affected by rocks in the raw clay that may cause vessels made with it to crack and break during drying and firing because of the different rates of expansion between the clay and the rocks. To alleviate this problem, the potter may just pick them out of the clay when it is drying and when he wedges the paste. If the rocks are small, the potter may have to modify the amount of temper added to the clay to achieve a paste with the appropriate working properties. Another alternative is to levigate the clay by soaking it with enough water so that the clay particles go into suspension (see Arnold 2008, 222; Curtis 1962, 492; Matson 1973, 124–25; Rice 1987, 118; 2015, 133; Rye 1981, 37; Shepard 1965, 52). The

FIGURE 5.1. The first stage of mixing temper with clay (1966). Temper is mounded up around a depression and the soaked clay is placed inside of it. Mixing clay with temper is not the simple materializing of a paste recipe. Even though potters will, if asked, provide such recipe, they begin with approximate amounts. Rather, the proportions of clay and temper result from the potter's engagement with the performance characteristics of the paste that provide sensory information (feedback) from the process.

rocks sink to the bottom of the vessel and are ultimately discarded. The liquefied clay is poured out and mixed with the temper.

Unlike the clay, temper requires no preparation before mixing with the paste because it is sifted during preparation at the temper mines (Arnold 2008, 193–214). For those potters who make small figurines, however, they sift their temper again to produce a finer paste.

PASTE PREPARATION BEHAVIOR AS MATERIAL ENGAGEMENT

Paste recipes are not precise nor immutable, but rather vary with the sensory feedback that the potter receives from his engagement with the preparation process. If asked for a recipe for mixing temper with clay for noncooking pottery, a potter will say that he mixes one part clay to two parts temper, but in reality the proportions for mixing temper with clay are only approximate because potters do not appear to measure the amounts of these materials precisely (figure 5.1). Rather, as they prepare the

124 THE POTTERS' ENGAGEMENT WITH PASTE PREPARATION

FIGURE 5.2. Potter evaluating the characteristics of the paste in an early stage of its preparation (1966). He tests the mixture of temper with the soaked clay from the feedback of the texture of the mixture. When the feedback indicates that the temper is inferior, for example, the potter modifies the mixture to achieve the desirable paste characteristics. In this case the potter needed to add more water.

paste, the ratio of clay and temper changes depending on the quality of the temper (i.e., depending on the amount of smectite in the temper; see the previous chapter), the quality of the clay, the presence of rocks in the clay, and how much additional temper or *sak lu'um* is necessary to achieve a satisfactory paste (figure 5.2).

If the potter encounters what appears to be the effects of poor temper in the early stages of the paste preparation, he can avoid damage to his vessels later on. If the mixture is very sticky, for example, it does not have strength (*muuk'*), the temper is inferior, and he must mitigate its potential negative effects. If he does not, the vessels he makes will not hold their shape. What the potters call "strength" (*muuk'*) thus allows the paste to cohere and hold its shape with enough plasticity to be formed into the desired vessel, but not so much that the newly formed vessel will collapse or sag (figure 5.3).

If the potter realizes that he has used poor temper in mixing his clay, or if after beginning fabrication he discovers that the quality of the temper is inferior, he grinds and sifts some *sak lu'um* and adds it to the clay (figure 5.4). Again, the potter does not imprint a mental template of a paste recipe onto mixing the clay, but

FIGURE 5.3. Adding more water to the mixture of temper and clay from figure 5.2 to achieve the appropriate texture and moisture content for wedging the clay (1966). The amount added must be evaluated relative to the tactile and visual feedback that the potter receives from the paste preparation process. Knowing how much water to add to the paste during preparation is critical because the clay mineral palygorskite in the temper functions as a nonplastic in the paste and is approximately 22 percent of the paste mixture.

his engagement with the visual and tactile feedback from the paste affects the amount of temper and/or *sak lu'um* that he adds to the clay to solve the challenges he encounters with paste preparation (see chapter 4 in this volume; Arnold 1971).

The flexibility of the paste preparation recipe based upon the potter's engagement with the raw materials is best illustrated by the changes in the clay that potters obtained from new sources that occurred between 1984 and 1997. In the late 1980s, the quality of the clay mined at Yo' K'at was changing, and potters modified the way that they prepared the clay and mixed it with temper. After clay mining at Yo' K'at ended in late 1991, Ticul potters repeatedly faced changing and highly variable clay quality, making it necessary for them to engage their raw materials in new ways in order to solve the problems with the properties of different clays (D. Arnold 2000, 346–51, 356; 2008, 153–89).

Potters solved this quality problem in several ways. One response consisted of discarding, or setting aside, inferior clay if the potter could afford to do that. Another response was to change suppliers. In the 1990s, for example, potters discovered that

FIGURE 5.4. Mixing the newly moistened clay/temper mixture (1966). At this point, the potter may need to add more temper if the mixture is too wet or too sticky. Or, he may add pure ground palygorskite (*sak lu'um*). If he feels rocks in the paste, he will pick them out and discard them.

the clay from one seller was consistently inferior, and they just stopped buying clay from him. Another response to inferior clay was to mix it with a better-quality clay in different ratios depending upon the potter's experimentation. Finally, because of the changing amount of nonplastics in the paste over time, potters simply changed their initial paste recipe (D. Arnold 2000; 2008, 221–28).

Potters mix the clay/temper mixture by wedging it (figure 5.5), and this activity is critical for the success in forming the vessels. It mixes the temper throughout the clay and increases its workability by reducing its plasticity so that the vessels will hold their shape after forming. Finally, thorough mixing speeds drying and reduces shrinkage of the vessels during drying and firing. If the paste is not wedged well, potters say that the pottery will shatter during the first stage of the firing process (*chokokinta'al*).

Mixing temper with the clay completely and evenly is critical because the clay from Yo' K'at consists of kaolinite and a random-mixed layering of kaolinite and smectite (Schultz et al. 1971). Smectite has the property of taking up water between the clay particles and crystal lattices. It thus tends to expand a great deal in the presence of water and shrinks greatly when it is dried and fired, causing

FIGURE 5.5. Wedging the newly mixed clay that has been formed into cylinders for making pottery (1966). The amount of wedging needed is determined by the tactile feedback the potter receives from the process. If clay cracks with the wedging process, wedging must continue. More temper may be added at this stage, if necessary, depending upon the feedback from the mixing process.

the vessels to crack and break. Consequently, incomplete mixing causes vessels to crack and break during forming, drying, and firing because of different rates of expansion and shrinkage between the tempered and untempered clay. Temper thus must be mixed both thoroughly and evenly with the clay to enhance drying and firing properties.

The proper consistency of the paste thus exists within a narrow range of proportions of temper and clay. If too much temper is added, the paste will be too stiff to work. If, on the other hand, the amount of temper is insufficient, the paste is too plastic and pots will not hold their shape and will sag. This range of workability is monitored by visual and tactile feedback that comes from potters' perception of the performance characteristics of the paste. If, during wedging, cracks (*bilil k'at*) appear in the paste near the basal working surface, then it must be wedged again (figure 5.6). A second test consists of rolling the paste between the palms to form a vertical sausage-shaped coil. If part of the coil breaks off and falls during this process, it has not been mixed sufficiently and must be wedged again. Once this visual feedback reveals that the clay is mixed well, the wedging process is complete.

FIGURE 5.6. The final stage of the wedging process in which the clay is rolled into cylinders in preparation for forming the vessels (1965). The potter engages the properties of the prepared paste at this stage by seeing if cracks appear at the base of the wedged clay. If so, it must be wedged again. When properly prepared, some of the cylinders are used immediately for forming, and the remainder are stored as shown here.

All of these behaviors reveal that potters' indigenous knowledge has no set plan, design, or immutable mental template that they use to mix their paste. Although their knowledge does consist of a basic strategy of mixing raw material categories in a ratio of two parts temper to one part clay, it does not cover unforeseen technical challenges to which they must respond during their engagement with paste preparation. Rather, they depend upon visual and tactile feedback from the process and make choices based upon their assessment of the challenges they face in order to ensure the ultimate success of forming their pottery. Paste preparation thus involves knowledge of the raw materials, the pottery-making process, and problem-solving skills to deal with their sensory feedback from the process to ensure their success in transforming their raw material into a finished object.

6

The Potters' Engagement with Vessel Forming

Forming a vessel is the most obvious step in changing a formless mass of clay into a useful object. This step best illustrates how culture imprints itself upon the plastic medium of the clay. This imprinting, however, does not constitute the entire picture of vessel construction, nor is it the simple result of materializing a mental template without intervening variables.

The potter has many choices at this stage, but forming the vessel is the result of the engagement of the potter's indigenous knowledge with the raw materials, the paste, and the process of fabrication. Potters do not just sit down and create the form they desire with no intervening variables, but rather, fabrication of a vessel involves the engagement of different kinds of indigenous knowledge such as their repertoire of vessel shapes and their various sizes, the customary muscular patterns required, and the sensory feedback that comes from the paste and the emerging vessel during the forming process. All of these components affect the how the potter engages the paste to make a vessel.

The first subset of indigenous knowledge necessary to form a pot consists of potters' repertoire of vessel shapes. An experienced traditional potter can produce many different shapes and various sizes of those shapes. In 1965, for example, one informant produced approximately 180 different named forms.[1] Most of these were no longer made, but potters did produce a few of them for ritual and for carrying and storing water.

TABLE 6.1. Nomenclature of the size categories for making traditional vessel shapes (e.g., *cántaros* [*p'uul*], *tinajas*, and *apastes* [*kat*]). (From "Factors Affecting Standardization" by Dean E. Arnold and Alvaro Nieves. In *Ceramic Production and Distribution: An Integrated Approach*, ed. by George J. Bey III and Christopher A. Pool, 1992, pp. 101. Westview Press, Boulder, Colorado. Used with permission [Arnold and Nieves 1992].)

English	Spanish	Yucatec Maya
small	*chico*	*chichan*
medium	*mediano*	*chan tan kelen* or *chuumak*
regular[a]	*regular*	*tup'is*
large	*grande*	*noboch*
	gigante	*hach noboch*

a A vessel larger than medium, but not large.

A second subset of the indigenous knowledge of forming consists of the potter's repertoire of the sizes of traditional vessels that are targeted for different uses and for different consumers. Specific sizes of water-carrying pots, for example, are produced for men, women, or children. Other sizes are targeted for a specific geographic area depending on the distance of the household to water sources (Arnold 2008, 103–4). Some populations, for example, desired medium rather than large water-carrying pots because medium vessels full of water were easier to carry longer distances than large ones.

A third subset of the indigenous knowledge of forming consists of operationalizing the sizes in making the vessels. Potters recognize five different sizes (*medidas*) of their vessels (table 6.1), and the potter chooses one of these sizes depending on the vessels' intended market. Each size varies according to a set of specific measurements for each stage involved in forming them.

Operationalizing these size classes involve two basic methods, but both may be combined on the same shape. The first method consists of the number of coils (called *vueltas* [literally "turns"]) used to create a vessel. Since potters draw up thick coils to form the vessel walls, and the potter knows the appropriate size of each coil, the number of coils required to build a vessel or portion thereof is a proxy measure of size.

The second method of measuring the parts of the emerging vessel consists of the hand and fingers (table 6.2). Although these units appear to use Spanish words, only the finger (*dedo*) and the hand span (*jeme*) were found in the online edition of the *Dictionary of the Royal Academy of the Spanish Language* (Real Academia Española 2012a, 2012b).

A third component of the forming process consists of the customary muscular patterns that the potter uses to create the intended form. Whereas the shape, size,

TABLE 6.2. The units of measurement that potters use to make traditional vessels (such as *p'uul* [*cántaro*], *tinajas* [no Maya name], and *kat* [*apaste*]). (From *Social Change and the Evolution of Production and Distribution in a Maya Community*, by Dean E. Arnold, p. 268, University Press of Colorado, 2008.)

Measurement	Definition	Metric equivalent for an adult male potter
jeme	The distance from the end of the extended thumb to the end of the extended index finger (fore finger)	15.5 cm
cuarta	The distance from the end of the extended thumb to the end of the extended little finger (i.e., a hand span)	20.5 cm
One *dedo*	The width of any of the three longest fingers of the hand; often the width of the index finger is used	About 1.5 cm
Three *dedos*	The combined width of the three longest fingers at the first joint from the palm	About 6.5 cm
Four *dedos*	The width of the four fingers at the first joint from the palm	9 cm

and units of measurements used to make a vessel are more conscious, the customary muscular patterns are unconscious and learned by doing. Learning these patterns involves strengthening the appropriate muscles that are used repeatedly in the fabrication process. They are the most difficult part of the pottery-making process to learn and thus take the most time to acquire (Arnold 2008, 42). They tend to be congruent with other activities in the culture and are reinforced by tools, furniture, and other material culture (or the lack thereof). Like customary muscular patterns everywhere, they are difficult to change (Arnold 1985, 147–51). In Ticul, they are the most enduring and most conservative aspect of pottery technology, persisting through more than four decades of massive social and technological change (Arnold 2008, 229–79).

Customary muscular patterns consist of at least two different types of patterns: postural patterns and the syntax of muscular patterns (called motor habits) that are involved with forming. The postural patterns used by the Ticul potter consist of the muscle patterns associated with sitting on a low stool, squatting, or perhaps squatting on one leg (figure 6.1a), and are consistent with postural patterns used in other activities among the Maya of Ticul (figures 5.1–5.4, 5.6, 6.1b–6.1d).

Postural patterns are culturally determined and not universal. I regularly demonstrated this principle in one of my anthropology classes. North Americans, for example, who usually use postures conditioned by using chairs usually cannot squat for any length of time with their feet planted flat on the floor. I found that students could not maintain that position for much more than a minute. Even though I

FIGURE 6.1A. Potters' working position while making a water-carrying jar in 1984. Even though this potter is using the ball-bearing turntable (the *tornete*) that was introduced in the 1970s (see Arnold 2008, 256–62), he still uses the same working position as he did with moving the traditional turntable (the *k'abal*) in the late 1960s.

demonstrated the position no more than twice a year, the duration of my squatting usually outlasted that of all of my students, even though I was twice to three times their age. Such a posture in Yucatán, however, is the traditional working pattern for potters and others, and an inventory of potters' working positions over the last sixty years reveals that this pattern has persisted through time even with massive social and technological change (table 6.3).

Finally, a fourth subset of indigenous knowledge of forming consists of knowing how to deal with the sensory feedback that comes from the forming process itself. Because the goal is to make a particular vessel, potters receive feedback from their senses about their progress in making that vessel. This feedback is critical for the potters' engagement in the process and consists of knowing how, and how much, to thin a vessel wall, how long to allow a portion of a vessel to dry before a new section is added, and how to attach a new coil to a vessel so that the junction will not separate during drying or firing. This kind of knowledge is acquired largely through practice and experience, though it may also be explicitly taught.

How then, does the potter operationalize the form given all of these subsets of knowledge? First, understanding the properties of the clay used is critical. All clays

FIGURE 6.1B. When a low stool is not available, potters still maintain the same working position. This potter (1988) is sitting on a sack of clay (or temper) and engages the same muscle patterns involved when using a low stool. In this case, the potter is moving the turntable with his foot as he smoothens the neck of a water storage jar (*tinaja*).

are not alike, and they have different properties and performance characteristics (see Rice 1987, 5–24, 43–50; 2015, 45–60, 61–73; Shepard 1965, 374–77). Similarly, the clays around Ticul have different properties from one another (see chapter 3), and forming a vessel must take these properties into account if the potter wants to be successful in making, drying, and firing a vessel. The potter learns these characteristics experientially by engaging the raw material properties by preparing the paste and forming a vessel. The traditional clay from Yo' K'at, for example, is plastic

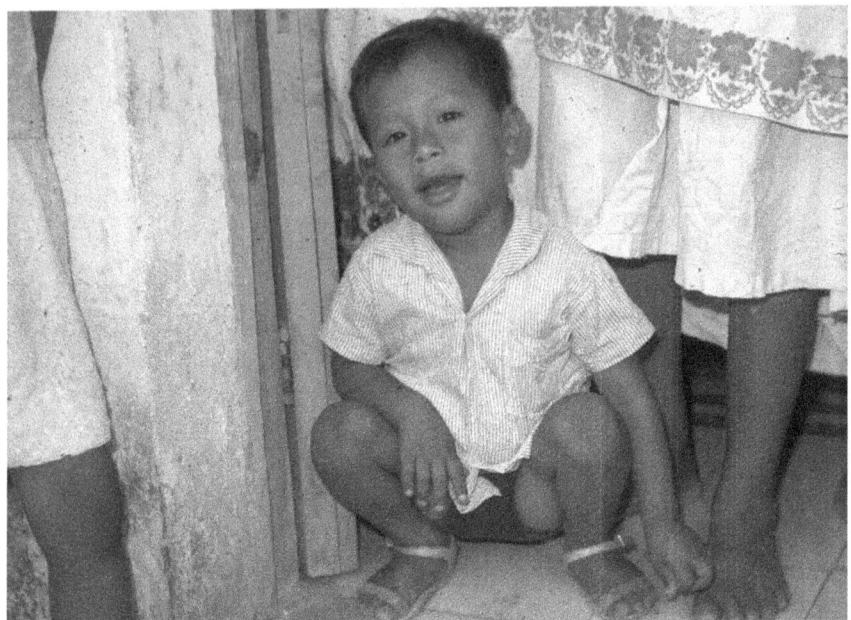

FIGURE 6.1C. A young boy resting in a squatting position in 1970 has already developed this muscular pattern that is learned at a young age by sitting on a low stool and is reinforced across different activities.

enough to make a complex shape such as the water-carrying jars (*cántaros*), but it is so plastic that most large vessels and those with concave profiles cannot be made in an uninterrupted continuous operation without them sagging and collapsing. Experienced potters thus never try to make a large vessel in one continuous sequence without drying between stages.

This same property is also illustrated by the use of vertical-half molding that was introduced during the 1940s. With this technique, the clay forced into each of the two molds must be plastic enough to stick together when the molds are combined, but not so plastic that the resulting vessel will sag after it is removed from the molds. This problem increases with the size of the vessel, so that vessels more than twenty centimeters high and those with sharp concave vertical profiles usually sag and collapse after being combined with the other half of the mold (Arnold 1999; 2008, 245–56). The only exceptions to this problem are large coin banks that are totally enclosed because, like the strength of a sphere or an egg, the walls mutually support themselves in a way that is impossible with an open vessel. Such large closed objects are dried in their molds for a longer period of time to further inhibit sagging.

FIGURE 6.1D. A man using a squatting position trims a *huano* palm frond for repairing a thatched roof of a house in 1984. Working positions pattern muscle use through repetition, and the pattern occurs in a variety of activities in a culture.

Consequently, except for enclosed coin banks, vessels over a height of twenty centimeters cannot be made using vertical-half molding without sagging (Arnold 1999; 2008, 254–55).

This plasticity of the Ticul clay thus places constraints on the forming process and upon the vessel's shape, its size, and the technique of fabrication because only smaller vessels can be made in one continuous sequence. As a consequence, potters fabricate larger vessels in more than one stage; each stage must dry sufficiently in order to support the weight of the next stage (Arnold 2008, 236). Using modified (slab) coiling and building vessels in stages thus is the potters' adjustment both to the benefits and the constraints of a highly plastic paste that contains so much smectite (see chapter 3). The potter's choices of these stages and their size may seem to be culturally determined, but in reality, the size of each stage (usually about 15–20 cm high) is the largest size that the potter can make at a time without it sagging because of the plasticity of the clay.

This adaptation to the plasticity of the local clay is reified in the potter's indigenous knowledge because each stage of forming traditional vessels is given a unique name in Yucatec Maya (table 6.4). Some named stages are the same from vessel to vessel and indicate that the potter uses the same choice even when crafting

TABLE 6.3. Postural patterns of making pottery in Ticul from 1951 to 2008 documented from published photographs.

Observation year	Posture	Activity	Figure	Reference
1951	Stool	Forming pottery	23g	Thompson 1958, 89
	Stool	Forming pottery	23h	Thompson 1958, 89
	Floor or stool	Forming pottery	23i	Thompson 1958, 89
	Floor	Forming pottery	25:a–c	Thompson 1958, 93
1965	Stool	Forming pottery	4.4	Arnold 2015a, 127
	Squatting	Sifting temper	6.4	Arnold 2008, 205
1966	Stool	Slipping pottery	3.10	Arnold 2015a, 78
	Stool	Forming pottery	3.12	Arnold 2015a, 83
1970	Stool	Forming pottery	8.1	Arnold 2008, 233
1970s (late)	Stool	Forming pottery	Frontispiece	Moseley and Terry 1980
1980s	Squatting (one leg)	Sorting clay		Ramírez Carrillo 1987, 5
	Kneeling	Forming pottery		Ramírez Carrillo 1987, 9
	Kneeling (?)	Mixing paste		Ramírez Carrillo 1987, 8
	Floor or stool	Forming pottery		Ramírez Carrillo 1987, 13
1984	Stool	Forming pottery	8.3	Arnold 2008, 236
	Stool	Molding pottery	8.5	Arnold 2008, 249
	Stool	Forming pottery	8.12	Arnold 2008, 259
	Stool	Forming pottery	8.16	Arnold 2008, 267
	Stool	Forming pottery	1.8	Arnold 2015a, 24
	Stool	Forming pottery	4.3	Arnold 2015a, 125
	Stool	Painting pottery	4.7	Arnold 2015a, 130
	Stool	Forming pottery	9.8	Arnold 2015a, 256
	Squatting	Showing turntable	8.10	Arnold 2008, 256
	Squatting	Mixing paste	2.8	Arnold 2008, 46
	Sitting on legs	Finishing molded	8.6	Arnold 2008, 256
	Floor	Forming pottery	4.1	Arnold 2015a, 122
	Floor	Forming pottery	9.11	Arnold 2015a, 263
	Cement block	Forming pottery	8.11	Arnold 2008, 258
	Cement block	Preparing to form	3.8	Arnold 2015a, 74
1990s?	Squatting	Sifting temper	9	Morales Valderrama 2005

continued on next page

TABLE 6.3—*continued*

Observation year	Posture	Activity	Figure	Reference
1997	Stool	Painting	4.6	Arnold 2008, 140
	Stool	Forming pottery	4.32	Arnold 2015a, 165
	Stool	Forming pottery	3.23	Arnold 2015a, 94
	Stool	Painting pottery	3.25	Arnold 2015a, 96
2008	Stool	Drying clay	9.16	Arnold 2015a, 268

different shapes. The first stage of three traditional vessels (table 6.5), for example, is called the *kat 'it*. After forming this first stage, the potter can choose to make any of three different vessels, but for each subsequent stage, the potter's options narrow. This same pattern of production choices occurs in Chinautla, Sacojito, and Durazno, Guatemala (Arnold 1978a, 1978b), and in Quinua, Peru (Arnold 1972a; 1972b; 1993, 91, 99).

As this chapter will demonstrate, Ticul potters *do* have a choice in the forming technique that they use, but many of the choices have already been made for them because their traditional knowledge has adapted their forming technology to the performance characteristics of the clay. These choices may, or may not, however, allow a wide latitude in what they make and how they make it (cf. Arnold 2008, 229–79; Van der Leeuw 1993). Nevertheless, given the mineralogy of the clays used, the forming technique and the vessel shape produced are interdependent. Potters are influenced by the performance characteristics of the clay and the prepared paste (Arnold 1971), and by the feedback resulting from the interaction of these factors when the vessel is being formed.

THE FORMING TECHNOLOGY

Since 1965, Ticul potters have used a variety of forming techniques: the traditional turntable, the wheel, vertical-half molding, slip casting, and, in a few cases, simple modeling. These techniques were treated elsewhere (Arnold 1999; 2008, 229–79; Arnold, Wilson, and Nieves 2008) and will not be repeated here except to say that each technique cannot be used to make every shape because of the limitations of the clay, the paste, and the shaping technology (Arnold 2008, 229–79). Slip casting, for example, requires a very different paste that is liquid and very fine grained. Molding cannot be used for larger vessels because they will sag after they are removed from the mold (see Arnold 1999).

TABLE 6.4. Sequence of the stages of fabrication for vessels with a concave profile. Each stage is the largest portion of a vessel that can be made without sagging. A period of drying is necessary between each of these stages. (The *winli'* or *nak'* consists of two parts: the *kat 'it* and the *kelem bal*.)

Yucatec terms for stages		Part of the vessel from base to mouth
winli' or *nak'*	*(sh) kat 'it*	From the base to the point just below the point of the greatest circumference
	kelem bal	The shoulder (*hombro*) or body (*cuerpo*) of the vessel from the point of greatest circumference to the mouth or the place where the neck is attached
kal		The neck of the vessel

TABLE 6.5. The stages of fabrication (see table 6.4) required to form the *apaste* (*kat*), the *tinaja*, and the *cántaro* (*p'uul*).

	Part of vessel		
Shape name in Spanish (Maya name)	**kat 'it** *(base)*	**kelem bal** *(shoulder)*	**kal** *(neck)*
apaste (*kat*)	Yes	Yes	None
tinaja	Yes	Yes	Wider
cántaro (*p'uul*)	Yes	Yes	Narrower

The only technique that is truly part of Maya traditional indigenous knowledge is the modified coiling technique used to build a vessel on a turntable, called a *k'abal* (figure 6.2–6.4; see also Arnold 2008, 234; Thompson 1958, 76–81). This device consists of a removable platform which rotates around a nail embedded in a thick piece of hard wood. The vessel is formed on this platform by adding thick coils to a pancake base and then drawn up with a gourd scraper. In order to facilitate movement, a circular metal disk is placed on top of the wood base and oil is added to it to reduce friction.

Except for a change in the turntable itself to a ball-bearing mechanism (Arnold 2008, 256–62), modified/slab coiling on a turntable has been used continuously for fabricating pottery since at least the late nineteenth century, when Henry Mercer (1897a, 1897b) first documented the technique in Yucatán. Of all of the fabricating practices used by Ticul potters, this technique is the most versatile, and potters have used it to produce all shapes that have a circular horizontal cross-section. During the late 1960s potters used it to produce traditional shapes such as the water storage pot (*tinaja*), the water-carrying jar (*cántaro*), and a vessel for soaking maize in lime water (*apaste*). Since then, potters have also used it to produce plant pots.

THE POTTERS' ENGAGEMENT WITH VESSEL FORMING   139

FIGURE 6.2. A potter using a traditional k'abal in Ticul, Yucatan, in 1984 using his foot to turn the turntable while he shapes the vessel with both hands. In this case, the potter works seated on the floor.

Understanding the details of the slab/modified coiling technique is crucial for recognizing the constraints that raw materials place upon fabrication and the changes in technique that occur as a result of those constraints. Because the amount of smectite in the clay from Yo' K'at (either alone and in a mixed layering with kaolinite; see chapter 5), the clay is very plastic and is easily formed into the potters' desired shape by drawing up large coils and thinning them.

To begin a vessel, the potter takes a handful of paste, rolls it between her hands to form a sausage shape (approximately 5 cm × 25 cm), and then flattens part of it into

FIGURE 6.3. Potters seated on stools while slipping pottery in 1965. This position and the muscles involved are used throughout the entire sequence of making pottery (see also table 6.3). The potter on the far right is slipping an *apaste* with a red slip.

a circular disk of the appropriate size of the base of the vessel and places it on the platform of the turntable. Then, taking another handful of paste, the potter rolls it into a sausage shape and flattens it into a coil.

With the palm of one hand placed inside the vessel, the potter uses the other to push the flattened coil onto the pancake of clay on the turntable. Often this motion moves the turntable, but it may also be moved by the toe or foot in order to free both hands to shape the vessel. The potter then draws up and thins the newly attached coil with a gourd scraper (Thompson 1958, 75, 81–82), using the palm of one hand inside the pot to support the vessel wall. This behavior moves the turntable, and the potter may move it first in one direction and then the other, occasionally propelling it gently with the foot. Additional coils are prepared, attached, and built up in a similar way.

Usually not more than one or two thick coils are used for each stage because of the plasticity of the clay. When the height of the vessel reaches the limit of the appropriate stage (about 15–20 cm), the potter thins the walls and allows them to dry partially before adding the next stage.[2]

FIGURE 6.4. Four women seated on low stools to slip pottery on a sunny day prior to firing in 1984. A traditional k'abal is in the center foreground of the image.

FOUR TRADITIONAL VESSELS

Four of the most frequently produced traditional vessels in the 1960s were used for carrying and storing water. Water-carrying vessels (*p'uul*) served as channels that brought water to the household. When the water arrived at the house, it was dumped into a large-mouthed storage jar with a high neck called a *tinaja* or into a neckless jar called an *apaste*.

When piped water was installed in Yucatán in the early 1970s, the need for water-carrying vessels diminished, and their production was largely abandoned (Arnold 2008, 104–7). Even after the adoption of piped water, however, some of the Maya still preferred to use the *apaste* or the *tinaja* for storing piped water because they kept the water cool. The water came out of the spigot warm because the pipes were laid close to the surface, and the sun heated the water before it arrived at the houses. Because these pottery vessels were slightly porous, water seeped through the walls, and when it reached the exterior surface, it evaporated, removing heat from the water and thus cooled it.

The *apaste* was also used to soak maize in lime water before it was ground to make the moist dough (*masa*) from which tortillas were made. Other traditional vessels such as food bowls and incense burners continued to be made because they were ritual vessels used for the Day of the Dead ceremonies (see figure 8.1).

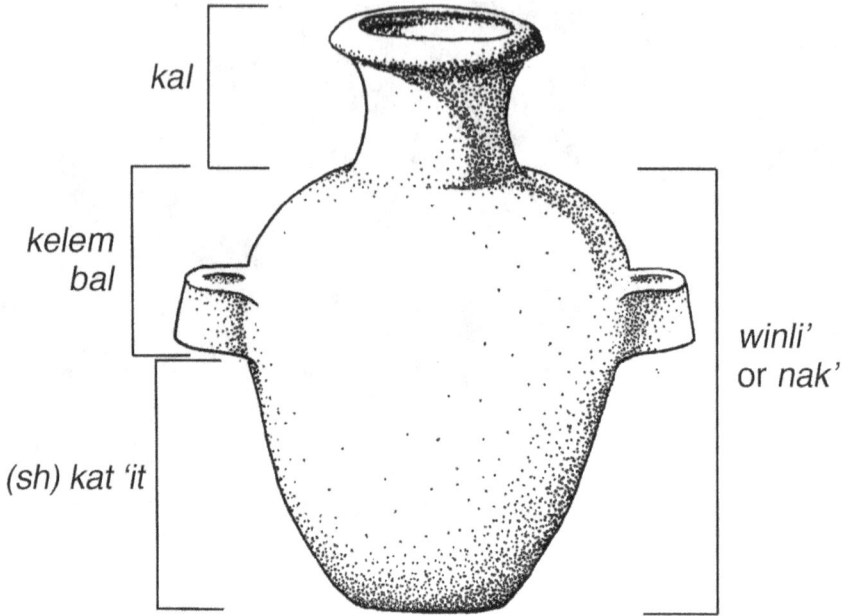

FIGURE 6.5. Named parts of a traditional water-carrying vessel (*p'uul*, or *cántaro* in Spanish). Each named part corresponds to a stage of fabrication that requires drying before the next stage can be added, so that the vessel will not sag. (Drawing by Michelle Arnold Paine.)

The Water-Carrying Jar (*P'uul* in Yucatec Maya, or *Cántaro* in Spanish)

Because of the karst topography in Yucatan, rain soaks into the ground quickly and little water is available on the surface. The principal water sources were sinkholes where surface rock had collapsed down to the level of the groundwater. In the southern part of Yucatán nearer the *puuk* ridge, however, sinkholes with water are rare because water lies deep below the surface. After the Spanish Conquest, explosives and metal tools were used to dig wells here, and subsurface water became more accessible. Even so, wells were expensive because water was more than twenty meters below the surface. Although they allowed access to subsurface water, their frequency was related to the depth of the water table, but they were not widely distributed.

Pottery vessels served to bring water from wells and sinkholes to households. Since water was often carried some distance, the water-carrying jar (*p'uul*) with a narrow neck and two strap handles provided a channel of water transport (see figure 6.5). Like all vessels intended for carrying water, this shape has a small-mouth

TABLE 6.6. Potters' choices of different sizes and the appropriate measurements used for forming the stages of the water-carrying jar (*cántaro* [*p'uul* in Yucatec Maya]). (Modified from table 8.10, *Social Change and the Evolution of Production and Distribution in a Maya Community*, by Dean E. Arnold, p. 269, University Press of Colorado, 2008.)

Vessel part	Size of vessel			
	Small	Medium	Regular	Large
Base diameter	4 *dedos* or 1 *jeme*	1 *jeme* or 1 *cuarta*	1 *cuarta*	1 *cuarta*
Body height (*winli'* or *nak'*)	1 *cuarta* or 4–5 *dedos*	1 *cuarta* and 5 *dedos*	1 *cuarta* and 1 *jeme*	2 *cuartas*
Neck Height (*kal*)	2 *vueltas* (a little more than 8 *dedos*, which is slightly less than one *jeme*)	A little less than 1 *jeme*	A little less than 1 *jeme*	1 *jeme* (three *vueltas*)
Mouth diameter (*hol*)	Depends on the size of the potter's hand	Depends on the size of the potter's hand	Depends on the size of the potter's hand	1 *jeme*

diameter relative to the maximum diameter so that water will not spill during movement (see Henrickson and McDonald 1983).

The distance to water sources also influenced the shape of the vessel that potters made for each market niche. Since unique motor habit patterns are required to carry water jars, those patterns affect the size and shape of vessels. Women have more of a hip shelf than men, so water-carrying jars are constructed with a flat base and horizontal strap handles so that they can be carried with the arm around the neck of the vessel with either the base or the strap handle resting on the hip. This pattern appears to facilitate carrying a larger amount of water longer distances than using other vessels (see Arnold 1985, 147–51; 2008, 101).

These carrying patterns have definite implications for the dimensional variability of the vessel, and the sizes of the parts of the water-carrying jar (*p'uul*) do not covary in the same way across its different sizes (table 6.6). The dimensions of some parts are more uniform between different sizes than those of other parts.

The neck, for example, has a similar height across most sizes so that the arm can fit around it while being carried on the hip (see Arnold 2008, 101). For little girls, however, the vessel is much smaller, and the neck is shorter so that the girl's arm can fit around it comfortably. Further, the mouth diameter is small enough so that the water will not spill, but large enough so that the potter's hand can be inserted to form the neck.

Strap handles are placed exactly opposite of one another approximately one hand span (*cuarta*) above the base, and the excess clay on top and below the handle is cut with a string to provide a flat surface so that the angle of the bottom of the handle can rest on the hip when the arm is placed around the neck. Both the angle on the horizontal strap handle and the angle between the flat base and the vessel wall allow the vessel to be carried easily on the hip.

Apart from this similarity of neck size and handle placement for all water-carrying jars, potters produce a particular size depending upon the target population. In this case, vessel size is a product of choice just as vessel shape is, and is dependent upon potters' knowledge of the market. Apart from these dimensions related to making and carrying of the vessel, the other dimensions vary with the size of the vessel (table 6.6) and may also vary from potter to potter.

Before piped water eliminated the need for water jars, consumer demand provided feedback for the potter to make sizes that targeted specific consumers. Different sizes of water jars, for example, were required for men and women, and for the age of the carrier. Women used two-handled jars and carried them on the hip (Arnold 2008, 101). A small size of this shape with a shorter neck height was produced strictly for little girls (table 6.6). The three-handled water-carrying jar (Thompson 1958, 57) was used only by men who cultivated milpa plots south of the *puuk* ridge, where water from natural sources such as sinkholes was rare and limited to wells dug during the historic period, or was obtained from rocks that held water from rainfall (such as *sarteneas* or *hal tuns*). When water was required for newly planted crops such as before the regular rains began, or during a drought, men carried this vessel on their back using a tumpline or carefully packed two of them on a horse, traveling as many as two kilometers to take water to their crops.

In addition to the importance of gender and maturity influencing the potters' production choice of the size of water jars, different sizes were targeted to different communities depending upon the distance that women needed to walk carrying a full vessel of water. Women in communities near the city of Tekax, for example, did not care about the size of their jars because water sources were relatively close to the houses. In Santa Elena, on the other side of the *puuk* ridge, however, consumers wanted medium-size jars because the water table there was seventy meters deep and only one well existed in the community. Women had to walk some distance to obtain their water and thus wanted a smaller jar.

RIM VARIATION AND ITS MEANING

Besides different sizes of water-carrying jars, potters' indigenous knowledge includes two choices of different rim forms that reveal both the use of the vessel and the potter who made it (figure 6.6).

The first form is an everted rim (figure 6.6A [right]); Thompson 1958, 37, fig. 6d) that simply flares outward from the mouth (the *tach' hol*). Potters choose this rim form for vessels used to make a fermented drink called *balche'* consumed

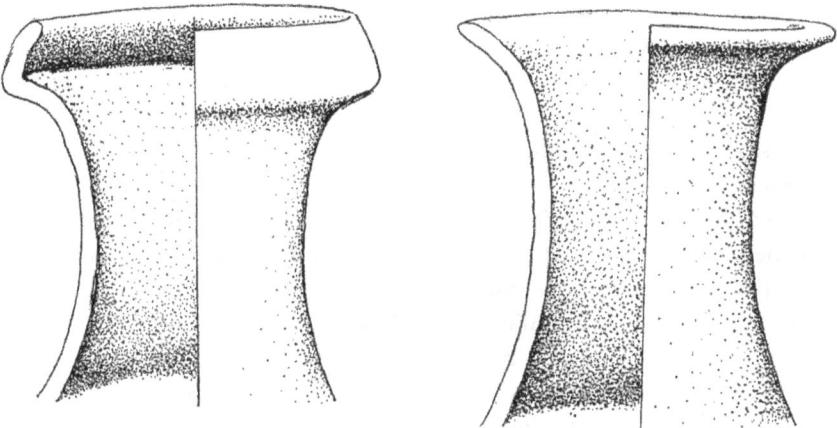

FIGURE 6.6A. Cutaway images of the two rim forms on the water-carrying jar (the *cántaro* or *p'uul*) in Ticul. The rim on the left is the Mani-style rim (*shmani hol*), and the rim on the right is the everted rim used in vessels to serve *balche'*. (Drawing by Michelle Arnold Paine.)

during two indigenous religious ceremonies. Performed by traditional Maya priests (*h-men*), these ceremonies, called the *chaachac* and the *huajikol* ceremonies, take place in the forest and are tied to traditional Maya religious beliefs. In Chan Kom in eastern Yucatán, the *chaachac* was performed for the spirits of the cornfield to bring rain (Redfield and Villa Rojas 1962, 83, 85, 138–43), whereas the *huajikol* ceremony (or *u hanli col*) establishes satisfactory relationships with the deities of the forest and assures health and agricultural success (Redfield and Villa Rojas 1962, 134–37). Three to eight days before these rituals, pieces of the *balche'* tree (*Lonchocarpus longistylus*, Pittier, Birman Furman 1996, 251; Roys 1976, 216; Souza Novelo 1940, 7; Steggerda 1943b) are washed and placed in a medium-sized water-carrying vessel with an everted rim. The vessel is filled with water and the mixture is allowed to ferment until one day before the ritual. Then, honey (or sugar) and anise are added to sweeten the brew and is consumed during the ceremony. This same rim form was also used for Christmas *piñatas* sold in Mérida and in the Ticul market during December.

The second rim form (the *shmani hol*) flares out slightly from the neck and is recurved back toward the mouth to form a concave profile (figure 6.6A [left], figure 6.6B; Thompson 1958, 36, fig. 5d–e). This rim form is chosen for vessels used for carrying water and is a further enhancement of its shape to ensure that water would not splash out of the vessel while it is being carried.

Potters attribute the introduction of this rim style to the influence of Doña Lol (Florencencia Rodríguez), who migrated to Ticul with her husband, Simon

Pech, from the village of Mama in the mid-nineteenth century (Arnold 2015a, 126). Before they arrived it was said that potters made water-carrying vessels with a rim that flared outward. Doña Lol, however, taught potters to recurve the rims of the vessels. Potters call this rim form the *mani hol* or, freely translated, "the Maní-style mouth." By the late 1960s it was the predominant rim form used on water-carrying vessels.

Potters also use this rim form on large water-carrying jars (called *p'uul ich kol*) that men use to carry water from sources in the forest (such as *sarteneas* or *hal tuns*, rocks that held water from rainfall) to their corn fields. These vessels are two to three times the size of the ordinary water jars (*osh p'uul*) and have a wider mouth and three handles (rather than two; see Thompson 1958, 37, fig. 6d).

Potters thus choose to make vessels with one rim over the other depending upon the vessel's intended use. If a liquid placed in a vessel is relatively small and limited (like *balche'*), then an everted rim is used. Pouring is easier, and less liquid is wasted. A vessel with a recurved rim, however, can be used for pouring *balche'* if no vessels with an everted rim are available. For water transport, however, the recurved rim is preferred because the rim prevents the spillage of water during transport. When a water-carrying jar with either type of rim is emptied into a storage vessel such as a *tinaja* or an *apaste*, no water is lost because the mouths of these storage vessels are larger than those of the carrying jars. The recurved rim is thus preferred for carrying water while the everted rim is preferred for preparing *balche'*.

This water-carrying shape has pre-Columbian antecedents in the Terminal Classic Period (AD 800–1100) and the Postclassic Period. It appears to be similar to jar shapes of Chichén Slate ware (Smith 1971, figs. 14: a–j, fig. 59a) of the Terminal Classic Period, and to Mayapán Red ware (Smith 1971, fig. 38: nos. 1–7, fig. 74: c–d), San Juaquín Buff ware (Smith 1971, fig. 50, figs. 75: i–j), Peto Cream ware (Smith 1971, fig. 52: a–b, fig. 75: l–m), and Mayapán Unslipped ware (Smith 1971, fig. 61) from Mayapán during the Postclassic Period.

Whenever the shape began in Maya prehistory, its association with carrying patterns suggest that it was an innovation that facilitated easier transport of water, perhaps over longer distances than previously (Arnold 2008, 101). What did the beginning of this shape in the ceramic sequence of Yucatán indicate? It might coincide with the arrival of a new population that developed an innovative motor habit pattern that facilitated carrying water over longer distances with greater ease than shapes used to carry water from cisterns (*chultuns*). Alternatively, it may have been borrowed from another population. Since water sources are scarce in southern Yucatán, except for cisterns (*chultuns*) that appear to be used for water storage during the Terminal Classic, the adoption of the *p'uul* shape may indicate a change in settlement in which people needed to travel greater distances to obtain water. This

FIGURE 6.6B. Ticul potters use a distinct variation of the recurved rim on the traditional water-carrying vessel (*p'uul*) as a unique signature of their work. In this image taken in 1984, a potter demonstrates how he makes his own unique angular rim signature by using his thumb nail.

may have happened when the rainfall decreased (as much as 40 percent) during AD 800–1000 (the Terminal Classic Period), resulting in failure to fill inhabitants' cisterns with enough water to sustain themselves through the dry season.[3] *Chultuns* also existed north of the *puuk* ridge, but rainfall still might have been insufficient to

FIGURE 6.6C. Rim style of Máxima Tzum de Uc in 1984. Note the consistency of the curve of the rim style on these vessels, and their contrast with angular rim signature of her nephew (Alfredo Tzum Camaal) in figure 6.6b.

fill them, and populations had to settle around more reliable sources of water such as *cenotes* (such as those in Maní, Sacalum, and Mayapán).

Is there, for example, a difference in shapes that could be used to carry water between the sites south of the *puuk* ridge and those north of it during the Terminal Classic? Since natural sources of water were scarce in the south, water was largely drawn from cisterns refilled from the rains of the rainy season, and it didn't need to be carried very far. It is already known that the populations moved northward during the Terminal Classic and Postclassic Periods and that the Xiu rulers from Uxmal, for example, settled in Maní, a community north of the *puuk* ridge with a reliable source of water—a sinkhole (*cenote*) with water. The only reliable water sources during the droughts of the Terminal Classic and Postclassic Periods were sinkholes (*cenotes*) like the one at Maní, and the high-necked water-carrying jar may have been developed in response to carrying water longer distances in settlements with a single water source. Unfortunately, the questions of changes in vessel shape cannot be answered using standard Maya ceramic typology alone. Water-carrying vessels continued to be made in Ticul and in Mama in the late 1960s and beyond until the demand for them ceased.

The recurved rim form on water-carrying jars, however, appears to be much more recent than the Terminal Classic Period and dates at least to the Colonial Period. Thompson (1958, fig. 5, 40) illustrates the recurved rim on water-carrying vessels excavated from colonial deposits at Maní and Telchacquillo (see Thompson 1958, 36, figs. 5: c–d, figs. 40: b–c), as well as vessels from Mama and Ticul made in 1951.

INDIVIDUAL VARIATION IN RIM FORM

Variations in the Maní-style rim also reflect a potter's own unique signature style. Some potters recurve the rim in a perfectly rounded fashion; others push the finger into the moist clay on the inside of the rim and draw it around so that the fingernail creates an angular indentation around the perimeter of the inside of the rim. Still others used other techniques to modify the rim form.

Potters can recognize their own rim signature on vessels months after they made and sold them. In 1967 I traveled to the town of Maní with a potter named Francisco Keh (Arnold 2015a, 78–81). At that time, water was drawn from the sinkhole in the center of the town, and during our walk to see it Francisco stopped a woman carrying a water pot and talked with her briefly. He remarked later that she was using a water pot that he had made, and he had recognized his own personal rim style.

In the 1960s, rim signatures on water-carrying vessels also served to identify individual potters when they shared the same kiln. After firing was completed, potters sorted individual vessels using the rim form of their makers. When Francisco Keh (Arnold 2008, 100 (fig. 3.5); 2015a, 78–81) fired his own vessels with those of his next-door neighbor (Eusevio Yeh, see Arnold 2015a, 123–24), for example, the vessels from the two potters were easily separated using the rim form after they were fired. Although it would seem that simply counting the number of vessels that each potter contributed to a firing event would work equally well as a method of separation, identifying the maker becomes more important if a vessel breaks during firing because of the inferior raw materials or insufficient drying. Identifying a vessel by the rim form thus may indicate that its creator may be responsible for the damage rather than the person who fired it.

OTHER TRADITIONAL SHAPES

Potters also apply their indigenous knowledge of measurement techniques to forming other shapes as well: the *apaste*, the *tinaja*, and the pitcher (*jarra*). The *apaste* shape (called *kat* in Yucatec Maya) is a common shape for storing water and for soaking maize kernels in lime water (figure 6.7, figure 6.3). It shares the same two basic forming stages with the water-carrying jar (*p'uul*, table 6.5), and comes in

150   THE POTTERS' ENGAGEMENT WITH VESSEL FORMING

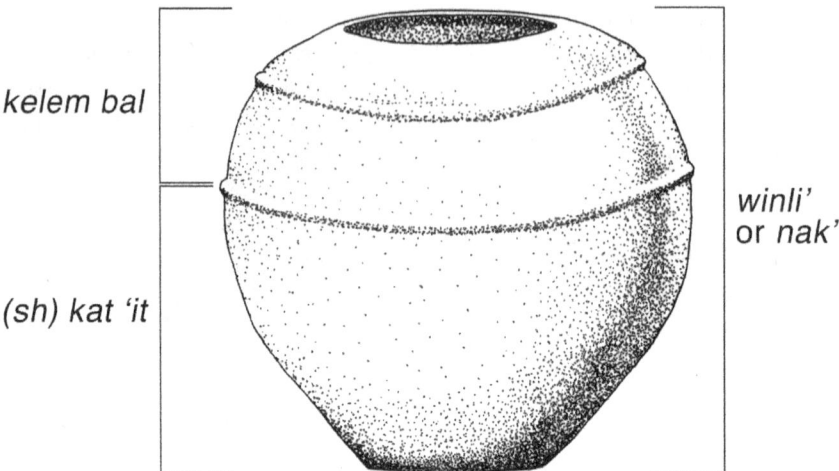

FIGURE 6.7. The traditional water storage jar (*kat*, or *apaste* in Spanish) made in Ticul showing the different named parts. Each named stage corresponds to a stage of fabrication that requires drying before the next stage can be added. Each stage consists of the amount of clay that can be formed without the stage sagging. The *apaste* was also used to soak kernels of maize in lime water to prepare the kernels before grinding them to make the dough (*nishtamal*, or *masa*) for tortillas. (Drawing by Michelle Arnold Paine.)

several different sizes depending on its use (table 6.7). An alternative set of sizes of the *apaste* uses a more limited number of categories (table 6.8).

The *tinaja* is a water storage jar (figure 6.1b, figure 6.8). It also shares two of the same forming stages and measurement units with the *apaste* and *cántaro* (table 6.5, table 6.9), and potters use the same measurement units for them. The *tinaja*, however, has no Maya name. Even so, it appears to be the same shape as the wide-mouthed Postclassic Mayapán Red ware jar (Smith 1971, fig. 38a: nos. 8–10, 18; fig. 74: j–l), and the San Juaquín Buff ware jar (Smith 1971, fig. 53: nos. 1–5) from Mayapán, but without the handles.

Traditional measurement units are also used with pitchers (*jarras*) that have a body height of one hand span (*cuarta*) plus either three or four fingers (*dedos*). They are the same size as the water carrying vessels (*cántaros*) used for *piñatas*.

Potters use a slightly different measuring method for the food bowl (*cajete, lak* in Maya) and the incense burner (*incensarios*). Both of these vessels are used primarily for the Day of the Dead rituals (see Arnold 2008, 107–10; Arnold and Nieves 1992). The food bowl is made with only one coil, and its height is trimmed to the width of four fingers. Its mouth diameter results from the size of the gourd scraper used to finish it and is slightly larger than that of the length of the scraper. One size of

TABLE 6.7. Potters' choices of different sizes, their use, and the appropriate measurements used for forming one variety of the *kat* shape (*apaste*). The mouth diameter is not measured, but it is always smaller than the greatest diameter. There are two different Maya names for a size translated into Spanish as *regular*. (Modified from table 8.12, in *Social Change and the Evolution of Production and Distribution in a Maya Community*, by Dean E. Arnold, p. 270, University Press of Colorado, 2008.)

	Size of vessel				
	Medium	*Regular*	*Regular*	*Large*	*Very large*
Body Height (*winli'* or *nak'*)	1 *cuarta* + 5 *dedos*	1 *cuarta* + 2 *dedos*	< 1 *cuarta* (but more than 1 *jeme*)	2 *cuartas* + 1 *jeme*	3 *cuartas*
Use	Soaking maize for preparing tortilla dough (*nishtamal*)	Bathing	Washing or soaking maize		
Maya Name	*kati pook kum*	*kati ich kil*	*kat bo'h a'*	*nohoch homa' kat*	*muy especial*

TABLE 6.8. Potters' choices and their measurements for making a second variety of the *kat* (*apaste*) shape. (Modified from table 8.12 in *Social Change and the Evolution of Production and Distribution in a Maya Community*, p. 270, University Press of Colorado, 2008.)

	Size of vessel		
	Small	*Medium*	*Large*
Height of first stage ([*sh*] *kat 'it*)	1 *jeme*	1 *cuarta* + 3 *dedos*	1 *cuarta* + 3 *dedos*
Height of second stage (*kelem bal*)	2.5 *dedos*	3 *dedos*	> 4 *dedos*

TABLE 6.9. Potters' choices of size categories and the appropriate measurements used for each stage of the water storage jar (*tinaja*). The body of the *tinaja* is the same as the body of the *apaste* (see table 6.7). (Modified from table 8.13 in *Social Change and the Evolution of Production and Distribution in a Maya Community*, p. 271, University Press of Colorado, 2008.)

	Size of vessel				
Vessel Part	*Small*	*Medium*	*Regular*	*Large*[a]	*Large*
Body height (*winli'* or *nak'*)	1 *cuarta*	2 *cuartas*	2 *cuartas* + 4 *dedos*	2 *cuartas* + 1 *jeme*	3 *cuartas*
Neck height (*kal*)	< 1 *jeme*	1 *jeme*	1 *cuarta*	1 *cuarta*	1 *cuarta* + 2–3 *dedos*
Mouth diameter (*hol*)	< 1 *jeme*	1 *jeme*	1 *cuarta*	1 *cuarta*	1 *cuarta*

a This size holds sixty liters and corresponds to the volume of three *cántaros* of water. This size was more popular than the larger size that consumers did not buy.

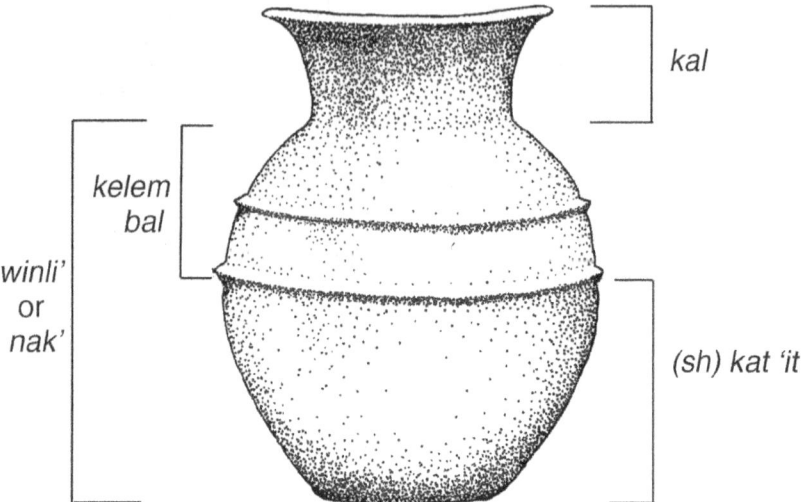

FIGURE 6.8. Another traditional water storage jar (*tinaja* in Spanish, no Maya name) made in Ticul showing the different named parts. Each named part corresponds to a stage of fabrication that requires drying before the next stage can be added. Each stage is the largest amount of clay that can be formed without the stage sagging. (Drawing by Michelle Arnold Paine.)

scraper was used for a large bowl and another size for the small bowl. Other sizes are possible depending on the size of the gourd scrapers, and some potters make several different sizes depending on the size of the scrapers that they have available.

The incense burner consists of a food bowl on top of a pedestal base, but with holes punched through the walls of the bowl. The bowl is made first and then allowed to dry partially before adding the base.

The sizes of bowls, incense burners, and other vessels (such as ashtrays) are susceptible to size variations due to the width of a potter's fingers used to measure them, and the sizes of the scraper used to shape them. Because scrapers eventually get smaller with wear, the mouth diameter of these vessels would be expected to change over time, and show great variability from potter to potter. The result of these practices produces a vessel in which the statistical variances of their dimensions are significantly larger than those of other vessels (Arnold and Nieves 1992).

NOTES

1. Made by Alfredo Tzum Camaal, these shapes were stored for years in the garage of the Instituto Interuniversitario para Investigaciones Fundamentales en Ciencias Sociales en

Yucatán, Calle 76, No. 455LL in Mérida. When the Instituto was dissolved and the facility became the School of Anthropology of the University of Yucatán, the vessels were moved into the Museum of Anthropology in the Palacio Cantón on the Paseo Montejo.

2. Thinning vessel walls evenly to the appropriate thickness is an acquired skill. When potters changed from making traditional vessels to making plant pots, they produced vessel walls that were thicker because they required less skill than thinning the walls. This change also accommodated changing clay sources with different performance characteristics that often included differing amounts of natural nonplastics in them and reportedly did not break as much as vessels with thinner walls.

3. The Maya response to decreased rainfall and ensuing droughts is a complicated issue that has great regional variation (Kennett and Beach 2013; Medina-Elizalde and Rohling 2012). Heather Pringle's (2009) news item in *Science* summarizes papers on this theme from the 2009 Society for American Archaeology meeting.

7

The Potters' Engagement with Drying and Firing

Although a less obvious part of potters' indigenous knowledge than shaping vessels, drying and firing them are the most risky steps in the production sequence (the *chaîne opératoire*). During these steps the potter faces a new set of challenges to fix the form of a fabricated vessel, and once again, these challenges illustrate the complex engagement of the potter's knowledge with the raw materials and with the pottery-making process. Like forming, drying and firing involve the relationship of the potter's indigenous knowledge and the feedback from raw materials and from the processes themselves. Like forming, the potters' knowledge about drying and firing also integrates feedback from the weather. All of these interactions profoundly influence the choices that the potter makes during these final stages of production.[1]

Maintaining the integrity of a shape by preventing damage to it during drying and firing requires considerable indigenous knowledge. Potters must know how long to dry their vessels: if they are not dried enough, they will break during firing because of the steam produced by the free water inside the vessel walls. Potters also must know the burning characteristics of wood, the parts of the kiln, the sequence of the process, how to respond to the visual feedback of inclement weather, and the changes in the pottery occurring during the firing process itself.

Potters recognize that success during these segments of making pottery does not just begin with the actual firing, but rather with the previous parts of the production process beginning with the choices that they make in selecting the clay and temper. If potters use poor quality clay (*ma' pahtal le k'atil*), for example, the results may not appear until after the firing process is over when the pots crack and will not hold water. On the other hand, if the clay used is very, very poor quality, the vessels made from it will crack severely even before they are put into the kiln. Consequently, it is important to choose good-quality clay.

This rootedness of firing success in the raw materials was one of the first things that I learned when I began to study firing in 1965. Originally, I thought that since I was learning about firing, I did not need to learn anything about making pottery before the actual firing process began. I was greatly mistaken. As soon as I began to immerse myself in both the language of firing and observations of the process, I learned that success was based upon the quality of all of the raw materials necessary to make pottery—especially the temper that was prepared by mining specialists. Temper quality could make or break firing success depending on whether or not it contained *sak lu'um* (palygorskite). At the time I had no idea about the complexity of the potter's knowledge of temper, about the importance of *sak lu'um*, and that it corresponded to the clay mineral palygorskite. Further, I had no idea that *sak lu'um* had medicinal uses, and, as I was to discover later, I was unaware that it was a critical component of the ancient pigment, Maya Blue (Arnold 1967a, 1967b; Arnold and Bohor 1976; Arnold et al. 2012).

Only experienced adult potters typically possessed the knowledge and skill of firing pottery. The complexity of these capabilities is further affirmed by the fact that firing was one of the segments of the process that some potters turned over to specialists after 1965. For them, it was simply easier to sell their pottery unfired and have someone else fire it than buy the firewood and go through the complicated and risky process of firing their vessels themselves (Arnold 2008, 286–90, 301–2).

GENDER AND FIRING

As with the gender of potters in general, the gender of those who fire pottery is related to their engagement with the process and with other activities. As described in cross-cultural studies of gender-based division of labor summarized in *Ceramic Theory and Cultural Process* (Arnold 1985, 99–108), potters tend to be women, as they tend to be elsewhere in the Maya area (see Arnold 1978a; Reina and Hill 1978, 200–1, table 2),[2] but this pattern appears to be tied to the practice of the craft in household contexts where women can easily make pots between fulfilling domestic responsibilities and childcare. Further, the gender of potters also tends to be related to subsistence scheduling such that when males perform agricultural tasks that take place when the weather does not significantly impact the intensity of pottery production, potters are women. When pottery making becomes economically more important, more frequent, and moves out of the household, males become involved in the craft—in some cases, without female participation.³

The gender of those who fire pottery is not necessarily the same as that of those who form it. When firing is done in the open and fuel and pottery are placed together before the process begins, potters tend to have few responsibilities during the process, and the gender of those who fire the pottery is the same as those who form it (as in the Valley of Guatemala, see Arnold 1978a, 354–57). Kiln firing in Ticul, however, is very different, and though women may assist in loading the kiln, once the fire is ignited, it requires constant vigilance over the roughly six hours of its duration, and one must abdicate all other responsibilities not related to firing. Such exclusive concentration is incompatible with women's responsibilities such as childcare and food preparation. Similarly, the physical exhaustion that results from firing and the long rest required after it (see the introduction) would also keep women from fulfilling their childcare and household responsibilities, just as it does with men. As a consequence, the six-hour task of firing with all of its accouterments such as splitting firewood and attending the kiln tend to be assigned to men rather than women.

Cross-cultural studies of gender division of labor (Arnold 1985, 99–108; Burton et al. 1977; Murdock and Provost 1973) indicate that activities that require absence from the household and that are dangerous are usually assigned to men. Ticul pottery production fits this probabilistic model because though both men and women are potters, only men mine clay and temper.⁴ Both are potentially dangerous activities (Arnold 2008, 172–78), and several fatalities and close calls with death have been reported in Ticul (Arnold 2008, 158) because of the collapse of overburden in the clay and temper mines (Arnold 1985, 62; 2008, 158, 172, 176; 2015a, 62, 260).⁵ In fact, the sherd-tool over a large lump of clay discovered in the Yo' K'at clay mine in 1968 may indicate that the overburden may have collapsed over a miner, leaving his tool on the mined lump of clay intact, only to be discovered a millennium later (see chapter 4). Certainly, a collapsed mine tunnel approximately three meters underground indicates the danger of mining the clay from Yo' K'at. Firing in Ticul is not as dangerous as mining clay and temper but requires constant vigilance over a period of about six hours that would take women away from domestic and childcare responsibilities. Men thus tend to fire pottery, even though both men and women are potters.

This pattern explains why even though women potters may know how to fire, they often prefer to sell their pottery unfired or ask a male relative to fire it for them. In 1965, for example, one woman (Domitila Tzum de Cima, see Arnold 2015a, 76–77) with a husband and six small children reportedly knew how to fire, but she did not like to do it and took her pottery across the street for her brother to fire.

Another woman potter (Máxima Tzum de Uc, see Arnold 2015a, 98–99) also had childcare and household responsibilities. She knew how to fire, but her husband or sons usually fired for her, though she occasionally asked her nephews next door to fire some of her vessels.

Women potters with no male potter available to fire for them, however, had no alternative except to fire for themselves or sell their pottery unfired. Making pottery, for example, was one way that single, abandoned, or widowed women could survive because it was compatible with their household and childcare responsibilities and could be done in the household (Arnold 2008, 73–78). If they had no man to fire for them, then they would have to fire their own pottery or sell it unfired to another potter. One woman, (María Mex, see Arnold 2015a, 140, 143, 199) reportedly fired for her father (Cesario Mex) when his broken leg was healing in the 1930s, and she continued making and firing her own pottery before she married. After she was divorced, she resumed making and firing her pottery until she was too infirm to work. Similarly, when a nonpotter (Manuel Martín, see Arnold 2015a, 151) married into a pottery-making family in the 1950s, his wife's unmarried half-sister fired his pottery for him until he learned how to do it himself. Another female potter who was unmarried (Guadalupe Tzum Tuyup, see Arnold 2015a, 107) fired her own pottery up until she died in 1965, and another learned how to fire after she was abandoned by her husband. All of these women were elderly or deceased by 1984, and most female potters usually had access to the firing expertise of males in the household or to that of male relatives nearby. Similarly, another elderly potter (Augusta Tzum de Segura, see Arnold 2015a, 82–84, 88), who, by 1997, had been widowed for eight years, supervised a male assistant who was firing plant pots at her daughter's production unit. Our conversation revealed that she had an impressive knowledge of firing, especially considering that few women fire.

FIRING COOKING POTTERY

Traditionally, Ticul potters used two types of firing technology: one for cooking pottery and another for noncooking pottery. Although both types utilize a beehive kiln of probable Moorish origin (Lister and Lister 1987; Thompson 1958, 96), great differences exist between the kilns and the behavior associated with each technology. Because cooking pots dry more quickly than the vessels of noncooking pottery, they can be dried in one day and then fired immediately thereafter. Further, in contrast to the kiln used to fire noncooking pottery, the kiln for cooking pottery has a larger doorway (Thompson 1958, 96) that is probably related to the firing technique. In contrast to firing noncooking pottery, the potter preheats the empty kiln by burning two or three bundles of firewood and then spreads the burning charcoal over its floor. Then, he carefully inserts the end of a long pole into a dry pot and places it on the coals. After he completes a single layer, he covers the top of the vessels with brush (*chilib, ramos*) to complete the firing. When the vessels are completely fired, he removes them using the same pole and replaces them with another set of pots, firing as many as three sets of vessels in the same episode. Firing noncooking pottery, however, takes much longer, is much more complicated, and appears to require more knowledge of firewood and about the process of firing itself.

BUILDING A KILN

Building a kiln requires specialized knowledge, a unique mortar, and a special kind of rock because all rocks do not have equal utility for constructing a kiln. So, the potter must know the different classes of rocks and their characteristics so that he can select those rocks that are most resistant to heat. The type of rock called *sah kab tunich* is too soft for kiln construction. Another type, called *tok' tunich*, is a harder flintlike rock (see chapter 4), but both types will crack and break when heated, and a kiln made from them will eventually crumble. Another type, called *sakel bach tunich* (literally *sakel bach* rock, or "white birds eggs rock"), however, is superior to other types of rocks for kiln building, but in order to obtain enough of such rocks, potters must purchase an abundant supply to be sure that they can select enough of the *sakel bach* type of rocks to build their kiln.[6]

Even with the most heat-resistant rocks available, however, they are still limestone, and over time, the heat from the fire causes them to disintegrate from calcination (see chapter 4). To forestall this problem for as long as possible, the potter uses a unique mortar to protect the rocks from the damaging heat of the fire.

To make this mortar, potters combine one part of *k'an kab* with two parts of *sah kab* temper (see chapter 4) that results in a durable kiln that lasts twenty to thirty years (Arnold 2008, 286–87). Alternatively, potters may combine *k'an kab* with tailings from sifted temper (*ta'achach* [*chichi'*]). It enables the plaster to adhere well, maintain its form, and endure the heat longer. Although *sah kab* (a natural marl) for construction purposes is more common, abundant, and available, and is used for kiln mortar in some cases, *sah kab* temper is preferred because potters say that the *sak lu'um* in the temper creates a harder plastered surface and resists the damaging heat of the fire longer than regular *sah kab* (natural marl). If one uses *sah kab* for construction purposes (or cement) for the plaster, however, it will slowly fall apart because the heat of the fire decomposes the calcite and dolomite in the plaster because of calcination. Since about one-third of the *sah kab* temper is the clay mineral palygorskite (table 4.3), using it in the mortar reduces the amount of carbonates (calcite and dolomite) in the temper that will disintegrate with heat.

The doorway of the kiln must be constructed with care. It must be large enough for a man to enter and load the kiln, but small enough to minimize heat loss. It is also the portal through which the potter adds firewood and stokes the fire during the process.

The direction that the door faces is critical. Because rain or a gust of wind can damage vessels on either side of the door, potters orient it in a direction from which there is no wind and rain. Potters say that rainy weather comes from the east from late May through November, whereas during January and February, storms (called *nortes*) come from the north across the Gulf of Mexico. During the months of March through May, on the other hand, hot dry winds blow from the south. West, they say, is the only direction from which there is no wind and rain. So, in order to keep rain and wind from entering the kiln and damaging the pottery, potters usually construct their kilns with the door facing west (table 7.1).

The potters' perceptions of wind direction fit well with the meteorological data from Mérida, located sixty-five kilometers north of Ticul, the only location from which data on wind direction was available (table 7.2). These data indicate that wind does indeed come from the north, south, and easterly directions, but not from the west (Cserna, Mosiño, and Benassini 1974, 168). These directions do not correspond precisely with potters' perceptions, but they do indicate that potters engage weather conditions and receive feedback from them to inform the way that they build their kilns.

The orientation of the kiln door has not changed much since 1965. Surveys in 1965, 1966, 1984, and 1997 revealed that almost all of the kilns in Ticul have their doorways facing west. Of the eighteen kilns observed in 1965–66, 89 percent ($N = 16$) faced west, and the remaining 11 percent ($N = 2$) faced west-southwest (table 7.1). This pattern continued in 1984 with 100 percent ($N = 22$) of the kilns observed facing west (table 7.1). By 1997, 90 percent (35/39) of the traditional beehive kilns faced west (table 7.3).

Potters' perception of wind direction and of its role in affecting the orientation of their kiln doors parallels the ethnoastronomical and ethnoclimatological knowledge of the Andean Quechua and its use to schedule their agricultural practices. Using the rise and intensity of the Pleiades constellation in the night sky, Andean farmers can successfully predict planting times, the onset of rains, and whether a crop year will be dry because of the effect of the El Niño (Orlove, Chiang, and Cane 2002). Andeans thus engage their environment and receive feedback from it in a way that affects their practice of agriculture much like the way in which potters receive feedback from weather and climate in the way that they orient the doors of their kilns because they must use different behavioral choices (as indicated below) when it rains during firing.

TABLE 7.1. Kilns and their characteristics for each production unit from 1965 to 1966 and 1984. Ranges in number of bundles of firewood usually (but not always) consist of the bundles required for firing in the dry season (the lower number) and the number of bundles required for firing in the rainy season (the higher number). In the case of Adrian Huicab (observed in 1966) and Justo Uc (observed in 1984), the ranges indicate the amount used when the kiln is not full and when it is full.

Household	Direction kiln faces (1966)	Number of bundles of firewood required to complete firing (1965–66)	Direction kiln faces (1984)	Number of bundles of firewood required to complete firing (1984)
Carmelo Chan	West	4–6		
Enrique Garma	West	17		
Elia Puuc Navarro	No kiln	N/A		
Carlos Itzá	West	–		
Carlos Itzá (used by father)	West	–		
Gonzalo Huicab	West	12		
Venancio Huicab	Uses Gonzalo's		West (3 kilns)	
Claudio Huicab	West	15	West	15
Celestino Huicab (kiln abandoned; used Gonzalo's)	No data	3–7		
Manuel Tzum	West	16		
Daniel Huicab	WSoW	10	No data	
Adrian Huicab	West	8–12		
Ramon Aguilar	WSoW	10		
Evusevio Yeh	West	10		
Jose María Keh (observed in 1965)	West	9–17		
Francisco Keh	West	10	West	
	West	18		
Miguel Segura	West	10	West (2 kilns)	
Jose Venancio Chan	West	8		
Casimiro Canul	No data	no data		
Domitila Tzum	No kiln		West	

continued on next page

TABLE 7.1—continued

Household	Direction kiln faces (1966)	Number of bundles of firewood required to complete firing (1965–66)	Direction kiln faces (1984)	Number of bundles of firewood required to complete firing (1984)
Alfredo Tzum Camaal	West		West	18–20
Ramon Xiu	West	no data		
Justo Uc	West		West	40–50
Gustavo Huicab			West	
Lorenzo Pech (household workshop)	West	18	West (2 kilns)	
Lorenzo Pech (highway workshop)			West (2 kilns)	
Miguel Tzum			West	18
Arturo Yeh			West	45
Raúl Martín			West	19
Norberto Ucan			West	12
Diego Tzum			West	
Fidencio Huicab (large kiln)			West	
Fidencio Huicab (small kiln)			West	

TABLE 7.2. Direction of the prevailing winds in Mérida, Yucatán (Cserna, Mosiño, and Benassini 1974, 168). No other data for weather stations closer to Ticul were available. No dates of observation were provided.

Month	Predominant wind direction	Month	Predominant wind direction
January	ESE	July	E
February	ESE	August	ESE
March	ESE	September	S
April	ESE	October	E
May	ESE	November	NE
June	ESE	December	NNE

A kiln must be built carefully because its shape affects firing success. It should have equal inside dimensions such as 2 × 2 × 2 meters (for a medium-sized kiln) or 3 × 3 × 3 meters (for a large-size kiln), and should not be constructed with vertical walls because the fire may not reach the back of the kiln, and the pottery there will remain black.

Potters start building the kiln with a ring of large rocks. After adding mortar to the top of them, they add the next row of rocks but place them slightly closer to the center of the kiln so that its wall slopes slightly inward. All subsequent rows follow this same pattern. As the row of stones begin to close the arch near the top of the kiln, some potters add a cylindrical piece of pottery as a vent (called an *'iik'*) at the rear to aid in cooling the kiln after firing (table 7.4). Finally, at the top of the kiln, the last stone is dropped in place. Then, they plaster the kiln on the inside and outside with the same mixture of *k'an kab* and *sah kab* temper used for the mortar.

If not built properly, a kiln will collapse. One informant reported that he hired a mason to build his kiln in 1956, but it collapsed shortly after completion. Similarly, when the Oaxaca potter came to Ticul in the 1940s (Arnold 2008, 238), he reportedly built a kiln made entirely with blocks of *k'an kab*. But, when it was fired, it collapsed.

Kilns are covered to keep off the rain in order to protect the exterior plaster and reduce maintenance. In the 1960s potters used palm leaves, metal sheeting, and tar-impregnated roofing scraps. By 1997, however, most potters covered the outside of the kiln with a facing of cement to protect it (Arnold 2008, 286–87); a few began this practice decades earlier.

If not covered in some way, the *k'an kab* plaster on the outside of the kiln will deteriorate over time, and moisture will seep into it, causing the plaster inside the kiln to fall apart and expose the rocks to the heat of the flames. As a result, the rocks in the wall will disintegrate because of the calcination of the limestone, and the kiln collapses.

Before potters fire a load of pottery in a newly constructed kiln, they prefire it empty to "warm" it, driving off the moisture from the mortar and plaster inside in order to prevent damage to the pottery during firing the kiln for the first time. Between firings, they block the door to keep out domestic animals and children to avoid introducing moisture and damaging the plaster on the interior of the kiln. Even so, if a kiln has not been used for a long time, potters prefire it so that the moisture in it does not damage the pottery. They may also do so in the rainy season because they believe that the kiln is cold at this time, and firing it empty also prevents damage from residual moisture within it.

TABLE 7.3. Kilns and their characteristics for each production unit in 1997. Ranges of amounts of firewood sometimes indicate the difference between the amount used in the dry season (the smaller value) and that used in the rainy season (the larger value). Sometimes amounts vary because of the size of the bundles.

Potter	Type of kiln	Size (in bundles [tercios]) of firewood)	Direction faces
Venancio Huicab	Beehive	30	West
Venancio Huicab	Beehive	18	West
Socorro Segura	Beehive	70	West
Socorro Segura	Large plant pot	—	East
Jorge Martin	Cylindrical	4	West
Miguel Segura (chico)	Beehive	60–65	West
Vacilio Ucan	Beehive	20	West
Elio Uc	Beehive	50	West
Miguel Tzum	Beehive	—	West
Andrés Mena	Beehive	40–50	West
Santiago Mena	Beehive	—	West
Moisés Canul	Beehive	50	West
Moisés Canul	Cement block	8	West
Humberto Segura	Beehive	10	West
Humberto Segura	Beehive	30–35	West
Diego Ayala	Beehive	40–45	West
Gonzalo Santa María	Beehive	70	West
Gonzalo Santa María	Beehive	36	West
Gonzalo Santa María	Beehive	20	WNW
Raúl Martín	Beehive	30	West
Raúl Martín	Beehive	12–15	West
Raúl Martín	Cylindrical	3	West
Manuel Alfaro	Beehive	20	West
Manuel Alfaro	Beehive	40	West
Antonio Cruz	Beehive	30–50	WSW
Julian Huicab	Beehive	—	WSW
Daniel Huicab	Beehive	40–45	West
Jeni Segura	Beehive	40–43	West
Luis Pech	Beehive	—	West

continued on next page

TABLE 7.3—*continued*

Potter	Type of kiln	Size (in bundles [tercios]) of firewood)	Direction faces
Lorenzo Pech	Beehive	—	West
Lorenzo Pech	Beehive	—	West
Lorenzo Pech	Beehive	—	West
Lorenzo Pech	Beehive	—	West
Ademar Uc	Beehive	—	West
Alfredo Tzum Camaal	Beehive	—	NW
Jose Iván Garma	Beehive	Large	West
Jose Iván Garma	Beehive	Large	West
Fidencio Huicab	Beehive	70	West
Fidencio Huicab	Beehive	30	West
Juan Chan	Beehive	30	West
Eusevio Tzum Caamal	Cylindrical	< 7–7	West
Carlos Gonzalez	Square	70	—
Carlos Gonzales	Square (cement block)	20	—
Francisco Keh	Beehive	—	West
Pedro Tzum Ortiz	Beehive (abandoned)	—	West
Pedro Tzum Ortiz	Square brick gas kiln	—	North (kiln indoors)
Luis Huicab	Beehive	15	West

Kiln Sizes

In 1965 it was obvious that kilns came in various sizes, and I wondered how potters described those sizes. So, thinking that the size of a kiln was related to the number of vessels it held, I asked my informant how many pots he placed in the kiln for a single firing episode. He replied that it held 15 large pots, 20 medium-sized pots, and 20 to 30 small pots plus as many figures that he could place inside the large vessels. Another potter described the size of his kiln according to the number of water carrying jars (*cántaros*) that could be placed in it. Still another described size as the amount of money that the kiln's contents would bring. He said that his kiln normally held 150 pesos' worth of figures, but if it was full, then the value of its contents was 250 pesos. Because the same kiln was used to fire various shapes, sizes, and amounts of pottery, however, measuring its size by the amount of pottery it held, or the price that its fired vessels brought, obviously provided no objective basis to compare the sizes of kilns between potters.

TABLE 7.4. Variability of kiln construction observed in 1965 except as noted in parentheses after the name.

Potter	Pach k'aak' (place for firewood behind kiln furniture)	Chun k'aak' (kiln furniture)	Relative size	Support over door	"iik' (vent)	Comment
Carmelo Chan	?	Yes	Small	Steel rail from railroad or tramway (*tranvía*)		Used only for firing figures
Ramon Xiu	No	No	Small	Steel rail from railroad or tramway (*tranvía*)		Built and used only for firing cooking pottery
Francisco Keh	Yes	Yes	Very large	Stone arch	No	
Jose María Keh	Yes	Broken *cántaros*	Large	Stone arch	Yes	Used by in DaHu (Manuel Martín), who did not own a kiln
Alfredo Tzum Camaal	Yes	Yes	Small-medium	Stone arch	Yes	
Julian Huicab	Yes	Broken *cántaros* and rocks	Medium	Stone arch		Covered with *buano* palms for protection from rain
Cesario Mex (Probably used by DaHu across the street, who formerly made cooking pottery)	No	No	Small	No data	No	Raised 0.5 meter off ground with doorway slanting down to floor of kiln; covered with sheet metal. Kiln must be warmed the day before firing by burning paper and palm fronds.
Ramon Aguilar (1966)	Yes	Rocks				
Lorenzo Pech	Yes		Large	Stone arch		
Justo Uc	Yes	Yes		Stone arch	Yes	Sunken floor 15 cm below ground level

166   THE POTTER'S ENGAGEMENT WITH DRYING AND FIRING

The only way around this problem was to describe the size of the kiln another way. So, later in that first field season, I simply asked potters how they described the size of their kilns, and they responded by saying that they measured it by the number of firewood bundles they need to complete the firing process (table 7.1, 7.3; see Arnold 2008, 302–4). So, it was clear that I previously had missed the way in which potters measured the size of their kilns. I had asked the wrong question based upon my own cultural assumptions before I was immersed in the culture and participated in the practice of firing. Such is the problem with doing ethnography and ethnoarchaeology: getting beyond one's cultural assumptions is probably one of the most difficult aspects of learning about another culture—no matter what the topic.

Parts of the Kiln

The parts of the kiln are elaborately classified with distinct terms for its parts and subparts (figure 7.1) because they relate to the potter's behavior in firing. Its inside is classified according to the location of the fire (*k'aak'*): center (*chuumuk k'aak'*), sides (*tsel k'aak'*), rear (*tan k'aak'*), and around the door (*ti u hol*). The words for the left and right sides reflect the preferred orientation of the door so that the left side is "north" (*shaman*) and the right side is "south" (*nohol*). The sections on either side of the door are also named because the temperatures are cooler there, and wind and rain can enter the kiln through the doorway and damage pottery near it. As a consequence, potters need to pay special attention to the pottery around the door during firing and add fuel there, if necessary.

Around the inside perimeter of the kiln, potters place a row of rocks (called the *chun k'aak'*) about twenty to twenty-five centimeters from the inside wall (figure 7.1).[7] The space between the rocks and the kiln wall is called the *pach k'aak'* (behind the fire), and they must place firewood there first before they load the kiln with pottery.

So, when potters load the kiln, they stack their pottery on the *chun k'aak'* that raises it about fifteen to twenty centimeters above the floor and away from direct contact with the fire in the center and underneath the stack between the *chun k'aak'* and the kiln wall (the *pach k'aak'*). Because the heat of the firewood varies in different parts of the kiln, the Maya names for the subparts reflect potters' concern that they must devote different amounts of attention to the vessels in each section. For example, the *tan k'aak'* is the hottest part of the kiln, whereas both sides of the door (*u tsel u hol*) are its coolest parts. The vessels stacked around the door require special attention at the end of the firing to be sure that they are adequately fired, whereas those stacked in the *tan k'aak'* must be monitored so that they are not overfired and damaged. Using different names for different parts

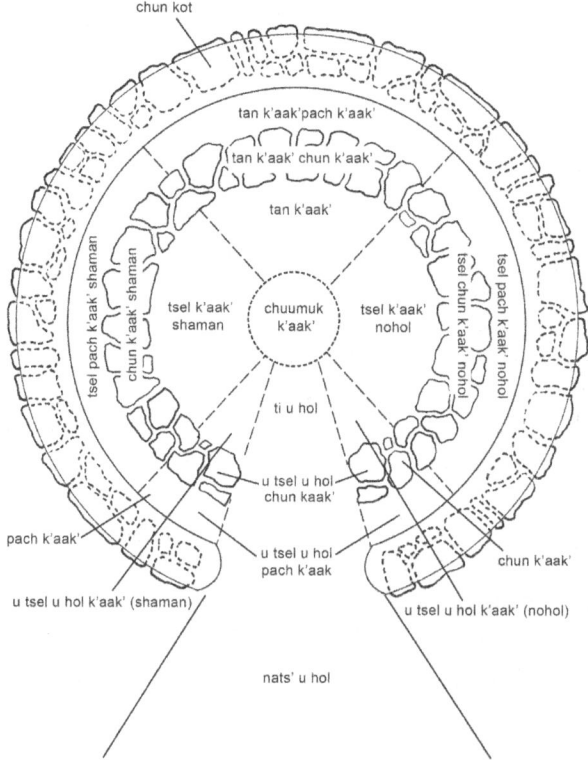

FIGURE 7.1. Diagram of a plan view of the Ticul kiln showing the named parts. Names for the center (*chuumuk k'aak',* literally "center fire"), side (*tsel*), rear (*tan k'aak'*), and sides of the door *(hol)* require special attention during firing. The sides (*tsel*) refer to the cardinal directions (*shaman* "north" and *nohol* "south") and reinforce the importance of a west-facing kiln. The rear part of the kiln (*tan k'aak'*) is the hottest, and potters must take care that this portion not get too hot. The parts of the fire toward the door (*ti u hol*), on either side of that area (*u tsel u hol k'aak'*), and the *pach k'aak'* near the door (*u tsel u hol pach k'aak'*) require extra care because they are the coolest parts of the kiln. The part outside of the kiln near its door (*nats' u hol*) is where the potter adds the fuel to the kiln. Early in the process he crouches to add fuel near the door, but near the end of the process, he may be as much as two meters from the door, but still in this same area. (These terms are transcribed as those that were originally elicited from a potter using a diagram of a kiln. The particle *u* is a grammatical particle often preceding a noun and may be translated as "its" or "the" depending on its context. It may also reveal the parts of the same noun phrase that go together: the word following the first *u* modifies those that follow the second *u*.) (Drawing by Michelle Arnold Paine.)

of the kiln thus aids in providing feedback for the potter, but these names are especially important for instructing others about how to fire and to solve problems that occur during the firing process.

PREPARING FOR FIRING

In addition to the parts of the horizontal section of the kiln, potters also had names for the vertical section of the kiln. The names for the parts in the vertical section, however, did not reveal much about the firing process and were purely descriptive. My informant, for example, referred to parts such as the "wall inside the kiln" (*u paakiil uichil le koto'*), the "high part of the wall of the kiln" (*u paakilil u yook'ol kot*), the "ceiling of the inside of the kiln" (*ka'anil ichil kot*), the "base of the kiln" (*chun kot*), and the "middle of the kiln" (*tan chuumuk le koto'*), as well as the vent (*'iik' kot*) and its cover (*u maak 'iik' kot*).

Preparation for firing involves five principal kinds of activities that are generally sequential but overlap with one another. Some of these activities (such as drying) are largely passive, do not require the potter's constant attention and engagement, and can cooccur with other activities, such as sorting and splitting firewood. Other activities required the potter's full attention.

DRYING POTTERY

After vessels are formed, they must be dried before firing. Drying is a critical step in pottery production so that the physically held water in the clay evaporates from the object (Arnold 1985, 61–98; Rice 1987, 63; 2015, 89–92; Shepard 1965, 72–74). The location and the amount of time necessary to dry the vessels completely are critical to maintaining the integrity of the shape of the newly formed pots (see Arnold 1985, 61–97). Vessels drying inside the house also can be damaged by careless adults, playing children, domestic animals, and ordinary household activities. During the rainy and hurricane season, violent storms can destroy houses, penetrate leaky roofs, and damage drying pottery (Arnold 2015a, 250–73).

Although vessels may dry inside a structure for a week or more after they are formed, they are always placed in the sun on the day of firing because they will crack during slipping and firing if they have not dried sufficiently. A warm sunny day is preferred, but in practice the potter often is satisfied with even a small amount of sunshine to prepare for firing.

Drying vessels outside in the sun on the day of firing still brings risks, however, and requires vigilance. Unfired vessels are very fragile and must be moved with care. Vessels placed outside must be moved back inside again when it rains and are susceptible to breakage because lifting them and setting them down may damage them. Since children often move the vessels outside, they may damage them because of inexperience and lack of care (Arnold 2015a, 257–59). Placing vessels in the sun may result in drying unevenly, and potters must monitor and turn them frequently so that they will not shrink unevenly and then crack as they dry. Feedback from weather in the form of sunshine and lack of rainfall thus is critical for the successful engagement of the prefiring preparations.

SLIPPING

Decoration of pottery vessels varies greatly across the world and is affected more by cultural imprint than any other part of the pottery-making process. Even so, the potters' indigenous knowledge of decoration involves feedback that comes from the engagement with the material agency of this part of the process as well.

Once a potter has chosen a decorative technique, however, further options are more limited. In Ticul, decoration on traditional vessels largely consists of slipping after the vessels have dried completely. Slips are placed on all objects except coin banks and vessels used on the fire,[8] and help seal the pores on the outside of the vessel, inhibiting the porosity of the vessel walls (Rice 1987, 231; 2015, 164, 418–19; Shepard 1965, 191). Slips should adhere to the body and have the same coefficient of expansion as the body and harden within the same temperature range, as they appear to do in Ticul.

In Ticul these requirements are met by using two kinds of materials for slipping (figure 7.2; see also Thompson 1958, 91–94, 116, 122, 124–28). One consists of red earth (called *k'an kab*; see chapter 4) and water, and fires to a dark rust color. The second kind of slip (called *sak kaab*) consists of body clay (*k'at*), shavings of hand soap, and water, and fires to a reddish-tan color. Besides its use as a binder for the clay slip, adding soap (sodium stearate) may also help seal the exterior from calcination of the calcium carbonates in the paste by lowering the flux temperature, just as sodium chloride does in the paste (Rye 1976; see also chapter 4 in this volume). This explanation, however, has yet to be tested experimentally.

Both slips are mixed with water, and potters use only the fine-grained portion suspended in water. The courser clay particles and any rocks present in the clay fall to the bottom of the vessel that contains the slip (see Shepard 1965, 68). Usually, potters cover the entire vessel with only one kind of slip, but occasionally they will use two different slips on the same vessel, placing each in different zones (e.g., *apastes* and *tinajas*). If one coat of a slip is insufficient to cover a vessel, it is slipped again; the red slip may require up to three coats in order to ensure adequate coverage.

FIGURE 7.2. Slipping a water storage vessel (*tinaja*) before firing in 1966. This image shows other *tinajas*, water storage/maize soaking vessels (*apaste*; *kat* in Yucatec Maya), and water-carrying jars (*cántaros*; *p'uul* in Yucatec Maya) in front of and to the potter's left (see chapter 6). Mold-made figurines (*far right*) are not slipped, but after firing, they are sanded and painted with a glossy oil-based paint. (See figures 6.3 and 6.4 for additional images of slipping pottery prior to firing.)

Final Drying

After the potter slips the vessels, they are placed in the sun again to dry before being loaded into the kiln. Potters say that slipped pottery must be "warmed" before firing.

When identical shapes from more than one potter are fired together, and the rim form is not distinctive enough to identify the wares of a potter (see chapter 6), each potter makes a unique mark on the underside to identify the maker of the vessel. In October 1984, for example, an informant's kiln included food bowls (*cajetes*) from two households. Those from one household were marked with a white dot (made of *sak lu'um*) on the underside of their vessels, whereas those from the other household (the father's sister next door) were marked with a red dot (made of *k'an kab*). Such maker's marks are used in some parts of highland Peru where they differentiate vessels when multiple potters fire their pottery together (Donnan 1971, see also Arnold 1972c).

Fuel Preparation

Usually, potters obtain their firewood well before the day that they fire their pottery. In the late 1960s they purchased it from local *milperos*, often from those who came to the potter's house to sell it, or they solicited it from neighbors who cultivated a swidden plot. This pattern changed, however, during the following twenty years as the practice of shifting agriculture decreased, and the number of production units increased. During this period, entrepreneurs in surrounding towns hired local *milperos* to cut and bundle firewood and brought it to Ticul in trucks to sell to potters (Arnold 2008, 282–84).

Firewood does not just consist of a few types, but rather many different types that have diverse burning characteristics (table 7.5). Knowledge of these characteristics enables potters to manipulate the firing process in order to produce the desired effect during each stage and use their firewood more efficiently. Potters also recognize the equivalency of the burning characteristics of the different types (table 7.6).

Detailed knowledge of firewood characteristics largely resided among older potters who were formerly *milperos*. Selecting a portion of the forest for a field and cutting down the trees for their cornfields gave them intimate familiarity with different kinds of wood. Cutting it into lengths for transport to their house provided familiarity with the distinctive characteristics of the wood from each type of tree. *Katsim*, for example, has thorns with white wood that has a little red in the center, whereas *chukum* has thorns on its bark and wood that is red in the center. Wood from *chon lok'* is heavy compared to other types.[9]

This same engagement with the trees, the wood, and its burning characteristics also occurred among *milperos* in the jungles of Quintana Roo, east of Ticul (table 7.7; Sánchez González 1993). Although their knowledge was not as extensive as that of the potters described here, the *milperos* in Quintana Roo also knew the forest. They used Maya names for twenty different kinds of trees and knew the burning characteristics of the wood, the amount of ash that each type produces, and the usefulness of each for cooking, for building houses, and for heating rocks to produce lime (Sánchez González 1993).

In order to test the Quintana Roo *milperos'* knowledge of the wood quality of each species, Sánchez González (1993) analyzed their burning characteristics in the laboratory using the following criteria: calories produced per gram, the grams per cubic centimeter, and the calories produced per cubic centimeter. These results were then compared to the qualities that the *milperos* themselves assigned to the wood. These data, however, did not always match their perception of wood quality. Generally, those categories of wood with poor burning qualities were validated, but the match of the *milperos'* perception of "good" firewood and the actual etic

TABLE 7.5. The burning characteristics of the varieties of firewood used for firing pottery. Data were produced by frame substitution of the tree name in the Yucatec Maya query: *Bish u yeetel _____ (tree name) _____ ti'a'al pook?* ("How does it (the wood) from _____ (tree name) _____ burn for firing?"). Responses were translated from Yucatec Maya. Columns were originally created from Maya terminology and then collapsed according to meaning. (The following gradations for meaning are given for small amounts: none [*mina'an* or *ma'*]; some [*yan* = "there is"]; a little bit [*um chan p'iit* = "a small bit"]; a little [*um p'iit* = "a little amount"; small amount [*chan* = "small"]; not much [*ma' hach* = "not very"]; very strong [*hach* = "very"]; very very very strong [*hach hach* = "very very"]; much [*hach yan* = "there is very much"/ "excessive").

Tree name	Intensity of fire (*chiich*)	Amount of smoke (*buuts'*)	Other characteristics
kaatsim	Very strong	None	
sak kaatsim	Very strong	None	
boosh kaatsim	Very, very strong	None	
ts'il ts'il che'		None	
sal che'		None	
sutup		None	
p'eres kuch	A little bit	None	
chukum		None	Very average fire (*hach tup'is*)
bakal che'		None	
shkitin che'		A little	
shu'ul	None	None	
k'ana siin	A little bit	None	
shpichi che'	Small amount	A little	
sa' its'al che'		None	Accelerates (*sebuka'antal*) the height of the flame
shpimienta che'		A little	No high flame
choon lok'	None	None	
ts'uts'uk		A little	
(sh)kan purus che'		A little	No high flame
ts'iw che'		Some	
bo' ch'iich'		None	
k'an che'	None	Some	
shapuch		A little	
shchak te'	Small amount		

continued on next page

TABLE 7.5—continued

Tree name	Intensity of fire (chiich)	Amount of smoke (buuts')	Other characteristics
ha'abin		A little	Burns very slowly (shan) with little strength (muuk')
tsalam		Some	No strength (muuk'), and burns slowly (shan)
tak'in che'		Much (ya'ab)	Burns very slowly (hach shan)
chakah		Some	Hinders the fire (tu t'ooch' u k'aak'il)
kiis		Only produces smoke	Hinders the fire
shpomol che'		Excessive	Doesn't burn well and not good for firing
ch'i'i maay		Some	Burns very slowly (ku'uch)
shtu'uha' che'	Small amount	A little	
shpak'aal che'	Small amount	None	
shya'ash ki'ish		A little	Flame not high (sen = "very"), but it is identified as a quality between "good" (ma'alob)' and "very good" (hach ma'alob)
silil		None	Good to very good quality of fire
sak beek		A little	Burns sufficiently as fire naturally does (kuyelel chan beel u k'aak'il)
sina'an che'		A little	Burns sufficiently as fire naturally does
sabak che'		None	
sak naa' che'		None	
chulul che'		None	
k'an chunup		None	
bohon che'		A little	

continued on next page

TABLE 7.5—continued

Tree name	Intensity of fire (chiich)	Amount of smoke (buuts')	Other characteristics
shya' che'		A little	No high flame
shu'che'		A little	No high flame
subin che'		Excessive	No high flame
shyash eek'		A little	No high flame
aak' si' (undried wood of any type)		Much	Slow to kindle and explodes in the kiln (shan u t'a'abal yeetel kuwaak'al)
shku' ch'el che'	Not very much	A little	

characteristics of burning were inconsistent. As with potters' perception of the burning characteristics of wood in Ticul, the differences between the perceived qualities of firewood for the Quintana Roo *milperos* and the actual etic burning characteristics determined by laboratory testing suggest that the perceptions of the Quintana Roo *milperos* probably involved a wider range of burning characteristics than were tested in the laboratory, such as height of the flame, the amount of smoke produced, and the speed of burning, just as they do in Ticul. Such indigenous knowledge is difficult to evaluate and validate experimentally, but it does indicate how deeply native peoples engage the details of their raw materials and rely upon feedback from their use to create, maintain, and revise their indigenous knowledge.

The indigenous knowledge of at least some Ticul potters was much greater than that of the *milperos* of Quintana Roo. When I elicited the data on firewood in 1965, my thirty-nine-year-old informant knew many types of firewood, but he asked his father to fill in the details. Together, they recognized forty-seven different types and knew the burning characteristics of each (table 7.5). Another potter, my informant's sister's husband, had learned the craft from his mother and knew only fourteen types of wood even after being asked to name the types of wood and how they were used on two separate locations. By 1984, however, another potter, my informant's cousin, only recognized seven types of wood. More than twenty years younger, he did not learn pottery making from his father but from his mother. Since women do not practice shifting agriculture, this man had not spent a sufficient amount of time in the forest to learn the types of wood from a potter who cultivated a milpa field and, as a result, did not know the relationship of the types of wood, their zone/s of origin, and their firing characteristics. When another younger cousin was asked to identify the different types of wood for firing, he replied that he only separated out

TABLE 7.6. Equivalent choices of firewood that have similar characteristics according to potters. These types of trees were provided in response to the frame: *Ba'ash che'il igual yeetel ulaak' che'?* "What type of wood is equal to another type of wood (for firing)?"

Type of tree for firewood	Equivalent firewood	Type of tree for firewood	Equivalent firewood
shyash eek'	shu'che'	chak te'	kan purus che'
ha'abin	subin/tsalam	ts'ilts'il che'	sa' its'al che'
tak'in che'	shpomol che	bakal che'	kaatsim
shya'che'	sak beek	bo' chiich'	chukum
ch'i'i maay	bohon	shkitin che'	ts'iw che'
sabak che'	k'an chunup	shya'ash ki'ish	shpak'aal che'
sak naa' che'	chulul	k'ana siin	shu'ul
shtu'uha' che'	sina'an che'	choon lok'	sak beek/siliil
chakah	kiis	shpichi' (che')	shpimienta che'

TABLE 7.7. The burning values for the firewood from different types of trees (with their Maya names) that were common to potters in Ticul and *milperos* in Quintana Roo and their perceived quality. The table also shows the calories available per gram as well as the density of the firewood in grams per cubic centimeter (Sánchez González 1993, 56, 57, 61, 63). Trees are listed in approximate order of their quality for firing from bad to good according to Ticul potters.

Maya name	Botanical name	Cal/ cubic cm	Quality for milperos (Quintana Roo)	Quality for potters (Ticul)	Cal/g	G/ cubic cm
chakah	Bursera simaruba	1195.5	Bad	Hinders the fire	3967.3	.30
shu'ul	Jatropha gaumeri	1494.1	Bad	No evaluation	3988.5	.38
shpomolol che'	Jatropha gaumeri	1494.1	Bad	Doesn't burn well; not good for firing	3988.5	.38
ts'ilts'il che	Hampea trilobata	1647.6	Good	No data	4079.7	.40
tsalam	Lysiloma Latisiliquum	2098.9	Very good	No strength; burns slowly	4047.2	.52
chukum	Pithecellobium albicans	2238.8	Good	Average fire	4298.8	.52
shkitin che'	Caesalpinia gaumeri	2319.9	Very good	No data	4074.2	.56

continued on next page

TABLE 7.7—continued

Maya name	Botanical name	Cal/ cubic cm	Quality for milperos (Quintana Roo)	Quality for potters (Ticul)	Cal/g	G/ cubic cm
chakah	Caesalpinia gaumeri	2319.9	Very good	Hinders the fire	4074.2	.56
ts'ilts'il che'	Gymnopodium floribundum	2458.3	Very good	No data	3985.9	.59
k'anasin	Piscidia piscipula	2709.3	Very good	A little	3498.5	.77
ha'abin	Piscidia piscipula	2709.3	Very good	Burns slowly	3498.5	.77
sa'itsa	Neomillspaughia emarginata	3122.8	Very good	Accelerates height of the flame	4383.5	.69
sa'itsa	Hampea trilobata	3122.8	Very good	Accelerates height of the flame	4079.7	.40
silil	Diospyros cuneata	3133.7	Good	Good to very good	4093.1	.77
sak kaatsim	Mimosa bahamensis	3367.5	Very good	Very strong	4337.3	.78
sutup	Helicteres baruensis	3756.9	Good	No data	4608.6	.82
bosh kaatsim	Acacia gaumeri	3840.9	Very good	Very very strong	4399.7	.87

Note: The botanical tree names listed here may not necessarily refer to the same trees that exist around Ticul because the tropical forest of Quintana Roo is very different from the forest around Ticul. As mentioned in the text, common names may not have a one-to-one correspondence to unique species, but may both underdifferentiate and overdifferentiate the actual species involved. Further, it is unknown whether the Maya share a common definition of names of common trees, especially when they live in such diverse areas. Nevertheless, the broad correspondence between the burning qualities of the common names of the trees named here with those in table 7.5 suggest some broad correspondence in definition. Given the link between Maya common names and botanical names in the botanical literature in table 3.3 suggests that the definition of at least some trees are widely shared throughout Yucatán.

the large and undried pieces of firewood for the first stage of firing and burned the split, smaller, and dried pieces later in the process. He had no specialized knowledge of the different types of firewood beyond these simple distinctions. This knowledge contrasts with another informant, my informant's wife's brother, who in 1965 knew nothing of pottery making but came up with fourteen types of wood because he had been a *milpero*, but without much nuance of the characteristics of the wood or how it was used in firing.

Selecting Wood for Firing

Just as the potter selects and engages the raw materials for forming pottery, and mixes the paste based upon the feedback from their physical characteristics, so he engages the characteristics of the wood before he actually places it in the kiln. Because the potter obtains the firewood in bundles and cannot see its overall quality, he doesn't always know the kinds of wood that he has purchased. Splitting the firewood enables him to assess its quality, providing visual and tactile information necessary to sort it into appropriate types for the different stages of the process. Splitting wood also helps it to catch fire and burn more quickly.

Ideally, potters' choices of firewood involves two major criteria: wood that has dried completely and the types of wood whose burning characteristics match the effects desired during each stage of the firing process. Because potters should not use undried wood, wood that burns with a low flame, produces a lot of smoke, or burns slowly for the final stage of the process, they use these kinds of wood for the initial stage of the firing, though they may also mix it with wood that burns very quickly (table 7.5, 7.6). Burning undried wood for this initial stage is acceptable, but using it for the latter stages of the process can result in grave consequences both for firing success and the amount of wood necessary to complete it properly. If potters discover that their firewood has not dried sufficiently, however, it may be too late to interrupt or postpone the process because they may need the financial returns from selling their vessels. In such cases they may try to buy dry wood from a neighboring potter.

Because the area behind the rocks around the interior perimeter of the kiln (called the *pach k'aak'*) is inaccessible once the potter loads the kiln, he allocates wood there first. Because he wants a strong, hot, quick-burning flame in this location with no smoke, he only uses split pieces of high-quality wood there that has these characteristics (tables 7.5, 7.6, 7.8).[10]

The engagement of the potter with the final stage of firing (the *ts'ooksa'al*), however, requires particular attention to firewood because the central focus of the potters' choices is to remove the black soot from the pottery acquired during the warming process. If he burns the improper kind of firewood, he may not be able to remove the soot from the pottery as quickly and may prolong firing. To avoid this problem, the potter sets aside a dry wood that burns with a high, rapid, and smokeless flame (such as *kaatsim*) to use for the final stage of the process.

Loading the Kiln

Once the potter fills the *pach k'aak'* with split firewood, he loads the kiln with pottery. Stacking must be done with care so that all parts of the vessels will be completely

TABLE 7.8. The ideal type of firewood used for each part of the firing process as elicited using the frame *Ba'ash paarte ti pook kutooka'al* _____ (tree name) ____? ("What part of firing do you burn _____ [tree name] ____?"). Some variation exists among informants for the kinds of wood used for the warming of the process. Qualities of each type were translated from the Yucatec Maya terms ("very good" = *hach ma'alob*, "good" = *ma'alob*, "small amount" = *u chan p'iit ma'alobil*, "bad" = *ma' pahtal*).

Tree name	Warming of kiln (chokokinta'al)	When the kiln is "hot" (hoopol)	After the pach k'aak' bursts into flame (ts'o'ook u hoopol pook)	Fire in the door of the kiln (hook'ol k'aak')	Attending to the sides of the door of the kiln (tanalta'al u hol pook)	Wood behind pots (pach k'aak')
kaatsim	Bad	Good	Very good	Very good	Very good	Very good
sak kaatsim	Bad	Good	Very good	Very good	Very good	Very good
boosh kaatsim	Bad	Good	Very good	Very good	Very good	Very good
ts'il ts'il che'	Bad	Very good	Very good	Good	Good	Good
sal che'	Small amount	Small amount	Good	Good	Small amount	Small amount
sutup	Small amount / bad	Very good	Good	Very good	Good	Good
peres kuch	Small amount / bad	Very good	Very good	Very good	Good	Very good
chukum	Bad	Good	Very good	Very good	Very good	Very good
bakal che'	Small amount	Very good	Very good	Very good	Good	Good
shkitin che'	Very good	Very good	Good	Good	Bad	Bad
shu'ul	Good / small amount	Very good	Small amount	Good	Small amount	Small amount
k'ana siin	Very good / small amount	Very good	Good	Good	Bad	Bad

continued on next page

TABLE 7.8—continued

Tree name	Warming of kiln (chokokinta'al)	When the kiln is "hot" (hoopol)	After the pach k'aak' bursts into flame (ts'oook u hoopol pook)	Fire in the door of the kiln (hook'ol k'aak')	Attending to the sides of the door of the kiln (tanaltaʼal u hol pook)	Wood behind pots (pach k'aak')
shpichi che'	Good	Very good	Small amount	Good	Bad	Bad
sa'its'al che'	Good / small amount	Good	Good	Very good	Small amount	No data
shpimienta che'	Very good / small amount	Small amount	Small amount	Small amount	Bad	Bad
choon lok'	Bad	Small amount	Very good	Good	Good	Small amount
ts'uts'uk	Very good / good	Small amount	Small amount	Small amount	Bad	Bad
kan purus che'	Good / small amount	Good	Good	Good	Good	Bad
ts'iw che'	Good	Small amount	Small amount	Small amount	Bad	Bad
bo' ch'iich'	Small amount / bad	Very good	Very good	Good	Good	Small amount
k'an che'	Very good / good	Small amount	Small amount	Small amount	Bad	Bad
shapuch	Good / small amount	Small amount	Small amount	Good	Bad	Bad
shchak te'	Very good / small amount	Small amount	Small amount	Small amount	Bad	Bad
ha'ahin	Very good	Bad	Bad	Bad	Bad	Bad
tsalam	Very good	Bad	Bad	Bad	Bad	Bad

continued on next page

TABLE 7.8—continued

Tree name	Warming of kiln (chokokintaal)	When the kiln is "hot" (hoopol)	After the pach k'aak' bursts into flame (ts'óook u hoopol pook)	Fire in the door of the kiln (hook'ol k'aak')	Attending to the sides of the door of the kiln (tanaltaal u hol pook)	Wood behind pots (pach k'aak')
tak'in che'	Very good	Bad	Bad	Bad	Bad	Bad
chakah	Very good	Bad	Bad	Bad	Bad	Bad
kiis	Very good	Bad	Bad	Bad	Bad	Bad
shpomol che'	Very good	Bad	Bad	Bad	Bad	Bad
ch'i'i maay	Small amount	Bad	Small amount	Small amount	Bad	Bad
shu'uha' che'	Good	Small amount	Small amount	Small amount	Bad	Bad
shpakáal che'	Good	Small amount	Small amount	Small amount	Bad	Bad
shya'ashb ki'ish	Good	Small amount	Good	Small amount	Small amount	Bad
silil	Bad	Very good	Very good	Very good	Good	Good
sak beek	Small amount	Very good	Good	Good	Small amount	Small amount
sinaán che'	Good	Small amount	Small amount	Small amount	Bad	Bad
sabak che'	Small amount	Very good	Very good	Very good	Small amount	Bad
sak naa' che'	Bad	Good	Very good	Very good	Small amount	Good
chulul che'	Small amount	Good	Very good	Very good	Small amount	Small amount
kán chunup	Bad	Good	Small amount	Small amount	Small amount	Small amount
bohom che'	Good	Small amount	Small amount	Bad	Bad	Bad

FIGURE 7.3. Loading a kiln with water storage jars (*tinajas*, left and right of the potter), water-carrying jars (*cántaros*, behind the potter), water storage/maize-soaking vessels (*center bottom*), and figurines (*bottom right*) in 1965. Reusable piles of wasters used for securing the pottery in the kiln are on the far left of the image and on the other side of the door.

fired. Potters thus place the vessels with their mouths facing downward and toward the center of the kiln. Smaller vessels are placed inside of larger vessels. If vessels are too close to one another and too far away from the fire, they may remain black and will have to be fired again. They also need be securely positioned so that they will not shift so much that the stack of pots will collapse when the chemically held water in the clay is driven off and the vessels shrink.

Loading the kiln usually requires a two-person team (figure 7.3). The potter enters the kiln, stacks the vessels inside, and requests specific vessels from a second person (sometimes a woman or child) outside of it. The second person finds the appropriate vessel, moves it into the door of the kiln, and the potter adds it to the stack inside.

As the potters stack the vessels, they carefully note the contact points between them. If they see that there are many rounded surfaces in contact with each other that would contribute to slippage and the collapse of the stack of pottery when it shrinks during firing, they request a waster from the pile outside the kiln and wedge it into the contact point to secure the vessels (figure 7.4). If a waster is not the proper size, the potters trim it appropriately.

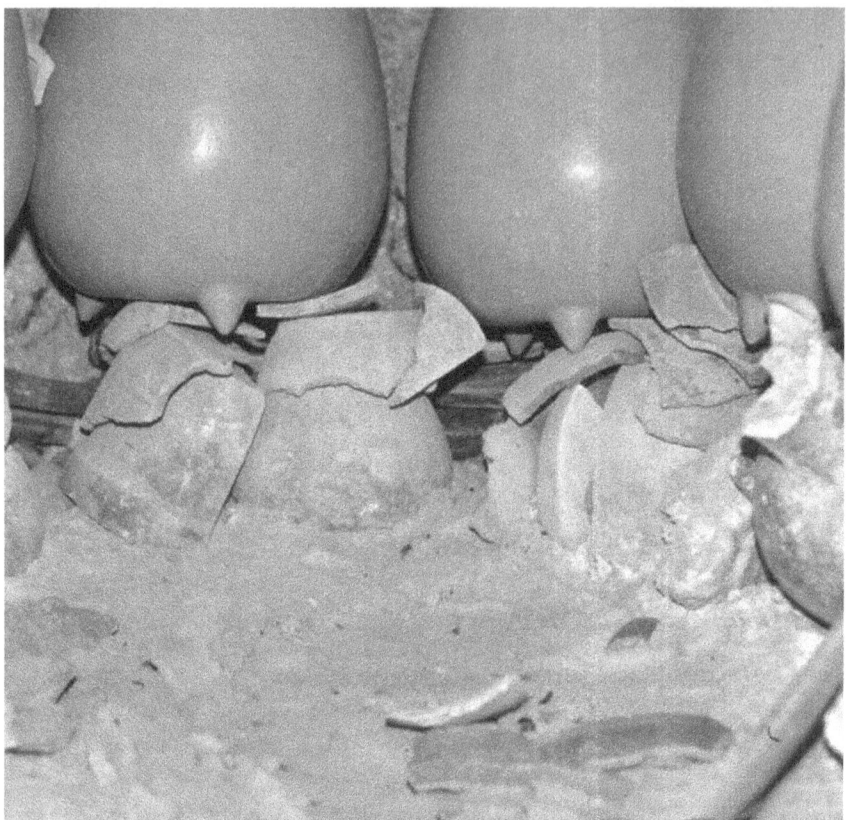

FIGURE 7.4. View inside a kiln showing flower pots resting on a foundation (*chun k'aak'*) of wasters awith waster fragments used to stabilize the pottery to keep it from collapsing. The dark in the center and at the far left center is the firewood in the *pach k'aak'* behind the *chun k'aak'* (1984).

Besides using broken wasters to secure the stacked pottery, wasters of complete vessels, or nearly complete vessels, may be used as saggars to hold small items if larger vessels cannot accommodate all of the smaller vessels. In any case, the amount and kind of wasters used varies with the shapes of the pottery being fired. Active kilns thus usually have a pile of wasters next to them, whereas abandoned kilns have none for reasons that are unknown. Wasters that are too small to use as wedges to secure the pottery are discarded in the yard and ultimately end up covering the potter's house lot. Ultimately, they may be gathered up and dumped in abandoned *sah kab* mines in the house lot, thrown in the rear of the lot, pushed off to the side of the heavily used area of the lot, or used to fill potholes in an adjacent street. When production units developed into workshops and their owners acquired trucks, they took their unusable waster fragments, charcoal, and ashes from firing to the sources of temper (e.g., Yo' Sah Kab) and *k'an kab* and dumped them there before they loaded up these raw materials to return to Ticul (figure 3.9).

FIRING

According to ceramic technologist Owen Rye, firing is divided into six stages: (1) water smoking, (2) low-temperature decomposition, (3) clay-mineral decomposition and sintering, (4) organic combustion, (5) vitrification, and (6) cooling (Rye 1981, 105–16). These stages represent a fixed sequence of what happens to pottery during firing. They also might be called objective and etic stages of firing. Although the firing process universally goes through these stages, the Maya potter classifies them differently, using different etic criteria based on feedback coming from the firing process. He does not recognize these stages per se.

Fundamental to the successful completion of firing is a relatively fixed behavioral sequence (the *chaîne opératoire*), but with a number of choices possible depending on the visual (and sometimes aural and tactile) feedback that the potter receives from the process. Although the duration of the stages and substages of this engagement vary, potters divide firing into two major stages: the warming stage (*chokokinta'al*) and the termination stage (*ts'ooksa'al*). The transition from one stage to the other depends upon the feedback that the potter receives from the fire in the kiln.

The Warming Stage (*chokokinta'al*)

The goal of the warming stage is to keep the fire burning and gradually increase the amount of heat until the kiln is "hot." To begin, the potter enters the kiln and crosses a few pieces of firewood in its center. After adding something that is easily combustible (such as grass, paper, cardboard, tar-impregnated roofing, or gasoline) to the wood, he ignites it with a match or a piece of burning charcoal from the hearth (*nah che'*). Then, he leaves the inside of the kiln and watches the fire to be sure that the wood catches fire.

Once the wood is ignited, the potter allows it to burn until the flames have diminished. This point provides visual feedback for the potter to add more wood, and he does so evenly, first from one side of the door and then from the other so that it is crossed on the fire and will burn easily (figure 7.5). Each time the potter adds firewood, he throws slightly more on the fire than he did previously and then

FIGURE 7.5. Potter throwing wood into the kiln at the very beginning of the firing process (the warming stage) in 1965. The potter can get close to the entrance to the kiln in this stage, because the kiln is not very hot. Excess kiln wasters on the right side of the door were used to secure the pottery inside the kiln and keep the stack from collapsing when the vessels shrink during firing.

waits until the flames diminish before he adds fuel again. Over time, this repeated behavior increases the height of the flame and gradually heats up the kiln.

Virtually any kind of wood can be used during the warming stage (table 7.8) without extending firing time, but potters normally use wood that is undried, burns slowly, or burns with a low and/or smoky flame that they should not use in the final stage. During the period between each addition of fuel, the potter continues to sort the firewood, setting aside the high-quality wood with excellent burning qualities to be split for the end of the process.

During the warming stage the pottery begins to blacken (*u kahal u booshtal*), and this stage ends when the pottery is completely black (*u la u booshtal*; figure 7.6a–7.6b). At this point the potter must engage the fire by throwing wood evenly in the center of the kiln (*yan u tanalt'a'al k'aak' ti*). Then, the potter waits until the wood placed underneath the pottery around the interior perimeter of the kiln (the *pach k'aak'*) spontaneously bursts into flame (*kucha'abal yeleh pach k'aak'*). The kiln is "hot" at this point, and it marks the end of the warming stage of the process.

 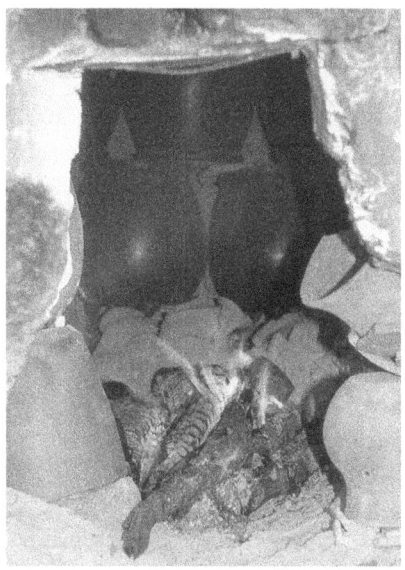

FIGURE 7.6A. Inside of a kiln in 1988 showing the pottery beginning to blacken in the early part of the warming stage (*chokokinta'al*).

FIGURE 7.6B. Inside of the kiln showing the blackening pottery (*u la u boshtal*) at the end of the warming stage of firing (*chokokinta'al*). At this point, the fire underneath the pottery around the internal perimeter of the kiln (*pach k'aak'*) should burst into flame, indicating the end of the warming process (1984).

The spontaneous combustion of the *pach k'aak'* provides critical visual feedback for the potter. Potters call it the *hoopol* and regard it as the significant turning point of the firing process; it is the "point of no return." If it begins to rain and the kiln has not yet reached the *hoopol* event when the *pach k'aak'* bursts into flame, they are able to abandon firing and start the process again another day. If the process has already reached this point and it begins to rain, potters cannot postpone firing because rain will cool the kiln prematurely and will affect firing success adversely. If they *must* continue firing in the rain,[11] they use an additional amount of wood to keep the fire hot and finish the process. This increase in fuel may range from 10 percent to more than 100 percent of the normal amount of wood required. As a consequence, firing in the rain increases firing costs and risk of loss, and extends the amount of time necessary to complete the process.

This stage of the firing appears to correspond to two of Rye's stages: the water smoking stage and low temperature decomposition (Rye 1981, 105–6). During these stages the pottery is heated gradually to drive off the remainder of the physically held water between the clay layers. Much of this water has already been removed by air drying, but should pottery be heated too quickly during this stage, the physically held water remaining in the pottery will form steam and break the vessels. The clay mineral smectite also begins to lose some of the water that is loosely bonded in the mineral structure during this stage. The Ticul potter, however, only knows that pottery must be heated slowly so that it will not break.

The Final Stage (*ts'ooksa'al*)

The final stage of firing removes the black soot from the vessels and heats them until they glow red. Potters divide this stage into two substages. Each substage is made up of subparts based on the visual feedback from the process, and the number of these subparts is determined by the potter's response to the overall sensory feedback coming from the kiln.

During each of these two substages, the potter uses wood that is dry and burns rapidly with a high, smokeless flame (e.g., *chukum* and *katsim*; see table 7.5, 7.8) in order to remove the black soot from the pottery. So, in order to achieve the best effect and conserve fuel, potters reserve wood with these burning qualities for this final stage of the process. Burning undried wood, or wood that burns slowly, or with a smoky flame is avoided in this stage, if at all possible.

After the *pach k'aak'* bursts into flame, the potter allows the fire to burn down to the embers (*kucha'abal u habah k'aak' ti*), and he levels them *(kuha'ache'ta'a)* using a long pole (figure 7.7). Then, he throws (*ku pu'ulu*) one bundle of firewood into the center of the kiln piece by piece and waits until the flames subside. When only glowing embers remain, he levels them again. He repeats this sequence of behaviors five times, increasing the number of firewood bundles thrown into the kiln each time by one. After the fifth repetition of the cycle, and the wood has burned down to the embers, the potter pulls them toward the door of the kiln with a scraper attached to a long pole (*ku kola'a u chuuki'*) and spreads out the remainder inside the kiln (*ha'ache'ta'a*).

At this point, the second substage of the final stage of firing begins. The flames from the kiln get so hot that one cannot stand within two meters of its door, and this substage is referred to as "fire in the door of the kiln" (*hok'ol k'aak'*, figure 7.8). With this visual and tactile feedback, the potter engages the process using a set of behaviors that is repeated at least two times.

The first part of each repeated cycle consists of throwing one bundle of firewood piece by piece into the interior of the kiln, increasing the amount by one bundle with each cycle. Because the heat of the fire is so intense at this stage, the potter

FIGURE 7.7. Potter leveling out the embers (*ha'ache'ta'a*) after the kiln is hot (the *hoopol*), the wood on the sides (*pach k'aak'*) has spontaneously burst into flames, and the fire in the center of the kiln has burned down to embers (1966).

must get close enough to throw the wood into the kiln but not so close to endanger him. Being so far away from the door affects the accuracy of the destination of the thrown wood. If he is careless, or throws too hard using his entire arm, the wood may hit the pots with a "thud" on the other side of the fire, and this auditory feedback means that he must modify the force of his throw so as not to hit the pottery and break it. To forestall this problem, the potter has developed a unique motor habit pattern that propels firewood into the kiln but with a lesser chance of damaging the pottery on the far side of the fire. Rather than extending his entire arm to throw the wood, he uses only his forearm with a wrist snap to position it precisely in the center of the kiln (see chapter 1).

The second part of each cycle of this substage involves attending to the pottery on the sides of the door of the kiln. Because the sides of the door are not as hot as parts deeper inside the kiln, the potter must pay special attention to the pots there (*tanalta'al u ts'el u hol kot*) and throw firewood into the *pach k'aak'* on either side of the door (*u pu'ulu che' tu pach k'aak' tu ts'el u hol kot*, figure 7.9), moving it

188 THE POTTER'S ENGAGEMENT WITH DRYING AND FIRING

FIGURE 7.8. Potter throwing split wood into the kiln in 1966 during the early part of the last half of the final substage of firing (*ts'o'oksa'al*) called "fire in the door of the kiln" (*hok'ol k'aak'*). At this stage the potters use split firewood that is quick burning and remain some distance from the door as they throw the wood into the kiln to avoid the heat of the fire. Notice that the throwing does not involve the entire length of the extended arm, but only the forearm using a wrist snap that is not visible here. The covering of palm fronds and corrugated tar-impregnated cardboard protects the kiln from rain.

into position behind the pots using a pole (*u tul ch'in ta'a si' tu ts'el u hol kot*, figure 7.10–7.11).

At the end of the second of these cycles, the potter levels out the embers using a pole and looks into the kiln. If the pottery glows red, this visual feedback indicates that the firing process is complete (*kuho' sa'a*). If not, he must add more wood, and firing must continue by repeating the cycle of adding firewood, spreading out the embers (figure 7.12), and checking the pots on the sides of the door of the kiln. After each cycle, the potter checks for the red glow of the pots. If present, he ends the process.

Since it is difficult to see the glow during daylight, many potters fire at night so that they can see the red glow more clearly, but nighttime is also cooler because the potter does not have to endure both the heat of the sun and the heat of the kiln. The more experienced the potter, however, the more easily he can assess the glow of fired pottery in daylight.

By looking into the kiln at this time, the potter can also determine if some of the pottery is overfired. If parts of the vessels nearer the fire (such as those in the *tan k'aak'*) are dark, and the remainder of them glow red, the dark vessels are overfired.

FIGURE 7.9. Throwing split wood into the area behind the pots (the *pach k'aak'*) on either side of the door during the "fire in the door of the kiln" phase (*hok'ol k'aak'*) of firing (1966).

If the red glow of the pots indicates that firing is finished, the potter wants to avoid overfiring his vessels. So, if there are glowing embers on the floor of the kiln at this time, he moves them to the door of the kiln (*kuho'sa'a* [*wa ya u shoot'o' si' ma'ahabo'*]) with a scraper attached to a long pole, and pulls them out of the doorway to cool the kiln more rapidly (*kolta'a' u chuuki' yola'a sista'a le koto'*). This activity limits the deleterious effect of the excess heat on the pottery that may result in more firing accidents (see table 7.9), and the kiln cools faster.

At this point the potter uncovers the vent (*'iik'*) at the back of the kiln (if there is one) to cool it, and he goes into seclusion to rest. Twenty-four hours later, the kiln is cool enough for someone to enter and remove the pottery.

Failure to engage the firing process properly without being cognizant of what is happening can result in deleterious consequences. Potters must act on the visual feedback from the process in order to decide how to engage the process at any given point and how to solve problems should they arise. This ability to assess feedback from the kiln and act on it appropriately reflects the level of a potter's skill. In August 1984 my informant, Alfredo, began firing and then left his son in charge of the process so that he could bathe and eat. When he returned about an hour and a half later, the fire was almost extinguished; his son had burned undried wood at the end of the process, allowed the fire to get too low, and risked damage to the pottery. In such circumstances he should have kept the flame high

FIGURE 7.10. Moving burning embers close to the door of the kiln in 1966 during the "fire in the door of the kiln" phase (*hok'ol k'aak'*) of firing before pushing them into the area behind the pots at the sides of the door of the kiln (*u tul ch'in ta'a si' tu ts'el u hol kot*).

and the fire hot in order to burn the undried wood. Because of his son's inexperience, the firing process was extended an hour and required at least 10 percent more wood to complete.

This incident also illustrates why so many potters stored a large supply of firewood after the 1960s. With more and more firewood coming from suppliers that brought truckloads of it to Ticul (Arnold 2008, 282–84), the wood was less likely to be adequately dried than it was when potters bought it from *milperos* who only brought it to Ticul a year after it was cleared from the field. Storing firewood assures potters that it will be as dry as possible when they actually need it, and that they will have plenty available should unforeseen consequences occur during the firing process.

VARIATIONS IN THE FIRING PROCESS

The most important variations in firing behavior take place during the final stage of the process. These variations consist of the number of steps in the two final substages of the process and how frequently the embers are leveled. The number of cycles in each substage is not fixed but dependent upon the potter's visual feedback

FIGURE 7.11. Pushing burning embers into the area behind the pots (the *pach k'aak'*) at the sides of the door of the kiln (*u tul ch'in ta'a si' tu ts'el u hol kot*) in 1966 during the "fire in the door of the kiln" phase (*hok'ol k'aak'*) of firing (1966).

from the red glow of the fired pots. At whatever point this occurs, the potter ends the process.

Another variation of firing concerns the way that the kiln is cooled after the completion of the process. Some kilns have a vent (*'iik'*); others do not. Rather than allowing the kiln to cool on its own, some potters may throw water on the burning embers in the kiln in order to remove the pottery more quickly. Others say, however, that if a kiln is consistently cooled in this way, the plaster inside it will crack and shorten the kiln's useful life. Such a practice limits kiln use to 10 to 12 years in contrast to a 30-year use-life if it is cooled without using water and properly maintained (Arnold 2008, 287). Other potters do not remove glowing coals from the kiln after the last stage of the firing process but let the fire burn down to ashes.

FIRING ACCIDENTS

In spite of all of the precautions that potters use to carefully tend the firing process and properly respond to the feedback from it, some vessels end up being damaged.

FIGURE 7.12. Leveling the burning embers in the kiln near the end of the "fire in the door of the kiln" phase (*hok'ol k'aak'*) of firing (1966).

Potters have a nomenclature for such failures and provide explanations for why they occur (table 7.9, figures 7.13–7.16). Some occur because of variation in the strength of the fire, and others result from overfiring. In other cases, poor-quality temper, a lack of homogeneity in the paste (a paste with rocks in it), or lack of sufficient drying before firing are responsible for the accidents.

Explanations of firing accidents provide feedback for the potters' assessment of the entire pottery-making process. If the accidents indicate that the potter has used poor-quality clay and temper, he may change suppliers, or in the case of temper, go to Yo' Sah Kab himself to prepare his own temper (Arnold 2008, 191–215). Because the quality of the temper purchased from specialists has declined since 1965 because of mining specialists who were not potters, one potter in 2008 mined pure *sak lu'um* at Yo' Sah Kab, soaked it, and dried and crushed it to sell to potters to improve the quality of their temper.

TABLE 7.9. Kinds of firing accidents identified by Ticul potters and the appropriate illustrations when available.

Maya term	Figure	Translation/Explanation
bosh ela'an	7.13	Black section with many tiny cracks
bu'ul	7.14	The vessel has broken apart, or broken in half (from *un buh* "portion")
waak'al	7.15	A circular-shaped flake that has popped off the surface, caused by a rock in the paste
k'e	7.16	A portion of the vessel has popped off the surface
man u k'aak'el	—	Literally, "the fire passes, or exceeds"; when the fire is too hot
hon nihil	—	A spot lighter in color than other parts of the vessel; it may dangerously damage a larger jar, but not a smaller one
es k'aak'	—	A vessel that has cracked from the firing process
sak ela'an	—	A light portion (white) of a vessel with tiny cracks
si'ik'il	—	A vessel that has cracked or broken into four or more parts

FIGURE 7.13. Illustration of the *bosh ela'an* type of firing accident in which the vessel has a large black spot with tiny cracks in it (1965).

FIGURE 7.14. Illustration of the *bu'ul* accident in which a vessel has broken apart during firing (1965).

FIGURE 7.15. Illustration of the *waak'al* firing accident in which a circular-shaped flake has popped off the surface that potters say was caused by a rock in the paste (1984).

FIGURE 7.16. Illustration of a *k'e* type of firing accident when a large portion has popped off a vessel (1965).

NOTES

1. The choices used by potters during firing have been noticed by others. Christopher Pool (2000), for example, noticed the different choices that potters made in firing in the Tuxtla Mountains of Mexico.

2. Based upon my survey of Yucatán potters in 1967, 1968, and 1994, except for Ticul and Tepakán, potters in Yucatán (Mama, Akil, Maxcanú) tended to be women. Ruben Reina and Robert Hill (Reina and Hill 1978, 200, table 2) found three communities in Guatemala (San Cristóbal Totonicapán, Santa María Chiquimula, and Rabinal) in which both males and females were potters. Potters in all of the remaining communities they surveyed were females.

3. This summary only superficially explains the gender of potters and needs to be understood in relation to a variety of factors. For a fuller and more complete discussion, see Arnold 1985, 99–108.

4. I know of only one example of a woman mining clay or temper in Ticul. In 1997 an older woman from Chapab was mining temper in an underground mine at the temper mines near there (Arnold 2008, 206). This exception, however, doesn't make clay and temper mining in Ticul any less dangerous, nor any less a male activity. It is likely that the cash from mining temper outweighed household responsibilities, which were probably performed by others.

5. Clay in Chinautla, Guatemala, is also extracted from a deep underground mine (Arnold 1978a, 364–66), and Ruben Reina noted that a miner was killed there during the years that he was studying the community (Reina 1966, 63).

6. The type of rocks used for building a kiln described here contradicts the data presented in table 3.4 for reasons that are unknown. It appears, however, that the emphasis of using *sakel bach* rocks for a kiln might be due to the loss of indigenous knowledge of rock types since 1965. The data in table 3.4 was collected in 1965, whereas the data described here came from 1997.

7. The composition of the *chun k'aak'* changed between 1965 and 1997, as the shapes of the pottery changed. In the late 1960s, water-carrying jars (*cántaros*) and water storage vessels (*tinajas, apastes*) were some of the most frequent vessels produced, and rocks were used for the *chun k'aak'*. The curved surfaces of the vessels fit well in the spaces between the rocks and provided a secure base upon which to stack upon them. With the change to the production of large plant pots (*maseteros*) in the 1980s, however, wasters of complete plant pots (and some *cántaros* and *apastes*) completely replaced the rocks. Plant pots have large open mouths and flat bases so that when turned upside down, they can support a stack of pots of the same shape. Vessels thus could be stacked higher and more securely on a flat surface than on rocks. On occasion, however, unfired plant pots, rather than wasters, were used as supports. In other kilns where small items of pottery were fired, *tranvía* rails from *henequén* haciendas (see Arnold 2008, 157), pieces of iron, or the top of fifty-five-gallon steel drums were used to support the pottery. By 1997, plant pots and other large vessels continued to be used for kiln furniture, but a few potters used cement blocks.

8. A few potters occasionally made water storage and water-carrying vessels in 1984, and those vessels, along with ritual pottery made for the Day of the Dead, still received the same slips as they did in the late 1960s. When production changed to making plant pots, they also received such slips. These same patterns continued in 1988, 1994, and 1997, though potters chose other alternatives for decoration as well.

9. In 1965 I started a line of questioning to elicit the characteristics of each type of firewood with the frame (*Bish u k'aota'al* ____[tree name]____? ["How do you know ____ (tree name)____?"), but I only obtained data on five types of wood. At the end of those responses, I wrote: "Incomplete, but not necessary." In going back over those five responses, and translating them from Maya, most of the data were about the trees, not the wood, and this was probably the reason that I suspended my elicitation. Some (*chukum, kaatsim* [probably *sak kaatsim*], and *boosh kaatsim*) had *ki'ishel* (thorns) identified as small in one case. Another (*bakal che'*) had no thorns but had a white flower that smelled very good. Still another tree (*ts'tsiil che'*) had slivers on its bark and did not have thorns, but had small partially rounded leaves and a flower that smelled very good and attracted bees. Its wood did not have a black center.

10. I have detailed data on what I think was the intersubjectivity of classifications of each type of firewood for each stage of the firing process, and I used codes to characterize that variability (or lack of it). The meaning of those codes (different firing events and different informants), however, was unclear after fifty years, and the meaning of the some of the codes that I used were incomplete. Consequently, I could not condense those data into chart form in any meaningful way beyond what was provided in table 7.8. Nevertheless, the wood qualities elicited with reference to stages of firing in table 7.8 appear to be generally consistent with the more complex chart of incomplete codes, but the structure of the variability (which is not very great) and its meaning are not clear.

11. Sometimes potters must take chances and fire in inclement weather because they need the financial returns from selling their pottery, and the need for such returns outweighed the risk of firing in poor weather.

8

Ticul Pottery as a "Distilled Landscape" / "Taskscape"

How does potters' engagement with the landscape, raw materials, and the production processes relate to archaeology? So far this work shows that this engagement has resulted in an elaborate indigenous knowledge that is not just cognitive but involves complexities of motor habits, feedback, and a working knowledge associated with the choices of critical raw materials (such as clay, temper, and wood) and those made during the actual production process. Besides an example of material engagement theory and its challenge to the notion that the potter merely materializes a mental template, pottery also is a material distillation of the local landscape and condenses, encapsulates, and materializes religious beliefs celebrated in the Day of the Dead rituals.

In his books *Making* and *Perception of the Environment*, Tim Ingold (2013, 2000) argued that perception of the landscape is a critical aspect of artifact production and is embodied within artifacts as a "distilled landscape" or a "taskscape." Following Ingold (2000), Michelaki and her colleagues (Michelaki et al. 2012; Michelaki et al. 2014) analyzed the raw materials collected in a resource area (less than 7 km) around a Neolithic site in Calabria (Italy), compared their analyses to the petrography of the pottery found there, and made test tiles of the clays to determine their suitability for making pottery. They found that some raw materials were used for pottery and others were not, and following Ingold (2000), they argued that pottery from the site consisted of a distilled (or congealed) landscape called a taskscape.

DOI: 10.5876/9781607326564.c008

In many respects, the results of Michelaki and her colleagues (Michelaki et al. 2012; Michelaki et al. 2014) parallel the data presented in this work except that theirs are archaeological, analytical, and experimental, and this work is ethnographic. In their work, as in Ticul, some features of the landscape provide raw materials used to make pottery, whereas other features yield materials that are rejected for that purpose. So, pottery is not a distillation of the entire landscape but only of those features that yield raw materials that possess the most suitable performance characteristics for making pottery. In terms of the landscape, seeing pottery as a taskscape recognizes that pottery does not distill all of those tasks used to engage the landscape, but rather encapsulates only those associated with features that provide the raw materials used to make it.

The reasons why pottery distills a portion of the landscape extend beyond selecting those raw materials that possess the best performance characteristics for making pottery. Rather, the difference between ancient pottery as condensed, congealed, or distilled landscape and its ethnographic context involves senses of place and the religious beliefs and practices associated with those sources that provide constituent raw materials. This added dimension strengthens the notion that pottery is not just a distillation of certain raw materials from particular critical features of the landscape, but it also embodies and encapsulates religious meaning of those sources and a sense of place in the present and probably in the past as well.

The clay and tempers in Ticul came from sources that had a sense of place for the potters. These places were unique locations that also provided unique raw materials superior to those obtained from other locations. The significance of these places was reified by religious meanings. Although these meanings no longer exist for many of these sources, the religious meanings for sources of clay, particularly, and temper (to a lesser extent) still existed in the late 1960s. The meaning of others, however, can be inferred from ethnographic, ethnohistoric, and archaeological data. Nevertheless, they do show that the notion of "pottery as distilled landscape" or "pottery as a taskscape" still has validity in the rich ethnographic data from Ticul and also may be applied to the past as well, reflecting both a sense of place and the religious meaning of the sources and the raw material that comes from them (table 8.1).

THE RELIGIOUS DIMENSIONS OF RAW MATERIALS AND THEIR SOURCES
Clay (Yo' K'at)

Of all of the sources of raw materials, Hacienda Yo' K'at (literally "over clay") possessed the strongest sense of place for potters. Mining clay, however, was relatively unimportant to the principal economic activity of the hacienda during the historic period, even though its managers believed that mining occasionally interfered

TABLE 8.1. The taskscape of the ancient and modern potters of Ticul and their religious association that are materialized into pottery as a distilled landscape used for the rituals for the Day of the Dead. Based upon the comparison of cross-cultural distances to ceramic resources, the modern distances to resources suggest that the ancient location of Ticul potters was likely San Francisco de Ticul, an archaeological site north of the city, and reveal that Ticul was a unique and long-standing community of practice that was reified in its pottery. Ticul pottery thus reflected a taskscape unique among other communities of potters in Yucatán.

Material	hi' (crystalline calcite)	sak kab with sak lu'um	Clay (k'at)	Firewood (si')	Water (ha')
Use	Temper for pottery used for cooking	Temper for pottery not used for cooking	Raw material for making pottery	Firing pottery	For mixing with clay and temper
Landscape source	Cave (*Aktun*)	Temper mines (*Yo' Sah Kab*)	Clay mine (*Yo' K'at*)	Forest (*K'ash*)	Wells (*Che'en*)
Distance from Ticul potters	1 km	4 km	5 km	> 2 km	< 0.1 km
Religious meaning	Gateway to the underworld	Archaeological site with sighting of feathered serpent	St. Peter was its patron saint; *novena* said in his honor each year until 1978	Location of nature spirits, guardians of the forest and fields. Non-Christian rituals always performed here.	*Chaak* was god of rain among contemporary and ancient Maya; inhabited ancient water sources (*cenotes*)
Distance from San Francisco de Ticul	3.5 km	3.5 km	5 km	Varying distances	*Chultuns* (extant there, but distance unknown)

with this activity (see Arnold 2008, 156–59).[1] Nevertheless, the association of clay with a place-name suggested that the clay source on the hacienda was very ancient (Thompson 1958, 66). This supposition was supported by archaeological evidence that indicated that potters were mining clay at Yo' K'at during the Terminal Classic Period (AD 800–1100), when a large sherd-tool was sealed inside a mining tunnel on top of a chunk of mined clay (Arnold and Bohor 1977; see chapter 4).

The clay mined at Yo' K'at was not just any clay, however, but rather a unique, high-quality clay that is found at few places in Yucatán (see chapter 4 in this volume;

see also Arnold 2008, 154–55). The potters' strong sense of place for Yo' K'at, however, was also reinforced and reified through the religious rituals associated with its patron saint, San Pedro. This association dates at least to the late nineteenth century, when the owner, Juaquín Espejo, reportedly brought the images of three saints to the hacienda: San Antonio, San Felipe, and San Pedro. Of these, San Pedro became its patron saint, and each year during late June and early July, nine nights of ritual prayers (a *novena*) were said in his honor.

Consequently, although the potters appeared to get their clay at Yo' K'at because of the strength of tradition (*habitus*), the practical superiority of the clay from there became overlaid with a sense of place and a strong religious meaning. So, the traditional choice of using the Yo' K'at clay to make pottery involved social, religious, and technological dimensions.

HISTORY

The oral history of relationship of potters with the patron saint of Hacienda Yo' K'at underscores the religious significance of the Hacienda's "sense of place" for potters. In the distant past, the rituals honoring San Pedro not only included a *novena* but also a full-fledged fiesta with food, music, and folk dances (*vaquerías*, see Arnold 2015a, xxiv–xxv) along with many other accouterments typical of Yucatecan fiestas. One potter (Agustín Tzum 1903–88; see Arnold 2015a, 63) recalled the first time he witnessed the fiesta about 1910 when he accompanied his father there. A sizable population lived at Yo' K'at at the time, and horse-drawn platforms brought people from Ticul on the Hacienda's tramway (the *tranvía*). At that time the Montes family owned the Hacienda (Arnold 2008, 157), and they provided financial support for a Mass, a *novena*, and a fiesta.[2]

At one point in the 1940s, however, the clay mine at the hacienda yielded only poor-quality clay and rocks (*sishk'at*) and threatened the potters' livelihood. At that time one potter named Emilio Tzum (Arnold 2015a, 81) was acquainted with the hacienda's manager, Humberto Herrera (see Arnold 2008, 158), because Emilio was renting some of the hacienda land as a *rancho* for his cattle. Emilio reportedly expressed his concern to Herrera about the loss of quality clay, and Herrera invited Emilio to pay for one of the nine nights of ritual prayers (*novena*) for the hacienda's patron saint (San Pedro). In doing so, Emilio would be making a promise to the saint and establishing a patron-client type of dyadic contract (Foster 1963, 1979), anticipating that the saint would reciprocate by restoring the quality of the clay. Subsequently, potters dug two new mines nearer the hacienda buildings and discovered good-quality clay. Because of this successful outcome, and to ensure the quality of future clay mined there, potters continued to participate more directly in the adoration of the saint at the hacienda by sponsoring one night of the *novena* there.

About 1953, two potters (Manuel Martín, see Arnold 2015a, 150–51, and Guadalupe Tzum, see Arnold 2015a, 107) wanted to assure a reliable supply of high-quality clay from Yo' K'at by reaffirming Emilio's original promise to San Pedro.[3] So, they approached the manager to ask if they could carry the saint to Ticul for a second *novena* after the one at the hacienda was finished. He consented, and potters began having their own *novena* for the saint in Ticul. Each night a different potter or group of potters paid for its expenses.

By the mid-1960s the fiesta for San Pedro had disappeared at Yo' K'at, and only a *novena* remained. When I witnessed the *novena* in late June 1965, it was a small affair. Potters were only invited for its first night (June 23), and they provided financial support for the *recidora* (the layperson who said the prayers), flowers, candles, and *horchata*[4] for the evening. They met in the "bronze store" of Manuel Martín (1928–90; Arnold 2015a, 150–51) and then walked to the west edge of town where a mule-drawn platform was waiting to take us to Yo' K'at on the rails of the narrow-gauge *tranvía* (Arnold 2008, 68). *Henequén* was grown and processed at the hacienda at the time, and our ride took us through *henequén* fields for the five kilometers to Yo' K'at.

The potters' *novena*s for San Pedro continued through the remainder of the 1960s and part of the 1970s, though the traditions surrounding the saint were declining. In November 1968, potters reported that a *novena* had taken place for San Pedro the previous June. In 1970 they attended the *novena* at Yo' K'at, but it was sponsored by those who mined clay there, rather than by all of the potters. When it ended, Manuel Martín again organized a *novena* in Ticul. Potters gathered at the west edge of town, while others took a truck to Yo' K'at to get the saint. When they returned, the image was carried in a procession from one potter's house to another, and each family was asked to pay for the expenses for one night of the *novena* or contribute what they could. After the saint made the rounds of the potters' households, it was taken to Manuel's bronze store to begin another round of nine nights of prayers for the saint.

When I wanted to return to Ticul in 1984, I deliberately planned to arrive before the day of San Pedro in the Catholic Calendar (June 29) because I wanted to see if the *novena* still existed, and then use it as a qualitative proxy measure for the changes in the craft since 1970. After I arrived, however, I discovered that there was no *novena* in honor of San Pedro that year and there was no attempt by the potters to organize one. Manuel Martín said that 1978 was the last year that it was celebrated, before the hacienda was sold, and the saint disappeared.

In the 1990s a *novena* to honor San Pedro was revitalized, but only by one family. In 1994 one potter reported that Lorenzo Pech (the son-in-law of Emilio Tzum, the potter who had made the original promise to San Pedro in the 1940s) had reestablished it in 1993, apparently in response to the exhaustion of clay at Yo' K'at in late 1991 (see Arnold 2008, 164).[5] This *novena*, however, was restricted to Lorenzo's immediate family and not open to other potters. It reportedly continued in 1997. By this time, however, no clay came from Yo' K'at.

By October 2014 the clay mines at Yo' K'at had been backfilled, and buildings of the hacienda had been remodeled and converted into a boutique hotel (see Hacienda YoKat 2014). The only remnant of its past as a source of clay was its name, meaning "over clay," and a small museum (called the "Museum of Clay," see Museo Casa de Barro 2015) that the owner had created in a structure that formerly housed the machinery for processing *henequén*.

The *novenas* formerly associated with the patron saint of Yo' K'at are paralleled by another religious ceremony that became associated with clay mining. When I visited Lorenzo Pech's clay source near Dzitbalché in Campeche in 1997, I noticed that he had constructed a roofed shelter near it. It seemed unusual to build a permanent shelter with open sides and cement roof supports in such a seemingly remote location. When I asked one of Lorenzo's sons about its purpose, he said that it was a shelter for eating lunch and the location where a Maya ceremony called *huaricol* was performed forty days before Good Friday of each year in order to say "thank you" to the spirits of the forest for the clay extracted on the property.

This ceremony appears to be what Redfield and Villa Rojas (1962, 112–13, 134) called the *u hanli col* ritual in the Maya village of Chan Kom, located southeast of the ruins of Chichén Itzá. It establishes satisfactory relations with the gods of the rain (the *chaacs*), the guardians of the milpa and the village (the *balams*), and the deities of the forest (the *kuilob kaaxob*), ensuring wealth, health, and a good harvest. If it was not performed, sickness would plague the community.

Fear of offending the spirits was also present among other potters in the 1990s, and thus placating them was perhaps another reason why such a ceremony was performed at Lorenzo's clay source. In 1989 Lorenzo's brother-in-law (Miguel Segura, his wife's sister's husband, see Arnold 2015a, 82–84) died suddenly, and when Miguel's son also passed away six years later, Miguel's wife (Lorenzo's wife's sister) suspected that witchcraft was involved, and she consulted a Maya shaman (*hmen*), paying him a large sum of money to provide spiritual protection for her family.

Temper for Cooking Pottery (Aktun Hi')

A second source of raw material with probable ancient religious meaning is a cave called Aktun Hi' located in the hill ridge above the Ticul cemetery. This cave was the source of macrocrystalline calcite (*hi'*) used as a temper for cooking pottery. Again, a place named for the material obtained from it suggests that it was an ancient source of that material just like Hacienda Yo' K'at described above, but its antiquity is also confirmed by archaeological evidence (chapter 4). Pottery tempered with crystalline calcite (*hi'*) is a variety of the Terminal Classic Puuc Unslipped ware (Smith 1971, 145–48) and is found locally at the archaeological site of Yo' Sah Kab (Arnold 2005a). Indeed, potters identify this ware as being tempered with *hi'*. Further, archaeological evidence in Aktun Hi' and other nearby caves revealed that *hi'* mining was associated with Terminal Classic pottery (see chapter 4).

Although caves had no religious meaning to the potters of Ticul in the 1960s and thereafter, caves were sacred to the ancient Maya. They were the gateways to the underworld (King et al. 2012) and frequently were the location of offerings. Further, some had great religious meaning associated with them, such as at Balankanché near Chichén Itzá (Andrews 1970), Oxkintok (near Maxcanú) and Loltun (near Oxkutzcab) in Yucatán, and elsewhere in the Maya area (Demarest 2013, 385–88; Hatt 1953, 18–19; King et al. 2012; Uc González and Canche Manzanero 1996).

Temper for Noncooking Pottery (Yo' Sah Kab)

Yo' Sah Kab (literally "over *sah kab*"), the source of the temper for the noncooking pottery, was a third raw material source with religious significance named for the raw material that came from it. Sources of natural marl (*sah kab* for construction purposes) are widespread around Ticul, and almost any anywhere is literally "over" *sah kab*. Yo' Sah Kab, however, is unique because it was the only source of the critical component of *sah kab* temper called "white earth" (*sak lu'um*) by potters. Up until about 1970, an archaeological site near the mines gave the area around it a special sacred meaning that kept potters and miners from digging around and under it (Arnold 2005a). Once demand for pottery increased, the intensity and extent of mining also increased, task specialization removed temper procurement out of the hands of potters, and these specialists were not aware of the religious significance of the site. As a result, miners churned through the site in order to obtain the materials to make pottery temper (chapter 4) and eventually destroyed all evidence of ancient occupation (Arnold 2005a).

Red Slip (*Tantan lu'um*)

The earth (*lu'um*) is the source of the rust red *k'an kab* that was used to slip pottery and is universal around Ticul, covering areas in which there is no surface rock. The earth is also the location from which the spirits of the dead reside when they come back to the land of the living during the Day of the Dead rituals between

October 30 and November 6. During this time these rituals focus on the household altar, and encounters with spirits may not just occur at the household altar. In 1984 one potter (José Uc) told me about his encounter with a disembodied spirit in his house lot several years previously during the Day of the Dead rituals. In the middle the night, he got out of his hammock to urinate outside, and as he left his house he saw a ghost. Troubled by the encounter, his family hired a shaman to discover the meaning of the apparition. The shaman determined that someone had been buried in the rear of their house lot (in *k'an kab*) and was the source of the ghost.[6] Digging there, they discovered human bones, and then gathered them up, took them outside of town, and threw them into the forest. They were never bothered by the ghost again.

WATER (*CHE'EN*)

Water is critical for making pottery, and in the 1960s it came from deep wells dug using a postconquest technology. In antiquity, however, many of the natural sources of water were sinkholes and sacred to the Maya, and one of these was the sacred *cenote* at Chichén Itzá, where the Maya made offerings to Chaak to request rain (Tozzer 1957, 192, 196).

Before the conquest, however, populations living along the *puuk* ridge and south of it had limited natural sources of water, but during the Terminal Classic Period, they used cisterns (*chultuns*) to hold rain water from the rainy season to sustain them into the dry season. *Chultuns* are also found around Ticul. In the mid-1960s they were visible at Yo' Sah Kab, near the *puuk* ridge on the edge of Ticul, and at the large archaeological site of San Francisco de Ticul, north of the city. It is likely that the ancient potters in the area drew their water from them to make pottery and used them as sources of water for domestic use.

FUEL FOR FIRING (*K'ASH*)

Wood (*si'*) was the fuel for firing pottery and was a byproduct of clearing a milpa plot in the forest (*k'ash*, see chapter 3). The forest also has great religious significance because it is inhabited by the spirits of nature such as the guardians of the milpa plot and the village (the *balams*), the gods of rain (*chaaks*), the deities of the forest (the *kuilob kaaxob*), and others such as the *alux* (Redfield and Villa Rojas 1962, 111–15). All of these spirits must be placated in some way, and such ceremonies always occur in the forest outside of settlements, even in modern Ticul.

RITUAL POTTERY AS SYMBOLS OF A DISTILLED LANDSCAPE: THE DAY OF THE DEAD RITUALS

Seeing pottery as a distilled taskscape is best illustrated in the pottery required for Day of the Dead rituals (on October 31, November 1, and November 6), when the spirits of the deceased ancestors come back to the land of the living.[7] To feed the returning relatives, one of the traditional accouterments for the appropriate performance of these ceremonies was to use pottery vessels to cook the food.[8] Then, the food was placed in pottery bowls and offered on the household altar to feed the returned spirits of the departed ancestors. Other items used on the household altar—such as incense burners, candle holders, and flower pots—should also be made of fired clay (figure 8.1). Making these vessels involved the use of raw materials from the local landscape described in this work and, as already described, these sources had religious meaning: Clay (*k'at*) from Yo' K'at, temper (*sah kab*) for noncooking pottery from Yo' Sah Kab, temper (*hi'*) for cooking pottery from Aktun Hi'. Water (*ha'*) also had a religious meaning coming from Chaak, the rain god. Further, a red slip (*k'an kab*) also came from an opening in the landscape (*tantan lu'um*), and a tan slip (*sak kaab*) was made from clay mined at Yo' K'at, both of which reinforce the link between the pottery and the soil (*k'an kab*) and clay (*k'at*) that exists in many areas of Yucatán. Wood (*si'*) for firing came from the forest (*k'ash*) where many of the spirits lived (table 8.1).

The use of pottery in these rituals thus appears to materialize the link between the present world of the Maya, their ancestors, and their landscape. Further, it distills much of the landscape and its products into a material item used in these sacred rituals, but it also appears to embody and distill the religious meaning of the raw material sources. The pottery used during the Day of the Dead rituals thus not only represents a distilled set of tasks of engaging the landscape as a taskscape, but it also distills and encapsulates the religious meaning from the sources of ceramic raw materials as well (table 8.1).

Modern Yucatecos do not appear to recognize this layering of meanings in using pottery vessels required for the Day of the Dead rituals. The link between pottery, the earth, deity, and spirits, however, probably existed in antiquity. Although the tradition of using clay vessels for the Day of the Dead ceremonies continues, the symbolic and religious significance of the raw materials and of their sources in the landscape is no longer part of the participants' conscious memory. Nevertheless, pottery used for the Day of the Dead ceremonies embeds the memory of the landscape and its raw materials, the sense of place of their sources, and their religious meaning, whether the potters or the participants in the rituals realize it or not.

FIGURE 8.1. Household altar for the Day of the Dead ceremonies in Ticul, Yucatán, on October 31, 1984. Proper altar preparation requires pottery food bowls and incense burners and may also include candle holders of pottery. All of these reflect the potters' taskscape that links the present ceremonies with return of the spirits of the dead ancestors from the earth. Collectively called the "Day of the Dead" (Día de los Difuntos), these rituals correspond to All Saints Day (October 31), All Souls Day (November 1) in the Roman Catholic calendar, and November 6. For the ethnic Maya of Yucatán, they mark the return of the spirits of the dead ancestors to the land of the living. This relationship between the living and the dead is symbolized and expressed by food bowls, candle holders (*right and left*), and an incense burner (*out of sight below in front of the altar*) that are made from clay and temper. Those constituents as well as the clay slip and the red slip come from the earth. Tortillas (*lower center*) and a turkey (*center*) are ancient foods of the Maya, and the yellow marigolds (*extreme upper right and left*) are also symbols of the return of the dead spirits. Marigold pedals are also used to mark the path to the household altar from the street so that the spirits can find the altar when then come down the street.

ANCIENT POTTERY FROM TICUL: A DISTILLED COMMUNITY OF PRACTICE

The conclusion that Ticul potters encapsulate and distill the local landscape raises another question: How big is this landscape, and how does it relate to other communities of potters in Yucatan? This question is especially salient because the geology of Yucatán is similar, and the most common minerals (calcite, dolomite, and smectite) are found throughout the peninsula. The random mixed layering clay from Yo' K'at and palygorskite (*sak lu'um*) from Yo' Sah Kab, however, are infrequent and much more localized.

The constellation of landscape features used for sources of pottery raw materials around Ticul are unique to the community, and potters have used the most important sources (Yo' K'at, Yo' Sah Kab, and Aktun Hi') for at least a millennium (see chapter 4). Whereas the geology and minerals may be similar from place to place in Yucatán, the socially defined and technologically meaningful landscape is not and is more restricted. The features of this landscape that serve as a source of pottery materials for potters, however, have "senses of place" for them and are not shared by other communities. Historically, these sources were different from those of other communities of potters in Yucatán, such as Tepakán, Mama, and Akil.

The constellation of Ticul sources thus do not just represent a different and unique utilization of the landscape but actually is a highly restricted socially perceived landscape that is embedded in their indigenous knowledge.[9] Other communities of potters use different sources and different Maya names for categories of raw materials (Arnold 1971; Thompson 1958, 65–104). Potters in Mama, for example, obtained all their raw materials from a large sinkhole 3.75 kilometers from the church along the road to Chumayel,[10] and their categories of raw materials are named differently than those from Ticul: *shlu'um hi'*, *sak k'at*, *chichi hi'*, and *sak sah kab* (D. Arnold 2000, 356). Topographic land forms, geological deposits, and some minerals used to make pottery may be similar and may be found around other communities of potters, but their sources are not the same as the culturally defined and socially perceived landscape of the Ticul potters.

Up until the 1990s, the Ticul landscape used as sources of raw materials for making pottery was bounded and did not exceed six kilometers from the potters' residence (see figure 8.2). If one uses five kilometers as the distance that most communities travel to get their raw materials worldwide (Arnold 1985, 2011; Heidke et al. 2007, 145–51), and instead use them as radii from the major sources of clay (Yo' K'at) and temper (Aktun Hi' and Yo' Sah Kab) in Ticul, they intersect both in modern Ticul and in the ancient site of San Francisco Ticul that lies north of the current city. As late as the 1960s, ruined mounds still existed there, and based upon the style of the stone architecture, San Francisco appeared to be a Terminal Classic site (see also Stephens 1996, 71–77; Velázquez and López de la Rosa 1988). Nicholas Dunning (1994, 20) lists it as a Rank I site in his settlement hierarchy.[11] It was the most likely location of the ancient potters that used the sources and raw materials described in this work (figure 8.3) and probably was the home of the remote ancestors of modern Ticul potters (table 8.1).

To put this perspective into a larger context, the distance to resources, most frequently fewer than five kilometers but seldom more than seven kilometers, not only circumscribes the resource area and the potters' raw material choices (Arnold 2005b), but it is also a limit of the socially perceived and culturally defined landscape that potters used to obtain their raw materials (figure 8.2).[12] This implies that

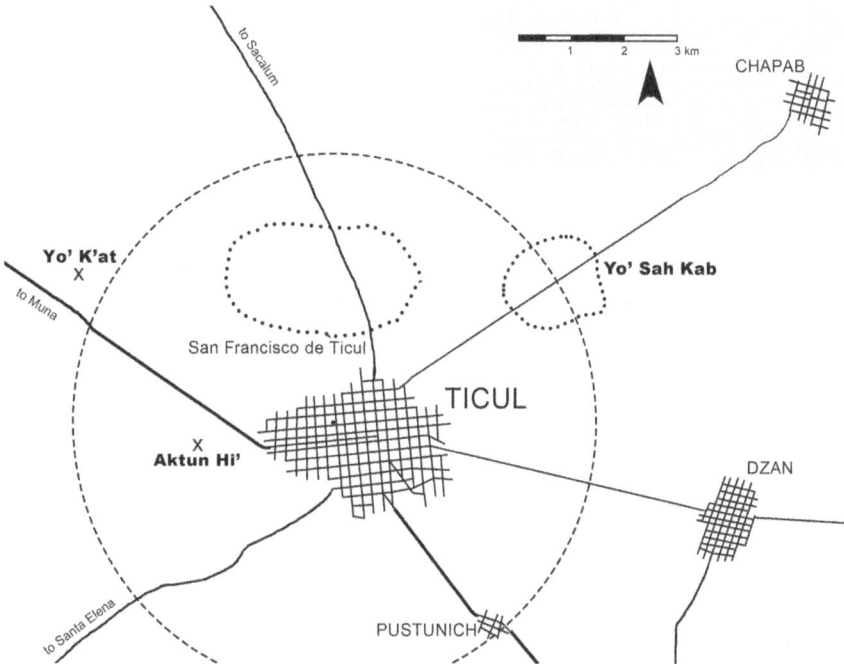

FIGURE 8.2. Map showing the taskscape of Ticul potters before 1970. The borders and extent of Yo' Sah Kab are approximate and change over time as miners dig new mines, expanding some mining areas and abandoning others. Some mining has moved nearer to Chapab since 1991 (see Arnold 2008, 193–220). The circle has a five-kilometer radius and is drawn around a point approximately in the center of the area in which potters lived between 1965 and 1970. It includes the resource area of the potters' socially perceived landscape that included most of the sources of their raw materials (except clay) during this time. (Map drawn by Michelle Arnold Paine, using basic features traced from Instituto Nacional de Estadística Geografía e Informática 1986.)

a community of potters such as Ticul not only utilizes the resources in a unique resource area, a point that has been made before (Arnold 2005b), but that these exploitative activities reflect the landscape, the sense of place, and religion of the community, and they encapsulate, distill, and congeal that landscape in the pottery in the form of the raw materials from the sources in that landscape. Further, this unique spatially bounded landscape indicates that Ticul potters are a unique "community of practice." Not only are the landscape, its raw material sources, their names and their meanings different, but before tourist demand changed the production of pottery and eliminated the need for traditional vessels, the shapes and decoration made in Ticul were different from those made in Mama and Tepakán

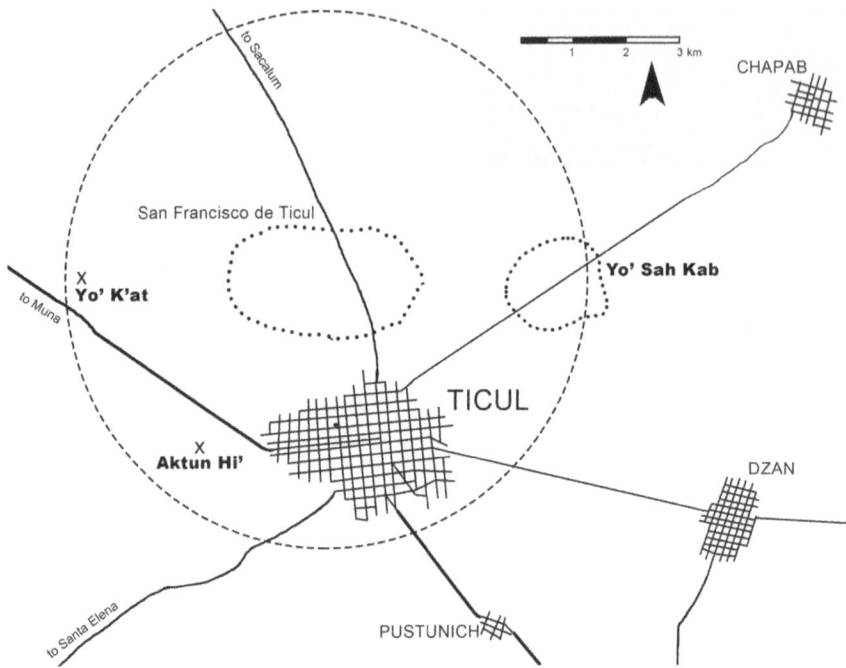

FIGURE 8.3. Map showing the taskscape of Terminal Classic potters of San Francisco de Ticul. The borders and extent of the ancient site of San Francisco de Ticul are approximate. Similarly, the borders for Yo' Sah Kab are also approximate and change over time as miners dig new mines, expanding some mining areas and abandoning others. Some temper mining has moved nearer to Chapab since 1991 (see Arnold 2008). The circle has a radius of 5 km and is drawn around a point approximately in the center of San Francisco de Ticul and includes the probable resource area of the ancient Terminal Classic potters of San Francisco de Ticul. (Map drawn by Michelle Arnold Paine, using basic features traced from Instituto Nacional de Estadística Geografía e Informática 1986.)

(see Thompson 1958, 105–37). For Ticul, at least, this spatially bounded and socially perceived landscape and the choices of raw materials from it are not just limited to Ticul before the 1970s, but appear to apply to the potters at the Terminal Classic site of San Francisco de Ticul as well. They were a community of practice much like that of modern Ticul potters.

The water-carrying jars (*p'uul*) made in Ticul described here and those described by Thompson from his 1951 research (Thompson 1958, 125, figs. 40a, d, and e) are different from those made in Mama (Thompson 1958, 125, figs. 40f, g, i, j, and k) and those made in Tepakán (Thompson 1958, 126, fig. 41). These differences were identical to those water jars made in those communities in the late 1960s. Water-carrying jars made in Tepakán appeared to be unslipped and were painted with black and red plant and animal designs. The water-carrying jars made in Mama, however, were slipped white and had red painted designs on them.

Pottery, however, does not distill the resources from the entire landscape around Ticul. It does not include clay (*k'at*) that occurs commonly in pockets in marl quarries and at the base of those quarries. Further, it does not distill the common marl itself (*sah kab*) that is used for mortars, plasters, and surfacing materials (chapter 4), that is found universally in Yucatán. So, pottery only distills those choices of materials that are excellent for using pottery—not those materials rejected for making pottery. In Ticul these choices reflect the materialization of a distinct landscape that is unique, using sources that are unique and that provide unique materials. This distillation thus is a subset of the Yucatán landscape, sources, and raw materials that are unique to Ticul and therefore are more appropriately called a "taskscape" than a "distilled landscape" in which the landscape is materialized in the pottery and exists in a greatly abbreviated form.

It could also be argued that the traditional pottery from Ticul is an encapsulated memory of landscape, significant places, and critical religious beliefs. This interpretation is, of course, hard to verify, because modern Yucatecos did not appear to see it that way. Even so, however, it does not mean that the religious meaning is not there. In modern Roman Catholic, Anglo Catholic, and Orthodox forms of Christianity, artifacts, liturgy, and behaviors during worship are loaded with religious meaning even though their congregants may not be aware of what that meaning might be except for that of the most obvious symbols.

The main problem with attributing a lot of meaning to pottery with respect to landscape and religion is that the pottery changes through time, and the sources of its raw materials change, and these new sources may not have a religious meaning at another place and time. In the case of Ticul, the pottery and the sources of its raw materials used for pottery made for the Day of the Dead rituals have changed so much that they no longer reflect (or distill) the landscape around Ticul but encapsulate a far different and more extensive landscape. This change means that attempts to reconstruct the taskscapes of the past matching pottery with local raw materials and those raw materials from distant sources may not reflect the local landscape at all. This consequence is less likely the case for traditional communities of practice but more reflective of modern communities that import their raw materials from distant sources using trucks and specialists that are not potters (see Arnold 2008, 154–182). Changes in raw materials and their sources thus do not always provide a clue to the local community of practice as an indicator of a taskscape.

NOTES

1. Clay mining at Yo' K'at has always been a footnote to the principal economic activity of the hacienda. In the Colonial Period the hacienda produced cattle and maize. As a result of the invention of the McCormick reaper in the mid-nineteenth century, the demand for fibers to make twine stimulated the production of *henequén* in Yucatán (Baklanoff 1980). The reaper cut the stalks of grain and mechanically used twine to bind them into shocks as it moved through the field. The bundled grain then was loaded on a wagon to be taken to the site of the threshing machine. As a result of the demand for twine to use in the reaper, Hacienda Yo K'at, like many haciendas in Yucatán, also began to grow *henequén* and produce fibers to make twine for export. This activity lasted into the mid-1960s at Yo' K'at, and some of that infrastructure still remains today (see Hacienda YoKat 2014).

Sometimes the owner, manager, or foreman of the hacienda regarded clay mining as too much of a bother, too dangerous (Arnold 2008, 154–59), or believed that it interfered with the hacienda's principal economic activity. When clay mining at the hacienda ended in December 1991 and the clay in the area designated by the owner for mining became exhausted, the owner refused to let clay miners expand it because he was afraid that digging more mine shafts would pose a danger to his cattle.

2. The Montes family still has a presence in Mérida and owns the Quinta Montes Molina on the Paseo Montejo (Paseo de Montejo No. 469 entre 33 × 35) in Mérida (Illescas 2013). Besides its spectacular setting, it includes a museum and is a testimony to the grand era of the *henequén* industry of the late nineteenth and early twentieth centuries. In this context it is also a setting for weddings and other catered events (www.laquintamm.com). When Hacienda Yo' K'at was converted to a boutique hotel in 2014, descendants of the Montes family (e.g., Alejandro Illescas) were present at the formal inauguration of the hotel, even though the Montes family were no longer the owners.

When Josefina Montes Molino inherited the hacienda, she reportedly sent money to the manager (Arturo Terello) to pay for a Mass and a fiesta.

3. The exact dates of the promises to San Pedro are uncertain, but the general outline of events appears to be consistent even though the details vary according to informants. In 1965, informants said that the date of the promise was twelve years beforehand, and initially, I thought that it represented only one event. In 1984, however, it become clear that the original promise by Emilio Tzum was a different event than its reaffirmation by Manuel Martín and Guadalupe Tzum. At that time the date of the renewed promise was said to have occurred more recently than the mid-1950s (as recently as 1963 according to some).

The existence of two promises to the saint was confirmed by other data. Sometimes informants said that the promise to San Pedro took place when Humberto Herrera was the manager of the Hacienda in the 1940s and very early 1950s, and sometimes they said it occurred when Enrique Valadez was manager between about 1952–62 (Arnold 2008, 158–59). This seeming discrepancy was resolved by recognizing that there were two promise events:

the original promise that occurred during the management of Herrera, when he encouraged Emilio Tzum to pay for part of the *novena* at the hacienda and the reaffirmation of the promise during the management of Valadez.

The date of the renewal of the promise in the early 1950s was consistent with Manuel Martín's move from the Barrio of Santiago to the "bronze store" across the street from some of the potters. He was a store owner originally, not a potter, and he had no reason to get involved with the concerns of potters until after he married a potter (who lived across the street) in March of 1950 (RCMTYM, 1950, p. 17, No. 27). Since the original promise was made to San Pedro in the 1940s, I am using 1953 as the approximate date for the renewal of the promise by Manuel Martín and Guadalupe Tzum Tuyup.

4. *Horchata* is a drink made from milk, rose water, and rice and flavored with vanilla.

5. Lorenzo Pech had extensive production facilities in Ticul (Arnold 2015a, 126–38) and was already obtaining clay from near Dzitbalché in Campeche.

6. Eusevio Tzum Dzul (AD 1869–1959, Arnold 2015a, 60), the ancestor of many Ticul potters, purchased this land from Finca Tabí that used it for the stables and corrals for the mules and horses that pulled sugar-laden carts from the Finca to Ticul (see Meyers 2012). Before the railroad the carts went over a wagon road from Ticul to Mérida, but after the railroad was built, the carts moved sugar from Tabí to the Ticul Railway Station (Arnold 2015a, 62). Since burials were placed in house lots before the cemetery was used, it is plausible that the burial was one of the ancestors of the Tzum family. José thought that the burial was one of his grandfather's (Eusevio Tzum Dzul) brothers or one of his great-grandfather's brothers (Arnold 2015a, 60).

7. These dates generally correspond to the rituals of "All Saints" in the Catholic calendar except that the dead children are ritually celebrated on October 31, and the dead adults are ritually celebrated on November 1. When the sprits return to the earth on November 6, they are shown the way to leave the household by a candle on the gatepost.

8. Making cooking pottery (tempered with *hi'*) was largely abandoned by 1965, though some was made seasonally to use for cooking food for the dead ancestors in 1970 (Arnold 2008, 110–12; 2015a, 177–96). One or two potters continued to make these vessels for the Day of the Dead rituals into the 1980s.

9. Although Thompson (1958) documented pottery making in Becal and Maxcanú in 1951, it had been abandoned in Becal by the time that Bruce Bohor and I visited there in 1968. Potters that we found in Maxcanú made only whistles for the Day of the Dead. When we visited Peto during that same year, we found several families that were formerly potters, but they said that they had stopped making pots six years earlier (1962).

10. In 1968 there was only a path to the sinkhole, but by 1994 a road had been built to Chumayel. Today the sinkhole (at approximately 20 degrees, 27' 50" N and 89 degrees, 20' 44.5" W) lies at a straight-line distance of 190 m south/southeast of the junction of the road to Chumayel and the highway from Mérida.

11. Dunning (1994, 18) says that sites in Ranks 1–3 are major sites that contain sociopolitical status markers, including ball courts and stelae, not found in smaller sites in Ranks 4–6. In 1968 a small pyramid structure and low mounds were observed at the site, but in later years these features disappeared and were apparently destroyed. More recently, Google Earth reveals that the area of the site consists of a planned suburban development of house lots.

12. Aktun Lara, another cave in which Mercer (1896, 66) found what seems to be Terminal Classic Pottery with *hi'* fragments, also appears to lie within six kilometers from Ticul and from the ancient site of San Francisco de Ticul (Mercer 1896, 5).

9

Conclusion

This work is the first book-length monograph that elaborates the indigenous knowledge involved with making pottery. Highlighted by fieldwork and reflection over a period of more than fifty years, it is also the first book-length monograph that uses material engagement theory to understand the components of that process from selecting the raw materials to firing the finished vessels. It brings together several different cognitive domains of the Maya potters: the forest, the earth, the materials that come from them, and the potters' choices used in the process. This knowledge is not just in the mind, however, but extends beyond it to the potters' engagement with their environment, to their materials for making pottery, and to the sequence of its production. This engagement recursively affects the potters' indigenous knowledge as feedback and influences their behavioral choices as they move through the process.

WHAT IS INDIGENOUS KNOWLEDGE?

At least some archaeologists assume that ancient craftsmen act on a mental template that is materialized in a media such as plastic clay, and that its fired product—pottery—exclusively reflects the society and culture of its makers. This work, however, illustrates how the Maya potters' engagement of their traditional knowledge challenges this notion. This knowledge is not just a mental template imposed on selecting raw materials and making pots. Neither is it determined by the landscape, the mineralogical components of the raw materials, nor by the phenomenological sequence of the pottery-making process. Rather, the potters' knowledge and practice result from their engagement with these features and provide feedback for creating and using their indigenous knowledge.

Using many examples and summarizing much of the literature on the subject, both Tim Ingold (2013) and Malafouris (2013) argue that knowledge is not just in the mind but also in the practice of engaging the world. Ingold calls this the process of transformation where the embodied mind meets the making of artifacts. Malafouris (2013, 3, 67, 227–39) argues that production is engagement with the physical world and that the mind is not just in the brain but extends outside of it as it encounters the external world. In the research presented here, it is certainly true that a great deal of knowledge exists in the head of the Maya potter, but this knowledge is the result of their engagement with the landscape, with the raw materials from it, with the pottery-making process itself, and with the weather and climate that affects it. Pottery is not just a materialization of what's in the mind inside of one's head, but rather is the result of the interaction of the cognitive categories, the internalized and embodied patterns of motor skills, and the engagement of those categories and skills with the production process. In the final analysis, all of these factors have some agency in making pottery. Making pottery thus involves the interaction of both human and material agency.

Documenting the indigenous knowledge of, and engagement with, the landscape and the raw materials that come from it indicate that in many respects, pottery is a material distillation of a portion of the landscape that can be best expressed as a taskscape (Ingold 2013; Michelaki, Braun, and Hancock 2014). Pottery thus consists of materials from a variety of sources, and the potter extracts and transforms these materials into a social product that represents a cultural modification of the landscape. The engagement of the potter with this landscape is usually circumscribed by a distance of no more than seven kilometers from the potters' residence and results in a community of practice unique from the engagement of other communities of potters in the area—in this case Mama, Tepakán, and Akil.

SUMMARY

Like the knowledge of plants sought by ethnobotanists and ethnopharmacologists to discover new drugs from the plants used by the indigenous peoples of the world, the potters of Ticul also have practical knowledge of the landscape, the forest, the geology, and the mineralogy of the materials that they use for making pottery.[1] This knowledge consists of the way in which they structure and make sense of their environment and use it to make pottery. It is derived from potters' repeated engagement with their living and nonliving environment that results in classifications of the culturally and socially perceived landscape and the raw materials that they obtain from it. These classifications are not just the action of a mental template on the environment, but rather result from the interaction of mind and thing, of mental category and action, and of cognition and sensory engagement.

The basic building blocks of the potter's landscape (their ethnoecology) consist of the topography, the forest, and the earth. The forest is divided into eight ecological zones that extend from an area near the north coast of the peninsula to the tropical forest to the south. A variety of different trees grow in these zones, and potters, who were also subsistence agriculturalists, knew the types of trees in each zone and the burning characteristics of the wood from each of them.

Like the local ethnoecology, the potters' indigenous knowledge also includes a sophisticated understanding of their raw materials. This knowledge forms the basis of their engagement in making pottery as they select, use, and mix these materials to make pottery. They operationalize this knowledge by classifying those raw materials using certain kinds of distinctive features. First, these features reflect the sources from which the raw materials come. Some sources have a unique "sense of place" in the local landscape, others do not. Second, the features reflect the potters' working knowledge that comes from the actual engagement of the physical properties of their materials relevant to making pottery. Some of these features reflect simple phenomenological characteristics such as color, texture, and crystallinity. Others reflect mineralogical differences (table 4.9) that arise from a working knowledge of their unique physical properties.

This working knowledge is not scientific or theoretical in that potters know nothing of the material's chemical or mineralogical composition. Similarly, they do not know a tree's botanical classification or the changing molecular structure of pottery during the firing process. Rather, potters have simply found that certain raw materials behave differently during their selection and use, and they regard them as different—whether or not their categories are terminologically distinct.

The relationship between the native and scientific categories is by no means universal among potters worldwide. Some communities have semantic categories of raw materials that do not reflect mineralogical distinctions. Daniel Miller (1985, 211), for example, failed to find a correspondence between indigenous categories of raw materials and minerals in India, and only one of the most obvious physical characteristics of potters' raw materials in Quinua, Peru, had a mineralogical basis (Arnold 1972b, 1993, 73–80).

The relationship of potters' classification of trees to biological taxonomy is equally complex, and the folk categories of plants generally do not always match up with scientific classifications. Folk taxonomies are often underdifferentiated or overdifferentiated relative to scientific taxonomies of botanical species (Berlin 1973, 267–69; Berlin et al. 1966).

Equally important, potters' ethnomineralogical knowledge is not just cognitive but also practical, consisting of their knowledge of the physical consequences of their choices and of problem-solving strategies that enable them to engage their raw materials, evaluate their suitability for making pottery, and change their selection behavior. Potters' ethnomineralogy thus is not just a mental template but a practical set of categories, guidelines, problem-solving skills, and strategies by which the potters use visual and tactile feedback from the raw materials to make their choices and to deal with the consequences.

This perspective has become clear to me over the last fifty years as potters' sources of raw materials have changed and potters have adapted to those changes using their extant indigenous knowledge (Arnold 2008, 153–228). These adaptations have highlighted the complex nature of the potters' knowledge and practice in the late 1960s and how that knowledge handles the changes in raw materials.

The assumption that pottery materializes a potter's mental template finds its clearest expression in forming and decorating a vessel. Potters' indigenous knowledge of forming pottery, however, consists of implicit knowledge of postural and motor habit patterns, knowledge of different vessel shapes, how to form those shapes using their units of measurement, and the knowledge of the populations that consume those shapes. Whereas potters' indigenous knowledge of forming a vessel certainly does imprint itself on the clay as a specific vessel shape, the process of doing so is much more complicated; the raw materials exert a compelling agency on the way vessels are formed. Even with the best clay available, excessive plasticity places constraints on the forming technique. On the one hand, the Ticul clay is plastic enough to allow potters to use slab coiling to draw up the clay to form the vessel walls. Conversely, potters cannot form large vessels in one continuous operation without them sagging and collapsing. So, potters adjust to this constraint by making a pot in stages, allowing each to dry before adding a subsequent stage. Each stage thus represents the largest portion of a vessel that can be added without sagging and collapsing, and each stage thus is roughly the same height from vessel to vessel. In order to incorporate this constraint into the potter's indigenous knowledge, each stage is named in Yucatec Maya. At least some traditional vessels begin with the same stage, but after this stage is formed and partially dried, the potters' choice of shape is restricted.

Consequently, because of the plasticity of the local clay and the vessel desired, some of the potters' technological choices have already been made for them in that the fabrication technique limits the size of the vessel or the stage that can be formed in one sitting (Arnold 1999; Arnold 2008, 254–56). These realities of the forming process have great implications for production organization because the larger the vessel and the more stages needed to complete it, the more drying time and drying space are required. This constraint increases the footprint of drying pottery and requires large structures for the increased frequency and intensity of production (Arnold 2008, 90; 2015a, 243–76).

The engagement of the potters with the firing process also involves a large corpus of indigenous knowledge. First, they know the different stages of the firing process and what happens to the pottery during each stage. Second, they know the different types of firewood and their burning characteristics and how to match those characteristics to the desired result of each stage. Third, they know the different parts of the kiln and how they affect the pottery during firing. Fourth, they understand the sensory feedback that comes from firing and how to use it as input to make the appropriate behavioral choices in management of the process. Finally, potters have developed a set of motor skills that allows them to throw wood into the fire without damaging the pots.

Examining the potters' engagement of the firing process again demonstrates why they do not simply materialize and implement a fixed mental template to fix the form of the pot with heat: firing may present unforeseen problems that must be resolved so the vessels are not damaged during the process. First, the transformation of the dried pot into a fired one requires careful monitoring to avoid blackening and overfiring vessels. Second, although potters may try to control the quality of wood they throw into the kiln, it may not be dry enough, and they simply may not be able to obtain and/or select enough high-quality wood that burns with a high flame and limited smoke. As a result, they must use slow burning wood and that which burns with a smoky flame, and must change their behavior by using more fuel to keep the flames high. Third, during the second part of the final stage when the fire is in the door of the kiln, the tactile feedback from the heat keeps potters two meters from the kiln door, and they use a particular motor habit pattern as they throw firewood on the fire in order to avoid hitting and damaging the vessels.

In summary, potters use visual, tactile and, to a lesser degree, auditory feedback from the firing process to modify their behavior to assure that all pottery in all parts of the kiln are properly and completely fired. Potters constantly monitor the process, and the visual feedback of the red glow of the pottery determines when the process is complete.

Firing pottery thus is not a simple process of just putting pots in a kiln and heating them, but rather involves knowing and choosing the different types of wood, knowing the parts of the process, the nature of the feedback from it, and how to solve unforeseen problems. All of this knowledge and skill allows potters to fully engage the process so that they can fix the form of their vessels without damaging them. The firing process is thus one more example of the potter's indigenous knowledge necessary to engage the process than just materializing a preexisting mental template.

INDIGENOUS KNOWLEDGE AND LEARNING

The Maya names of the categories of raw materials, landscape, parts of the process of making pottery, and parts of the kiln are critical parts of potters' indigenous knowledge in that they facilitate its transmission to those who learn the craft, whether they are children in the household or adults who marry into it. It also enables potters to identify and communicate the effects of their engagement with the weather, the environment, ceramic raw materials, and the pottery-making process to others. Both the language and the engagement with the process are critical, just as they were with me when I learned much of the process by participant-observation.

In the preface, I stated that this book is a prequel to my two other books on Ticul. Both were diachronic pictures of the changes in Ticul over a period of thirty-two years (Arnold 2008) and forty-three years (Arnold 2015a). In the first, *Social Change and the Evolution of Ceramic Production and Distribution in a Maya Community* (Arnold 2008), I discussed the changes and continuity of the demand, consumption, distribution, and production of pottery between 1965 and 1997. The longest chapter of that book chronicled the quantitative changes in the population of potters and the mechanisms of selection as ways to explain those evolutionary changes. In an attempt to identify changes in the personnel of production units over time, I plotted the most frequent type of individual in the production units for each year of observation and then tried to identify patterns over time using trend lines. The number of points (year of observation) on each graph was small (< 10) and the R^2 did not reveal any significant trends over time except an increase in the number of laborers who were not relatives of production unit owners. The graphs did reveal, however, that almost all of the potters in the production units were members of the nuclear family (Fa, Mo, So, Da, Wi), related to one another either lineally or through marriage (Wi). Clearly, production units continued to consist of members of the nuclear family with no significant changes through time.

This conclusion was reinforced in my second book, *The Evolution of Ceramic Production Organization in a Maya Community* (Arnold 2015a), in which I used narrative to describe the history of the production units and their continuity (and lack of it) through time focusing on personnel and production space. In both books I described the composition and structure of production units and their organization. Using both quantitative (Arnold 2008, 31–91) and qualitative (Arnold 2015a) data, I showed that ceramic production in Ticul is household based, and the nuclear family (Fa, Mo, So, Da, Wi) makes up the majority of the potters in the production units (Arnold 2008, 42–67; 2015a). Households, however, do not just consist of nuclear families but sometimes consist of extended families of lineal, collateral, and affinal relatives. Learning the craft is, of course, a social process, and though a list of those from whom potters learn the craft sometimes was a seemingly bewildering corpus of different relatives (Arnold 2008, 43), potters almost always learn from someone within their own household. Patrilineal inheritance of household land, procreation, and patrilocal residence ensured a continuation of the infrastructure of the craft and provided a pool of teachers and learners (Arnold 2008; Arnold 2015a). Sometimes, variability of learning types exists when the inheritance of the house lot includes collateral relatives already in it. Similarly, postnuptial residence patterns may bring affinal relatives into the household who are not related to the groom but lineally or collaterally related to his wife. Even so, not all those in the household want to learn the craft, and a variety of mechanisms select for and against household members continuing the craft (Arnold 2008, 40–48; 2015a).

Although almost all learning of pottery making in Ticul took place within the household in the 1960s, the types of production units since then have changed (Arnold 2015a). Most continue to be household based, and potters continue to learn in the household, but changes in demand and the market have diminished the indigenous knowledge necessary to make pottery. The loss of access to traditional raw materials (such as clay) has resulted in changes in paste preparation. New shapes required less skill to fabricate and, except for the creation of two-piece molds, the making of mold-made objects required virtually no skill at all (Arnold 1999). Potters no longer produced the shapes they made in the 1960s, but they still relied on the base of traditional indigenous knowledge described here for making large vessels by using stages of construction with a period of drying between each stage.

ETHNOARCHAEOLOGY AS CULTURAL HERITAGE

Ethnoarchaeology and more generally studies of contemporary pottery making can also be seen as preserving Cultural Heritage. Cultural Heritage is more than the archaeological sites, burials, landscapes, and artifacts of native peoples but also involves the knowledge and process of creating those artifacts called the "Intangible" Cultural Heritage (see UNESCO 2016; see also Biagetti and Lugli 2016; Han and Antrosio 2016a, 2016b). In Serbia (Djordjević 2007, 2013, 2016) and Mexico (López Varela 2014; López Varela and Aguilar Escobar 2014), for example, those who study pottery making describe it as the preservation of Cultural Heritage. In a rather unique approach to Cultural Heritage, the Inter-American Foundation in Colombia funded the scaling-up of pottery production and turned villages into "Living Museums" (Goff 1990).

The modern concern about Cultural Heritage and Intangible Cultural Heritage has deep roots in American anthropology. Although not known as "Cultural Heritage" at the time, much anthropological research in the late nineteenth and early twentieth centuries was driven by a concern to preserve information about the language, culture, and artifacts of the indigenous societies in North America before they disappeared or changed.

The ethnoarchaeological research among Maya potters in Ticul during the last fifty years presented in this work and others is thus part of the preservation of their unique Intangible Cultural Heritage (e.g., Arnold 2008, 2015a; Arnold et al. 2012).[2] Ceramic technologist Anna O. Shepard realized the importance of this task by trying to convince me that preserving the Cultural Heritage of Yucatec Maya pottery making before it disappeared was so critical that it should take precedence over my concerns about fulfilling the requirements for the PhD (letter quoted in Arnold 1991, 321).[3] Although some of my research in ethnoarchaeology has consisted of answering a priori archaeological questions, this work has focused on the Maya potters' indigenous knowledge embedded in their language, supplemented with participant-observation of selecting and mining raw materials and of firing pottery. This approach has revealed three implications for understanding, preserving, and discovering Yucatec Maya Cultural Heritage.

First, this multifaceted approach has demonstrated that a culture's native language, Yucatec Maya in this case, is key to understanding local indigenous knowledge and that language is, in itself, part of the Maya Cultural Heritage. Engaging this knowledge provides unique insights about landscape, raw materials, and the process of making pottery that reveals a deep knowledge of, and engagement with, the local ecology found in its trees, rocks, and minerals as well as in the pottery-making process itself. This knowledge, however, embraces more than just the native categories, but should also be understood as the potters' engagement of a locally and socially defined landscape that has religious meaning. This meaning is encapsulated and distilled in pottery that is used during the traditional Day of the Dead ceremonies.

Second, this approach to indigenous knowledge provided a platform for seemingly accidental and serendipitous archaeological discoveries that are also part of the Maya Cultural Heritage. These discoveries reveal that at least some of that knowledge had deep roots in the prehistoric past. Such discoveries, for example, indicated that Ticul potters knew about, and used, a material they called "white earth," known mineralogically as the clay mineral palygorskite. The contemporary Maya used it for a variety of ailments such as burns, stomach problems, and diarrhea (Arnold 1967a, 1967b, 2005a, 55).[4] Perhaps related to its healing properties (Arnold et al. 2008), the ancient Maya also used it to create the unusual clay-organic pigment called Maya Blue. Blue was the color of sacrifice for the ancient Maya, and it symbolized the god of rain, Chaak, invoked to bring healing rain to a drought-stricken land (Arnold et al. 2008).

Third, this research has also resulted in the discovery of ancient sources of raw materials for making pottery (clay and temper), for making medicine (palygorskite), and for making Maya Blue (palygorskite), further contributing to understanding and preserving the knowledge of the Cultural Heritage of the Maya. Unfortunately, much of this heritage has now disappeared because of great social changes, changes in demand, and the segmentation of the tasks of making pottery from those who procure raw materials and from those who fire and distribute it. As was said before, the loss of Cultural Heritage also results from the loss of the Yucatec Maya language (see preface) and from the death of those potters who possessed this knowledge but did not pass it onto the next generation. The loss of Cultural Heritage has also come from the alteration of the landscape for housing, orchards, and agriculture.

IMPLICATIONS FOR METHODOLOGY

This research did not begin by asking archaeological questions or by using an agenda that might be important archaeologically. Rather, it began with studying the pottery-making process itself and the cognitive domains that the potter used to practice the craft. I first learned about the firing process by eliciting information about it in Yucatec Maya, observing the process, and then by doing it myself. As a result, I learned that understanding technological processes from the potter's perspective is possible by performing those processes by the tried-and-true method of anthropological research, participant-observation.

This work thus presents an alternative approach to ethnoarchaeology. There are those who think that ethnoarchaeology should be done by archaeologists rather than ethnographers or other kinds of anthropologists. Certainly, most social and cultural anthropologists have not been interested in studying material culture in a way that is relevant to archaeological questions. Nevertheless, there are important questions that archaeologists have about the relationship between the cognition, behavior, and artifacts that can only come from the present. How can one know the cultural and social patterns of an ancient society that are reflected in pottery without understanding them in the ethnographic present, even if the present is different from the past? As this work shows, and as I argued in *Social Change and the Evolution of Ceramic Production and Distribution in a Maya Community* (Arnold 2008), when one engages in long-term diachronic research in a community, it is possible to separate those factors responsible for the great changes in production brought on by a global economy from those that have relevance for archaeology.

This work thus illustrates those more traditional aspects of pottery making that can be filtered out of a dynamically changing craft affected by tourism and globalization through long-term diachronic study—now over a period of fifty years. As the last chapter demonstrated, however, this approach has not only shown those aspects relevant for archaeology, but it has actually identified ancient patterns of raw material use and led to the discovery of sources used a thousand years ago in the Terminal Classic Period. Long-term ethnoarchaeological research in an area, when combined with a survey of sources of raw materials and with comparison with archaeological pottery from the area, can reveal that some of the contemporary patterns of pottery production are actually very ancient.

By focusing on archaeological questions a priori in ethnoarchaeology, however, it is possible to unconsciously ask questions that are ethnocentric, result from the cultural values of the archaeologist, and may be irrelevant to the culture itself. During my original research in Yucatán in 1965, the Midwest Universities Consortium sponsored much research in Yucatán with funding administered through the Social Psychology Laboratory at the University of Chicago (see preface). This funding brought many students from several different universities to the towns of Ticul and nearby Pustunich. One group of psychology graduate students was interested in developing cross-cultural measures of maleness and femaleness and had developed a set of questions to try to measure it cross-culturally. They asked us to translate the questions into Spanish and use our informants to translate them into Yucatec Maya. As I recall the incident, we were frustrated because some of the questions that they wanted translated made no sense in the context of Maya culture. One of the items on the questionnaire was: "Do you like to take a bath or a shower?" The semantic distinctions that the students wanted to capture, however, were irrelevant in Maya culture. The Maya bathed every day, but did so sitting on a low stool, just like the stool used for making pottery.[5] They dipped heated water out of a bucket with a metal cup, poured it over themselves, soaped themselves down, and then rinsed off their body with more cups of water. Was this a bath or a shower? There were no other alternatives for bathing. Even the Spanish translation of bathing, *bañarse* (to bathe yourself), had no semantic or behavioral variation for the Maya.

I faced a similar problem in studying firing. I initially assumed that elapsed time was important in the firing process and recorded the hour and minute each time the potter did something so that I could calculate the elapsed time. It seemed to be the empirical way to do ethnography. I soon discovered that completion of the process was not about time but about the engagement of potters with the process that was based upon the visual feedback that they received from the fire and the pottery in the kiln. They possessed indigenous knowledge about a set of categories associated with conscious and unconscious behaviors, but these were modified based upon the visual (and to some extent, tactile and aural) feedback received from their engagement of the firing process. It wasn't until I learned how to fire myself that I began to put the Maya linguistic categories of the process into an actual context, observed the potters' behavior, and then learned how to see, hear, and feel what was happening in the kiln. I learned by experience that the potter's indigenous knowledge was more than just linguistically labeled semantic categories. Without using the Maya language in learning about firing, observing the process, and then actually firing myself, I would have gotten a very skewed and ethnocentric perspective of firing pottery.

Learning about the sizes of kilns also challenged my ethnocentric categories. I had noticed that there were different sizes of kilns, and it seemed their size was related to the number of vessels that a potter could fire in a kiln of each size. My informants even cooperated with my perceptions by suggesting that kiln size was based upon the selling price of the pots stacked inside it. Eventually, I discovered that potters measured their kiln sizes by the number of firewood bundles required to fire the kiln successfully and was determined through their engagement of the firing process by calculating the number of bundles used after the kiln was fired for the first few times.

So, it was clear that I had missed the way in which potters measured the size of their kiln. I asked the wrong question based upon my own cultural assumptions before I was immersed in the culture and experienced the technology of firing. Such is the problem with doing ethnography and ethnoarchaeology: getting beyond one's cultural assumptions is probably one of the most difficult aspects of learning about another culture—no matter what the topic.

My own approach to doing ceramic ethnoarchaeology in Ticul first consisted of understanding the craft itself, its context, and its production organization, and then relating those results to archaeology. Approaching the present with specific archaeological questions, though not as ridiculous as asking the Maya questions about their preference for a bath or a shower, may result in asking questions that are irrelevant to the society. Similarly, focusing on responses to questionnaires and surveys written a priori before immersion in the culture, and without consideration of the context of the behavior, may produce abundant data that is convenient for cross-cultural comparative purposes, but does that information reflect actual behavior and the larger context of production? Information gained by using only verbal data may not be as empirically valid as it could be unless one can demonstrate that informants behave in the way that they said they do. Knowledge cannot represent behavior unless it is seen in relation to actual performance—how that knowledge is learned and manipulated to produce action. For an ethnographic description to have theoretical and practical significance, a representation of the cognitive content of a culture can only be meaningful in terms of its relation to action. From my own experiences in studying pottery making, like those presented here, engagement theory is a necessary perspective for adequately describing the informant's knowledge.

WHAT DRIVES CHANGES IN INDIGENOUS KNOWLEDGE?

I have already suggested that as potters who possessed the knowledge presented here pass from the scene, much of their knowledge will disappear. But, this factor only explains the disappearance of indigenous knowledge, not its change.

When I created the title of this work, I wanted to represent all of the dimensions that I had learned about the potters' knowledge: cognition, engagement, and practice. After going back through my abundant underlining, notes, and highlighted portions of Malafouris's (2013) book, and reflecting on this manuscript after multiple passes through it, I realized that engagement is the key to, and the link between, cognition and practice. This was brought home to me as I contemplated the changes in the practice of pottery making in Ticul and in the disappearance of much of its cognitive dimension. If, as Malafouris argued, the mind (cognition) extends beyond the brain and reflexively influences the potter's engagement with the physical and social world, then changes in that physical and social world will change the potters' cognition and practice. That consequence is precisely what has happened in Ticul since 1965. Indeed, the changes in the physical and social world that the potters engage has greatly diminished their indigenous knowledge (see Arnold 2008, 2015a).

Another factor that changed the indigenous knowledge is the development of task segmentation that separates those who actually make the pottery from those who mined raw materials, from those who painted the pottery, and from those who distributed it. Originally mined by potters, former potters, and the relatives of potters, more recent mining specialists had no relationships with potters, no traditional knowledge of raw materials, and no contact with potters except at the point of sale (Arnold 2008).

The potters' loss of access to traditional source locations of raw materials complicates this change,[6] and the potters can no long rely upon their traditional knowledge of categories for acquiring raw material. The exhaustion of clay at Yo' K'at, for example, required potters to get their clay from elsewhere, and soon entrepreneurs were coming to Ticul to sell clay from Campeche (Arnold 2008, 153–80). Furthermore, temper preparation has largely, but not completely, moved from its traditional location (Yo' Sah Kab) to an area nearer Chapab (Arnold 2008, 193–204). Rather than selecting raw materials of the highest quality as a potter would do, procurement specialists were no longer potters or relatives of potters, and they did not know (or did not care to know) how to select the raw materials of the highest quality. They simply wanted to sell as much clay or temper as possible, regardless of its quality. Most of these procurement specialists (for clay, temper, and wood) were not from Ticul but from other towns such as Chapab, Santa Elena, Calkiní, and Dzitbalché. This task specialization moved Ticul potters away from engaging the landscape and raw materials themselves and has pushed quality control into the production units, creating new challenges (Arnold 2008, 153–220).

Potters thus needed to engage the clay and temper in new ways, rejecting raw materials from some specialists, mixing some raw materials with other materials of higher quality, and buying different materials from other specialists. One potter, for example, developed a new specialty in which he did no more than mine *sak lu'um* to sell to potters to improve the quality of their temper (Arnold 2015a, 101–2; see also chapter 4).

As potters encountered these new materials and the new organization of raw material procurement, they no longer engaged them in the traditional ways as they had in their traditional taskscape around Ticul. As a consequence, their indigenous knowledge changed. As their traditional resource niches in the landscape were destroyed or became unavailable, they had to engage new sources and the materials from them in new ways.

Another way to say this is that as the social and physical landscape of resource procurement has changed, the indigenous knowledge necessary to make pottery also changed. Although the traditional landscape has not disappeared, it has been rendered unusable, inaccessible, or irrelevant. Specifically, the traditional clay source at Yo' K'at has become inaccessible and unusable. The temper source at Yo' Sah Kab has changed because of limited access and declining number of potters who mined and prepared temper there. Finally, the temper source for cooking pottery at Aktun Hi' has become irrelevant because demand no longer exists for cooking pottery, and the knowledge of making that kind of pottery has disappeared as the former makers of those vessels passed from the scene.

On the other hand, some aspects of the potters' working memory are responsible for the continuity of whatever traditional indigenous knowledge still remains. This memory involves the way in which potters receive and interpret sensory feedback from the raw materials. As they engaged these new materials and their performance characteristics, they were challenged to problem-solve and adjust their behaviors to produce a viable pot, adjusting paste recipes and changing what formerly seemed to be immutable categories and behavioral syntax.

FINAL REFLECTIONS

Whereas I have already said that this book is a prequel to my two books about the changes in Ticul pottery production and distribution (Arnold 2008, 2015a), it is also a sequel to *Ceramic Theory and Cultural Process* (Arnold 1985). In writing that book, I was trying to move away from the relativism of both my experience of using cognitive anthropology in 1965 and away from my relativistic and descriptive field research on pottery making in Quinua, Peru, and the Valley of Guatemala.

As I began to see patterns of similarity derived from my experience studying pottery making in Yucatán, Peru, and Guatemala, I discovered patterns that I had not seen before and that they were derived from the basic universal sequence of making pottery based upon the characteristics of clay minerals and the process necessary to turn them into a fixed form (see Arnold 2011). The overall point of that book was to elucidate universal feedbacks that existed between ceramic raw materials, the pottery production process, the environment, and some cultural patterns that could be useful to archaeological interpretation.

In *Ceramic Theory and Cultural Process*, I thus wanted to focus on more generalizing concerns, not that there weren't more culturally particular aspects of ceramics, but that archaeological interpretation might benefit from an empirical understanding of the relationships between cultural patterns and the universal production sequence of making pottery. There are, of course, culturally relative sequences of choices that may reveal unique social patterns, but the universal sequence of making pottery provides a baseline of understanding the cultural and environmental context of production within which such social patterns exist.

Archaeologists, of course, always use some sort of generalization that links archaeological data and cultural patterns. This link is usually based upon theory and tradition rather than an understanding of how, where, and under what circumstances people make pots. It is always easier to use generalizations that others cite rather than the probabilistic interpretations of making pottery based upon the complicated relationships with the material agency of raw materials, the constraints of the pottery-making process, and its relationships to the weather and the physical environment.

Consequently, archaeological interpretation of ceramic production seems to be mired in tradition and abstract theory that appear to be untethered to the universal realities of the ceramic production sequence. Focusing on the exceptions of low probability to those probabilistic cross-cultural patterns developed in *Ceramic Theory and Cultural Process* has left explanations of ancient ceramic production as an artifact of theory, tradition, and imaginative creativity that gives explanatory priority, if not exclusivity, to sociopolitical explanation (e.g., state or elite control of production) that often (but not always) bears no relationship to patterns of making pottery and how they relate to environment and culture. Such approaches assume that pottery is simply a product of a mental template that varies in a relativistic way from community to community and culture to culture.

Now, with more than thirty years of reflection about *Ceramic Theory and Cultural Process*, and the work of Ingold (2000, 2013) and Malafouris (2013), I realize that what I was trying to do in that book was parallel to what Malafouris did in showing what he termed as the "material agency" of raw materials and the pottery-making process—except that I extended this agency to weather and climate, sedentism, scheduling, and relationship to the marginality of subsistence, among others. Like Malafouris' (2013) book, *How Things Shape the Mind*, *Ceramic Theory and Cultural Process* (Arnold 1985, 1–19) was written as an antidote and challenge to the relativistic view of pottery that potters materialize a mental template because its principal raw material, clay, is so plastic that cultures uniquely express their culture through it.

As this work shows, however, potters do not just use a mental template in making their pots. So, to work out the culturally unique and relative aspects of pottery production (of which there are many), one must first understand the material agency of the environment, raw materials, and the intersecting cultural patterns that affect pottery production. Now, this book joins *Ceramic Theory and Cultural Process* and the work of Ingold (2013) and Malafouris (2013) to challenge the notion of the unicausality of the mental template. I trust that it will make a contribution to that task.

NOTES

1. Many modern drugs (Aspirin, Digitalis, and Curare [which consists of several muscle relaxants]) used in the twenty-first century originally came from the indigenous knowledge of plants. Most recently, a powerful antimalarial drug, Artemisinin, came from sweet wormwood (*Artemisia annua*), a plant used in traditional Chinese medicine (Stokstad and Vogel 2015). Similarly, the drug Metformin, an extract derived from goat's rue (*Galega officinalis*), an herb used since the Middle Ages in Europe and China, is currently an important treatment for diabetes and prediabetes and is being considered as a potential drug for preventing other diseases associated with aging (Hall 2015).

2. See also Arnold 1971, 2005a, 2015b; Arnold and Bohor 1975, 1976, 1977, 2008; Alfredo Barrera Vásquez 1937; Brainerd 1958; Silvia Rendón 1947; Silvia Terán and Christian Rasmussen (Terán and Rasmussen 1981); Thompson 1958; Carmen Varela Torrecilla 1990.

3. Letter from Anna O. Shepard to Bruce F. Bohor, March 27, 1967. Copies of the complete letter can be found in the Dean E. Arnold correspondence in the Wheaton College Archives and Special Collections (Series 2, Box 1, Folder 4) and in the papers of the Anna O. Shepard Collection in the University of Colorado Museum of Natural History, Boulder (Drawer 13, File F13, as referenced in the "Anna Osler Shepard Papers: Content and Organization" flier from the museum).

4. Palygorskite (attapulgite) is also used in over-the-counter medicine in the modern world as a treatment for diarrhea (MedicineNet 2015).

5. There were no tubs or showers in Maya houses. When I stayed with a Maya family and wanted to bathe, my host gave me a pail of warm water, a bar of soap, a cup, and a towel. They put me in one of their outbuildings with a low Maya stool (a *k'an che'*), instructed me how to bathe, and then closed the door to the structure, leaving me alone to accomplish the task.

6. The factors responsible for this are multicausal and described elsewhere (Arnold 2008).

References

Aimers, James John. 2012. *Ancient Maya Pottery: Classification, Analysis and Interpretation*. Gainesville: University Press of Florida.

Alisky, Marvin. 1980. "The Relations of the State of Yucatán and the Federal Government of Mexico, 1823–1978." In *Yucatán: A World Apart*, ed. E. H. Moseley and Edward D. Terry, 245–63. Tuscaloosa: University of Alabama Press.

Amundson, Ronald, Asmeret Asefaw Berhe, Jan W. Hopmans, Carolyn Olson, A. Ester Sztein, and Donald L. Sparks. 2015. "Soil and Human Security in the 21st Century." *Science* 348 (6235): 647–53. https://doi.org/10.1126/science.1261071.

Andrews, E. Wyllys, IV. 1970. *Balankanche, Throne of the Tiger Priest*. Middle American Research Institute Publication 32. New Orleans: Tulane University.

Arnold, Dean E. 1967a. "Maya Blue: A New Perspective." MA thesis, University of Illinois, Urbana.

Arnold, Dean E. 1967b. *Sak lu'um in Maya Culture and Its Possible Relation to Maya Blue*. Department of Anthropology, Research Reports No. 2. Urbana: University of Illinois, Urbana.

Arnold, Dean E. 1970a. "Ethnomineralogical Studies in Yucatán: Archaeological Implications." General Session, Annual Meeting of the Society for American Archaeology, Mexico City, May 1.

Arnold, Dean E. 1970b. "The Emics of Pottery Design from Quinua, Peru." PhD diss., University of Illinois, Urbana.

Arnold, Dean E. 1971. "Ethnomineralogy of Ticul, Yucatán Potters: Etics and Emics." *American Antiquity* 36 (1): 20–40. https://doi.org/10.2307/278020.

Arnold, Dean E. 1972a. "Native Pottery Making in Quinua, Peru." *Anthropos* 67 (5–6): 858–72.

Arnold, Dean E. 1972b. "Mineralogical Analyses of Ceramic Materials from Quinua, Department of Ayacucho, Peru." *Archaeometry* 14 (1): 93–101. https://doi.org/10.1111/j.1475-4754.1972.tb00053.x.

Arnold, Dean E. 1972c. "Mold-Made Potters' Marks from Andahuaylas, Department of Apurimac, Peru." *Ethnos* 37 (1–4): 81–87. https://doi.org/10.1080/00141844.1972.9981051.

Arnold, Dean E. 1975a. "Ceramic Ecology of the Ayacucho Basin, Peru: Implications for Prehistory." *Current Anthropology* 16 (2): 183–205. https://doi.org/10.1086/201538.

Arnold, Dean E. 1975b. "Reply to Haaland and Browman." *Current Anthropology* 16 (4):637–40.

Arnold, Dean E. 1978a. "The Ethnography of Pottery Making in the Valley of Guatemala." In *The Ceramics of Kaminaljuyu*, ed. Ronald K. Wetherington, 327–400. University Park, PA: Pennsylvania State University Press.

Arnold, Dean E. 1978b. "Ceramic Variability, Environment and Culture History among the Pokom in the Valley of Guatemala." In *Spatial Organization of Culture*, ed. Ian Hodder, 39–59. London: Duckworth.

Arnold, Dean E. 1983. "Design Structure and Community Organization in Quinua, Peru." In *Structure and Cognition in Art*, ed. Dorothy Washburn, 56–73. Cambridge: Cambridge University Press.

Arnold, Dean E. 1984. "Social Interaction and Ceramic Design: Community-Wide Correlates in Quinua, Peru." In *Pots and Potters: Current Approaches in Ceramic Archaeology*, ed. Prudence M. Rice, 133–61. Monograph XXIV. Los Angeles: Institute of Archaeology, University of California.

Arnold, Dean E. 1985. *Ceramic Theory and Cultural Process*. Cambridge: Cambridge University Press.

Arnold, Dean E. 1989. "Patterns of Learning, Residence and Descent among Potters in Ticul, Yucatan, Mexico." In *Archaeological Approaches to Cultural Identity*, ed. Stephen Shennan, 174–84. London, UK: Unwin Hyman.

Arnold, Dean E. 1991. "Ethnoarchaeology and Investigations of Ceramic Production and Exchange: Can We Go Beyond Cautionary Tales?" In *The Legacy of Anna O. Shepard*, ed. R. L. Bishop and F. W. Lange, 321–45. Boulder: University Press of Colorado.

Arnold, Dean E. 1993. *Ecology of Ceramic Production in an Andean Community*. Cambridge: Cambridge University Press.

Arnold, Dean E. 1999. "Advantages and Disadvantages of Vertical-Half Molding Technology: Implications for Production Organization." In *Pottery and People: A Dynamic*

Interaction, ed. J. M. Skibo and G. M. Feinman, 50–80. Salt Lake City: University of Utah Press.

Arnold, Dean E. 2000. "Does the Standardization of Ceramic Pastes Really Mean Specialization?" *Journal of Archaeological Method and Theory* 7 (4): 333–75. https://doi.org/10.1023/A:1026570906712.

Arnold, Dean E. 2005a. "Maya Blue and Palygorskite: A Second Possible Pre-Columbian Source." *Ancient Mesoamerica* 16 (01): 51–62. https://doi.org/10.1017/S0956536105050078.

Arnold, Dean E. 2005b. "Linking Society with the Compositional Analyses of Pottery: A Model from Comparative Ethnography." In *Pottery Manufacturing Processes: Reconstitution and Interpretation*, ed. Alexandre Livingstone Smith, Dominique Bosquet and Rémi Martineau, 15–21. BAR International Series 1349. Oxford: British Archaeological Reports.

Arnold, Dean E. 2006. "The Threshold Model for Ceramic Resources: A Refinement." In *Ceramic Studies: Papers on the Social and Cultural Significance of Ceramics in Europe and Eurasia from Prehistoric to Historic Times*, ed. Dragos Gheorghiu, 3–9. BAR International Series 1553. Oxford: British Archaeological Reports.

Arnold, Dean E. 2008. *Social Change and the Evolution of Ceramic Production and Distribution in a Maya Community*. Boulder: University Press of Colorado.

Arnold, Dean E. 2011. "Ceramic Theory and Cultural Process after 25 Years." *Ethnoarchaeology* 3 (1): 63–98. https://doi.org/10.1179/eth.2011.3.1.63.

Arnold, Dean E. 2012. "The Social Evolution of Potters' Households in Ticul, Yucatán, Mexico 1965–1997." In *Ancient Households of the Americas: Conceptualizing What Households Do*, ed. John G. Douglass and Nancy Gonlin, 163–87. Boulder: University Press of Colorado.

Arnold, Dean E. 2015a. *The Evolution of Ceramic Production Organization in a Maya Community*. Boulder: University Press of Colorado. https://doi.org/10.5876/9781607323143.

Arnold, Dean E. 2015b. "Maya Blue." In *Encyclopaedia of the History of Science, Technology, and Medicine in Non-Western Cultures*, 2866–70. Dordrecht, The Netherlands: Springer-Science Business Media. https://doi.org/10.1007/978-94-007-3934-5_10170-2.

Arnold, Dean E., and Bruce F. Bohor. 1975. "Attapulgite and Maya Blue: An Ancient Mine Comes to Light." *Archaeology* 28 (January): 23–29.

Arnold, Dean E., and Bruce F. Bohor. 1976. "An Ancient Attapulgite Mine in Yucatán." *Katunob* 8 (4): 25–34.

Arnold, Dean E., and Bruce F. Bohor. 1977. "The Ancient Clay Mine at Yo' K'at, Yucatán." *American Antiquity* 42 (4): 575–82. https://doi.org/10.2307/278930.

Arnold, D. E., and B. F. Bohor. 2008. "Maya Blue: Where Did Its Palygorskite Constituent Originate?" *La Tinaja: A Newsletter of Archaeological Ceramics* 10 (1): 2–8.

Arnold, Dean E., Bruce F. Bohor, Hector Neff, Gary M. Feinman, Patrick Ryan Williams, Laure Dussubieux, and Ronald Bishop. 2012. "The First Direct Evidence of Pre-Columbian Sources of Palygorskite for Maya Blue." (July) *Journal of Archaeological Science* 39 (7): 2252–60. https://doi.org/10.1016/j.jas.2012.02.036.

Arnold, Dean E., Jason R. Branden, Patrick Ryan Williams, Gary M. Feinman, and J. P. Brown. 2008. "The First Direct Evidence for the Production of Maya Blue: Rediscovery of a Technology." *Antiquity* 82 (315): 151–64. https://doi.org/10.1017/S0003598X00096514.

Arnold, Dean E., Hector Neff, and Ronald L. Bishop. 1991. "Compositional Analysis and 'Sources' of Pottery: An Ethnoarchaeological Approach." *American Anthropologist* 93 (1): 70–90. https://doi.org/10.1525/aa.1991.93.1.02a00040.

Arnold, Dean E., Hector Neff, Ronald L. Bishop, and Michael D. Glascock. 1999. "Testing Interpretative Assumptions of Neutron Activation Analysis: Contemporary Pottery in Yucatán, 1964–1994." In *Material Meanings: Critical Approaches to the Interpretations of Material Culture*, ed. Elizabeth Chilton, 61–84. Salt Lake City: University of Utah Press.

Arnold, Dean E., Hector Neff, and Michael D. Glascock. 2000. "Testing Assumptions of Neutron Activation Analysis: Communities, Workshops and Paste Preparation in Yucatán, Mexico." *Archaeometry* 42 (2): 301–16. https://doi.org/10.1111/j.1475-4754.2000.tb00883.x.

Arnold, Dean E., Hector Neff, Michael D. Glascock, and Robert J. Speakman. 2007. "Sourcing the Palygorskite used in Maya Blue: A Pilot Study Comparing the Results of INAA and LA-ICP-MS." *Latin American Antiquity* 18 (1): 44–58. https://doi.org/10.2307/25063085.

Arnold, Dean E., and A. L. Nieves. 1992. "Factors Affecting Standardization." In *Ceramic Production and Distribution: An Integrated Approach*, ed. G. J. Bey III, and C. A. Pool, 93–113. Boulder, CO: Westview Press.

Arnold, Dean E., Jill Huttar Wilson, and Alvaro L. Nieves. 2008. "Why Was the Potter's Wheel Rejected? Social Choice and Technological Change in Ticul, Yucatán, Mexico." In *Pottery Economics in Mesoamerica*, ed. Christopher A. Pool and George J. Bey III, 59–87. Tucson: University of Arizona Press.

Arnold, Dean E., Hayley Schumacher Wynne, and Josiah Ostoich. 2013. "The Materiality of Social Memory: The Potters' *Gremio* in Ticul, Yucatán, México." *Ethnoarchaeology* 5 (2): 81–99. https://doi.org/10.1179/1944289013Z.0000000007.

Arnold, Phillip J., III. 1988. *Ceramic Production and Consumption in the Sierra de los Tuxtlas, Veracruz, Mexico*. Research Paper Series, No. 21. Albuquerque: Latin American Institute, University of New Mexico Press.

Arnold, Phillip J., III. 1991a. *Domestic Ceramic Production and Spatial Organization: A Mexican Case Study in Ethnoarchaeology*. Cambridge: Cambridge University Press. https://doi.org/10.1017/CBO9780511598395.

Arnold, Phillip J., III. 1991b. "Dimensional Standardization and Production Scale in Mesoamerican Ceramics." *Latin American Antiquity* 2 (4): 363–70. https://doi.org/10.2307/971784.

Arnold, Phillip J., III. 2000. "Working without a Net: Recent Trends in Ceramic Ethnoarchaeology." *Journal of Archaeological Research* 8 (2): 105–33. https://doi.org/10.1023/A:1009452310915.

Arthur, John W. 2006. *Living with Pottery: Ethnoarchaeology among the Gamo of Southwest Ethiopia*. Salt Lake City: University of Utah Press.

Baddeley, Alan. 1992. "Working Memory." *Science* 255 (5044): 556–59. https://doi.org/10.1126/science.1736359.

Bailey, S. W., G. W. Brindley, W. D. Johns, R. T. Martin, and M. Ross. 1971. "Summary of National and International Recommendations on Clay Mineral Nomenclature: 1969–70 CMS Nomenclature Committee." *Clays and Clay Minerals* 19 (2): 129–32. https://doi.org/10.1346/CCMN.1971.0190210.

Baklanoff, Eric N. 1980. "The Diversification Quest: A Monocrop Export Economy in Transition." In *Yucatán: A World Apart*, ed. E. H. Moseley and Edward D. Terry, 202–44. Tuscaloosa: University of Alabama Press.

Balfet, Hélène. 1965. "Ethnographical Observations in North Africa and Archeological Interpretation." In *Ceramics and Man*, ed. F. R. Matson, 202–17. Chicago: Aldine.

Ball, Joseph W. 1994. "Northern Maya Archaeology: Some Observations on an Emerging Paradigm." In *Hidden among the Hills: Maya Archaeology of the Northwest Yucatán Peninsula: First Maler Symposium, Bonn, 1989,* ed. Hanns J. Prem, 389–96. Mochmuhl, Germany: Verlag von Flemming.

Barrera Marín, Alfredo, Alfredo Barrera Vásquez, and Rosa María López Franco. 1976. *Nomenclatura ethnobotánica maya: Una interpretación taxonómica*. Colección Científica 36. Mérida, Yucatán, Mexico: Instituto Nacional de Antropología e Historia, SEP, Centro Regional del Sureste.

Barrera Vásquez, Alfredo. 1937. "Cerámica maya." *Obre, Organo de la Universidad Nacional del Sureste de México* 1 (3): 162–64.

Barrera Vásquez, A. O., J. Ramón Bastarrachea Manzano, W. Brito Sansores, Refugio Vermont Salas, D. Dzul Góngora, and Domingo Dzul Poot. 1980. *Diccionario maya cordemex: Maya-español, español maya*. Mérida, Yucatán, Mexico: Ediciones Cordemex.

Bates, R. L., and J. A. Jackson, eds. 1987. *Glossary of Geology*. Alexandria, VA: American Geological Institute.

Bateson, Gregory. 1958. *Naven*. 2nd ed. Stanford, CA: Stanford University Press.

Beck, Margaret E. 2006. "Middle Ceramic Assemblage Formation: A Case Study from Kalinga, Philippines." *American Antiquity* 71 (1): 27–51. https://doi.org/10.2307/40035320.

Begossi, A., M. Clauzet, J. L. Figueiredo, L. Garuana, R. V. Lima, P. F. Lopes, M. Ramires, A. L. Silva, and R. A. M. Silvano. 2008. "Are Biological Species and Higher-Ranking Categories Real? Fish Folk Taxonomy on Brazil's Atlantic Forest Coast and in the Amazon." *Current Anthropology* 49 (2): 291–306. https://doi.org/10.1086/527437.

Benz, Bruce, Hugo Perales, and Stephen Brush. 2007. "Tzeltal and Tzotzil Farmer Knowledge and Maize Diversity in Chiapas, Mexico." *Current Anthropology* 48 (2): 289–300. https://doi.org/10.1086/512986.

Berlin, Brent. 1970. "A Universalist-Evolutionary Approach in Ethnographic Semantics." In *Current Directions in Anthropology* 3 (3, Part II): 3–18.

Berlin, Brent. 1973. "Folk Systematics in Relation to Biological Classification and Nomenclature." *Annual Review of Ecology and Systematics* 4 (1): 259–71. https://doi.org/10.1146/annurev.es.04.110173.001355.

Berlin, Brent. 1992. *Ethnobiological Classification: Principles of Categorization of Plants and Animals in Traditional Societies*. Princeton: Princeton University Press. https://doi.org/10.1515/9781400862597.

Berlin, Brent, Dennis E. Breedlove, and Peter H. Raven. 1966. "Folk Taxonomies and Biological Classification." *Science* 154 (3746): 273–75. https://doi.org/10.1126/science.154.3746.273.

Berlin, Brent, Dennis E. Breedlove, and Peter H. Raven. 1968. "Covert Categories and Folk Taxonomies." *American Anthropologist* 70 (2): 290–99. https://doi.org/10.1525/aa.1968.70.2.02a00050.

Berlin, Brent, Dennis E. Breedlove, and Peter H. Raven. 1974. *Principles of Tzeltal Plant Classification: An Introduction to the Botanical Ethnography of a Maya-Speaking People of Highland Chiapas*. New York: Academic Press.

Berlin, Brent, and Paul Kay. 1969. *Basic Color Terms: Their Universality and Evolution*. Berkeley: University of California Press.

Biagetti, Stefano, and Francesca Lugli, eds. 2016. *The Intangible Elements of Culture in Ethnoarchaeological Research*. New York: Springer International. https://doi.org/10.1007/978-3-319-23153-2.

Binford, Lewis R. 1965. "Archaeological Systematics and the Study of Culture Process." *American Antiquity* 31 (2): 203–10. https://doi.org/10.2307/2693985.

Birman Furman, Raquel, ed. 1996. *Recetarios de indios en lengua maya: Índices de plantas medicinales y de enfermedades coordinados por D. Juan Pío Pérez con extractos de los recetarios, notas y añadiduras por C. Hermann Berendt, M. D. Mérida 1870. Serie de Fuentes Para el Estudio de la Cultura Maya*, 13. Mexico City: Universidad Nacional Autónoma de México.

Black, Mary. 1963. "On Formal Ethnographic Procedures." *American Anthropologist* 65 (6): 1347–51. https://doi.org/10.1525/aa.1963.65.6.02a00100.

Black, Mary, and Duane Metzger. 1965. "Ethnographic Description and the Study of Law." *American Anthropologist* 67 (6): 141–65. https://doi.org/10.1525/aa.1965.67.6.02a00980.

Blair, Robert W. 1964. "Yucatec Maya Noun and Verb Morpho-syntax." PhD diss., University of Chicago.
Bohor, Bruce F. 1975. "Attapulgite in Yucatán." *Guidebook to Field Trip No. 4*. International Clay Conference, Mexico City, July.
Bourdieu, Pierre. 1978. *An Outline of a Theory of Practice*. Trans. Richard Nice. Cambridge: Cambridge University Press.
Bourdieu, Pierre. 1980. *The Logic of Practice*. Trans. Richard Nice. Stanford, CA: Stanford University Press.
Bowser, Brenda J. 2000. "From Pottery to Politics: An Ethnoarchaeological Study of Political Factionalism, Ethnicity, and Domestic Pottery Style in the Ecuadorian Amazon." *Journal of Archaeological Method and Theory* 7 (3): 219–48. https://doi.org/10.1023/A:1026510620824.
Bowser, Brenda J. 2005. "Transactional Politics and the Local and Regional Exchange of Pottery Resources in the Ecuadorian Amazon." In *Pottery Manufacturing Processes: Reconstitution and Interpretation*, ed. Alexandre Livingstone Smith, Dominique Bosquet, and Rémi Martineau, 23–32. BAR International Series 1349. Oxford: Archaeopress.
Bradburn, Anne S. 1998. "Botanical Index." In *A Dictionary of the Maya Language: As Spoken in Hocabá Yucatán*, ed. V. Bricker, Eleuterio Po'ot Yah, and Ofelia Dzul de Po'ot, 320–28. Salt Lake City: University of Utah Press.
Brainerd, George W. 1958. *The Archaeological Ceramics of Yucatán*. Anthropological Records, vol. 19. Berkeley: University of California.
Bricker, Victoria, Eleuterio Po'ot Yah, and Ofelia Dzul de Po'ot. 1998. *A Dictionary of the Maya Language: As Spoken in Hocabá Yucatán*. Salt Lake City: University of Utah Press.
Brondizio, Eduardo S., and Francois-Michel Le Tourneau. 2016. "Environmental Governance for All." *Science* 352 (6291): 1272–73. https://doi.org/10.1126/science.aaf5122.
Brouwer, Jan. 1998. "On Indigenous Knowledge and Development." *Current Anthropology* 39 (3): 351. https://doi.org/10.1086/204739.
Brush, Stephen B. 1980. "Potato Taxonomies in Andean Agriculture." In *Indigenous Knowledge Systems and Development*, ed. David Brokensha, Dennis M. Warren, and Oswald Werner, 37–47. Washington, DC: University Press of America.
Bunzel, Ruth L. 1929. *The Pueblo Potter: A Study of Creative Imagination in Primitive Art*. New York: Columbia University Press.
Burton, M. L., L. A. Brudner, and D. R. White. 1977. "A Model of the Sexual Division of Labor." *American Ethnologist* 4 (2): 227–51. https://doi.org/10.1525/ae.1977.4.2.02a00020.
Butler, James, and Dean E. Arnold. 1977. "Tzutujil Maize Classification in San Pedro La Laguna, Guatemala." In *Cognitive Studies of Southern Mesoamerica*, ed. Helen L. Neuenswander and Dean E. Arnold, 182–205. Publication No. 3. Dallas: SIL Museum of Anthropology.

Caamal-Fuentes, Edgar, Luis W. Torres-Tapia, Paulino Simá-Polanco, Sergio R. Peraza-Sánchez, and Rosa Moo-Puc. 2011. "Screening of Plants Used in Maya Traditional Medicine to Treat Cancer-Like Symptoms." *Journal of Ethnopharmacology* 135 (3): 719–24. https://doi.org/10.1016/j.jep.2011.04.004.

Carmean, Kelli, Patricia A. McAnany, and Jeremy A. Sabloff. 2011. "People Who Lived in Stone Houses: Local Knowledge and Social Difference in the Classic Maya Puuc Region of Yucatán, Mexico." *Latin American Antiquity* 22 (2): 143–58. https://doi.org/10.7183/1045-6635.22.2.143.

Carneiro, Robert. 1994. "The Knowledge and Use of Rain Forest Trees by the Kuikuru Indians of Central Brazil." In *The Nature and Status of Ethnobotany*, 2nd ed., ed. Richard I. Ford, 201–16. Anthropological Papers, Museum of Anthropology No. 67. Ann Arbor: Museum of Anthropology, University of Michigan.

Chimello de Oliveira, Luiz Eduardo, Tainá Barreto, and Alpina Begossi. 2012. "Prototypes and Folk Taxonomy: Artisanal Fishers and Snappers on the Brazilian Coast." *Current Anthropology* 53 (6): 789–98. https://doi.org/10.1086/667717.

Clement, Amy C., Robert Burgman, and Joel R. Norris. 2009. "Observational and Model Evidence of Positive Low-Level Cloud Feedback." *Science* 325 (5939): 460–64. https://doi.org/10.1126/science.1171255.

Conklin, Harold. 1961. "The Study of Shifting Cultivation." *Current Anthropology* 2 (1): 27–61. https://doi.org/10.1086/200160.

Costin, Cathy Lynne. 2000. "The Use of Ethnoarchaeology for the Archaeological Study of Ceramic Production." *Journal of Archaeological Method and Theory* 7 (4): 377–403. https://doi.org/10.1023/A:1026523023550.

Couzin, Jennifer. 2007. "Opening Doors to Native Knowledge: Scientific and Local Cultures Seek Common Ground for Tackling Climate-Change Questions in the Arctic." *Science* 315 (5818)::1518–19. https://doi.org/10.1126/science.315.5818.1518.

Cserna, Zoltan de, Pedro A. Mosiño, and Oscar Benassini. 1974. *El escenario geográfico: Introducción ecológica (primera parte)*. Mexico City: Instituto Nacional de Antropología e Historia, Departamento de Prehistoria.

Curtis, F. 1962. "The Utility Pottery Industry of Bailén, Southern Spain." *American Anthropologist* 64 (3): 486–503. https://doi.org/10.1525/aa.1962.64.3.02a00020.

D'Andrade, Roy. 1995. *The Development of Cognitive Anthropology*. Cambridge: Cambridge University Press. https://doi.org/10.1017/CBO9781139166645.

David, Nicholas. 1972. "On the Life Span of Pottery, Type Frequencies, and Archeological Inference." *American Antiquity* 37 (1): 141–42. https://doi.org/10.2307/278897.

David, N., and H. Hennig. 1972. *The Ethnography of Pottery: A Fulani Case Seen in Archaeological Perspective*. Addison Wesley Modular Publications No. 21, 1–29. Reading, MA: Addison Wesley.

David, Nicholas, and Carol Kramer. 2001. *Ethnoarchaeology in Action*. Cambridge: Cambridge University Press. https://doi.org/10.1017/CBO9781316036488.

de Jager, Monique de, Franz J. Weissing, Peter M. J. Herman, Bart A. Nolet, and Johan van de Koppel. 2011. "Lévy Walks Evolve through Interaction between Movement and Environmental Complexity." *Science* 332 (6037): 1551–53. https://doi.org/10.1126/science.1201187.

de Pablo, Liberto. 1964. "Las Arcillas: 1. Clasificación, identificación, usos y especificaciones industriales." *Boletín de la Sociedad Geológica Mexicana* 28 (2): 49–91.

Deal, Michael. 1998. *Pottery Ethnoarchaeology in the Central Maya Highlands*. Salt Lake City: University of Utah Press.

Demarest, Arthur A. 2013. "Ideological Pathways to Economic Exchange: Religion, Economy, and Legitimation at the Classic Maya Royal Capital of Cancuén." *Latin American Antiquity* 24 (4): 371–402. https://doi.org/10.7183/1045-6635.24.4.371.

DeMarrais, Elizabeth, Chris Gosden, and Colin Renfrew. 2004. *Rethinking Materiality: The Engagement of Mind with the Material World, McDonald Institute Monographs*. Cambridge: McDonald Institute for Archaeological Research, University of Cambridge.

Djordjević, Biljana. 2007. "Ethnoarchaeological Research as a Method of Protection of Traditional Ceramics Technologies." In *Proceedings of the Regional Conference "Condition of the Cultural and Natural Heritage in the Balkan Region,"* vol. 1: 87–99. Belgrade: National Museum in Belgrade.

Djordjević, Biljana. 2013. "Pottery Making in Zlakusa: First Ethnoarchaeological Research Project in Serbia." In *Ethnoarchaeology: Current Research and Field Methods: Conference Proceedings, Rome, Italy, 13th–14th May 2010*, ed. Francesca Lugli, Assunta Alessandra Stoppiello, and Stefano Biagetti. BAR International Series 2472. Oxford: Archaeopress.

Djordjević, Biljana. 2016. "The Manufacture of Traditional Bread-Baking Pans: Ethnoarchaeology and the Safeguarding of Intangible Heritage." In *The Intangible Elements of Culture in Ethnoarchaeological Research*, ed. Stefano Biagetti, Francesca Lugli, 313–20. Cham: Springer International Switzerland. https://doi.org/10.1007/978-3-319-23153-2_26.

Doehring, D. O., and J. H. Butler. 1974. "Hydrogeologic Constraints on Yucatán's Development." *Science* 186 (4164): 591–95. https://doi.org/10.1126/science.186.4164.591.

Donnan, Christopher B. 1971. "Ancient Peruvian Potters' Marks and Their Interpretation through Ethnographic Analogy." *American Antiquity* 36 (4): 460–66. https://doi.org/10.2307/278466.

Donnan, Christopher, and C. W. Clewlow, Jr., eds. 1974. *Ethnoarchaeology, Monograph IV. Los Angeles*. Los Angeles: Institute of Archaeology, University of California.

Druc, Isabelle. 2013. "What is Local? Looking at Ceramic Production in the Peruvian Highlands and Beyond." *Journal of Anthropological Research* 69 (4): 485–513. https://doi.org/10.3998/jar.0521004.0069.404.

Duin, Renzo S., Kilian Toinaike, Tasikale Alupki, and Aimawale Opoya. 2015. "Archaeology of Engagement: Indigenous People, Social Memory, and Making History in the Upper Maroni Basin (Northern Amazonia)." *Current Anthropology* 56 (5): 753–61. https://doi.org/10.1086/683251.

Dunning, Nicholas. 1988. "The Yaxhom Conurbation." *Mexicon* 10 (1): 16–19.

Dunning, Nicholas. 1994. "Puuc Ecology and Settlement Patterns." In *Hidden among the Hills: Maya Archaeology of the Northwest Yucatán Peninsula: First Maler Symposium, Bonn, 1989*, ed. Hanns J. Prem, 1–43. Anlage, Mochmuhl, Germany: Verlag von Flemming.

Ehrich, Robert W. 1965. "Ceramics and Man: A Cultural Perspective." In *Ceramics and Man*, ed. F. R. Matson, 202–17. Chicago: Aldine.

Erasmus, J. Charles. 1965. "Monument Building: Some Field Experiments." *Southwestern Journal of Anthropology* 21 (4): 277–301. https://doi.org/10.1086/soutjanth.21.4.3629433.

Fahrenkamp-Uppenbrink, Julia. 2015. "On Top of the World." *Science* 347 (6217): 37. https://doi.org/10.1126/science.aaa3167.

Faust, Betty Bernice. 1998. *Mexican Rural Development and the Plumed Serpent: Technology and Maya Cosmology in the Tropical Forest of Campeche, Mexico*. Westport, CT: Bergin and Garvey.

Felger, Richard, and Mary Beck Moser. 1973. "Eelgrass (*Zostera mariana L.*) in the Gulf of California: Discovery of Its Nutritional Value by the Seri Indians." *Science* 181 (4097): 355–56. https://doi.org/10.1126/science.181.4097.355.

Folan, William J. 1978. "Cobá, Quintana Roo, Mexico: An Analysis of a Prehispanic and Contemporary Source of *Sascab*." *American Antiquity* 43 (1): 79–85. https://doi.org/10.2307/279634.

Folan, William J. 1982. "Mining and Quarrying Techniques of the Lowland Maya in Mining and Mining Techniques in Ancient Mesoamerica." *Anthropology Stony Brook, NY* 6 (1–2): 149–74.

Ford, Anabel. 2008. "Dominant Plants of the Maya Forest and Gardens of El Pilar: Implications for Paleoenvironmental Reconstructions." *Journal of Ethnobiology* 28 (2): 179–99. https://doi.org/10.2993/0278-0771-28.2.179.

Ford, Anabel, and Ronald Nigh. 2009. "Origins of the Maya Forest Garden: Maya Resource Management." *Journal of Ethnobiology* 29 (2): 213–36. https://doi.org/10.2993/0278-077-129.2.213.

Foster, George M. 1948. "Some Implications of Modern Mexican Mold-Made Pottery." *Southwestern Journal of Anthropology* 4 (4): 356–70. https://doi.org/10.1086/soutjanth.4.4.3628584.

Foster, George M. 1955. *Contemporary Pottery Techniques in Southern and Central Mexico*. Middle American Research Institute Publication No. 2. New Orleans: Tulane University.

Foster, George M. 1960a. "Life-Expectancy of Utilitarian Pottery in Tzintzuntzan, Michoacan, Mexico." *American Antiquity* 25 (04): 606–9. https://doi.org/10.2307/276647.

Foster, George M. 1960b. "Archaeological Implications of the Modern Pottery of Acatlán, Puebla, Mexico." *American Antiquity* 26 (2): 205–14. https://doi.org/10.2307/276199.

Foster, George M. 1963. "The Dyadic Contract in Tzintzuntzan, II: Patron-Client Relationship." *American Anthropologist* 65 (6): 1280–94. https://doi.org/10.1525/aa.1963.65.6.02a00040.

Foster, George M. 1965. "The Sociology of Pottery: Questions and Hypotheses Arising from Contemporary Mexican Work." In *Ceramics and Man*, ed. F. R. Matson, 43–61. Chicago: Aldine.

Foster, George M. 1979. *Tzintzuntzan: Mexican Peasants in a Changing World*, rev. ed. New York: Elsevier.

Frake, Charles O. 1962. "The Ethnographic Study of Cognitive Systems." In *Anthropology and Human Behavior*, ed. T. Gladwin and W. C. Sturtevant, 72–85, 91–93. Washington, DC: Anthropological Society of Washington.

Gates, William. [1937] 1978. *Yucatán before and after the Conquest, by Friar Diego de Landa, Translated with Notes by William Gates*. New York: Dover Publications.

Gettens, Rutherford J. 1962. "Maya Blue: An Unsolved Problem in Ancient Pigments." *American Antiquity* 27 (4): 557–64. https://doi.org/10.2307/277679.

Gillespie, Susan D. 2000a. "Rethinking Ancient Maya Social Organization: Replacing 'Lineage' with 'House.'" *American Anthropologist* 102 (3): 467–84. https://doi.org/10.1525/aa.2000.102.3.467.

Gillespie, Susan D. 2000b. "Beyond Kinship: An Introduction." In *Beyond Kinship: Social and Material Reproduction in House Societies*, ed. Rosemary A. Joyce and Susan D. Gillespie, 1–21. Philadelphia: University of Pennsylvania Press.

Gillespie, Susan D. 2000c. "Lévi-Strauss, Maison and Société à Maisons." In *Beyond Kinship: Social and Material Reproduction in House Societies*, ed. Rosemary A. Joyce and Susan D. Gillespie, 22–52. Philadelphia: University of Pennsylvania Press.

Goff, Brent. 1990. "Mastering the Craft of Scaling-Up in Colombia: An NGO is Preserving Crafts by Investing in Artisans and Turning the Nation's Rural Schools into 'Living Museums.'" *Grass Roots Development, Journal of the Inter-American Foundation* 14 (1): 12–22.

Goodenough, Ward. 1957. "Cultural Anthropology and Linguistics." In *Report of the Seventh Annual Round Table Meeting on Linguistics and Language Study*, ed. Paul L. Garvin. Monograph Series of Languages and Linguistics, No. 9, 167–73. Washington, DC: Georgetown University.

Goodenough, Ward. 1964. "Cultural Anthropology and Linguistics." In *Language, Culture, and Society*, ed. Dell Hymes, 36–39. New York: Harper and Row.

Goodman, Steven N. 2016. "Aligning Statistical and Scientific Reasoning: Misunderstanding and Misuse of Statistical Significance Impede Science." *Science* 352 (6290): 1180–81. https://doi.org/10.1126/science.aaf5406.

Gosselain, Olivier P. 1992. "Technology and Style: Potters and Pottery among Bafia of Cameroon." *Man* 27 (3): 559–86. https://doi.org/10.2307/2803929.

Gosselain, Oliver P. 1998. "Social and Technical Identity in a Clay Crystal Ball." In *The Archaeology of Social Boundaries*, ed. Miriam T. Stark, 78–106. Washington, DC: Smithsonian Institution Press.

Gosselain, Olivier P. 2000. "Materializing Identities: An African Perspective." *Journal of Archaeological Method and Theory* 7 (3): 187–217. https://doi.org/10.1023/A:1026558503986.

Gosselain, Oliver P., and Alexandre Livingstone Smith. 2005. "The Source: Clay Selection and Processing Practices in Sub-Saharan Africa." In *Pottery Manufacturing Processes: Reconstitution and Interpretation*, ed. Alexandre Livingstone Smith, Dominique Bosquet, and Rémi Martineau, 33–47. BAR International Series 1349. Oxford: British Archaeological Reports.

Gould, Richard A., ed. 1978. *Explorations in Ethnoarchaeology*. Albuquerque: University of New Mexico.

Gould, Richard A. 1980. *Living Archaeology*. Cambridge: Cambridge University Press.

Grim, R. E. 1962. *Applied Clay Mineralogy*. New York: McGraw-Hill.

Grim, R. E. 1968. *Clay Mineralogy*. 2nd ed. New York: McGraw-Hill.

Hacienda YoKat. 2014. Accessed August 29, 2015. http://www.haciendayokat.com.

Hall, Stephen S. 2015. "A Trial for the Ages: Nir Barzilai Wants to Launch the First Rigorous Test of a Drug That Could Put the Brakes on Aging." *Science* 349 (6254): 1274–78. https://doi.org/10.1126/science.349.6254.1274.

Han, Sallie, and Jason Antrosio, eds. 2016a. "Cultural Heritage." *Open Anthropology: A Public Journal of the American Anthropological Association* 4 (1). http://www.americananthro.org/StayInformed/OAIssueTOC.aspx?ItemNumber=13428.

Han, Sallie, and Jason Antrosio. 2016b. Cultural Heritage: The Editors' Note. In *Cultural Heritage. Open Anthropology: A Public Journal of the American Anthropological Association* 4 (1). http://www.americananthro.org/StayInformed/OAArticleDetail.aspx?ItemNumber=13443

Harris, Marvin. 1964. *The Nature of Cultural Things*. New York: Random House.

Harris, Marvin. 1968. *The Rise of Anthropological Theory*. New York: Thomas Y. Crowell.

Harris, Marvin. 1979. *Cultural Materialism: The Struggle for a Science of Culture*. New York: Random House.

Harris, Marvin. 1990. "Emics and Etics Revisited." In *Emics and Etics: The Insider/Outsider Debate*, ed. Thomas N. Headland, Kenneth L. Pike, and Marvin Harris, 48–61. Frontiers of Anthropology, Vol. 7. Newbury Park, CA: Sage Publications.

Hatt, Robert T. 1953. "Introduction." In *Faunal and Archaeological Researches in Yucatán Caves*, by Robert T. Hatt, Harvey I. Fisher, Dave A. Langebartel, and George W. Brainerd. Bulletin No. 33. Bloomfield Hills, MI: Cranbrook Institute of Science Bulletin.

Headland, Thomas N., Kenneth L. Pike, and Marvin Harris, eds. 1990. *Emics and Etics: The Insider/Outsider Debate*. Frontiers of Anthropology, vol. 7. Newbury Park, CA: Sage Publications.

Hegmon, Michelle. 2000. "Advances in Ceramic Ethnoarchaeology." *Journal of Archaeological Method and Theory* 7 (3): 129–37. https://doi.org/10.1023/A:1026502419007.

Heidke, James M., Susan Leary, Sarah A. Herr, and Mark D. Elson. 2007. "Alameda Brown Ware and San Francisco Grey Ware Technology and Economics." In *Sunset Crater Archaeology: Ceramic Technology, Distribution, and Use*, ed. Scott Van Keuren, Mark D. Elson, and Sarah A. Herr, 145–83. Anthropological Papers No. 32. Tucson, AZ: Center for Desert Archaeology.

Henrickson, Elizabeth, and Mary McDonald. 1983. "Ceramic Form and Function: An Ethnographic Search and an Archaeological Application." *American Anthropologist* 85 (3): 630–43. https://doi.org/10.1525/aa.1983.85.3.02a00070.

Hewes, Gordon W. 1955. "World Distribution of Certain Postural Habits." *American Anthropologist* 57 (2): 231–44. https://doi.org/10.1525/aa.1955.57.2.02a00040.

Hewes, Gordon W. 1957. "The Anthropology of Posture." *Scientific American* 196 (2): 122–32. https://doi.org/10.1038/scientificamerican0257-122.

Hirota, Marina, Milena Holmgren, Egbert H. Van Nes, and Marten Scheffer. 2011. "Global Resilience of Tropical Forest and Savanna to Critical Transitions." *Science* 334 (6053): 232–35. https://doi.org/10.1126/science.1210657.

Hirschhorn, Howard H. 1981. "Botanical Remedies of South and Central America and the Caribbean: An Archival Analysis, Part I." *Journal of Ethnopharmacology* 4 (2): 129–58. https://doi.org/10.1016/0378-8741(81)90032-5.

Hirschhorn, Howard H. 1982. "Botanical Remedies of South and Central America and the Caribbean: An Archival Analysis, Part II, Conclusion." *Journal of Ethnopharmacology* 5 (2): 163–80. https://doi.org/10.1016/0378-8741(82)90041-1.

Holden, Constance. 2007. "Gene Variant May Influence How People Learn from Mistakes." *Science* 318 (5856): 1539. https://doi.org/10.1126/science.318.5856.1539a.

Hudson, J. 1997. "Urban Pottery Workshops in North Africa." In *Pottery in the Making: Ceramic Traditions*, ed. Ian Freestone and David Gaimster, 134–39. Washington, DC: Smithsonian Institution Press.

Hunn, Eugene S. 1999. "The Value of Subsistence for the Future of the World." In *Ethnoecology: Situated Knowledge/Located Lives*, ed. Virginia D. Nazarea, 23–36. Tucson: University of Arizona Press.

Illescas, Alejandro. 2013. *Los fantasmas de la Quinta Montes Molina. México*. Mérida, Yucatán, Mexico: La Quinta.

Ingold, Tim. 2000. *Perception of the Environment: Essays on Livelihood, Dwelling and Skill.* London: Routledge, Taylor and Francis Group. https://doi.org/10.4324/9780203466025.

Ingold, Tim. 2013. *Making: Anthropology, Archaeology, Art and Architecture.* London: Routledge, Taylor and Francis Group.

Instituto Nacional de Estadística Geografía e Informática. 1986. *Carta Topográfica, 1:50,000: Ticul, Yucatán, Mapa F16C72.* Mexico City.

Isphording, Wayne C. 1975. "The Physical Geology of Yucatán." *Transactions: Gulf Coast Association of Geological Societies* 25:231–62.

Isphording, Wayne C., and E. M. Wilson. 1974. "The Relationship of 'Volcanic Ash' *Sak Lu'um*, and Palygorskite in Northern Yucatán Maya Ceramics." *American Antiquity* 39 (3): 483–88. https://doi.org/10.2307/279441.

Johnson, Allen. 1974. "Ethnoecology and Planting Practices in a Swidden Agricultural System." *American Ethnologist* 1 (1): 87–101. https://doi.org/10.1525/ae.1974.1.1.02a00050.

Joseph, Gilbert M. 1980. "Revolution from Without, the Mexican Revolution in Yucatán, 1910–1940." In *Yucatán: A World Apart*, ed. Edward H. Moseley and Edward D. Terry, 142–71. Tuscaloosa: University of Alabama Press.

Justman, Quincey A., Zach Serber, James E. Ferrell, Jr., Hana El-Samad, and Kevan M. Shokat. 2009. "Tuning the Activation Threshold of a Kinase Network by Nested Feedback Loops." *Science* 324 (5926): 509–12. https://doi.org/10.1126/science.1169498.

Kelly, Sophia E., Christopher N. Watkins, and David R. Abbott. 2011. "Revisiting the Exploitable Threshold Model: 14th Century Resource Procurement and Landscape Dynamics on Perry Mesa, Arizona." *Journal of Field Archaeology* 36 (4): 322–36. https://doi.org/10.1179/009346911X13140904575585.

Kennett, Douglas J., and Timothy P. Beach. 2013. "Archaeological and Environmental Lessons from the Anthropocene from the Classic Maya Collapse." *Anthropocene* 45 (December): 88–100. https://doi.org/10.1016/j.ancene.2013.12.002.

Kensinger, Kenneth M., Phyllis Rabineau, Helen Tanner, Susan Ferguson, and Alice Dawson. 1975. *The Cashinahua of Eastern Peru, Studies in Anthropology and Material Culture.* Vol. 1. Providence, RI: Haffenreffer Museum of Anthropology.

Kerr, Richard A. 2009a. "Joining Forces to Pump up a Variable Sun's Climatic Effects." *Science* 325 (5944): 1058–59. https://doi.org/10.1126/science.325_1058b.

Kerr, Richard A. 2009b. "Clouds Appear to Be Big, Bad Player in Global Warming." *Science* 325 (5939): 376. https://doi.org/10.1126/science.325_376.

Killion, Thomas W. 1999. "Review of *Mexican Rural Development and the Plumed Serpent: Technology and the Maya Cosmology.*" *American Anthropologist* 101 (4): 847–48. https://doi.org/10.1525/aa.1999.101.4.847.

King, Eleanor M., James E. Brady, Leslie C. Shaw, Allan B. Cobb, C. L. Kieffer, Michael L. Brennan, and Chandra L. Harris. 2012. "Small Caves and Sacred Geography: A Case

Study from the Prehispanic Maya Site of Maax Na, Belize." *Latin American Antiquity* 23 (4): 611–28. https://doi.org/10.7183/1045–6635.23.4.611.

Klein, Tilmann A., Jane Neumann, Martin Reuter, Jürgen Hennig, D. Yves von Cramon, and Markus Ullsperger. 2007. "Genetically Determined Differences in Learning from Errors." *Science* 318 (5856): 1642–45. https://doi.org/10.1126/science.1145044.

Kolb, Charles C. 1976. "The Methodology of Latin American Ceramic Ecology." *El Dorado: A Newsletter Bulletin on South American Anthropology* 1 (3): 44–82.

Kolb, Charles C., ed. 1988. *Ceramic Ecology Revisited, 1987: The Technology and Socioeconomics of Pottery*. BAR International Series 436. Oxford: British Archaeological Reports.

Kolb, Charles C. 1989. "Ceramic Ecology in Retrospect: A Critical Review of Methodology and Results." In *Ceramic Ecology, 1988: Current Research on Ceramic Materials*, ed. Charles C. Kolb, 261–375. BAR International Series 513. Oxford: British Archaeological Reports.

Kramer, Carol, ed. 1979. *Ethnoarchaeology: Implications of Ethnography for Archaeology*. New York: Columbia University Press.

Kramer, Carol. 1985. "Ceramic Ethnoarchaeology." In Bernard J. Siegel, A. R. Beals, and S. A. Tyler, eds., *Annual Review of Anthropology* 14 (1): 77–102. https://doi.org/10.1146/annurev.an.14.100185.000453.

Kramer, Carol. 1997. *Pottery in Rajasthan: Ethnoarchaeology in Two Indian Cities*. Washington, DC: Smithsonian Institution Press.

Kunstadter, Peter. 1994. "Ecological Modification and Adaptation: An Ethnobotanical View of Lua' Swiddeners of Northwestern Thailand." In *The Nature and Status of Ethnobotany*, 2nd ed., ed. Richard I. Ford, 169–200. Anthropological Papers, Museum of Anthropology No. 67. Ann Arbor: Museum of Anthropology, University of Michigan.

Kurjack, Edward B. 1994. "Political Geography of the Yucatán Hill Country." In *Hidden among the Hills: Maya Archaeology of the Northwest Yucatán Peninsula: First Maler Symposium, Bonn, 1989*, ed. Hanns J. Prem, 308–15. Anflage, Mochmuhl, Germany: Verlag von Flemming.

La Barre, Weston. 1947. "Potato Taxonomy among the Aymara Indians of Bolivia." *Acta Americana* 5:83–103.

Lansing, J. Stephen, James N. Kremer, and Barbara B. Smuts. 1998. "System-Dependent Selection, Ecological Feedback and the Emergence of Functional Structure in Ecosystems." *Journal of Theoretical Biology* 192 (3): 377–91. https://doi.org/10.1006/jtbi.1998.0664.

Lauer, Matthew, and Shankar Aswani. 2009. "Indigenous Ecological Knowledge as Situated Practices: Understanding Fishers' Knowledge in the Western Solomon Islands." *American Anthropologist* 111 (3): 317–29. https://doi.org/10.1111/j.1548-1433.2009.01135.x.

Lee, Jun Hee, Andrei V. Budanov, Eek Joong Park, Ryan Birse, Teddy E. Kim, Guy A. Perkins, Karen Ocorr, Mark H. Ellisman, Rolf Bodmer, Ethan Bier, et al. 2010. "Sestrin as a

Feedback Inhibitor of TOR that Prevents Age-Related Pathologies." *Science* 327 (5970): 1223–28. https://doi.org/10.1126/science.1182228.

Lemonnier, Pierre. 1986. "The Study of Material Culture Today: Toward an Anthropology of Technical Systems." *Journal of Anthropological Archaeology* 5 (2): 147–86. https://doi.org/10.1016/0278-4165(86)90012-7.

Lemonnier, Pierre. 1992. *Elements for an Anthropology of Technology*. Anthropological Papers, Museum of Anthropology No. 88. Ann Arbor: Museum of Anthropology, University of Michigan.

Lemonnier, Pierre. 1993. *Technological Choices: Transformation in Material Cultures since the Neolithic*. New York: Routledge.

Lett, James. 1987. *The Human Enterprise: A Critical Introduction to Anthropological Theory*. Boulder, CO: Westview Press.

Lett, James. 1990. "Emics and Etics: Notes on the Epistemology of Anthropology." In *Emics and Etics: The Insider/Outsider Debate*, ed. Thomas N. Headland, Kenneth L. Pike, and Marvin Harris. Frontiers of Anthropology Vol. 7: 127–42. Newbury Park, CA: Sage Publications.

Lindholm, Maléne E., Stefania Giacomello, Beata Werne Solnestam, Helene Fischer, Mikael Huss, Sanela Kjellqvist, and Carl Johan Sundberg. 2016. "The Impact of Endurance Training on Human Skeletal Muscle Memory, Global Isoform Expression and Novel Transcripts." *PLOS Genetics* 12 (9): e1006294. https://doi.org/10.1371/journal.pgen.1006294.

Lister, Florence C., and Robert H. Lister. 1987. *Andalusian Ceramics in Spain and New Spain: A Cultural Register from the Third Century B. C. to 1700*. Tucson: University of Arizona Press.

Littmann, E. R. 1958. "Ancient Mesoamerican Mortars, Plasters, and Stuccos: The Composition and Origin of *Sascab*." *American Antiquity* 24 (2): 172–76. https://doi.org/10.2307/277478.

Littmann, E. R. 1960. "Ancient Mesoamerican Mortars, Plasters, and Stuccos: the Puuc Area." *American Antiquity* 25 (3): 407–12. https://doi.org/10.2307/277528.

Loney, Helen L. 2000. "Society and Technological Control: A Critical Review of Models of Technological Change in Ceramic Studies." *American Antiquity* 65 (4): 646–68. https://doi.org/10.2307/2694420.

Long, Patrick, and Gabriel Corfas. 2014. "To Learn is to Myelinate." *Science* 346 (6207): 298–99. https://doi.org/10.1126/science.1261127.

Longacre, William A., ed. 1991. *Ceramic Ethnoarchaeology*. Tucson: University of Arizona Press.

Longacre, W. A., and J. M. Skibo, eds. 1994. *Kalinga Ethnoarchaeology: Expanding Archaeological Method and Theory*. Washington, DC: Smithsonian Institution Press.

López Varela, Sandra L. 2014. "Clay Griddles, Analytical Techniques, and Heritage: An Ethnoarchaeological Perspective of Economic Development Policies in México." In

Social Dynamics of Ceramic Analysis: New Techniques and Interpretations: Papers in Honour of Charles C. Kolb, ed. Sandra L. López Varela, 95–105. BAR International Series 2683. Oxford, UK: Archaeopress.

López Varela, Sandra L., and Daniel Aguilar Escobar. 2014. "Building Landscapes of Memory with Pots: Hermeneutic Expressions of Tlaloc in a Festivity of the Valley of Morelos, Mexico." In *Social Dynamics of Ceramic Analysis: New Techniques and Interpretations: Papers in Honour of Charles C. Kolb*, ed. Sandra L. López Varela, 79–86. BAR International Series 2683. Oxford: Archaeopress.

MacLean, Evan L., and Brian Hare. 2015. "Dogs Hijack the Human Bonding Pathway." *Science* 348 (6232): 280–81. https://doi.org/10.1126/science.aab1200.

Malafouris, Lambros. 2004. "The Cognitive Basis of Material Engagement: Where Brain, Body and Culture Conflate." In *Rethinking Materiality: The Engagement of Mind with the Material World*, ed. Elizabeth DeMarrais, Chris Gosden, and Colin Renfrew, 53–62. McDonald Institute Monographs. Cambridge: McDonald Institute for Archaeological Research, University of Cambridge.

Malafouris, Lambros. 2013. *How Things Shape the Mind: A Theory of Material Engagement*. Cambridge, MA: MIT Press.

Masson, Marilyn A., and Carlos Peraza Lope. 2014. "Chapter 6: The Economic Foundations." In *Kukulkan's Realm: Urban Life at Ancient Mayapán*, 269–423. Boulder: University Press of Colorado.

Matson, Frederick R., ed. 1965a. *Ceramics and Man*. Chicago: Aldine.

Matson, F. R. 1965b. "Ceramic Ecology: An Approach to the Study of the Early Cultures of the Near East." In *Ceramics and Man*, ed. F. R. Matson, 202–17. Chicago: Aldine.

Matson, Frederick R. 1973. "The Potters of Chalkis." In *Classics and the Classical Tradition*, ed. E. N. Borza and R. W. Carruba, 117–42. University Park: Pennsylvania State University Press.

Mauss, Marcel. [1950] 1976. *Sociology and Psychology*. London: Routledge and Kegan Paul.

Mayer, Audrey L., and Azad Henareh Khalyani. 2011. "Grass Trumps Trees with Fire." *Science* 334 (6053): 188–89. https://doi.org/10.1126/science.1213908.

MBG (Missouri Botanical Garden). 2014. Accessed February 20, 2014. Tropicos.com.

McAnany, P. A. 1990. "Water Storage in the Puuc Region of the Northern Maya Lowlands: A Key to Population Estimates and Architectural Variability." In *Precolumbian Population History in the Maya Lowlands*, ed. T. P. Culbert and D. S. Rice, 263–84. Albuquerque: University of New Mexico Press.

McCullough, John M. 1973. "Human Ecology, Heat Adaptation and Belief Systems: The Hot-Cold Syndrome of Yucatán." *Journal of Anthropological Research* 29 (1): 32–36. https://doi.org/10.1086/jar.29.1.3629623.

McKenzie, Ian A., David Ohayon, Huiliang Li, Joana Paes de Faria, Koujiro Tohyama, and William D. Richardson. 2014. "Motor Skill Learning Requires Active Central Myelination." *Science* 346 (6207): 318–22. https://doi.org/10.1126/science.1254960.

MedicineNet. 2015. "Attapulgite." http://www.medicinenet.com/attapulgite/article.htm.

Medina-Elizalde, Martin, and Eelco J. Rohling. 2012. "Collapse of Classic Maya Civilization Related to Modest Reduction in Precipitation." *Science* 335 (6071): 956–59. https://doi.org/10.1126/science.1216629.

Meehl, Gerald A., Julie M. Arblaster, Katja Matthes, Fabrizio Sassi, and Harry van Loon. 2009. "Amplifying the Pacific Climate System Response to a Small 11-Year Solar Cycle Forcing." *Science* 325 (5944): 1114–18. https://doi.org/10.1126/science.1172872.

Menzies, Charles R., ed. 2006. *Traditional Ecological Knowledge and Natural Resource Management*. Lincoln: University of Nebraska Press.

Menzies, Charles R., and Caroline Butler. 2006. "Introduction: Understanding Ecological Knowledge." In *Traditional Ecological Knowledge and Natural Resource Management*, ed. Charles R. Menzies, 2–17. Lincoln: University of Nebraska Press.

Mercer, H. C. 1896. *Hill-Caves of Yucatán: A Search for Evidence of Man's Antiquity in the Caverns of Central America*. Philadelphia: J. B. Lippincott Company.

Mercer, H. C. 1897a. "The *Kabal*, or Potter's Wheel of Yucatán." *Bulletin of the Free Museum of Science and Art* 1 (2): 63–70. Philadelphia: University of Pennsylvania.

Mercer, H. C. 1897b. "The Potter's Wheel in Ancient America." *Science* 5 (128): 919–20. https://doi.org/10.1126/science.5.128.919.

Merkle, Bethann Garramon. 2016. "Drawn to Caribou." *American Scientist* 104 (1): 16–19. https://doi.org/10.1511/2016.118.16.

Metzger, Duane, and Donald W. Lathrap, consultants. 1965. *Ollero Yucateco*. 16 mm, 22 min. Urbana, IL: Motion Picture Service, University of Illinois.

Metzger, Duane, and Gerald E. Williams. 1963a. "Tenejapa Medicine 1: The Curer." *Southwestern Journal of Anthropology* 19 (2): 216–34. https://doi.org/10.1086/soutjanth.19.2.3629170.

Metzger, Duane, and Gerald E. Williams. 1963b. "A Formal Ethnographic Analysis of Tenejapa Ladino Weddings." *American Anthropologist* 65 (5): 1076–101. https://doi.org/10.1525/aa.1963.65.5.02a00070.

Metzger, Duane, and Gerald E. Williams. 1966. "Some Procedures and Results in the Study of Native Categories: Tzeltal 'Firewood.'" *American Anthropologist* 68 (2): 389–407. https://doi.org/10.1525/aa.1966.68.2.02a00060.

Meyers, Allan. 2012. *Outside Hacienda Walls: The Archaeology of Plantation Peonage in Nineteenth-Century Yucatán*. Tucson: University of Arizona Press.

Michelaki, Kostalena, Gregory V. Braun, and Ronald G. V. Hancock. 2014. "Local Clay Sources as Histories of Human-Landscape Interactions: A Ceramic Taskscape." *Journal of Archaeological Method and Theory*. https://doi.org/10.1007/s10816-014-9204-0.

Michelaki, Kostelena, Ronald G. V. Hancock, and Gregory V. Braun. 2012. "Using Provenance Data to Assess Archaeological Landscapes: An Example from Calabria, Italy." *Journal of Archaeological Science* 39 (2): 234–46. https://doi.org/10.1016/j.jas.2011.08.034.

Miller, Daniel. 1985. *Artefacts as Categories*. Cambridge: Cambridge University Press.

Miller, Mary, and Simon Martin. 2004. *Courtly Art of the Ancient Maya*. London: Thames and Hudson.

Mistry, Jayalaxshmi, and Andrea Berardi. 2016. "Bridging Indigenous and Scientific Knowledge." *Science* 352 (6291): 1274–75. https://doi.org/10.1126/science.aaf1160.

Morales Valderrama, Carmen. 2005. "La alfarería de Yucatán: Una tradicción al finalizar el Siglo XX." In *La producción alfarera en el México Antigua*, ed. Beatrix Leonor Merino Carrión and Angel García Cook, vol. 1: 121–42. Mexico City: Instituto Nacional de Antropología e Historia.

Morris, Earl, J. Charlot, and Ann Axtell Morris. 1931. *The Temple of the Warriors at Chichén Itzá, Yucatán*. Washington, DC: Carnegie Institution of Washington.

Moseley, E. H., and Edward D. Terry, eds. 1980. *Yucatán: A World Apart*. Tuscaloosa: University of Alabama Press.

Murdock, George P., and C. Provost. 1973. "Factors in the Division of Labor by Sex: A Cross-Cultural Analysis." *Ethnology* 12 (2): 203–25. https://doi.org/10.2307/3773347.

Museo Casa de Barro. 2015. Accessed on August 28, 2015. museocasadebarro.com/.

Nagasawa, Miho, Shouhei Mitsui, Shiori En, Nobuyo Ohtani, Mitsuaki Ohta, Yasuo Sakuma, Tatsushi Onaka, Kazutaka Mogi, and Takefumi Kikusui. 2015. "Oxytocin-Gaze Positive Loop and the Coevolution of Human-Dog Bonds." *Science* 348 (6232): 333–36. https://doi.org/10.1126/science.1261022.

Nash, June. 1966. "Review of *Ollero Yucateco*." *American Anthropologist* 68 (4): 1093–94. https://doi.org/10.1525/aa.1966.68.4.02a00750.

Nazarea, Virginia D., ed. 1999a. *Ethnoecology: Situated Knowledge/Located Lives*. Tucson: University of Arizona Press.

Nazarea, Virginia D. 1999b. "Introduction." In *Ethnoecology: Situated Knowledge/Located Lives*, ed. Virginia D. Nazarea, 1–20. Tucson: University of Arizona Press.

Neuenswander, H. L., and S. D. Souder. 1977. "The Hot-Cold Wet-Dry Syndrome among the Quiche of Joyabaj." In *Cognitive Studies of Southern Mesoamerica*, ed. H. L. Neuenswander and D. E. Arnold, 96–125. SIL Museum of Anthropology, Publication 3. Dallas, TX: SIL Museum of Anthropology.

Oltrogge, David F. 1977. "The Ethnoentomology of Some Jicaque (Tol) Categories of the Order Hymenoptera." In *Cognitive Studies of Southern Mesoamerica*, ed. Helen L. Neuenswander and Dean E. Arnold, 160–81, SIL Museum of Anthropology, Publication No. 3. Dallas, TX: SIL Museum of Anthropology.

Orlove, Benjamin S., John C. H. Chiang, and Mark A. Cane. 2002. "Ethnoclimatology in the Andes." *American Scientist* 90 (5): 428–35. https://doi.org/10.1511/2002.33.791.

Orosa Díaz, Jaime. 1994. *Historia de Yucatán*. (Decimo tercera reimpresión). Mérida, Yucatán, Mexico: Universidad Autónoma de Yucatán.

Ortiz de Montellano, Bernard. 1975. "Empirical Aztec Medicine." *Science* 188 (4185): 215–20. https://doi.org/10.1126/science.1090996.

Oswalt, W. H., and J. W. VanStone. 1967. *The Ethnoarchaeology of Crow Village, Alaska*. Bulletin No. 199. Washington, DC: Smithsonian Institution Bureau of American Ethnology.

Pelto, Pertti, and Gretel H. Pelto. 1978. *Anthropological Research: The Structure of Inquiry*, 2nd ed. Cambridge: Cambridge University Press. https://doi.org/10.1017/CBO9780511607776.

Peniche Barrera, Roldan. 1992. *El libro de los fantasmas Mayas*. Mérida, Yucatán, Mexico: Maldonado Editores.

Peñuelas, Josep, This Rutishauser, and Iolanda Filella. 2009. "Phenology Feedbacks on Climate Change." *Science* 324 (5929): 887–88. https://doi.org/10.1126/science.1173004.

Pike, Kenneth L. 1990. "On the Emics and Etics of Pike and Harris." In *Emics and Etics: The Insider/Outsider Debate*, ed. Thomas N. Headland, Kenneth L. Pike, and Marvin Harris, 28–47. Frontiers of Anthropology, Vol. 7. Newbury Park, CA: Sage Publications.

Pool, Christopher. 2000. "Why a Kiln? Firing Technology in the Sierra de Los Tuztlas, Veracruz (Mexico)." *Archaeometry* 42 (1): 61–76. https://doi.org/10.1111/j.1475-4754.2000.tb00866.x.

Pringle, Heather. 2009. "A New Look at the Mayas' End." *Science* 324 (5926): 454–56. https://doi.org/10.1126/science.324_454.

Quiñones, H., and R. Allende. 1974. "Formation of the Lithified Carapace of Calcareous Nature Which Covers Most of the Yucatan Peninsula and Its Relation to the Soils and Geomorphology of the Region." *Tropical Agriculturist* 51 (2): 94–101.

Ramírez Carrillo, Luis Alfonso. 1987. "De Como los Campesinos Se Vuelven Artesanos." *Revista de la Universidad Autonoma de Yucatán, Mérida, Yucatán, Mexico* 162 (September): 3–22.

Ramsey, Kathryn Moynihan, Jun Yoshino, Cynthia S. Brace, Dana Abrassart, Yumiko Kobayashi, Biliana Marcheva, Hee-Kyung Hong, Jason L. Chong, Ethan D. Buhr, Choogon Lee, et al. 2009. "Circadian Clock Feedback Cycle through NAMPT-Mediated NAD+ Biosynthesis." *Science* 324 (5927): 651–54. https://doi.org/10.1126/science.1171641.

Rancho el Porvenir. 2014. "Manifestación de impacto ambiental, modalidad particular, Rancho El Porvenir, Municipio de Solidaridad, Quintana Roo." Accessed March 26, 2014. http://sinat.semarnat.gob.mx/dgiraDocs/documentos/qroo/estudios/2004/23QR2004T0062.pdf.

Ratner, Nancy C., and Davin L. Holen. 2007. "Traditional Ecological Knowledge: Applying Principles of Sustainability to Wilderness Resource Management." USDA Forest Service Proceedings RMRS-P-49, 45–50.

RCMTYM (Registros Civiles del Municipio de Ticul, Yucatán, Matrimonios). 1950.
Real Academia Española. 2012a. "Dedo." *Diccionario de la lengua española*. Accessed on July 25, 2015. http://lema.rae.es/drae/?val=dedo.
Real Academia Española. 2012b. "Jeme." *Diccionario de la lengua española*. Accessed on July 25, 2015. http://lema.rae.es/drae/?val=jeme.
Redfield, Robert. 1941. *The Folk Culture of Yucatan*. Chicago: University of Chicago Press.
Redfield, Robert. 1950. *A Village That Chose Progress: Chan Kom Revisited*. Chicago: University of Chicago Press.
Redfield, Robert, and Alfonso Villa Rojas. 1962. *Chan Kom, a Maya Village* (Abridged ed.). Chicago: University of Chicago Press. (Originally published by Carnegie Institution of Washington, Publication No. 448, 1934.)
Reina, Ruben. E. 1966. *The Law of the Saints: A Pokomam Pueblo and Its Community Culture*. New York: Bobbs-Merrill.
Reina, Ruben E., and Robert M. Hill. 1978. *The Traditional Pottery of Guatemala*. Austin: University of Texas Press.
Rejón, Patrón L. 1981a. "Hacienda Tabí: Un cápitulo en la historia de Yucatán." *Cuadernos de Cultura Yucateca* No. 3.
Rejón, Patrón L. 1981b. "Tabí, una Hacienda azucarerea de Yucatán a fines del siglo XIX." In *Yucatán: Peonaje y liberación*, ed. Raúl Maldonado Coello, 117–40. Mérida, Yucatán, Mexico: Comisión Editorial del Estado, INAH.
Rendón, Silvia. 1947. "Notas sobre la alfarería indígena de la Peninsula de Yucatán." *Revista Mexicana de Estudios Antropológicos* 9 (1–3): 106–23.
Renfrew, Colin. 1998. "Mind and Matter: Cognitive Archaeology and External Symbolic Storage." In *Cognition and Material Culture: The Archeology of Symbolic Storage*, ed. Colin Renfrew and Christopher Scarre, 1–6. McDonald Institute Monographs. Cambridge: McDonald Institute for Archaeological Research, University of Cambridge.
Renfrew, Colin. 2004. "Towards a Theory of Material Engagement." In *Rethinking Materiality: The Engagement of Mind with the Material World*, ed. Elizabeth DeMarrais, Chris Gosden and Colin Renfrew, 23–31. McDonald Institute Monographs. Cambridge: McDonald Institute for Archaeological Research, University of Cambridge.
Renfrew, Colin, and Christopher Scarre, eds. 1998. *Cognition and Material Culture: The Archeology of Symbolic Storage*. McDonald Institute Monographs. Cambridge: McDonald Institute for Archaeological Research, University of Cambridge.
Rice, Prudence M. 1987. *Pottery Analysis: A Sourcebook*. Chicago: University of Chicago Press.
Rice, Prudence M. 2015. *Pottery Analysis: A Sourcebook*, 2nd ed. Chicago: University of Chicago Press. https://doi.org/10.7208/chicago/9780226923222.001.0001.
Rodríguez, Arellano, J. A. R. Rodríguez Rivera, and P. Uhu Chi. 1992. *Glosario de términos agrícolas Maya-Español*. Etnoflora Yucatanense, Fascículo 7. Mérida, Yucatán, Mexico: Universidad Autónoma de Yucatán, Sostenibilidad Maya.

Roux, Valentine. 2007. "Ethnoarchaeology: A Non-Historical Science of Reference Necessary for Interpreting the Past." *Journal of Archaeological Method and Theory* 14 (2): 153–78. https://doi.org/10.1007/s10816-007-9030-8.

Roys, Ralph L. [1931] 1976. *The Ethno-Botany of the Maya*. Philadelphia: Institute for the Study of Human Issues. (Repr. of the 1931 ed., Middle America Research Series Publication 2. New Orleans, LA: Department of Middle American Research, Tulane University.)

Rye, O. S. 1976. "Keeping Your Temper under Control: Materials and the Manufacture of Papuan Pottery." *Archaeology and Physical Anthropology in Oceania* 11 (2): 106–37.

Rye, O. S. 1981. *Pottery Technology: Principles and Reconstruction*. Washington, DC: Taraxacum.

Rye, O. S., and Clifford Evans. 1976. *Traditional Pottery Techniques of Pakistan: Field and Laboratory Studies*. Washington, DC: Smithsonian Contributions to Anthropology, No. 21.

Sabloff, Jeremy A., and Robert E. Smith. 1969. "The Importance of Both Analytic and Taxonomic Classification in the Type-Variety System." *American Antiquity* 34 (3): 78–85. https://doi.org/10.2307/278410.

Sánchez González, María Consuelo. 1993. *Uso y manejo de la leña en X-uilub, Yucatán*. Fascículo 8, Etnoflora Yucatanese. Mérida, Yucatán, Mexico: Universidad Autónoma de Yucatán Sostenibilidad Maya.

Schiffer, Michael Brian. 1975. *Behavioral Chain Analysis: Activities, Organization, and the Use of Space*. In *Chapters in the Prehistory of Eastern Arizona, IV*. Fieldiana. Anthropology 65:103–19. Chicago: Field Museum of Natural History.

Schiffer, Michael Brian. 2005. "The Devil is in the Details: The Cascade Model of Invention Processes." *American Antiquity* 70 (3): 485–502. https://doi.org/10.2307/40035310.

Schultz, L. G., A. O. Shepard, P. D. Blackmon, and H. C. Starkey. 1971. "Mixed-Layer Kaolinite-Montmorillonite from the Yucatán Peninsula, Mexico." *Clays and Clay Minerals* 19 (3): 137–50. https://doi.org/10.1346/CCMN.1971.0190302.

Shepard, Anna O. 1952. "Ceramic Technology." *Carnegie Institution of Washington Yearbook* 51:263–66.

Shepard, Anna O. 1958. "Ceramic Technology." *Carnegie Institution of Washington Yearbook* 57: 451–55.

Shepard, Anna O. [1956] 1965. *Ceramics for the Archaeologist*. Publication 609. Washington, DC: Carnegie Institution of Washington.

Shepard, Anna O. 1967. Letter to Bruce F. Bohor, March 27, 1967. Letter abstracted in Arnold 1991, 329–30. Copy of original letter available in Wheaton College Archives and Special Collections, Dean E. Arnold Papers, 1965–2003. Also available in the Anna O. Shepard Papers in the Library of the University of Colorado. http://archon.wheaton.edu/index.php?p=collections/controlcard&id=44

Shepard, Anna O., and H. B. Gottlieb. 1962. "Maya Blue: Alternative Hypotheses." In *Notes from a Ceramic Laboratory No. 1*. Washington, DC: Carnegie Institution of Washington. https://doi.org/10.2307/277680.

Sillar, B. 2000. *Shaping Culture: Making Pots and Constructing Households. An Ethnoarchaeological Study of Pottery Production, Trade and Use in the Andes*. BAR International Series 883. Oxford: British Archaeological Reports.

Sillar, Bill, and Michael Tite. 2000. "The Challenge of 'Technological Choices' for Materials Science Approaches in Archaeology." *Archaeometry* 42 (1): 2–20. https://doi.org/10.1111/j.1475-4754.2000.tb00863.x.

Sillitoe, Paul. 1998. "The Development of Indigenous Knowledge: A New Applied Anthropology." *Current Anthropology* 39 (2): 223–52. https://doi.org/10.1086/204722.

Smith, Robert E. 1971. *The Pottery of Mayapán*, vol. 66 (parts I and II). Papers of the Peabody Museum of Archaeology and Ethnology. Cambridge, MA: Harvard University.

Souza Novelo, Narciso. 1940. *Plantas melíferas y políniferas que viven en Yucatán*. Mérida, Yucatán, Mexico: Talleres Linotipográficos 'El Porvenir'. (Edición facsimilar reacondicionada, hecha por José Díaz-Bolio, Mérida, 1975).

Spier, Robert F. G. 1967. "Work Habits, Postures and Fixtures." In *American Historical Anthropology: Essays in Honor of Leslie Spier*, ed. C. L. Riley and W. W. Taylor, 197–220. Carbondale: Southern Illinois University Press.

Standley, P. C. 1930. *Flora of Yucatan*. Field Museum of Natural History Publication No. 279. Botanical Series, vol. 3, no. 3. Chicago: Field Museum of Natural History. https://doi.org/10.5962/bhl.title.2354.

Stanislawski, Michael B. 1977. "Ethnoarchaeology of Hopi and Hopi-Tewa Pottery Making: Styles of Learning." In *Experimental Archaeology*, ed. D. Ingersoll, J. E. Yellen, and W. MacDonald, 378–408. New York: Columbia University Press.

Stanislawski, Michael B., and Barbara B. Stanislawski. 1978. "Hopi and Hopi-Tewa Ceramic Tradition Networks." In *The Spatial Organization of Culture*, ed. Ian Hodder, 61–76. London: Gerald Duckworth.

Stark, Miriam T. 1991a. "Ceramic Change in Ethnoarchaeological Perspective: A Kalinga Case Study." *Asian Perspective* 30 (2): 193–216.

Stark, Miriam T. 1991b. "Ceramic Production and Community Specialization: A Kalinga Ethnoarchaeological Study." *World Archaeology* 23 (1): 64–78. https://doi.org/10.1080/00438243.1991.9980159.

Stark, Miriam T. 2003. "Current Issues in Ceramic Ethnoarchaeology." *Journal of Archaeological Research* 11 (3): 193–242. https://doi.org/10.1023/A:1025079730891.

Steggerda, Morris. 1941. *Maya Indians of Yucatán*. Carnegie Institution of Washington, Publication 531. Washington, DC: Carnegie Institution of Washington.

Steggerda, Morris. 1943a. *A Description of Thirty Towns in Yucatán, Mexico*. Anthropological Papers, No. 30. Bureau of American Ethnology Bulletin 136: 227–48. Washington, DC: Smithsonian Institution.

Steggerda, Morris. 1943b. *Some Ethnological Data Concerning One Hundred Yucatecan Plants*. Anthropological Paper No. 29. Bureau of American Ethnology Bulletin No. 136. Washington, DC: Smithsonian Institution.

Stephens, John L. [1843] 1996. *Incidents of Travel in Yucatán* (New ed. by Karl Ackerman). Washington, DC: Smithsonian Institution Press.

Steward, Julian H. 1955. *Theory of Culture Change*. Urbana: University of Illinois Press.

Stokstad, Erik, and Gretchen Vogel. 2015. "Neglected Tropical Diseases Get the Limelight in Stockholm." *Science* 350 (6257): 144–45. https://doi.org/10.1126/science.350.6257.144.

Strickon, Arnold. 1965. "Hacienda and Plantation in Yucatán: An Historical-Ecological Consideration of the Folk-Urban Continuum in Yucatán." *America Indigena* 25 (1): 35–63.

Sturtevant, William C. 1964. "Studies in Ethnoscience." In *Transcultural Studies in Cognition. American Anthropologist* 66 (No. 3, Part 3), 99–131.

Terán, Silvia, and Christian Rasmussen. 1981. *Artesanías de Yucatán*. Mérida, Yucatán, Mexico: PESIP/Arte y Comunicación, Dirección General de Culturales Populares/SEP.

Thieme, Mary S. 2007. "Changes in the Style, Production and Distribution of Pottery in Santa María Atzompa, Oaxaca, Mexico during the 1990s." *Museum Anthropology* 30 (2): 125–40. https://doi.org/10.1525/mua.2007.30.2.125.

Thieme, Mary S. 2009. *Continuity and Change in Domestic Industry: Santa María Atzompa, A Pottery Making Town in Oaxaca, Mexico*. Fieldiana Anthropology, New Series, No. 41, Publication 1553. Chicago: Field Museum of Natural History.

Thompson, Edward H. 1895. *The Chultunes of Labná, Yucatán*. Memoirs of the Peabody Museum of American Archaeology and Ethnology, Vol. 1, No. 3. Cambridge: Peabody Museum of American Archaeology and Ethnology.

Thompson, Raymond H. 1958. *Modern Yucatán Pottery Making*. Memoirs of the Society for American Archaeology No. 15. Salt Lake City: Society for American Archaeology.

Tite, M. S., and Y. Maniatis. 1975. "Scanning Electronic Microscopy of Fired Calcareous Clays." *Transactions and Journal of the British Ceramic Society* 74 (1): 19–22.

Tozzer, Alfred M. 1941. *Landa's Relación de las cosas de Yucatán: A Translation*. Papers of the Peabody Museum, vol. 18. Cambridge, MA: Harvard University.

Tozzer, Alfred M. 1957. *Chichén Itzá and Its Cenote of Sacrifice: A Comparative Study of the Contemporaneous Maya and Toltec*. Memoirs of the Peabody Museum of Archaeology and Ethnology, Harvard University. Vols. 11 and 12. Cambridge, MA: Peabody Museum.

Tyler, Steven A. 1969. *Cognitive Anthropology*. New York: Holt, Rinehart, Winston.

Uc González, Eunice, and Elena Canche Manzanero. 1996. "Las grutas de Monte Bravo, Campeche." *Investigadores de la Cultura Maya* 3. Publicaciones de la Universidad Autónoma de Campeche (II), 305–10.

Underhill, Anne. 2003. "Investigating Variation in Organization of Ceramic Production: An Ethnoarchaeological Study in Guizhou, China." *Journal of Archaeological Method and Theory* 10 (3): 203–75. https://doi.org/10.1023/A:1026035706326.

UNESCO. 2016. United Nations Educational, Scientific and Cultural Organization: Intangible Cultural Heritage. http://www.unesco.org/culture/ich/en/home.

Vallo, Michael. 2002. *Die Keramik von Xkipché: BAR International Series 1056*. Oxford: Archaeopress.

Van der Leeuw, Sander. 1993. "Giving the Potter a Choice: Conceptual Aspects of Pottery Techniques." In *Technological Choices: Transformation in Material Cultures since the Neolithic*, ed. Pierre Lemonnier, 238–88. London, UK: Routledge.

Van der Leeuw, S., and A. C. Pritchard, eds. 1984. *The Many Dimensions of Pottery: Ceramics in Archaeology and Anthropology*. Amsterdam: Universiteit van Amsterdam, Albert Egges van Giffens Insituut voor Prae- en Protohistorie, Cingvla VII.

Van Olphen, H. 1963. *An Introduction to Clay Colloid Chemistry*. New York: Interscience Publishers.

Varela Torrecilla, Carmen. 1990. "La producción alfarera artesanal del occidente de la Península del Yucatán: Un ejemplo de cambio cultural." *Revista Española de Antropología Americana* 20:183–220.

Velázquez, Adriana Morlet, and Edmundo López de la Rosa. 1988. "Atlas arqueológico de Yucatán." In *Zonas arqueológicos: Yucatán*, ed. Adriana Velázquez Morlet, Edmundo López de la Rosa, María del Pilar Casado López, and Margarita Gaxiola, 63–91. Mexico City: Instituto Nacional de Antropología e Historia.

Weiner, Norbert. 1948. *Cybernetics*. New York: Wiley.

Weiner, Norbert. 1954. *The Human Use of Human Beings: Cybernetics and Society*. Anchor books ed.. Garden City, NY: Doubleday and Company.

Wells, E. Christian, and Lorena D. Mihok. 2009. "Ancient Maya Perception of Soil, Land and Earth." In *Soil and Culture*, ed. E. R. Landa and C. Feller, 311–27. Netherlands: Springer. http://dx.doi.org/10.1007/978-90-481-2960-7_19.

West, R. C. 1964. *Surface Configuration and Associated Geology of Middle America*. Handbook of Middle America Indians. Vol. 1: 33–83. Austin: University of Texas Press.

White, W. Arthur. 1949. "Atterberg Plastic Limits of Clay Minerals." *American Mineralogist* 34 (7–8): 508–12. (Internet Archive Volume Report of Investigations No. 144, Illinois Geological Survey, Illinois State Government Document. Accessed September 23, 2013. http://archive.org/details/atterbergplastic144whit.)

Whitley, David S. 2007. "Indigenous Knowledge and 21st Century Archeological Practice: An Introduction." *SAA Archaeological Record* 7 (2): 6–8.

Wijnen, Herman. 2009. "A Circadian Loop asSIRTs Itself." *Science* 324 (5927): 598–99. https://doi.org/10.1126/science.1174132.

Williams, Eduardo. 1992. "Pots, Pans and People: Ceramic Ecology in West Mexico." *Papers from the Institute of Archaeology, University College, London* 3 (March): 44–51. https://doi.org/10.5334/pia.32.

Williams, Eduardo. 1994a. "Organización del espacio doméstico y producción cerámica en Huáncito, Michoacán." In *Contribuciones a la arqueología y etnohistoria del Occidental de México*, ed. Eduardo Williams, 189–225. Michoacán, Zamora, México: El Colegio de Michoacán.

Williams, Eduardo. 1994b. "Ecología cerámica en Huáncito, Michoacán." In *Arqueología del occidente de México*, ed. Williams Eduardo and Robert Novella, 319–62. Michoacán, Zamora, Mexico: El Colegio de Michoacán.

Williams, Eduardo, ed. 2006. *Ethnoarqueología: El contexto dinámico de la cultura material a través del tiempo*. Michoacán, Zamora, Mexico: El Colegio de Michoacán.

Wilson, E. M. 1980. "Physical Geography of the Yucatán Peninsula." In *Yucatán: A World Apart*, ed. E. H. Moseley and Edward D. Terry, 5–40. Tuscaloosa: University of Alabama Press.

Wynn, Thomas, and Frederick L. Coolidge. 2010a. "Beyond Symbolism and Language: An Introduction to Supplement 1, Working Memory." In *Working Memory: Beyond Language and Symbolism. Current Anthropology: The Wenner-Gren Symposium Series* 51, Supplement 1, S5–S16. https://doi.org/10.1086/650526.

Wynn, Thomas, and Frederick L. Coolidge, eds. 2010b. "Working Memory: Beyond Language and Symbolism." *Current Anthropology: The Wenner-Gren Symposium Series* 51, Supplement 1.

Zapata Peraza, Renée L. 1989. *Los Chultunes: Sistemas de captación y almacenamiento de Agua Pluvial*. Colección Científica, Serie Arqueología. Mexico City: Instituto Nacional de Antropología e Historia.

Index

Page numbers in italics indicate illustrations.

accidents, firing, 191–95
agency. *See* material agency
agriculture, 5, 61; shifting, 54–57; water-carrying vessels and, 143–44, 145; *ya'ash k'ash* zone, 62–63
aguadas, 71
Aguilar, Ramón, *110*
Akil, 48, 217
aktun, 73, 112, 113
Aktun Boosh, 73
Aktun Ch'ak Tale'en, 73, 112, 113
Aktun Hi', 73, 108, 112, 113, 120(n17); religious meanings of, 203–4; temper from, 206, 208
Aktun Lara, 73, 108, 112, 113, 214(n12)
Aktun Osh, 73
Aktun Shmak, 73, 113
Aktun Tzunu'um, 73
altars, household, 205, 206, *207*
apaste, 138, *140*, 141, 149–51, 151(tables). *See also* water-storage jars
archaeology, 206, 214(n11); and pottery production, 13–14, 198–99. *See also* Terminal Classic Period; *various sites by name*
artifacts, and cognition, 8–9
attapulgite. *See* palygorskite

Balankanché, 204
balche' tree (*Lonchocarpus longistylus*), 144
balche' vessel, rim form for, 144, 146
Becal, 48, 213(n9)
Belize, 4–5, 57
bilil k'at, 126, *127*, *128*
Binford, Lewis, xxiv
Black, Mary, 31
Bohor, B. F., on raw material collection, 47–48, 49
Bourdieu, Pierre, 17
bowls, food 103, 141, 150–51, 206–7
brain, and motor learning, 18
brush, used in firing, 158
Bunzel, Ruth, 25; *The Pueblo Potter*, xxv

Caesalpinia platyloba, 100
cajetes, 103, 141, 150–51, 206, *207*
calcination, 109, 110, 111, 169
calcite: crystalline, 108–11, 204; in *sah kab*, 90, 91, 102; in Terminal Classic pottery, 111–13
calcium hydroxide, in pottery, 82–83
Calkiní, 81, 227
Campeche, clay from, 80, 81, 203, 226
Canadian Northwest Territories, caribou in, 4
candle holders, 206, *207*

257

258 INDEX

cántaro. *See* water-carrying jars
Canul, Gómez, 85
categorization, in pottery production, 15–17
caves, 72–73, 204; crystalline calcite from, 108–9, 112–13
cenotes, 71, 205
ceramics. *See* pottery
Ceramics for the Archaeologist (Shepard), xxvi
ceremonies, 144–45, 203
chaachac, 145
Chaak, 206, 207, 224
chaîne opératoire, xxiv, xxvi, xxx(n4), 9, 14–15, 29(n7), 154, 183
chak'an zone, 52, 53, 54, 59
chak te' (*Caesalpinia platyloba*), 100
Chan Kom, 145, 203
Chapab, 94, 113, *209*, 226, 227
ch'è'en, 71–72
chen sah kab, for construction, 90, 91–94, 102, 119(n12)
Chichén Itzá, 93, 205
Chichén Slate Ware, 146
Chinautla, 137, 196(n5)
choice, 122, 211; in pottery production, 20–22, 218–20; technological and social, 23–26
chokokinta'al, 183–86
chultuns, 62, 72–73, 205; and water-carrying jars, 146, 147–48
chun k'aak', 166, 196(n7)
Ch'u'uyu', hacienda, 59
cisterns. *See chultuns*
clay, 16, 22, 75, 79, 80, 157, 226; choices of, xxv, xxvi, 24, 84–88; controlling quality of, 154–55; mining, 11–12, 195(n4), 196(n5); and paste preparation, 121, 122–*23*, 125–26; plasticity of, 14–15, 25; potters' classification of, 80–85, 118(n4); properties of, 118(n5, n8), 132–35; sampling in Yucatan, 47–48; Ticul uses of, 44–46; Yo' K'at source of, 199–200, 206, 207, 212(n1)
clay-mineral decomposition and sintering, 183
climate, 56–57, 159
Cobá, 94
cognition, xxiv, 27–28; and material culture, 8, 9; and practice, 34–35, 36, 226
cognitive anthropology, 26
cognitive archaeology, 47
coiling techniques, modified/slab, 138, 139–40
coin banks, 134

Colombia, 221
Colonial Period, rim forms, 150
colors: clay, 80; *sah kab*, 91–92, 117(n1)
communities: distance to water, 144; and pottery characteristics, 210–11
community of practice, 216; raw material use, 49, 115–16; Ticul as, 208–10
congealed landscape, 27
construction, *sah kab* for, 74, 75, 90, 91–94, 102–3
consumers, of water-carrying vessels, 143–44
cooking pots, 122, 206, 213(n8); crystalline calcite used in, 108–11, 112; temper sources for, 203–4
crafts, craft production, 4, 6
cubanos, 99, 138, 196(n7)
cuevas (man-made caves), 74
Cultural and Personality School, xxv–xxvi, 25
Cultural Heritage, xx, xxvii; ethnoarchaeology and, 27, 221–23
culture: definition of, 36–37; learning, 32–33; practice theory and, 41–42; determinative role in ceramic production, 25–26

dangerous activities, men and, 156
data collection, 50; ethnoscience, 30–31
Day of the Dead, 213(n7); pottery made for, 206–7, 211, 213(n9); raw material sources and, 200(table); spirits and, 204–5; vessels for, 141, 150, 196(n8)
deities/spirits, forest, 144, 203, 205
Dene First Nation, 4
design structures, 25
determinism, 23, 25, 29(n6)
development programs, 4
distilled landscape, 27
division of labor, in pottery making, 155–57
dolomite, 75, 90, 91, 102
droughts, 148
drying, 122, 190; choices in, 21, 22; vessel, 154, 168–69, 170; of Yo' K'at clay, 83–84
Duranzo, 137
Dzitbalché, 117(n4), 203, 227

earth, 79; religious importance of, 204–5, 206
ecology, xxiii; folk and scientific, 50–51
Ek Balam, 93
emic perspective, 16–17, 51
energy use, feedback loops, 22

engagement, 39–40, 121; ethnoarchaeology and, 223–26; vs. knowledge, 34–35, 36, 38; with landscape, 216–17; of potters with raw materials, 26–27; in vessel formation, 129–35

engagement theory, xxv, 8; archaeology and, 13–14; and *chaîne opératoire*, 14–15; environment and landscape and, 9–10; feedback, 18–23; muscular patterns, 17–18; participation and, 11–13; semantic structure, 15–17; technological choice in, 23–26

environment, 9–10, 21

Espejo, Juaquín, 201

ethnoarchaeology, xxv, 31, 48; ceramic, xxi–xxiii; as Cultural Heritage, 27, 221–23; and engagement, 223–26

ethnocentrism, and methodology, 224–25

ethnoecological zones, 58(table), 61–62; trees and, 57, 59, 64, 65–71(table)

ethnoecology, 50–51, 217–18; in Belize, 4–5

ethnogeology, 64; opening classification, 71–77

ethnomineralogy, 4, 26, 79, 219; of *k'at*, 80–88; *sah kab*, 89–108; *sak lu'um*, 88–89; in Ticul, 43–44

ethnopetrology, 77–78

ethnoscience, 15, 30; informants and, 31–32

ethnotaxonomy, 32

etic perspective, 16–17, 51

everted rims, on water-carrying vessels, 144, *146*

families, knowledge transmission, 220–21; farms, commercial, 61–62, 63, 213(n6)

feedback: in engagement theory, 10, 18–23; firing process, 183, 189–91, 192, 225; paste preparation, 105–6, 123–28; of raw materials, 79, 100, 121; for sizes of water-carrying vessels, 143–44; in vessel formation, 130–31, 132

fermented beverages, 144

fieldwork: participant-observation, 35–36; qualities of, 42–43; Yucatán, 32–35

fiestas, at Hacienda Yo' K'at, 201

figurines, 99, 103, *170*

final drying, 170

fincas, 61–62, 63, 213(n6)

fire in the door of the kiln phase (*hok'ol k'aak'*), 186–91, *192*

firewood, xix, 38, *55*–56; characteristics of, 37, 154, 171–77; classification of, 196(n9), 197(n10); in firing process, 157–58, 183–84, 186–*87*, *188*, *189*–90; and kiln size, 166, 225; knowledge of, 59, 174, 178–80(table), 219; religious aspects associated with, 205, 206

firing process, xix, 162; accidents during, 191–*95*; choices in, 21, 197(n11), 219–20; cooking pots, 111, 157–58; documenting, 35–36; engagement in, 13, 37, 38–39, 224–25; final stage, 186–*90*; fuel preparation and characteristics, 171–77; kiln loading, *181*–83; knowledge of, 40–41, 154, 155; men and, 156–57; at night, 188; raw materials and, 33–34; stages in, 183–*90*; variations, 190–91; warming stage, 183–86

flower pots, 206

Folan, William, 93

folk taxonomy, 32, 33; of *sah kab*, 90(table), 96–97; trees, 64, 65–71(table), 217–18

food bowls, 103, 141, 150–51, 206, *207*

forests: deities/spirits of, 144, 203, 205; shifting agriculture in, 54–57

Franklin, John, 4

gender, firing, 156–57; pottery-making process, 155–56, 195(n2)

geology, Yucatán Peninsula, 51–53

ghosts, 205

Goodenough, Ward, 36–37

groundwater, sodium chloride in, 82

Guatemala, 41, 137

habitus, 10, 17–18

haciendas, 59, 212(n1). *See also* Yo' K'at, Hacienda

halloysite, 87, 117(n3), 118–19(n9)

handles, water-carrying vessels, 143

hands and fingers, measuring by, 130

Hatt, Robert, 112

henequén production, 59, 212(n1)

Herrera, Humberto, 201, 212–13(n3)

Hewes, Gordon, on postural patterns, 17

hi': in cooking pots, 108–11, 122; as temper, 108–9, 214(n12); Terminal Classic use of, 111–13

hill country, 63

hill zone, 52, *53*, 59, 78(n1)

hi' nooy, 98, 99

hi' tunich, 108

hok'ol k'aak', 186–91, *192*

hole in the earth (*tantan lu'um*), 76–77; slip from, 204–5, 206

hoopol, 185

households: altars, 205, 206, *207*; pottery-making, 220–21
huajikol, 145
huaricol, 203
Huicab, Fidencio, 83
Huicab, Julián, 85–86
humidity, and clay preparation, 123

identification marks, 170
incense burners (*incensarios*), 141, 150, 151, 206, *209*
indigenous knowledge, xvii–xviii, xix, 3, 39, 53, 159, 215–16, 217, 229(n1); archaeology, 4–5; changes in, 226–27; of drying and firing, 154–55, 157; vs. engagement, 34–35; engagement theory and, 9–10; of firewood quality, 171, 174, 176, 178–80(table); of raw materials, 105–7, 115–17; semantic structure of, 15–17; specialized, 113–14; transmission of, 220–21; on vessel formation, 129–30, 132–33, 135–36, 138, 218–19; and water-carrying vessels, 142–44
informants: using ethnoscience with, 31–32; eliciting about pottery production, 32–36
information flow, and feedback loops, 20–21, 22–23
Ingold, Tim, 199; *Making*, xxv, xxvi, 25, 28(n2)
Intangible Cultural Heritage, 221–22
Inter-American Foundation, 221
Inuit, 4

jarras, 149, 15
jars. *See* water-carrying jars; water-storage jars

Kabah, 52, 63
kabal che' (*kaba' che'*) zone, *52*, *53*, 55, 59
kakab zone, *54*, 55; soils in, 59, 61–62
k'an kab che zone, 63–64
k'an kab soil, 63–64, 74, *76*, 158, 169
kaolinite, 80, 84, 87, 104(tables), 106, 117(n3), 118–19(n9)
k'at. *See* clay
Keh, Francisco, 35, 149
kilns, xix, 41, 76, 149, 225; beehive, 41, 157–58; building, 158–59, 162, 196(n6); characteristics of, 160–61(table), 163–64(table), 165(table); cooking of, 159; cooling, 183, 191; doorways, 159; firing process, 38–39, 154, 183–91; heating, 183–84; loading, 177, *181*–83; parts of, 166–68
knowledge, 5, 79, 121, 186; active engagement and, 10–13, 37–38, 40–41; and behavior, 6, 225; ecological, 50–51; practice theory and, 41–42; specialized, 113–14. *See also* indigenous knowledge
kut nooy, 99–100
kut sah kab, 91–92

Labná, 52, 62
land, agricultural, 57
Landa, Diego de, on *sah kab*, 93
landscape, 26, 27, 49, 198, 206, 211; ecological knowledge of, 50–51; engagement with, 216–17; geology of, 52–53; and pottery production, 6, 10, 16; raw material sources in, 207–9. *See also* taskscapes
Lathrap, Don, 31, 42
learning, indigenous knowledge and, 220–21
levigation, 122
lime, production of, 93, *94*, *95*
limestone, on Yucatán Peninsula, 51, 52–53
linguistics, field techniques, 32–33
Loltun, 204
Lonchocarpus longistylus, 144
low-temperature decomposition, 183, 185–86
lu'um, 79; religious importance of, 204–5, 206. *See also sak lu'um*

maize, swidden agriculture, 54, 55, 62
maize-soaking vessels (*apaste*), 138, *140*, 141, 149–*51*, 151(tables)
maker's marks, 170
Making: Anthropology, Archaeology, Art and Architecture (Ingold), xxv, xxvi, 25, 198
Malafouris, Lambros, 229; on engagement theory, xxvi, 8–9, 28(n1)
Mama, 47, 48, 208, 210, 211, 216
Maní, 148, 149
Maniatis, Y., 111
Mani-style rims, 145, *146*, *147*, *148*, 149
marketing, 13
marl. *See sah kab*
Martín, Manuel, 35, 157, 202, 212(n3)
material agency, 22, 25, 229; of raw materials and pottery-making process, 14–15; and sensory feedback, 19–20
material culture, 25; engagement theory, 8–10
material engagement theory, xvii, xxvi
Mauss, Marcel, on *habitus*, 17
Maxcanú, 47, 48, 213(n9)
Maya Blue, xxiii, xxiv–xxv, 43, 46, 47, 223

Maya Cordemex Dictionary, 5
Mayapán, 148; *sah kab* mines at, 93, 117–18(n4)
Mayapán Red Ware, 146, 150
Mayapán Unslipped ware, 146
measurements, units of, 130–31
measuring: kiln size, 225; vessel size, 130, 150–51
medicine, palygorskite as, 120(n19), 222, 223, 229(n4)
Mejorada, clay from, 85–88
memory: and landscape, 211; working, 20, 28–29(n5), 79
men, 156, 195(n2, n4); water-carrying vessels used by, 143–44, 145. *See also* gender
Méndez, Alonzo, 31
Mercer, Henry, 112
Mérida, 144
methodology, engagement and, 223–26
Metzger, Duane, 31, 32
Mex, Cesario, 85, 157
Mex, Josefina, 85
Mex, María, 157
Mexico, Cultural Heritage in, 221
Midwest Universities Consortium, 224
milpas, 143–44
milperos, firewood selection, 171, 174, 176
mining, 156, 195(n4), 196(n5), 212(n1); challenges of, 11–13; distance to sources, *209*; marl, 73–75
molding, vertical-half, 134–35, 137
Montes family, 201, 212(n2)
montmorillonite. *See* smectite
Morris, Earl, 93
mortars, 158; *k'an kab* for, 76, 81; *sah kab* for, 91–94
motor learning/skill, 18, 38–39
muscular patterns, 28(n3); in firing, 187, *188*; of pottery making, 17–18, 38–39; in slipping vessels, *140*; squatting, *134*, *135*; in vessel formation, 130–*32*, *133*
Museum of Clay (Museo Casa de Barro), 117(n2)
mutually causal relationships, 19–20

necks, water-carrying jars, 142
noncooking pottery, 122, 204
nonplastics 126
nooy, 74, 90, 101; good-quality (*nooy ma'alob*), 96–99; poor-quality (*kut nooy*), 99–100
Northwest Passage, 4
novenas, for San Pedro, 202, 203–4

Ollero Yucateco (film), 31
openings, classification of, 64, 71–77
organic combustion, 183
overfiring, 188–89
Oxkintok, 204
Oxloch, *finca*, 63

pach k'aak', 166; in firing process, 184, 185, 186–87
paleopsychology, 47
palygorskite, 44–45, 49, 78(n2), 90, 101, 118(n11), 155; and Maya Blue, xxiii, xxiv–xxv, 43, 46, 47; as medicine, 120(n19), 222–23, 229(n4); properties of, 88–89, 104(tables), 106, 107; specialized knowledge about, 115–16
participant-observation, xxiii, 35–36, 37; and engagement theory, 11–13
paste, 122; preparation of, 121, *123–28*
patrilineal inheritance, of house lot, 221
patrilocal residence, after marriage, 221
patron saints, Hacienda Yo' K'at, 201–6
Pech, Lorenzo, 202–3, 213(n5)
Pech, Simon, 145–46
Pedro, San, xxi, 212–13(n3); and Hacienda Yo' K'at, 201–3
Perception of the Environment (Ingold), 198
Peru, 41, 137
Peto, 48, 213(n9)
Peto Cream ware, 146
piñatas, Christmas, 144
pitchers (*jarras*), 149, 15
place(s): importance of, 199; sacred, 204, 205
plant pots, 99, 138, 196(n7)
plasters: *k'an kab* for, 76; *sah kab* for, 81, 91–94
plasticity, xxv; of clay, 25, 104(tables), 126; 'managing, 14–15, 105–7; and vessel formation, 133–35, 218
pok che' zone, 59
pole, to crush temper, 100
Polfus, Jean, 4
Postclassic Period, 146, 148, 150
postural patterns, 17; for carrying water-carrying jars, 142, 143; in slipping vessels, *140*, *142*; squatting, *134*, *135*; in vessel formation, 130–32, 136–37(table). *See also habitus*
potters, xxiii, 39, 170; in households, 220–21; knowledge and sensory feedback of, xxvi, 217–18; and raw material choices, 26–27, 44–46; and subsistence agriculture, 55–57

262 INDEX

pottery, 27; Day of the Dead, 206, *207*, 211, 213(n9). *See also* cooking pots; noncooking pottery
pottery production, xxi, xxiv, 27, 33, 216, 226; agency in, 14–15; archaeological descriptions of, 13–14; cognition and practice, 34–35, 37; families and, 220–21; landscape and, 198–99, 207–8; scheduling, 56–57; sensory feedback loops in, 20–21; technological choices within, 218–19; Yucatec Maya and, xx, 6, 43–44. *See also* firing process; raw materials; vessel formation
Pottery Technology (Rice), xxvi
Pottery Technology: Principles and Reconstruction (Rye), xxvi
practice, and cognition, 34–35, 38, 226
practice theory, 7, 41–42
processual archaeology, 47
production units, 220–21
Pueblo Potter, The (Bunzel), xxv
Pustunich, 224
Puuc Slate Ware, *87*, 112
Puuc Unslipped Ware, 96, 112, 111–13, 120(n18)
puuk zone, 52, *53*, 59, 78(n1)
p'uul. *See* water-carrying jars

quality: clay, 122, 125–26, 154–55; firewood, 171, 174, 176, 178–80(table); temper, 100–107
quarries, *sah kab*, 73–75, 92–94, 117–18(n4)
Quechua, 160
Quintana Roo, firewood from, 171, 174
Quinua (Peru), 25, 137

rainfall, 72, 122, 185
raw materials, 24, 71; changing access to, 226–27; choices of, 44–46, 211; collection of, 47–48; distance to, 208–9; engagement with, 26–27; and firing, 33–34; from forest, 54–57; knowledge of, 79, 115–17, 121; and landscape, 198, 216; preparation of, 122–23; procurement of, 10–11; religious dimensions of, 199–206; sources of, 53, *72*, 207–8, 217
recipes, paste, 123–24
rectos, 99, 138, 196(n7)
recurved rims, 145, *146*, *147*, *148*, 149
red earth/soil, 63–64, 74, *76*, 158, 169
religion, religious associations, 144, 211; and Hacienda Yo' K'at, 199–206; and red slip, 204–5; and temper sources, 203–4

Renfrew, Colin, on engagement theory, 8–9
Rice, Prudence, *Pottery Technology*, xxvi
rim forms, in water-carrying jars, 144–49
rituals: pottery production and, 200(table), 206–7; for San Pedro, 201–3
ritual vessels, 129, 141, 144, 196(n8)
roads, *sah kab* used in, 92, 113–15
rocks, 75, 79, 88; classification of, 74, 77–78; in kilns, 158, 166, 196(n6)
Rodríguez, Florencia (Doña Lol), 145–46
Rohn, Art, 31
Rye, O. S., 82; firing stages, 184, 186–87; *Pottery Technology*, xxvi

Sacalum, 148
Sacojito, 137
sagging, 107
sah kab (white powder), xviii, 73, 89–90, 108, 119(n12), 122, 158, 204; for construction, 74, 75, 81, 91–94; folk taxonomy of, 96–97; and *nooy*, 97–100; preparation of, 100–101; properties of, 81–82; quality tests for, 103–7, 118(n5); Ticul potters' use of, 44, 45–46; variability of, 101–3; at Yo' Sah Kab, 95–96
sah kabo'ob (*sascaberas*), 73
sah kab tunich, 158
sak beh, 92
sakel bach tunich,158
sak kaab, 169
sak lu'um (white earth), 46, 114, 119(n10), 120(n19), 204, 227; knowledge of, 115–16; palygorskite in, 43–45; in paste preparation, 124, 125, 126; properties of, 88–89, 104; at Yo' Sah Kab, 95–96
salts: and calcite, 110–11; in clay, 81–82, 118(n5, n8)
San Francisco (*finca*), 63
San Francisco de Ticul, 205, 208, 214(n12)
San Juaquín Buff ware, 146, 150
San Juaquín quarry, *75*
Santa Elena, 144, 227
sascab, xviii, 89. *See also sah kab*
sascaberas, 73
Sayil, 5, 52, 63
scheduling, of agriculture and pottery production, 56–57
scrapers, and vessel mouth size, 151–52
Segura, Miguel, 203
semantic structure, of indigenous knowledge, 15–17

sense of place, 199, 217; Hacienda Yo' K'at, 199–206
Serbia, Cultural Heritage in, 221
shamans, use of, 203, 205
Shepard, Anna O., xxi, xxx(n1), 109, 222; *Ceramics for the Archaeologist*, xxvi
shmani hol (Mani-style rims; recurved rims), 145, *146*, *147*, *148*, 149
signatures, rim, *147*, *148*, 149
sinkholes, 71, 141, 148, 205, 213(n10)
sitting position, slipping, *140*, *142*; and vessel formation, 131, *132*, *133*
Skayum, 63
slavery, 61
slip, slipping, 76; religious aspects of, 204–5, 206; of vessels, *140*, 169–70
slip casting, 137
smectite, 49, 75, 80–81, 84, 87, 117–18(n3, n4), 118–19(n4); properties of, 107, 127–28; in *sah kab*, 90–91; in temper, 104–6
soap (sodium stearate), in slip, 169
sodium chloride: and calcite, 110–11; in clay, 81–82, 83, 118(n5, n8)
soils: *kakab* zone, 59, 61–62; *k'an kab* (red), 63–64, 74, 76, 158, 169; Yucatán Peninsula, 52–53
Spier, Robert, 17
spirits, 203; Day of the Dead and, 204–5, 207, 213(n7); forest, 144
squatting, muscular pattern of, 131–32, *134*, *135*
stools: in slipping, *140*, *142*; and vessel formation, 131, *132*, *133*
sugar plantations, 61–62, 213(n6)

ta'achach, 98, 99, *103*; use of, 102, 113–15
ta'anooy, 99–100
Tabí, Finca, 61–62, 213(n6)
tailings: in kiln mortar, 158; mining of, 100–*103*; weathered, 98, 99, 102, 113–15
tan k'aak', 166, *167*
tantan lu'um (hole in the earth), 76–77; slip from, 204–5, 206
taskscapes, 27, 198, *209*, *210*, 216; pottery as, 199, 206, 211; religious associations of, 200(table)
technology, 41; choices in, 23–26, 218–19; in vessel formation, 137–40
Tekax, 144
Telchacquillo, 149
temper, 22, 155, 207; choices of, 24, 122; classification of, 16; collection of, 47–48; for cooking pots, 108–11; mining of, 156, 192, 195(n4); *nooy*, 96–100; and paste preparation, 121, *123*, 124, 125, 127; preparation of, 100–103, *110*; protection of sources, 113–14; quality tests for, 103–7, 118(n5); religious aspects of, 203–4, 206; *sah kab* for, 44–46, 90, 94–107
temper mines, mining, 11, 12–13, 156. *See also* Yo' Sah Kab'
Tepakán, 47, 48, 210, 211, 216
Terminal Classic Period, xix, 120(n18); raw material use, 47, 85, 108, 111–13, 200, 204, 208, 214(n12); use of *chultuns*, 62, 73, 205; vessel forms used during, 146, 147, 148; at Yo' Sah Kab, 95–96
testing, of temper, 103–8, 118(n5)
thinning, vessel wall, 140, 153(n2)
Thompson, Raymond, 5, 47
Ticul: *chultuns* around, 205; clay and temper use, 43–46; as community of practice, 208–10; ethnoarchaeology in, 224; government programs, 4; raw material sources, 207–8, 214(n12); taskscape of, *210*; women miners in, 195(n4)
tinajas, 99, 129, 138, 141, 149, 150, *152*, *170*. *See also* water-storage jars
Title, M. S., 111
tok' nooy, 120(n14); use of, 97–99
tok' tunich, 75, 99, 120(n14), 158
tradition, 17
travel, transportation, of clay and temper, 12–13, 22
trees: and ethnoarchaeological zones, 57, 59, 60–61(table), 63; folk taxonomies of, 217–18; identification and classification of, 64, 65–71(table), 218–19; used for firewood, 171–76
tsek'el zone, 59
ts'ooksa'al, 186–90. *See also* firing process
tunich. *See* rocks
turntables, *132*, 137, 138, *139*–41, *142*
Tzum, Emilio, 201, 212–13(n3)
Tzum, Guadalupe, 202, 212(n3)
Tzum Camaal, Agustín, 63
Tzum Camaal, Alfredo, 31, 63; firing, 189–90; as informant, 32, 35, 36, 37; pottery production, 33–34, 38–39, 40; raw material acquisition, 43, 49
Tzum de Cima, Domitila, 156
Tzum de Segura, Augusta, 157
Tzum de Uc, Máxima, 157; rim style of, *148*

Tzum Dzul, Eusevio, 213(n6)
Tzum Tuyup, Guadalupe, 157

Uc, Elio, 35
Uc, José, 35, 205, 213(n6)
u hanli col ritual, 203
underworld, caves and, 204
University of Chicago, 224
University of Illinois, 31, 40, 42
Uxmal, 52, 63, 148

Valadez, Enrique, 212–13(n3)
vertical-half molding, 134–35, 137
vessel formation: choices in, 218–19; postural patterns in, 130–32, 136–37(table); size and shape selection, 129–30; stages in, 135, 138(table); technology of, 139–40
vessels (pots): drying, 168–69; forming, 129–35; parts and proportions of, 145, *150*–51; slipping, *140*, 169–70
vessel shapes, 129, 198(n7); traditional, 130, 141–52. *See also by type*
vessel sizes, 130; apaste, 15(table); proportions, 150–51; variability of, 151–52; of water-carrying jars, 142, 143(table)
vitrification, 110, 183
volcanic ash, 52, 78(n2)

warming stage (*chokokinta'al*), 183–86. *See also* firing process
wasters, in kiln firing, *181*–*83*
water, 104, *125*, 141, 205
water-carrying jars, 99, 129 134, 138, *170*, 196(n7, n8); characteristics of, 141–43; community differences in, 210–11; consumers of, 143–44; rim forms, 144–49
water smoking, 183, 185–86
water sources, 62, 71–73, 141, 205; and water-carrying jars, 143, 144, 145, 146–48

water-storage jars: *apastes*, 149–*50*, 151(tables), *170*, 196(n8); *tinajas*, 99, 129, 138, 141, 149, 150, 152, *170*
weather, 10; and pottery production, 56–57, 122, 197(n11)
wedging (*bilil k'at*), 126, *127*, *128*
wells, 62, 71–72, 141
wheel, for forming pottery, 137
white earth. See *sak lu'um*
white powder. See *sah kab*
Williams, Gerald, 31
wind direction, 159, 161(table)
wits zone, 63
women, 195(n4); as potters, 56, 155, 156–57, 195(n2); and water-carrying vessels, 142, 143, 144
wood. See firewood
working positions. See postural patterns

Xkipché, 52
Xtabay, xx–xxi
Xtepén, 59

ya'ashom (green deep) zone, 63
ya'ash k'ash zone, *54*, 55; swidden agriculture in, 62–63
Yaxcopoil, 59
Yo' K'at, Hacienda, 212(n1); clay from, 24, 48, 81–85, 110–11, 119(n9), 125, 126, 133–34, 206, 207, 208, 226; clay mine at, 11, 12, 72, 156; Museum of Clay at, 117(n2); San Pedro and, 201–3; sense of place for, 199–201
Yo' Sah Kab, 49, 74, 77, *209*, 226; *hi'* from, 204, 206; *sah kab* from, 90, 113–14; temper from, 24, 45, 94–96, 192, 207, 208; temper mining at, 95–96, *102*, 113–14
Yucatán Peninsula, 32; ethnoecological zones, 57–64; geology, 51–53
Yucatec Maya language, xviii, xix, xx, 33, 113

www.ingramcontent.com/pod-product-compliance
Lightning Source LLC
Chambersburg PA
CBHW070912030426
42336CB00014BA/2388